The Chronicles of Aerah

Mind-link Communications across the Universe

by
Bonniol, Salumet, & George E. Moss

Love to Daph + Rod

George

Order this book online at www.trafford.com
or email orders@trafford.com

Most Trafford titles are also available at major online book retailers.

Printed in Victoria, BC, Canada.

ISBN: 978-1-4269-1857-5 (sc)
ISBN: 978-1-4269-1858-2 (hc)

Library of Congress Control Number: 2009936930

Trafford rev. 11/06/09

Trafford PUBLISHING® **www.trafford.com**

North America & international
toll-free: 1 888 232 4444 (USA & Canada)
phone: 250 383 6864 • fax: 812 355 4082

The light which we have gained was given us, not to be ever staring on, but by it to discover onward things more remote from our knowledge.

John Milton, Aeropagitica (1644).

A Timely Endorsement:

Sitting atop Cissbury Ring in West Sussex with colleagues on 28th June 1994, I was unaware that Salumet's very first visit to the Kingsclere Group had just occurred the evening before. David Russell and I dowsed details of the Cissbury location from information I had received by psychic means. A tall standing stone had once marked the spot, that the Romans had destroyed and replaced by a small temple to Diana—Goddess of hunting—also long-since gone. Local people had used the standing stone as a *communicating* device. We decided to replicate it by erecting a pole with a large amethyst crystal strapped on top of it; when all were assembled and with a brief invocation I put my hand on the top of the crystal and closed my eyes. I use 'light trance' and so was aware of what followed, and it was all recorded. Suddenly a powerful being radiated his personality on mine. It was the most intense yet at the same time a 'gentle being' that took hold of me. The voice that came out of my mouth was firm and strong. In answer to questions from Michael Green he gave his name as *JEUZ*, of the star system *Sirius—the Dog Star.* He insisted that he is not of human form, but similar.

Jeuz spoke of 'crop circles': "*The reason that they are here is because your Earth now needs to change. The knowledge of this we have known for thousands of years and we have hinted at it through various mediums and channels for so long, so long—this is only the beginning. The spirit of the land rises and blossoms and there will be signs in the sky. You will see this. The circles are here to help with this so-called 'rising of the Earth'. She must rise up now and join us. She is like a child to us in space, a jewel waiting to flourish, to become who she really is and take you all with her. It is such a journey, such a fantastic journey! And you are part of that journey and you must ride with her and keep the love of God, whatever you conceive that energy to be, in your heart and keep it alive, KEEP IT ALIVE!"* This was a big statement, to which Jeuz then added: *"There is only so much that we can do—yes, we ARE miracle workers—but there are limits. We cannot change the mind of man—he must do that. And it is only the beginning of vast changes. Please continue to work in the light—please do this, not for yourself but for the whole of the Earth, for she is beautiful, far more beautiful than you will know. But given time you WILL KNOW—"*

More was said, more fully accounted elsewhere [16]. I was left in tears—there was such love, such love. And this book is a part of that journey, aided by others in this universe. Our planetary jewel with all of us on board is rising to join and communicate with wondrous beings beyond our earlier imaginings. Read on—be mindful and always keep the love of God alive.

Paul Bura
Writer / Broadcaster / Poet / Psychic

PRE-NOTE:

IT WAS SUMMER1989—WE sat on the topmost step of the Mayan Sun Temple, Palenque, Mexico. I looked up with drifting thoughts at myriad stars in their extraordinary brightness and the cosmic message just zapped in from somewhere up there:

"It's alright to tinker with the mechanics of the universe—to try to figure things out—as did Newton, as did Einstein. It's a kind of appreciation, a kind of homage—BUT—the—most—important—thing—in all the universe—is—LOVE."

The moment was magical and a turning point. Firstly it was Mark, and then a series of synchronistic events led the way, not least when Ann and I bumped into Paul, our youngest on getting off the overnight bus from San Cristobal. The boys were each on six months vacation and Paul had travelled four Central American countries and no news from him for 2-months. We—had experienced a burning desire to get to Palenque; he—was waiting 24-hours for the next bus out. Our meeting was outside probability limits and doubtless meant, so Paul also this night was at the Sun Temple, a structure of truly imposing grandeur beneath those same starry heavens that in times past, mantled the Mayan night; but not in our wildest dreams did we imagine the pathway that now lay ahead.

Once back home, meaningful encounters began, leading naturally enough to the séance group at Kingsclere, Hampshire, UK meeting Monday evenings. It was Monday 27th June 1994, when the Light Being and Ascended Master SALUMET first began his mission to Earth. He spoke through Eileen, an accomplished medium who then rapidly assumed full-trance status. This master of all-knowledge chose this time to enter dense Earthly matter to teach the truth of existence and as I write, his approaching 500 visits continue still. This dear master brings much love, knowledge, upliftment and answers our many questions. The voice that issues from Eileen's briefly borrowed larynx and vocal process is richly vibrant with love and compassion. And the stage was now set for momentous happenings.

14th July 1997: A question placed to Salumet concerned our hopes for the future of the human race. His reply relates to what is happening now. Then, it appeared a bold statement but now, as we navigate into the 21st-century, his words resonate with crystal clarity:

~ "—Why should you confine your hopes, your wishes, to the population of this planet? My wish for you would be, that you could become more aware, more universally aware, more cosmically aware, rather than stay in the confines of Earthly population—I want you my dear friends to be children of the cosmos, because that is what you are. I would wish that you can grow enough whilst we are together, to realise that what you are, and what you have been, is spirit which has been confined to one planet in this lifetime. We have spoken much about this, but now the time is coming, when all of your population, all peoples, no matter what colour, what race, what religion, all will come to the realisation, that we belong to the much wider scheme of life, of living, of love, of that eternal energy to which we all belong."

We should then look beyond ourselves, beyond Earthly horizon, and this endearing master would soon bring others to speak—from beyond that horizon.

Mayan Temple of the Sun, Palenque, Mexico

Following the many wondrous happenings that have since transpired and the writing of this record, Salumet graciously gave his endorsement to the work in a profound style as befits a light-being from that deeper spirit:

~ "—I feel my dear friends that this book is self-explanatory. But I wish to say this to you: Bonniol has demonstrated to all that mind transference has no boundaries—has no limits. Of this we are assured. And I say this: Bonniol has brought to you these things: BEGINNINGS—OPENNESS—NASCENCE—NARRATIVES—INDIVIDUALITY—ORIGINALITY and the essence of all life—LOVE. These things belong to each and every one of you."

Salumet—29th June 2009—
Light-being, Master of All-knowledge and beloved Teacher

Also by George E Moss and Salumet:

A Smudge in Time

SALUMET – His Mission to Planet Earth

DEDICATION:

To all who know instinctively there is more to life than simple Earth-bound one-planet-logic.

To all who accept that humanoid others may wish to say 'hello'.

To those who would boldly venture forth across the universe in mind-linked brotherhood.

Foreword

It was the twin fears of death and infinity that started me on the journey to seek the truth. I could not believe that everything ended with death and yet all things appeared to be finite, even the Earth and the sun would end. Yet at the same time infinity was completely beyond our understanding; so most of my life has been a search to understand the great truths of existence.

Orthodox religion gave me no satisfactory answers, nor did teachers and elders that I asked along the way. But somehow I knew that I would recognise the truth when I heard it, and indeed I did when I met a great teacher, one considered to be a Master.

I was in need of help mentally, emotionally and spiritually when a friend told me about a homoeopathic doctor, and then added, "… but I think he's something more." How true this proved to be! On the second occasion that I saw him homoeopathically he told me that he held evening meetings in his surgery every other Thursday and that I would be welcome to come along. The first meeting was like coming home, every word was like a drop of water in a desert thirsting for knowledge. One night, a few days after that meeting, when I was due to see him as a homoeopath next day, I had a dream.

In the dream he was sitting behind his desk in his untidy study, he leant towards me and said, "Why don't you come and join us Bill?" It was one of those vivid dreams that stayed with me. Later that day I arrived at his house and as I walked into his untidy study he leant towards me with a knowing smile and said, "Did you get my message?"

That was the first of many spine tingling moments that are the wonderful gifts of walking the spiritual path.

After a few years he returned to his true home and I moved on. But always my preferred reading was that of the Ascended Masters, like Silver Birch who spoke through the medium Maurice Barbanell in the Hannen Swaffer Group. On going back to read them there was always something to learn, something that had been missed or something that I was now ready to understand; they were still my teachers.

You can imagine then the depth of my joyful excitement on receiving a letter from the Kingsclere Group, two of them having read my autobiography "Soul on the Street", telling me of their group and the Ascended Master Salumet, an Ascended Master of today, answering the questions of today: terrorism, global warming, the financial crash, as well as delivering all the arcane wisdom, and speaking with the gentleness and love that is always present with these wonderful light beings. What unspeakable joy!

The Kingsclere Group are blessed with his ongoing visits, having been prepared and having been together in previous incarnations; with Eileen as a full-trance medium and George Moss as the dedicated chronicler. Salumet has been with them since 27th June 1994, teaching, nurturing and expanding consciousness, through regular Monday evening meetings that, in addition to the evening plan, are often filled with delightful humour. He said to them during an early visit that his wish was for them to become more universally aware, more cosmically aware, rather than stay in the confines of Earthly population.

The incredible sequel to this was that on the night of 4th October 2004 Salumet introduced a visitor. This time the visitor was not one from the discarnate spiritual realms, as quite often happens on these occasions, but an incarnated humanoid being from a distant planet; a planet from beyond our observable universe! That planet is known to its inhabitants as "Aerah" and the visitor: "Bonniol".

Now, the most cynical of scientists will admit that merely by the law of averages there will be other inhabited planets, and indeed some of them even send out radio messages in the hope of one day receiving a reply. They choose to ignore the presence of UFOs, and likewise the increasingly complex messages in crop circles that are way beyond the abilities of two men and a plank!

But despite modern conventional patterns, suddenly we have it, not through radio or any means acceptable to orthodox science, but nonetheless we have a direct communication with another being from a distant planet. The word "alien", although once correct, has become a vague description with derogatory connotation; and these beings are spiritually much advanced. It is Salumet's advice that "space brother" would be apt expression and we are all of us children of the cosmos.

For those ready to accept and understand what is happening it is an occurrence of mind blowing magnitude, an unbelievable source of scientific, intellectual, spiritual and mind expanding information, not to mention the sheer joy of finding such cosmic companionship.

It is impossible to express our gratitude to the Kingsclere Group and Salumet for bringing us Bonniol, and indeed other visitors, and also to George who has written this amazing, unique chronicle in such a clear and easily understandable way.

This will be the most breath-taking read of your life!

William Roache, MBE

Preface

To project a mind across the countless light-years of this universe and speak with another was once merely a dream. Not so now; it has become today's full-fledged reality. The means is to hand and understood at last; that is, understood so far as Earthly intellect is capable of the knowing, for what must now be told, has for too long rested *remote from our knowledge.* John Milton's expression well describes the absence of such a concept from present day thinking. What follows is an account of how an advanced civilisation, living on a planet in a far galaxy has managed to establish communication with a group here on Earth. I speak for that latter group and in fact it might be said, I speak for both. Included in the narrative are details of how this has come about, why at this time, and then most important of course, there are the verbal exchanges themselves. These are quite detailed and for the most part presented as separate chapters. They take the form of conversations between the mind-projected one from afar and our Earthly group, all digitally recorded during evening sessions, as was meant to be. We are told we are the eighth planetary culture to have been reached in this way, and our mutual interests continue to be fired, as more and more astounding details come to light. The dialogues are well authenticated by others, not least the light-being and Ascended Master SALUMET whose essential and clarifying commentaries are also presented. Earth does not stand alone in the starry heavens. Did we ever really think that? There is much planetary life and love throughout all of existence, and our place in the grand pattern of divine creation now becomes strikingly clear as never before.

This first account of mind-link communication across the universe is set out in three parts with interim résumé chapter concluding Part One.

Contents

APPENDICES

REFERENCES

ILLUSTRATIONS

Acknowledgements

To this work of historic record and fresh understandings there have been many contributors. None has contributed more of course than our dear friend and universal mind traveller, Bonniol, who says so much in these pages; there is also his support team living on Planet Aerah gathered in his house there. We are indebted to many beings, both physical and non-physical. In the non-physical realms embracing both our planets are the 'guides' who facilitate connections, those who work the energies and the 'controls' who speak during séance with timely advice. All have made valuable contribution towards this record of intergalactic exchange. We value all that has been given and our Earthly team give sincere thanks.

We are indebted to Salumet for, in the first place, steadily and patiently raising our awareness through years of wonderful teaching and dialogue, and then arranging-through-spirit-connection the Bonniol visits; this to clarify our place in the universe and the part this planet plays within the *whole* of creation. I suspect also a further motive: to endorse the truth of our existence as taught, by exposing humans to other physical beings of the universe *that are more spiritually advanced* than present day humanity. This might be seen as an incredible gift that should assist Earth in taking a necessary giant pace forward.

The team who regularly sit in séance are listed in Appendix I, but we also acknowledge with thanks all those who have taken the trouble to 'sit in' on occasions in order to share in the experience and feel the dynamic of connection. There have been those from near and far, the latter including visitors from Canada, USA, Japan, Denmark, Finland, New Zealand and Australia. Thank you also to those who stay in touch through the free email service, and to all who help spread news.

Our thanks to William for much appreciated support, for reading the first draft, sending questions for Salumet and for contributing a Foreword—our heartfelt thanks for being there.

And thank you dear ones who watch over homes and families, enabling those of us who meet, to speak across the universe. There is one other: Leslie—Leslie Bone our group founder. We owe so much to the one who began these séance meetings.

Introduction

Bonniol, as do many of us, lives in a house on a planet in this universe. His appearance has similarities yet he is nonetheless different; bigger, more hairy, larger eyes and his people are more advanced in several ways. We might fairly describe them as humanoid. But the important point is: our dear friend has the most beautiful, loving and wonderfully-developed mind that can launch into interplanetary travel and communicate with others. There is a mode of interlocution not caught up in the fabric of space-time. It is beyond the Einstein continuum, so that the constraint of light-speed simply has no grip. Here, *instantaneous* mind connection can be made with another with total disregard to physical astronomic distance. The physical format of space-time is severely limiting but there is much that simply lies beyond that controlling presence, much that is free from any tangible imposition from that spatiotemporal construct. Details of this and explanation for the phenomenon of mind projection, in scientific language, are given in the appendices. The text that follows is very much a log of wonderful exchanges that have taken place through 4-years of regular encounter. What Bonniol has to say should uplift as well as astound all who read; it is A REVELATION that should influence for the better, life on Earth, and the way we perceive the cosmos in its entirety. So much more can now be understood of what is oft described as the PERFECT PLAN and how we on this planet are a small integral part of the living, growing creation. It is true we can only think of the starry void that envelops as infinite, yet all its bounds are within our easy reach. It is curious the way 'infinity' dwells just outside the exactness of imagination and reason. Infinity extends forever and therefore must be inexact, yet there, just beyond the crisply ordered, everyday comprehension is a domain of paramount importance. The rational brain perhaps understandably, at first approaches with caution. But that endless 'place' of the deeper spirit holds our kismet and access to all else and now draws us as never before.

Bonniol speaks carefully articulated words during séance using the voice mechanism of Paul, a medium to whom he is mind-linked. All dialogue is digitally recorded—three recorders—stored on computers and transcribed. Full records as sound files, hard copy and discs are kept and valued as nothing on Earth!

A chronicle is defined as a continuous register of events placed in time order; some would add that it is a recital of facts. What follows is certainly a recital; of events that are without any shadow of a doubt true facts, albeit facts which are a little strange for this world. In truth they are not of this world, nor even of this galaxy; indeed, they concern much further reaches of this universe. Yet you will agree as what is said unfolds, that the account can in no way be fiction, even though its strangeness may tempt one at times to dismiss it as such. But made-up fantasy it most certainly is not and perhaps we should now open our minds to the notion that all things are possible within this wondrous cosmos. The 'time order' is standard Earth-time and refers to the date sequence of communications. But the chronicles themselves concern a planet known to its inhabitants as 'Aerah', the correct pronunciation of which is as 'aero' but with 'o' replaced by an extended 'ah!'. I well remember how Bonniol carefully stressed the sound so that we should get it right—A-e-r-a-a-a-a-h!

Aerah is a doorway of opportunity that has opened at a time when we, the people of Earth, need to look far beyond ourselves. Opening this doorway will aid world-awareness of our true place within the vastness of the cosmos, a place always held. But only now, do we begin to acknowledge that ours is just one small planet within the much grander pattern of a very much alive and living infinite creation.

But how can we possibly know what a culture living on a planet in some far off galaxy call their home? The simple answer is: we speak with them. Nevertheless, the average rational person will immediately say, and understandably so, that such a thing is simply impossible. And it is true that just to go beyond our own Milky Way star system means travelling *thousands* of light-years. In fact, the physical universe seen in the night sky has its fixed 'speed limit' contained within itself. Nothing, under any circumstance, travels faster than light, not even radio waves or TV—and the distances across the universe are so vast as to be measured in 'light-years'—the cosmic yardstick known as one light-year being the distance travelled by light in one whole year. That velocity, as taught when *I* was at school: 186,000 miles per second. It is indeed fast! And the number of seconds in one year is vast. Therefore one light-year is a difficult-to-imagine distance. It follows from this that, if we have a chat with someone out there, each time we speak, it takes thousands of years for words to reach target, and further thousands of years for a reply to get back. And that is just the first 'hello'! Even locally, it takes any electromagnetic waveform 16 minutes to get to the sun and back, and more than eight years for the two-way journey to our nearest star—the *very local* heavens. So chatting across the *galaxies* surely must be reasoned as ludicrous; utter, complete, impossible nonsense! Well not quite. There is as it happens, a shortcut that avoids the speed limit.

Turning aside from that for one moment, let us further place the matter into perspective by considering our efforts in rocketry. The recent years have seen a manned moon rocket and unmanned probes exploring inner solar system planets; sufficient to warrant media headlines. Quite rightly so, and this is no small achievement. In retrospect however, this has been at huge and alarming cost, and already the limitations of such endeavours are plain to see. We cannot, by this means, expect to go beyond our own little solar system, which forms but a mere smidgen of one single arm of this, our very own galaxy. To visit by mechanical contrivance, or even to communicate by radio beyond this galaxy with others, is outrageously unthinkable! Certainly it is—just so long as we think of ourselves as purely physical beings, living in an entirely physical universe that is subject to the relentless, controlling physical laws, which the old 20th-century science has placed so elegantly before us. But, in the words of John Milton, these are facts *not to be ever staring on*. That was yesterday, today it is time to *discover onward things*.

So let us pursue the shortcut. We are *not* purely physical beings and it would be quite wrong also, to think of the universe as entirely physical. It is not. It has its other side, in general not at all well observed or understood and hence often labelled 'mystical'. This other side is not subject to the physical laws of our scientific and more immediate knowing, and there is no imposed 'speed limit' within its bounds. To put it in a nutshell, the visible universe has its non-physical or spiritual counterpart where physical laws have no place, and it can be accessed by beings such as humankind and various other mind-developed beings throughout the cosmos, once the protocol of access is understood and activated. This leads to the amazing revelation that conversations are indeed possible across limitless astronomic distance with no time delays whatsoever. Question-and-answer chats are instantaneous with no waiting-gaps. It would be no exaggeration to think of it as an in-place, instant, cosmic telephone system. But this all requires a much fuller and more detailed explanation. This will be forthcoming, but like so many worthwhile deep matters, we must go one step at a time.

The 'cosmic telephone system' is in the nature of a spiritual attribute but what do we mean by 'spiritual'? Perhaps we should peer beyond the 'blinkered view' of one-planet-single-religion-spirituality that once dominated while we were growing up. Let us now leap straight into a grand, celestial overview and consider the teaching that *all progressing cultures throughout the entire universe* recognise and serve the one Creative Principle or Universal Consciousness; there are many alternative names. And here on Earth, 'God' is often still much favoured and cherished. If we can overlook for one moment language, astronomical placement and trivial details, then much conformity will be seen to exist across the many light-years of spiritual enlightenment. If we are ever to be more than just simple single-planet-dwellers with little thought for aught else, then this is the hurdle we must leap to find the true 'universal' spirituality. It is a mega-hurdle.

We have progressed to the first significant point: that spirituality is *not* confined to one religion or to this one planet alone but runs throughout all God's creation, regardless of galaxy, planetary system, language, sect, creed or humanoid mind. And any who accept that all is indeed of divine creation must surely be ready to accept the rationale that all has spiritual identity and origin. It might be good to pause and just reflect for one moment, for this is one big statement. Spirituality and physicality each extends throughout all existence, both seen and unseen. In fact, we may think of the universe as being not one but two, one physical and one spiritual, two universes that co-exist. They inextricably entwine. But each is as if separate from the other in the laws that prevail. This duality is a factor that our limited brains must now encompass. Yet, I feel sure none would challenge the principle that the laws that govern spirit are different from those that control the material world. That is an obvious truth.

There are laws for the material domain that control weather pattern, planetary motion, light speed and such. But since the spiritual universe is essentially without material form, without dimensions of space and without time dependence, it is subject to a different rule book. Spiritual laws do indeed exist, as any who habitually access that realm via meditation, prayer or séance will know. Those spiritual laws, centring on love as they do, are ever an influence upon the material world. This was strikingly evident at that time when *The Commandments* were delivered to Moses. This event, I would point to, as one excellent example of the way in which spiritual and material domains interact. There are many ways in which the two universes (spiritual and material) can and do interact, and the mind projection process is one of them.

Thus far I have simply laid down a fabric of facts and observations that provide a sketchy approach to mind projection. There are many I know, who would prefer a more objective scientific introduction. Those readers are referred to the paper: *A Case for Two Universes*, Appendix II. Briefly, significant issues emerging from this are:

The physical brain functions as: a generator of intellectual reason, as a transmitter of information located elsewhere and as a transmitter of other information from elsewhere that is 'personally guided'. (Information held elsewhere would include conscience, inspiration, guidance from spirit and divine teaching.)

1. Personally guided transmissions come under the collective heading of 'mediumship', four distinct types of which are listed.

2. Three types generally occur during group séance, and especially where a group of dedicated ones meet regularly, so that some permanency of connection is established.
3. A *partial-trance* medium will be able to allow one from spirit to speak and will be aware of what is said, while the medium's own personality takes a back seat, so to speak. This is a frequent happening within séance groups.
4. A *full-trance* medium has no awareness of what transpires. The one who comes through takes over completely, the personality of the medium being placed entirely to one side. This arrangement is rare, but becomes necessary when one from a very much higher level descends to dense Earthly matter. Salumet regularly visits the Kingsclere Group, via the full-trance medium Eileen Roper.
5. *Mind Projection* is another remarkable form of mediumship. As above, the knowledge given will be unknown to the mind of the medium. In this phenomenon, the mind of one physical being links with the mind of another physical being via the realm of spirit. Spirit guides and spiritual protocol are involved in making and allowing the mind-connection. Unimaginable distance in terms of *physical* universe may be encompassed. More details are given later, much better explained during séance by Bonniol.

   One further issue: spirit entities and mind projection are not solely the preserve of séance and meditation groups. The United States Military Surveillance Program, coming from completely different direction and motive, has made parallel and documented discovery. That completely different bodies, seeking entirely different goals should make matching spiritual discoveries, is astonishing. This remarkable concordance should help reassure any who may have reservations concerning séance groups.

We are now in a position to proceed with the 'chronicles'. These involve many speakers. To help clarify, the prefix symbol '~' denotes speech received via a medium, and a different font is assigned to each speaker source:

~ ***"Bonniol is always presented in bold italic script."***
~ **"Salumet is in bold standard font."**
~ *"Others from spirit are in plain italic."*
"Human speech is presented thus."

References to Earthly literature have superscript numbers with appendix listing. In the dialogues, an inconsequential word in brackets has sometimes been included to improve sentence flow.

Just one further comment—this is a huge project; a first in space-exploration and new technique, employing hitherto undreamt of design—we did not design it—it just happened. Hence, as we of necessity feel our way, early chapters are hesitant and slow. But then, as momentum gathers, things really begin to happen! And as the pace of life accelerates it is a blessing that guidance is close by, currently delivered by Salumet and Bonniol with many others in attendance. I think we may rejoice in our good fortune.

George E Moss

E. Wittering, W. Sussex—November, 2008

PART ONE: *Incredible Reality, Love Thy Neighbour, a Highroad to Energy-superabundance and Mind in an Infinite Universe*

This kind of knowledge is a thing that comes in a moment like a light kindled from a leaping spark which, once it has reached the soul, finds its own fuel.

Plato 428 BC

CHAPTER: 1
Travellers and Journeys ... 4th October 2004

As usual we had travelled from locations in Hampshire, Berkshire, Dorset and West Sussex to gather in Lilian's home. Following initial 'hellos', delivery of paperwork from last week and setting up recorders, we filed into the darkened room set aside for weekly séance. Names and addresses were voiced to those in spirit for healing; then silence as prayers and greetings were given mentally. One from spirit came through Sarah to say there were messages for the two gentlemen. That would be Paul and me, others being ladies this time.

Between lengthy spells of supply teaching, Paul often travels, not in any living-it-up luxury style, but more to imbibe and experience life in faraway places as the student and inveterate traveller; this time parts of China and Tibet, calling at several monasteries on the way. In fact he was already packed and ready to leave next day—for five months. The first message was for Paul. They clearly knew the intricacies of his journey and wished him safe passage through the mountains. And he was to watch his step!

The second message was for me but addressed equally to the group; a timely 'thank you' for the Salumet book[1], going to publishers on Thursday. Our dialogue clarified that many had contributed, both from spirit as well as group. Our visitor continued: ~ "*Yes, indeed for us it is a great pleasure to see people who stay together for so long. The dedication that each of you gives to this work is not forgotten and we help you in any way we can. We may not speak to you as often as we would like, but of course, we know you understand the teaching that* ***comes to you as a book.***"

The book, had been a combined effort, from 'above' and 'below', with Salumet duly named as principle author, hence the expression: *the teaching that comes to you as a book*. And in typing the connecting-work, I have to say that sometimes ideas have just floated in that have not seemed to be my own conscious effort! And so it is all teamwork. Our knowing visitor went on to say more, thanking Lilian for hosting the meetings, and (correctly) noting how I have sometimes struggled with the computer. We asked if she was here often: ~ *"Since I last came to you I have observed many times and of course I too am still learning. But I always return to those who speak the simple word truthfully. I am always drawn to the simplicity of the word. I feel that it might seem, how shall I say—very appropriate at times to use the longer words, (but) the simple word as you well know, sometimes has greater impact."*

I had to agree but felt obliged to add: "I am trying to write for some of us who are more scientific as well—and I must admit that I have put in just a few longer words."

Knowing chuckles broke out as our visitor went on:

~ *"Well, we would not expect anything other than that from **you**!"*

That was the punch line that got everyone going. The truth is I have for many working years written scientific reports and my little foible of using the occasional long word has been noticed by our friends in spirit! What else!? There was mention of how our dear friend Leslie was a valued 'stepping stone' in our endeavours, and how in his day there had been a change in the pathway forward. This led to the observation: ~ *"It is not the individuals. It is the word and the truth and the love that continues to exist—but always we need people such as your selves, who are prepared to sit and allow the spirit to come forward."*

Then a Chinese lady speaking through Sue said one would be coming via Paul. Now this was surprising, because thus far Paul had been little used as a medium. And as is often the way with new developments, there was faltering at first: ~ ***"I—"***

Lilian: "Hello. Welcome! Can you tell us your name?"

~ ***"Yes—it's Erra—justa mejua—"***

Lilian: The first time you've done this?

~ ***"Yes."***

Lilian: "It must be rather strange."

~ ***"It is. We are very, very—careful."***

At this stage, of course, Lilian very reasonably assumed it to be a visitor from spirit learning to speak through a medium and went on reassuringly: "We are used to receiving people from your side of life..."

~ ***"I—I have to be patient I think. If I am here a little longer, it should get easier."***

A few more struggled words and Lilian was saying: "We won't ask too much of you this time."

But our guest made the surprise announcement: ~ ***"I could stay—forever!"***

A pause followed. In a bid to make more relaxed conversation, Lilian lightly ventured: "This instrument (medium) is going on a journey soon. Did you ever travel?"

It was one of those little forays that turned out to be rather more on target than intended, and it provoked a response, delivered humorously and midst our laughter: ~ ***"I am travelling now! This is an INCREDIBLE journey—to here!!!"***

Lilian: "You've been going for quite a while, have you?"

~ ***"I think it's best to say, I am not from this place. I come from another—PLANET—I think that's the word. I am testing the water, you might say—for future exchanges—then we can teach each other things. At first, we are meant to get to know each other."***

This is exactly the way it began. We now know 'Erra' to have been an attempt at the *planet* name and I rather think that 'justa mejua' was an attempt at 'just a minute'. But after the faltering start, we now had acceptable dialogue, a little slow and hesitant at times. But this after all, has to be seen as one huge step in language and mind connection. It surprised us at the time that there was any trace of fluency at all. But it is best that we let our new friend explain in due course, in his own good time, in his own way, why this should be and how it all works. We asked about the position of his planet:

~ ***"I think—from a galaxy you will not know yet—farther than you could imagine."***

Eileen asked: "Are you of the same form as humans here on Earth?"

~ "Very similar, very similar—only a little bigger—and perhaps thicker—and with longer hair—and—bigger eyes—but very similar in other ways."

Eileen: "And are you more advanced than we are?"

~ "Yes and no—we have trodden the shores—areas—you are still behind in."

Eileen: "You've obviously learned to speak our language, to communicate. What language do you use on *your* planet? Is it with words?"

Lilian: "Or do you communicate by thought?"

~ "It's the language of—Erra."

Lilian: "On this planet we have many languages."

~ "It's the language that has evolved on our planet. It is not like anything I have heard on yours."

Lilian: "Is yours a beautiful planet?"

~ "Yes—we have so much in common."

George: "Do you wear clothing as we do?"

~ "Yes—we have our own—fashions!"

Incredible! Spoken like he comes from Carnaby Street! And I think we all began to feel that here was a humanoid being with whom we might seriously identify.

We asked more about language but there was difficulty.

~ "It may be better to wait for this—link to improve. Then I can try—I think it's time for me to go now."

So with thanks and farewells that was it, Lilian adding: "We shall look forward to next time."

We were left with many thoughts. If on their planet, they have evolved to a single language, then they are indeed advanced. (But we should not jump to any hasty conclusion at this early stage. The development of lingua franca in some form would not necessarily exclude regional languages; on this, more will be said later.) Then there is the question of his knowing Earth languages. That was puzzling, and by what process does he know 'English' with such expressions as 'testing the water'? It was altogether too clever for one who is not even humankind! How can this be? But this for us was unknown territory. There would be much yet to unfold. We must be patient and take one step at a time. There is also endorsement of the principle of mind being unencumbered by material distance, and if, as our visitor says, we do not even *know* his galaxy, then it must be far indeed. Here on Earth during the past century, we have developed sophisticated travel systems, cars and motorways, mobile phones and a spread of electronic media. These have already made this world appear smaller. Under sail, it once took months to navigate an ocean. Powered flight now does it in, not months, but hours. Now, with mind-to-mind communication across immense universal expanse, the entire creation comes closer.

This chapter is about beginnings—the embarking upon several journeys: that of mind-travel across the universe and that of Paul setting out for China and Tibet. But by far the most important, is that ever-present one; our spiritual journey forward, and this now beckons as never before.

CHAPTER: 2

Salumet and a Synchronicity ... 11th October 2004 ... 24th January 2005

Our teacher was with us the following week and quickly observing that we still thought hard on last week's encounter, invited questions. There was one from Eileen, delivered by Lilian (since, as explained, Eileen's personality is elsewhere on Salumet evenings). She was concerned that beings were coming via spirit from beyond the galaxy, and why should this be? After all, most people still have difficulty accepting the idea of visits from ordinary UFO space-travellers? This led to a number of points being made by Salumet, providing useful general clarification.

Firstly he explained: Paul is inexperienced in the role of medium. True, but where extragalactic communication is concerned there is also widespread lack of familiarity amongst *mediums*, equally in the broader population (a subject still largely ignored by press, scientific circles and religious bodies alike). Paul it appears is the one *chosen by Bonniol.* He is the favoured instrument for this particular assignment. The selected method of communication is 'spiritual mind projection'. This involves the spiritual mind, which is very different from intellectual brain function that some might loosely think of as 'intellectual mind'. A reason for choosing the Kingsclere Group is the good standard of protection and safety that has built over the years of working together. It is an established group with excellent spirit connections. This is a new link that has been achieved and Salumet assures *there will be further communications.* Then in more specific reply to Eileen's question, the point was made that whilst the vast majority of Earth's population would not have ready acceptance of extragalactic communication, *this group* in Salumet's estimation is indeed ready. I was aware that Paul, now in China, had thought much on the matter and considered it to have been a 'real event' and something to be excited about, and I conveyed this to Salumet. He replied that Paul now has much time to reflect, and the timing of the event *was not accidental.*

In a subsequent session Salumet added that Paul has been primed for this work for quite some time. And in reply to a question concerning suitability of energy: ~ **"And it does not happen just like that—although I know sometimes as you sit within this room, you feel that communication is an instant thing. It does not happen in that way. There is much work on both sides."**

In fact, the more we continue the more we realise the need for lengthy preparations. But Salumet's words had substantially confirmed our nebulous thoughts and inner feelings, not least that this project will indeed continue.

Moving on to mid-November, I usually take a holiday break then. This involves driving across France with Ann and two friends Sheila and Alan, to Timeshare apartments at Tignes, in the French Alps. The high-level resort always has snow, and it is so exhilarating to ski down La Grande Motte. The mountainous terrain, a sparkling white wonderland with here and there a windswept rock face, has immense beauty. On this occasion Alan drove, while Ann and I were back-seat passengers and I found my knee was against something solid in the seat-pouch. It turned out to be a synchronicity in the shape of Courtney Brown's book: *Cosmic Voyage* [2]. Alan had borrowed it from the public library for holiday reading. After taking appropriate notes from this *very* interesting book, I then had a lengthy question for Salumet on returning. It concerned the espionage work of US Military Surveillance, to which he replied: ~ **"I will answer your question. Firstly, let me say this to you: the purpose of their work was to begin with, not for good, as you have quoted to us. But they have discovered much to their amazement, what many of you Earth people already know through mediumship. This is not new to those who have worked with our world for much of their human lives. That is the first point I wish to make. Let us now come to what you feel is a new concept to you—nothing comes to you by accident!"**

This we have heard before and I readily agreed, explaining, largely for the benefit and amusement of my colleagues, how the book had been virtually planted in my lap during the journey across France.

~ **"But my dear friend, we had spoken had we not, of mind projection? Well, our young gentleman friend (Paul) was used for that very purpose! It is the beginning of letting you know that whatever I bring to you, will be verified from many other sources. Therefore I think that your amazement is now a little dulled! We have, as I have told you previously, reached a point where you can now accept the fuller picture."**

I replied: "I appreciate that this adds on wonderfully to our recent introduction to 'mind projection communication.'"

~ **"And mind projection is nothing new. It has always existed, but it is only in your time, may I say, that all of this information is being gathered, and there are pockets of people on your planet who are wishing to strive for ever-increasing knowledge, and these include your scientific communities. Your question about those beings that take care of the cosmos, that also is not new, but they are given a new title (in the book: The Galactic Federation)—you may use whatever words you wish, but to us they are 'spiritual beings working for the good of all planets.'"**

So, to our teacher, mind projection is 'old hat'! I went on: "And in their mind projection, they refer to encounter with 'Midwayers' and point out they should not be confused with angels. I think *they* would be what *we* know as 'spirit guides' (and in an earlier teaching, Salumet had pointed out that some are apt to confuse 'spirit guides' with 'lower angels'.)"

~ **"Perhaps a question for them would be: midway to what?"**

I suggested midway between physical Earth and deeper spirit.

~ **"But they have a long way to travel."**

It is of course the midwayers or spirit guides who play important roles in mind projection, facilitating the connection between spirit and physical being, so either name has some point. But of course, 'spirit guide' is the time honoured, widely known functional name, while 'midwayer' is equivalent military jargon. The 'fuller picture' referred to is the total connectedness of spirit and physical universe, accounting for phenomena such as 'synchronicity', or that 'designed coincidence' that cannot be described by mathematical laws. It refers to a 'synchronising' of spirit and material realm. Hence, it is in no way chance, but a between-worlds designed connection and the probability laws of mathematics simply do not apply.

On 24th January 2005, Salumet declared that he was pleased to see our continued preoccupation with mind projection, and I mentioned that we had heard from Paul and expect his return in the following month. Our teacher repeated that he had been given the quiet time to ponder, and added: ~ **"We have so much time—we must never rush this kind of knowledge. It is for you to absorb, in order my dear friends that you may teach others, step by step, in the same way that I have endeavoured to bring to you knowledge. If you but help one human being on their journey, you have done much my dear friends."**

It is appropriate then, that what follows, be presented step by step without undue haste, in the order as received. These are the guidelines given, and this shall be our aim.

There are times at Salumet's bidding, when Sara guides us on a meditative journey, whilst she herself is moved by the spirit. We hear her gently spoken words as we go within. It was so on this occasion, and our experience was to have awareness of and imbibe a vista of vast, starry heavens: the wider picture. What an awesome journey that was! At the following meeting I put it to Salumet that it seemed to connect with our thoughts on mind projecting through the cosmos. He replied simply: ~ **"That was our intention."**

CHAPTER: 3

Travellers Return ... 7th March 2005

EILEEN WAS AWAY, which meant no Salumet. Paul had just returned from a tour of Tibetan monasteries and hiking through the Himalayas. A control spoke through Sarah to say how the time would be used on this particular evening: ~ "*The one, who is to come to you, will be the one who came before the gentleman went on his travels. We have organised those of us to be with you all this evening, so that we too can join with the information to be brought to you. This experience is not only something different for you, but it is also of interest to us in spirit. So if you will permit this one to come, I will take my leave of you now.*"

As she withdrew, Lilian thanked her and there followed a pause of several minutes before '*the one*' began to speak through Paul: ~ ***"I—will be able to speak—"***

Lilian reassured that we could hear the words, and our visitor continued with some faltering: ~ ***"It gets easier—I am happy though—it's—it's—"***

George: "We realise how difficult it is, and you must obviously take your time—and you are very, *very* welcome to our group!"

~ ***"It is good work—and it is always a help to hear that heart-feeling—with all the help available."***

Lilian: "Yes."

George: "Very good. I think what is happening is what we would call 'mind projection'. Does that sound right?"

~ ***"Yes. That is the way that we've been told, and that is the way we have understood it. I will not say much here (now)—but another time. The way it's done is far beyond your understanding at THIS time."***

George: "Yes, we can *easily* accept that! The last time you indicated that we could learn from each other. We can ask you questions, or you can ask us questions, or you may prefer just to speak."

On reflection, my statement may have seemed pushy, but I had the feeling our visitor welcomed exchange of words to aid the link. But in fact, he steadily became more voluble. He continued ever more positively, managing to string more words together: ~ ***"First I need to acclimatise, with the help—and enjoy the communication and exchange. More information comes later. Then we should say something about the times to come. There is going to be arranged—a series of talks, about a number of ah—ah—ah—"***

George: "I think I understand—a series of talks about a number of *subjects*?"

~ ***"I am thinking of the arrangements for the coming year—and I am allowed to come for other (further) visits—ah. If I bring more equipment here—it's—ah—ah—"***

George: "I imagine there has to be some more experience before moving on?"

~ ***"Yes, experience—and—ah—"***

A break in transmission of several minutes came at this point, then our visitor went on to explain he was making adjustments that might improve things.

~ ***"With the right adjustments made, it will be much more—better for us—both for this work, and leaving the opportunities to experiment and find the best arrangement, and such. We should then feel this has blossomed. And if there (still) is a problem, we will leave it for this time. Let us continue now—it's now fixed."***

We expressed gratitude for his efforts, and I ventured that it was wonderful that this exchange was happening at all. Lilian added that our group for this evening was smaller than usual and power would likely be low.

~ ***"Yes, good things always take time—but every step brings us together a little closer—closer to finding the truth of life and our true natures. I come from the farthest reaches beyond your galaxy ... and there is so much life and pure energy in the farthest reaches. I can bring some of the power load and—"***

As another long pause lengthened I ventured: "Last time, I think you mentioned the planet 'Erra'. Is that your planet—Erra?"

~ ***"Yes—Aerah."*** It was now given to us as a more expressive rendering than before.

Lilian: "Thank you. It sounds just a little like 'Earth'"

~ ***"She is con-scious-s-s, like a brother."***

I sought more precise meaning: "The planet has consciousness?"

~ ***"As has your Earth."***

Lilian, recalling a Salumet teaching: "Yes! And you said she was a brother. What do you mean by that?"

~ ***"We are all brothers."***

Lilian: "Yes, I do agree with you there!"

~ ***"Yes!"***

George: "We that live on the planets—all brothers." (Salumet had once suggested the term 'brother' as so much more satisfactory than 'alien', which has an unfriendly feel.)

~ ***"Then—we are all one!"***

Lilian: "Yes, and those on all planets, we think of as our brothers."

~ ***"As your Master—more than I—can show you!"***

Much agreeing and knowing laughter followed. Lilian was then saying how well our visitor had done, and asked for a name to know him by. That was the point at which the transmission abruptly terminated. Our new friend had rejoined us at the very first opportunity following Paul's return. At the outset there was intermittency and slowness, and we were reminded of the first occasion with Salumet. One cannot expect instant, flowing dialogue when amazing pioneering channels first open. As has been said, it is wonderful really that this happens at all. There was indication towards the end, that our friend has knowledge of our master and his teaching. He has indeed. These facts may appear curious, but let me just say that all will become clear and rational as we proceed.

CHAPTER: 4
More from Salumet – A Few Details ... 28th March 2005

ANOTHER MEMORABLE EVENING began with Salumet who some way into his session was saying: ~ **"Do you have questions this time?"**

We had, and Lilian signalled that I should go ahead. It concerned space-travel in the general sense. I attempted a summary of travel modes: using physical travel, rocketry, we can explore the solar system but no further; using the spiritual attribute of de-materialisation we can go beyond but still within the galaxy; but using mind projection we can go much further again. So I asked: "Is there a limit for mind projection or is it dependent upon the mind?"

~ **"Yes, I understand your question. When we speak of mind, we are speaking of course about spirit. We know that spirit is (spiritual) energy. Therefore there cannot be limits for mind projection as far as travel (distance) is concerned. There is limitation within the spiritual realms of all time, but there is no limitation for the projection of mind when it comes to travel within all that exists."**

The wording is a little curious, but I think Salumet is saying that there is no governance by time within *deeper spirit*, and no limit to the distance that may be covered in mind projection work, within that deeper spirit. I went on: "So the mind does not have to be a particularly developed mind?"

~ **"We can take an infant who can mind-travel. This is a topic that we have not touched upon as yet, but I assure that we shall."**

George: "That would be interesting! Our friend—who reaches us from the planet Aerah—I understand that they operate as a team, and I imagine the team help to control, or stabilise the mind that travels?"

~ "Whenever there is a collective consciousness, there is always that ability to help or control in any way that is necessary."

George: "So we can think of that in terms of a collective consciousness?"

~ "Yes, where an energy is collected together. Again, we are using Earthly words, but 'collective consciousness'—that is as far as I can say. Is that clear?"

George: "Yes, thank you. I was thinking: at least, we have got as far as being able to *detect* our own planetary collective consciousness." I was trying to make connection between Salumet's words and our slowly progressing science. (Computer-linked 'random number generator' (RNG) work, has actually detected and recorded fluctuations in our planetary consciousness. And world events such as 9/11 and New Year celebrations show up as energy peaks. This is today's 'cutting edge' research that demonstrates the existence of planetary collective consciousness as a fluctuating energy.)

~ "Yes, that is but a small drop in the ocean. Nevertheless, you have approached this knowledge in great detail—even upon your planet (you) are working *towards* 'spiritualised space' for the planet."

George: "And every drop in the ocean helps in our progress forward—"

~ "Yes, and there are many drops in one ocean!"

On thanking our teacher for his words, I was left with the feeling that he views the scientific method as tediously long and perhaps unnecessary. We can no doubt experience 'spiritualised space' for ourselves without dotting each 'I' and crossing every 'T' of intellectual thoroughness. Even so, it may be reassuring to many that *science has proved the existence of planetary collective consciousness* using physical apparatus, and this beyond any shadow of doubt. And if this exists as one *drop in the ocean*, then other energy collectives are surely likely; that could equally be detected and measured in the fullness of time. The topic of energy was further discussed in relation to feelings Sarah had experienced during our new friend's visit:

~ "Yes—you were used for a charge of energy. But although you feel the closeness of the one you are helping, it does not always mean that there has to be a connection between you."

In this work we are often aware that the availability of power is an important factor, and there are various ways in which this may be boosted. In this instance, one from spirit had remained with Sarah expressly to give power for the connection. The evening continued with Salumet, during which a typical assortment of topics was discussed, from self-development to fox-hunting and aggression in general.

One next came through Sarah speaking on environmental issues and as that one departed, Lilian again welcomed our new extraterrestrial friend. This time the dialogue became really chatty. What a truly splendid evening this time!

~ "I am doing all I can from our side—and it's becoming clearer—I hope."

George: "It is very clear."

~ "Good."

Lilian: "And I do thank you and your friends for the effort that you put into this, and the pleasure you give to others—unlimited!"

~ "I am trying to imagine what YOU must be thinking about US—because it must be harder for you. We are a little more used to speaking with other worlds."

Lilian: "Are you?"

George: "We very much admire your ability to do this. That is the first thing that comes to mind. And if we are in receipt of this communication, that is an honour for us. We very much appreciate what you are doing."

~ "We are very happy and excited to be linking more worlds—like this."

George: "I imagine you know much more about *our* world than we know about yours—"

Lilian: "Well, we know nothing really."

~ "We have the advantage there."

A few facts emerged. Aerah has three moons in the night sky revered as beautiful orbs, one colonised; the atmosphere described as 'thick'. Then we were asking about way of life and how we might compare: ~ ***"There are people in my world who would fit in with yours and there are many—who would not. We are beginning to find that the average person lives—needs—more space for themselves than previously thought."***

George: "Space—do you live in families, or do you have a different kind of unit?"

~ ***"We share the same buildings with our—offspring—the same houses as our children, until they marry, as with yours."***

George: "So you have male and female, and you marry and you have children, and live together as a family, very much as we do?"

~ ***"We have many children at the same location. We believe in bringing them (up) together—to bond and to grow together. So families are mixed together more."***

Lilian: "Something like a kibbutz. Do you know what that is?"

George: "So would it be like a live-together school?" I thought I was helping to clarify a difficult word but our friend surprised—startled us: ~ ***"I think that word (kibbutz) is right—yes!"***

Eileen had just 'returned' from her faraway full-trance, and would now enjoy the rare treat of being able to place questions. This is of course simply not possible during Salumet time when her consciousness is elsewhere; a period is also required for her return. Now she was with us and saying: "Can you tell us what you look like? Can you describe your features? Are they similar to ours, or are they completely different?"

The reply came with knowing good humour and appropriate voice intonation:

~ ***"I've been waiting for that!"***

Our good natured laughter was clearly anticipated: ~ ***"We are larger—a little taller and bigger. We are thicker set, and our hair is blond—all of us. And larger eyes—and the main—ah—ah—"***

Eileen: "Can you describe your feet?"

~ ***"We are—hairy around there—and lower regions are hairier—like horses."***

George: And do you have—we have five toes on each foot. Do you have toes, or is it a different arrangement?"

~ ***"The feet are larger and without toes. They are like—flippers—like a frog."***

George: "I wonder how this relates to the gravity of your planet. Is your planet larger than ours?"

~ ***"Our planet is greater—about three times bigger."***

Lilian: "And do you have computers as we do? I'm sure you do—you are more advanced than we are."

There was a substantial pause at this point, and then the answer: ~ ***"We are trying to develop something LIKE your computers."***

George: "Yes, I think I would be right in saying, you have developed spirit and mind much further than we have. We have developed in a different way—"

~ ***"There are some things that we do not have yet, which we are learning to bring about. We are perhaps a little behind you in your technology."***

George: "I see—but you are ahead of us in other fields—"

~ ***"There are certain things that we have at our disposal that you have not developed yet. There is an energy—ah—"***

George: "We do not yet understand all energies."

~ ***"There is a lot of energies we don't understand either. But there is one that is of great importance—and has allowed us to draw on it. That energy comes from the earth—ah—"***

George: "That would be an energy that comes from within your planet?"

This was clearly a question that was difficult to answer in an intelligible way. Our friend struggled with words, finally saying: ~ ***"I think I have to leave that one for another time."***

George: "Yes, we understand. There is a question I wanted to ask: do you have one language on your planet, or do you have several?"

~ ***"We have many tongues—many different languages."***

George: "So we are similar in that."

~ ***"Yes."***

Lilian: "Do you have different religions as we do, and teachers who started the religions?"

~ ***"We have different ways of worshipping the creation. But the overall beliefs are more together—more united in the acceptance of the Creative Force."***

Lilian: "Hopefully, we shall get there one day."

The diversity of Earth religions is bothersome to many, and I think we all felt it refreshing to learn that a more advanced culture is more united in reverence. This surely is true advancement. There would be so much to compare.

Eileen: "Could you give us one of your words that you use for 'LOVE'?"

There was a pause followed by several attempts. (We now realise that our throat and vocal arrangements are rather different, so that presenting a word foreign to them, could be extremely difficult.)

~ ***"ANCHEELIA."***

Eileen: "Thank you."

~ ***"And it's the same as we say when we are—ah—I am trying to find the words."***

George: "Yes, we appreciate that must be difficult sometimes."

~ ***"It's—sacred".***

George: "Yes, I was going to say: do you equate *love* to *God* or to the *Creative Force*?"

~ ***"I will say—these words are similar, but we have different ones for CREATIVE FORCE—it's not quite so easy now, to form the words. I am having—distractions—I will try once more—and I will have to leave it after this."***

We declared it to have been a very good session, and thanked our friend. Shortly after, the link terminated abruptly and we were left chatting excitedly. Words had flowed quite smoothly and with a good feel.

Curiously, when Salumet joined us the following week he continued the religion theme, prompted by the death of Pope John Paul II. He spoke of the tremendous outpouring of grief from Earth. Much was said of this much-loved pope; also of the state of Christendom, of prophecies concerning pope lineage, and the position of our planetary religions. We listened intently to a sweeping prophetic pronouncement: ~ **"Your Earthly religions cannot last forever—because this time, when so many of us (from spirit), including myself—we come to bring truth—and truth and love cannot fail this time. Therefore, Earthly religions will have their day, when people realise that there is but *one* truth, *one* creator, *one* who loves and nurtures all things—*all* experiences—*all***

planets—*all* universes—*all* of life. Yes, this religion (Christianity) has limited time. The people of your world are now able to think and to feel and to see for themselves. This I gave to you previously, when I told you that each successive generation, will not take any form of religion at its face value. Each individual will decide as time continues, what is right."

The statement is dramatic, profound and directed at *all* Earthly religions. One might conjecture: at first there had to be chosen people, then the Eastern religions, then Western religions, then splinter groups formed as parent religions became confused and lost their way. All should ideally be the same but they are not. Uniting as one would still not be enough. The entire universe; all planets; all creation must be as one—and that oneness must relate to each and every individual. The time *must* come, when old faiths will have served their purpose as stepping stones, crutches and centres of encouragement that once led many. But separatist endeavours are fast becoming superfluous to the more complete, unified awareness. And towards that more complete awareness is where the words of Ascended Masters from deeper spirit now lead. It is time to take account. This statement will rest uneasy with some but ultimately it must be so, or Earth isolates herself from the wider vista of God's work. There is but one creation and one Creative Principle. Recognition of the totality of creation is what this is about.

CHAPTER: 5
The Next Week's Nexus and New Perspective ... 11th April 2005

SALUMET NOW SPOKE of energy, spirit and mind projection. I report salient fragments of a lengthy discourse: ~ **"How is it possible for the thoughts of another from so far to travel through space to reach you here upon this planet? I say to you: it is simple when you know how it is done!"**

We countered that since it does not happen often, the 'knowing how' is perhaps difficult to grasp.

~ "It is being aware of the spirit self rather than the physical; you must let go of all things physical, in order to use the energy which, after all, is spirit—it is the clarity of the thought energy that makes it (mind projection) successful."

Paul: "And the distance is irrelevant—"

~ "You took the word I was about to use!"

George: "So the actual distance does not exist?"

~ "As the young gentleman has said, it is irrelevant. What I wish you to try to understand, is that when you have mind projection from other planets and someone giving you information, it is *instantaneous* in thought. Try not to think of great distance within your universe, because you can only become confused."

George: "Yes, we can *think* intellectually. We can also *feel,* and of course, the *feeling* is allied to spirit."

~ "Yes, of course. Always you must use your heart, you must *feel,* you must use what is given in a spiritual way, because once you begin to analyse, then you will lose your way. Always *feel* when unsure."

We spoke further on the instantaneous nature of the dialogues that have no significant time intervals between question and answer.

~ **"Yes. I am so pleased that you are as accepting as you are in your understanding, because for many these questions and answers would seem so far-fetched."**

Paul: "We accept that there is no time in spirit, and it looks like there is no space either."

~ **"These are difficult topics for you to understand and, as I have said to you so many times, it is difficult to equate spirit with the physicality of living."**

George: "We are talking of spirit in the sense of beyond the near Astral Planes, where there is still some consideration for time?"

~ **"Of course, the plane of existence of which you speak—because you are still so close to the physical plane (Earth), there has to be some *sense* of time, in order for the spirit to adjust. But again, it is a *sense* of time, as you know it—it is a feeling and a *sense* of time."**

And in reply to a question about 'thought communication' on Aerah: ~ **"Yes, it comes with evolvement, and each planet as well as each individual, has its own evolutionary time. And remember, the planet from whence he comes is still a planet of (physical) beings and not (pure) spirit. Please keep this in mind. They may be different, they may have different ways, they may have different voices and speech, but they are still *of existence* and not (pure) spirit as you would think of it. Does that make sense to you? And there are many, many planets with life upon them."**

To clarify further, Sarah was saying: "Life on these planets—is that physical, or spiritual, or both? I was thinking of the beings that make crop circles." (Our previous information on this was that these are physical beings, but they have mastered de-materialising physical matter as and when necessary. This enables them to travel at huge speed across the galaxy.)

~ **"All of existence is spiritual, yes—but of course, they have as *you* do, 'form'—so they are physical beings. There are some (physical) beings who, within your own space-time, can travel—space-travel."**

George: "So there are really two types of being in the universe, *physical beings* who have spiritual counterparts as our selves, and there are beings who are *entirely spirit*. Would that be a fair comment? So broadly, there are two types of being."

~ "If you are speaking of spirit, they would have no overcoats of flesh. Yes, as I am speaking now, I am a being from spirit, but I come not to you by mind projection, but for your own understanding, I come to you using a human instrument whose voice and body I borrow for such a short time."

George: "We are so happy with that!"

~ "I am so happy to be able to join with you and to help you in your understanding and your knowledge—and of course, I have to say to you, I would not have made an appearance until such time as you were ready to hear me."

We were glad of Salumet's discourse and now felt just a little less out of our depth.

Next, the powerful, clear voice of a control, speaking through Sarah, said: ~ *"Once again, I would like to bring to you, the one from the planet you call Aerah. The connection this time will be of a different nature, and we hope that your understanding will be as clear as we can bring it to you."*

As she was thanked, I quickly re-positioned a recorder.

Lilian: "Good evening—welcome to you."

~ "We are improving the link between our worlds. It is a beginning that will bring us together a little more at each point."

George: "Thank you. We do appreciate your efforts, and welcome!"

~ "There are so many things to talk about—I am unsure again, where to start—"

George: "Yes, could I suggest—could you have another go at telling us your name, because that is something that we have not got clearly yet?"

~ "I am called (There were several attempts before arriving at the final expression.) ***'Bonniol'—Bonniol, that is how it sounds—yes."***

George: "Thank you! Welcome Bonniol!"

~ "It is a common name where I come from. It is the name of a star."

Lilian: "Is it? And our spirit friend was this evening explaining more about the 'travelling of the mind'".

~ ***"It's a useful thing to do. It is used so much in our world."***

At this stage, 45-minutes into the evening, the recorder clicked 'off' and I turned the tape around. We would very shortly change to digital recorders that will transfer direct to a computer file. But this evening, we had the old cassette type. Bonniol noticed the adjustment and referred to the recording process. We of course do not have exact words on this, but we asked if, on Aerah, they record the sessions. His reply, now picked up on side B, was interesting: ~ ***"At the moment we are not using one, because there is no voice to record from our end."***

Lilian: So it's when you go back you can tell them—"

~ ***"No, they are shown the 'views' that I have. We are linked."***

All: "Wow!"

Sara: "So they can *see* us as well!"

~ ***"So they are able to share this mind—the memories of it—as well."***

Lilian observed that it is rather dark in our séance conditions, and I suggested they might see us spiritually rather than physically, so that lack of physical light matters not.

~ ***"We do not see with the eyes. We only see what has already happened and is in memory."***

Sarah: "Oh right!"

~ ***"It transmits as a memory. So now we know what you all look like—from the memories!"***

I am not sure why we all laughed at this, perhaps relief of built tension as we now understood just a little more. But laugh we did and it occurred to me that Paul's memory banks were functioning rather like a satellite relay station, only for spirit.

Lilian: "We'll have to get someone—"

Graham: "To draw a picture of what we think *you* all look like, and you can tell us if it's anywhere near."

~ ***"You will I'm sure, have a clearer picture of our world as time goes by."***

George: "Good. That raises a point—if we were able to draw a physical picture, would you be able to see it?"

~ ***"I may be able to use the eyes at some point. But at the moment, it's better to use the thought only."***

Sarah: "But if your instrument, Paul, were to look at the picture, then you would be able to see it from his memory, would you?"

~ ***"Yes, if you show it to him before the meeting, I can have a look."***

All: "Yes!"

(In fact, with a rather shaky hand, I tried a computer drawing from the brief details we had, but it was like a cross between Fred Flintstone and a frog. I think Paul was none too happy about committing it to memory, and perhaps it is just as well that idea got abandoned.)

~ ***"But I can send you all thoughts of what we look like—and maybe you will have a glimpse of it in your minds!"***

Bonniol seemed a little concerned that we would see big differences. I said it may help that our science fiction writers have given some conditioning re acceptance of other possible forms.

~ ***"I think that can help—and hinder things!"***

All: "Laughter!"

Lilian: "The other planets that you have visited—are they all completely different?"

~ ***"We are finding out how different they are, and it is an amazing thing, how diverse life is on all these planets."***

Lilian: "How many other planets did you visit?"

~ ***"There are eight altogether—and we hope to have others in the near future."***

Sarah: "How did you start this mind-travel?"

~ ***"It is something that has been with us for a long time, but only with our nearest planets."***

George: "It would be interesting to know how you measure time. Does your planet travel around your sun, and do you use this as a means of measuring time, as we do?"

~ ***"We do count time—and talking about that—the Earth orbits the sun—"***

George: "And that gives us our year."

~ ***"And it takes 24-hours, yes?"***

George: "That is the *rotation* of the Earth, to give night and day, and it takes 24-hours. Do you have a similar method of time measurement?"

~ ***"There is more daylight in our world, and the nights are shorter. Our sun is a brighter one—and the atmosphere—ah—ah—"***

George: "Yes, you described your atmosphere last time, as 'thick'. Does that mean it is like cloud? Are you aware of our clouds of moisture?"

~ ***"The atmosphere is thick sometimes—I think I said. It can be thinned, and this is an unusual thing for you I think. I think the atmosphere is like your water, but it is not wet."***

George: "Is it clear? Can you see a great distance?"

~ ***"It is clear."***

Graham: "Do you ever have rain, as we have on this planet, from high cloud?"

~ ***"We have something LIKE your rain. It's not quite the same as water. It has other elements in it, as well as the—hydrogen—and other ones (oxygen?). I would say it is thicker than water—and it moves more slowly in the air."***

Sarah: "We humans are made up of a large percentage of water. Are you made up of the same sort of system?"

~ ***"The recipe is a little different."***

Sara: "Is your skin rougher in texture?"

~ ***"It is rougher, yes."***

Sara: "Brownish colour?"

~ ***"I am—I have brownish eyes, but the skin is pinker, pinker than yours."***

Sarah: "Is the colour of your skin affected by the sun? Does it change colour like ours."

~ ***"It cannot change, from the sun. It stays pink throughout our lives. But the older you are, the paler the skin."***

There was difficulty in getting answers to some questions on time comparisons but it seems that life expectancy on Aerah would be 100-plus of *our* years.

Eileen returned us to spiritual matters with her question: "Before you projected your mind to this planet, did you have to seek permission from anyone?"

~ ***"Yes, there is a 'policeman'. There are beings who deal with this, and we have to be careful and ask permission, before we approach another planet, yes."***

Eileen: "Can you tell us how they would be able to stop you?"

~ ***"If you do it and they wanted to stop us, they could—block the flow—they could block the thought being projected."***

Eileen: "So there are those in spirit who could block the mind projection, is that what you are saying?"

~ ***"Yes, because it is all thought, and these can be changed or blocked easily, by spirit."***

Eileen: "Have you ever known of anyone who has tried to use mind projection to another planet in a negative way?"

~ ***"I haven't, no. There are those who have used it in OUR world, in a negative way towards others. It can be used destructively for selfish reasons. But never between worlds have I known that. This is not something that would enter our thoughts, when doing this work."***

In general spirit communication work, we are familiar with those designated 'gatekeeper', who look after protocol and see to it that only those permitted, get to use the mediums. Perhaps Bonniol is speaking of a similar policing arrangement for interplanetary work. One might also consider if those who cultivate such a spiritual attribute would be at all likely to then *run off the rails* of accepted protocol. I think not, at least, as Bonniol says: never between worlds. But here on Earth we know of voodoo spells, and perhaps this is an example of negative usage within a world.

Eileen: "When we humans are stripped of flesh, there is a skeleton. Can you tell us if you are made in the same way?"

~ ***"Yes, there is a skeleton. It is something similar, yes."***

Much followed from Graham's next line of questioning: "You seem to know an awful lot about our planet. Have you accessed this information from the one you're using?"

~ ***"That's it, yes!"***

Graham: "That's interesting."

Sarah: "So whilst Paul your instrument, was on holiday, you collected all the information—or does it not take very long to collect?"

~ ***"We were working towards THIS TIME. We were not aware of the holiday. We were waiting for something—we did not know that***

was it—that it was a holiday. But we had an idea of the time when it would be possible, from our own guides."

(Perhaps I should reiterate that it was in fact rather more than just a holiday; and without doubt a conditioning period for Paul.)

George: "You obviously know our language quite well. Has this been a difficult matter? Do you pick up language from consciousness, as a spiritual process?"

~ ***"The thoughts go in our own language, it is projected. When it reaches the recipient, it is translated into (recipient's) own language. So it is a question of the thought being translated at this end—thought behaving as a universal language—interpretation."***

George: "I understand, so there doesn't have to be any physical language interpretation?"

~ ***"There is an interpretation, but it is a natural thing."***

George: "It's almost automatic—"

~ ***"Yes, it's the language of thought. This is what allows us to do this."***

Sara: "And do you have humour, like us?"

~ ***"There is much humour throughout the universe! This is what keeps us all going!"***

We laughed and I added: "We could devote an evening to swapping jokes!"

~ ***"We could try! And now I think it's time to leave once more, and I hope we shall be together again soon—for some jokes!"***

George: "This has been a *very* good session! And *thank you* to all the team!"

~ ***"Thank you."***

All: "Thank you!"

The sessions and our understanding were steadily improving. There was a little deep philosophy as well as light-hearted chat, which seemed about right. It all felt friendly and with a mutual trust befitting spiritual encounter. Perhaps the lighter comments worked towards strengthening the link in some way. It is now becoming clear that *thought* is a communicative awareness, void of any language. And our wonderful brains are able to receive thought input from Bonniol for instant conversion to current English. So that is the mechanism!

CHAPTER: 6

How It All Works ...18th April 2005

It was clear from Bonniol's opening words that it was becoming easier each time, and happily his excitement at the prospect of exchanging news and views matched ours. I voiced the thoughts of all in stating: "We feel very excited about this and we do look forward to these meetings."

~ ***"We also look forward to them from our world."***

And in reply to a question from Lilian concerning the extent of their work:

~ ***"We only work with your group on Earth and are working with other worlds, as you know—as we explore this universe—and we wish always to learn more. And this is what this is about, sharing our knowledge and wisdom, and working towards creating better worlds through their sharing."***

George: "Information exchange working towards the common good. Wonderful!"

~ ***"There is a lot to learn for us both. And I would begin by answering your questions and see where they lead us."***

Lilian: "Well, have *you* any questions you would like to ask *us*?"

~ ***"We always have questions. We can find the answers without voicing them often, though not always."***

I asked if that would be through Paul's consciousness: ~ ***"It is memories, as I said before, of the one I speak through. We can access much information. It takes time, but we are gradually working with this one."***

George: "So in order to access *other* information, that *others* in this group have, that would have to be through the dialogue—"

~ ***"This would have to be through dialogue, yes—if it is not in this one's mind, this one's memories."***

Graham's questioning then sought precise description of the process: ~ ***"We are projecting our thoughts from our world to here—and you are 'speaking' your thoughts, which can then be understood as they come through this one. This is hard to explain—the thought projection from you to us is not required, because we are able to access this one's memories. And that is how words from you are changed back to the thoughts that they are."***

Graham: "Yes, that's a very clear explanation. Thank you for that!"

A clarification indeed! And if memory is stored as *wordless thought* to be accessed without language difficulty, this explains much. Wordless thought as memory is a key factor. Perhaps we might compare Paul to a well-ordered public library that allows information retrieval in any language.

~ ***"We hope that you will be able to learn more of this thought projection yourselves. There is no reason why you shouldn't be able to project to us, like we do to you."***

We mentioned 'telepathy' and how just a few people on Earth experience this: ~ ***"These people you speak of are no different I think. It is only that they have practised and have been trained in the method of thought projection from a young age, and it is natural to them now, and if you practise, you may also find it becomes natural to YOU."***

Graham: "Is thought projection something that can be achieved, only through the meditative state?"

~ ***"It requires concentration, focus on the thought in as much detail as you can, so that your whole focus is this thought—that thought which you wish to project. Nothing else should exist in your mind, as you send it forth to your chosen recipient."***

Eileen, having returned from trance: "As you focus your mind to project towards us, is it possible for those thoughts to be intercepted?"

~ ***"We are not able to intercept another's thoughts. If they are clearly aimed at another person, then it is only for them."***

George: "Yes—so there are two factors in this. There's developing the ability to really focus the thought, and there is the target?"

~ "Yes, you send the thought whilst using your mind's eye to visualise that person."

George: "Does the other person have to have the awareness that this might happen?"

~ "If the other person is open, then he will receive the thought. If they are not aware in that way, then the thought will still go to them, but they will be unaware of it—the thought will still reach them though."

Graham: "Could you be aware of a thought that wasn't targeted towards you?"

~ "We can pick up thoughts that are sent out without any clear direction. These are often in the form of ideas."

Graham: "It could get a bit noisy with all these thoughts going around. Do you just close down when you've had enough?"

~ "That is why you should be discerning—only opening in the direction that you wish, and this is again a natural thing. If you are wishing to connect with a certain person, you will naturally open that channel. If you are fishing for ideas—concepts—on a certain theme, you will open to those thoughts which are not directed at another person specifically. It can be useful to do that. You can 'hear' or perceive ideas from the latest thinkers on certain areas—new ideas, more knowledge—"

Graham suggested 'Google Search' as a comparable physical process.

~ "It also narrows things down in a similar way. But the clarity of those thoughts that you send will make the difference. These thoughts are 'living things'. They have their own awareness, if you like. Once you've sent them to someone, that someone may pick them up, may think on them further—they may send them out. The thought is no longer the thought that you sent. It has grown and may continue to grow, as others connect with it and develop it. And one day, that little thought you sent out, may become something of incredible size or shape—maybe an object, and even then, its journey may not end."

Salumet has taught, as have others, how thought powers the creation process. This statement is a description of precisely that.

Thought lies at the cutting edge of evolutionary change. Thought powers all.

Graham: "How do you *receive* a thought? Is it like a voice?"

~ ***"You feel something—it is not something that has a 'physical' feeling. But it is like a light being switched on in our heads, and the thought is changed into language."***

George: "This is very interesting! I rather fancy that something like that has happened in the past on our planet, when people in different countries have invented the same thing at the same time. Unfortunately, this has sometimes been confusing and embarrassing. There was a particular branch of mathematics that a gentleman named Leibniz in Germany invented, at the same time as one named Newton in England. They spoke different languages, they called their invention by different names, but it was the same invention. I think this must have been due to thought interaction—"

~ ***"We cannot always tell you the answers, but I am being told that this one happened—two people picking up the same thoughts, which were sent out to your world by the spirit realms."***

George: "Perhaps this is what we would call 'inspiration'?"

~ ***"Yes."***

[During our 17th-century, the 'calculus' of Gottfried Leibniz was essentially the same as the 'fluxions' invented by Isaac Newton. Ill feeling and suspicion that followed, was it seems unfounded.]

Lilian saw the opportunity for a broader statement on spirit: "Do you believe in the spirit world as we do?"

~ ***"We have our spirit helpers—guides—and we work with them in similar ways that you do. Our connection to them—that can be more direct at times, because we can project our thoughts and receive them more clearly. So that is (how it is) with us, even in our daily lives, but they don't tell us ALL the answers. We have to make our own mistakes, just as you."***

Eileen: "When we've had communication from spirit, we've learned of the way *they* live. Have you had information regarding that? It would be interesting to see if there are comparisons."

~ ***"We have Masters, like the one that comes to you, who have told us many things about the spirit world and this is something that is a vast area. I am not able to say how much of your knowledge***

is the same as ours, at the moment, but I am thinking that it will be in harmony with ours, because truth is the same wherever you are—it's the same universe!"

Eileen: "But your expectation must be different, because you come from a different planet—"

~ ***"Initially, the realms that we pass to when we first go over, will seem different (from Earthly realms)—tailor-made to make the (Aeran) transition easy. Once we are through those lower realms—as we progress, then there is less and less difference—as we move towards that purer energy."***

So it appears that Earth's connection to deeper spirit via Astral Planes is similar in principle to Aerah's connection to deeper spirit. Both planets have a transition zone to the universal deeper spirit. Important facts were now coming quickly, but once again it was time to depart: ~ ***"I think for this time, we should finish. I hope that you have found something of interest tonight?"***

George: "Yes indeed and thank you. It has been *most* interesting, and thank you team!"

~ ***"They also send their love and wishes—hope we can meet again like this soon."***

And there was our general agreement to that!

CHAPTER: 7

Deep Philosophy and Small Talk ... 25th April 2005

NOW BEGAN AN evening of, firstly Salumet who launched straight into a cheering message for Earth, followed by Bonniol who again brought much to think on.

~ **"What I would like to say to you this time my dear friends is that at this moment in time, there is a great outpouring of love directed to your planet. Always within your planet, there are turbulent times. Therefore it is necessary that we clothe you in much love, which will be duly felt by many. I can therefore say to you also that within five years there will be discoveries made—within your medical fields, your scientific fields, and also facts of historical value. There is much for you to look forward to in the gaining of knowledge, and that knowledge is for the good of mankind."**

Later he was speaking on the powerful nature of thought and the need for its control. And we commented that Bonniol's visits had very much endorsed the fact that spirit simply has no time or space.

~ **"Yes. Always this has been a difficult subject for you, but we do feel by this example, you are now ready to receive and accept that there is much more (within creation) than you at first recognised."**

Very true, and I felt there was a chance here to amplify the point and further clarify: "Could I just refer back to that time when we mentioned 'big bang theory', and in relation to that, scientists came up with the idea of a 'singularity'. And the singularity would be visualised as a point-without-space-or-time. And of course that is viewing in physical terms. But if that singularity were viewed with *spiritual* eyes—without space or time—it might well be seen as simply spirit. So perhaps scientist's only mistake is viewing the absence of space and time, with physical eyes instead of spiritual eyes?"

~ **"Yes. You are correct with your thinking. After all, much of what happens, many things that happen upon your planet, have been because individuals have seen life through physical eyes, rather than seek the spiritual explanation. That is true in many aspects of your living—even in the way that you view your own planet! For so long, individuals could see nothing other than what stood before them, but all that is changing. Gradually mankind has awoken to the spiritual aspect of all life. We no longer speak of planets or individuals, but of 'spirit' as it truly exists. And after all, remember that SPIRIT HAS ALWAYS BEEN, and whatever mankind places before itself, it cannot change the ultimate truth. No matter what words or discussions are used within your scientific community, it cannot be altered—no matter which words are used, which intelligences are embarked upon."**

Salumet's statement indeed clarifies, whilst also encouraging us to see things from our inner and more fundamental knowing. Quite simply, the absence of time and space equates to spirit, but if we think in a purely physical way, backtracking through time to the very beginning, then all we perceive is the intellectual point source. But a point source in physical terms is nothing, and that 'nothing' contains a whole squashed universe! How bizarre! The misconception is plain to see. Past errors in science are not unknown and disposing of them has sometimes been a lengthy process. And of course, not so very long ago there was a Flat Earth Society!

Salumet withdrew, with the closing words: ~ **"Until we come together once more, I will leave you encompassed in my love and with those who wish to be here with you."**

Bonniol began: ~ ***"We are happy to be with you this evening."***

Lilian: "We are very happy to have you with us."

~ ***"Thank you—you have many beings around you—"***

Following Salumet's closing sentence, we wondered if Bonniol could see the others: ~ ***"I am not aware of them, because they are a different vibration from the ones we are familiar with. They are for your conditions here."***

Sarah: "How do you know they are here—because Paul's memory/ mind knows?"

~ ***"Yes, and we have been listening to your last one this evening. We arrived a little early."***

We laughed at the thought; as if a cosmic tour-bus had arrived ahead of schedule!

Lilian: "And did you hear Salumet?"

~ ***"I think it was the one through you"***, said looking with closed eyes towards Eileen.

Sarah observed: "You could come earlier and listen to Salumet, and maybe you would learn something as well—"

George: "Enjoy the full package!"

Lilian: "I expect you have that on your planet anyway."

~ ***"Well, it's always a pleasure to meet these special beings of light."***

All: "Yes!!!"

Then we got onto family matters, which became just slightly difficult. Lilian asked if Bonniol had children and he replied emphatically: ~ ***"I have—yes, I have a lot! I think you would be surprised how many!"***

Families are large and parents it seems have more than one partner but there are different kinds of individual.

Sarah: "So you have more than just male and female?"

~ ***"Yes."***

Sarah, not being one to beat about the bush, then came straight to the point with: "What else do you have?"

~ ***"We have a peculiar—we have something you won't have. It's basically asexual—not one or the other."***

Further questions met with awkward difficulty: ~ ***"You are—the problem is—I am unable to choose, the right way to describe. Ah—ah—ah—"***

It was time to change the subject, but we would return to family matters. There was a small item that needed sorting. We had recently heard mention of a planet named 'Erra' in the Pliaides star system and wanted to confirm that this was indeed different, so we first asked Bonniol for a careful pronunciation, which he was pleased to give several times with wonderfully clear emphasis: ~ ***"A-e-r-a-a-a-a-h."***

It is quite evidently a more extended name than simply 'Erra', and Bonniol added that there are twelve planets in Aerah's system.

Graham pursued with further questions: "Is your planet in the Milky Way galaxy like ours, or is it in a different galaxy?"

~ ***"It is a different galaxy—far, far away."***

Graham: "Are there many galaxies between here and where you are?"

~ ***"There are many."***

Graham: "That's amazing!"

We would later discover that the above is gross understatement!

~ ***"We could NEVER travel physically. It's easy with thought though."***

Next, we sought more details about Aerah, this leading to a more straightforward spell. The dialogue flowed while the muse was fickle with topics: "Do you have mountains and plains—flat plains?"

~ ***"We have plains and mountains."***

George: "How about seas?"

~ ***"There are oceans."***

George: "Oceans—right. Are they oceans of water?"

~ ***"Yes, water and they are lighter—I think—than your water."***

George: "And do things live in the oceans?"

~ ***"Yes, there are many things alive in our oceans—big and small."***

Lilian: "Our planet is mostly blue and green. Is that similar to yours?"

~ ***"Our planet is purple—purple and blue. The sky is blue. The ocean is purple in colour."***

Lilian: "And you have plants? Do they have green leaves?"

~ ***"Yes, it is green, and the trees are green. The birds are many colours."***

Eileen: "Do your people have disease in the same way as we do?"

~ ***"Yes, there are diseases and some of them are serious. We have many doctors—but some diseases are still very serious. It is something that we have to accept."***

Eileen: "Do you use your mind projection to heal?"

~ ***"There are people who heal using the energy that comes THROUGH us—so it's a kind of projection."***

George: "Do you do healing when close together, also 'absent healing' at a distance?"

~ ***"There is absent healing, yes. It's like thought projection."***

We moved onto food. It seems that Aerans are vegetarian or virtually so:

~ ***"It is something that has taken many years. The vegetables have not always been sufficient, but we have more now than ever before."***

Sarah: "We get our vegetables from many countries. Do you do the same sort of thing on your planet?"

~ ***"We have many different ones—yes—from different areas. We try to eat the local ones, because they are the FRESHEST."***

George: "Yes, you are similar to us again. We are moving towards vegetarian diet, but I have to say, most of us (on the planet), are meat-eaters at the moment."

Lilian: "Do your countries live in harmony or do you have wars as we do?"

~ ***"There are many countries, and there are always one or two who have problems. War is rare. There has not been one for many aeons."***

This last fact was greeted with exclamations of both approval and surprise, and this led Graham to wonder if there was any money in circulation: ~ ***"We have money. It's different."***

Eileen returned us to matters spiritual: "Could I ask, if a number of people are projecting their thoughts at the same time, does it get rather busy?"

~ ***"They are arranged—outside of our knowing. They come one by one, as arranged by the angelic realms—I think that is the right words. They help to organise their arrival, so it is not too chaotic. Thoughts, as we said, are alive, and they need looking after. There are SHEPHERDS of thoughts."***

George: "Good word! Yes!"

Sarah: "Are you able to use your mind projection when you are doing your building—do you make use of de-materialisation?"

~ "There are people that use a vibration, which allows objects to be moved and manipulated easily."

Sarah: "So you don't need all the heavy machinery that we have, to move things about?"

~ "We can 'manipulate'—even better."

George: "I think you are using 'levitation' that we have used in our ancient world, but we have since lost that ability. But you are able to use levitation in your building, I think you are saying?"

~ "We can move objects of enormous size, and it is the vibrations that are changed to allow this to happen."

As briefly described, this is perhaps more in line with what we might think of as 'de-materialisation', a subject discussed in the earlier days of Salumet in relation to UFO-travel; also in relation to building projects achieved by ancient civilisations. That rocks weighing thousands of tons have been worked and transported in past times is obvious, yet many still find this to be unthinkable.

George: "The vibration of the object is changed—"

~ "Yes, and that can be done by a change that can project—that—"

George: "Would that be 'thought pattern'?"

~ "Thought—coupled—yes, thought pattern. That allows light—and through meditation—I am being told that this is not new to you."

Again, guides had made their contribution.

I replied: "That is right. That is something that has happened in our past, but present-day humanity is not able to do that."

Bonniol continued:

~ "Would you like to be able to do this?"

All: "Yes!!!"

Lilian: "Are you going to tell us how?"

George: "We have been told that it is a spiritual attribute."

~ "You—we are being guided to instruct you that this is already with some of your planet. You have the atmosphere that would make this a big advantage. So you could practise by projecting—much lightness—onto a brick and try to imagine that brick floating and weightless like a—flower in the breeze—like it was a hollow brick."

Sarah: "And it's thought that makes it weightless or makes it move?"

~ ***"Yes, and even if nothing happens, you can weigh the brick and see if it has become a little lighter. It is not something that everyone can do in our world. It is possible. It does happen. Allow your minds to accept that it can happen."***

On reflection, I feel that Bonniol's final suggestion is a *very* important first step—the mental acceptance that it *can or will* happen. There were appreciative comments for his words. And we were asking if he could take more questions, or should they wait?

~ ***"It's a little difficult this time. I think we will have to leave it there. I am sorry it was more difficult at first."***

George: "Well, never mind—we do realise that conditions change, and it will not always be the same. But it has been *very good* again, and we do appreciate your being with us."

~ ***"We can be clearer next time, with your questions on our breeding"***, delivered with distinctly humorous tremor and followed by our good natured laughter. Warm farewells were exchanged, and all felt it had been a remarkably informative session with only minor hitches. And we just had to keep telling ourselves that this was from huge unimaginable distance. In fact, we shall be learning how Aerah is even much, much further away than our present hazy impressions.

CHAPTER: 8

Plant Energy – Elementals – Gender Facts ... 16th May 2005

IN VICTORIAN TIMES, Emma Hardinge Britten was a remarkable pioneer in the cause of spirit communication, and in the group, we occasionally enjoy her presence as a visiting control. And so it was from this dear lady of recorded Earthly history that we learned Bonniol would be on the agenda for this evening. How very nice! A double treat, and the more so since it had been three weeks since last time!

Soon, Lilian was saying: "Good evening—welcome," adding following a substantial pause: "I hope it's not too difficult this evening."

~ ***"How are you?"***

Lilian: "Nice to be together again."

~ ***"Yes, we've missed you."***

Lilian: "We're so pleased to have you with us, I don't think we could describe just how pleased."

~ ***"There is still much you don't know about our world, and you might not like—"*** and midst our laughter, ***"—it."*** And then, ***"I am happy to give you any information you would like to know about our world."***

Lilian: "Thank you!" and she gestured across the darkened room towards Graham for his question.

Graham: "Do your people live together in cities, towns and villages, as we do, or do you spread around in a different way?"

~ ***"Yes, we have cities, but the majority prefer to live in the countryside, with nature. I think you have more cities than we do."***

Graham: Yes, that's where the work is. Is that the case in your world—it's where the people work?"

~ ***"We have very different lives. Work for us is of a very 'earthy' nature. The work is more to do with nature than so much of your work that does not involve nature. We work with plants and animals."***

George: "This would be partly agriculture for food production, would it?"

~ ***"Yes, the purpose is for food production, also for making our clothes, and houses and utensils. It all comes from the plant kingdom."***

Sarah asked if houses have appliances and decorative things, as ours.

~ ***"Our houses are more basic than yours—we choose to live more simply."***

George: "I'm sure that's very wise."

There was general agreement to that. Thus far, our questions had skipped along, probing this way and that with not a great deal of depth. It seemed to be what was required. And that was interesting enough, but then we homed in on a topic that really fired up our attention and I think we leaned forward in our seats as a fresh picture unfolded.

Graham was suggesting: "This is a way of achieving a balance with your living planet. You are aware of the balance with all the wildlife. The way *we* are conducting ourselves at the moment, we cannot go on for long before the resources of the planet run out. You've gone through these lessons now, and have gone back to a more simple life—is that your history?"

~ ***"We have ALWAYS worked closely with the plants in our world. There have been times when too much has been taken and not enough given. Your world is on a slightly different pathway, as all worlds are. You will no doubt return to a more balanced lifestyle."***

George: "Thank you! We need to change direction, certainly!"

~ ***"You will find all these answers you need, as soon as you start looking for them."***

It may seem an obvious statement on the surface, but the seeking is a vital first step that every world needs to take.

Graham: "One of the ways we are out of balance with our planet is with travel. We drive our cars, and we burn up the resources of oil. How do you travel?"

~ ***"We have automobiles with engines."***

George: "Might I ask what fuel you use for the engines?"

~ ***"They are run on the energies of the plant kingdom."***

Several exclaimed: "Oh!" "Ah!" "Ooh!"

~ ***"This is something new for you!"***

Sarah: "Perhaps you can tell us how you do it, so that we can save our resources!"

I think this was said tongue in cheek, but being aware of possible protocol-infringement, I felt obliged to quickly add: "That might be an unfair question!" and we all had to laugh at the idea. But Bonniol continued: ~ ***"You have the potential for this. This is an easy form of energy to use, but you will need to work with the elementals."***

Several: "Ah!"

Well it was bound to be not straightforward!

~ ***"They can help you with this."***

George: "So this is not a matter of converting plant material to alcohol, and using alcohol as a fuel? This is direct use of plant energy. Is this what you are saying?"

~ ***"Yes, it is an energy that is produced by the plant, but it is not one you are able to use unless you have an arrangement with the elementals. They are able to release it in a form that will produce the clean energies that your world would benefit from."***

Sarah: "So when you use these plant energies, is the plant destroyed in the process?"

~ ***"The plants are 'milked', you could say. They give off their energies willingly."***

George: "And can you say if this energy relates to the aura of the plant, which we are able to see and detect in various ways?"

~ ***"The aura that you can see is an aspect of the energy, but it is not the entire thing. It is only a shadow of this very powerful energy."***

Graham: "I see. I wonder—if the plants on our planet, if we look after them—with the elementals—would they be able to provide the energy for us?"

~ ***"I cannot speak for your elementals, but it would seem a solution from where we are standing."***

Sarah: "When you say the plant is milked—you collect the energy from the plant, and then you can store it can you?"

~ ***"We do not collect it. The elementals collect it and they harness it in a way to make it useful for us. We can then dip into it and power our machines and houses."***

George: "That is very, very interesting, but I do have to say, that the major part of our population does not even *believe* in elementals—so we have a few bridges to cross."

Well there had to be a catch, and this was it. How do you get to know and bond with the little folk so well that they help you in this way if you *do not even believe in them*? This is indeed a delicate bridge that has to be crossed! As to the energy itself, there is a half-understood parallel here. The extremely rare phenomenon of 'spontaneous combustion' that can result in near instant conversion of a human being to residual ash is accepted as a real event, because regardless of plausibility, it is *known to happen*. It indeed happens, and accounts of these extremely rare events have been presented in scientific journals. Explanatory theories have been attempted, but the phenomenon arises from a distortion within the 'energy body', and it is proof that the energy therein IS INDEED HUGE. (This has been the subject of earlier discussions with Salumet who has confirmed this to be so [1, 3]). Equally, plants also have their energy body, part of which can be seen or revealed as an aura, and this would have similar power within. Energy bodies are indeed energy bodies after all, whether human or plant. Bonniol aligns to this when he says that the observed aura is a mere shadow of the plant's powerful energy. Both plants and humans will likely share this same energetic property. But conventional science as yet does not accept that spontaneous combustion of humans arises in this way, and so, we have another bridge yet to be crossed. But the illuminating dialogue clearly indicates that this would be a sensible route for us, towards wonderfully clean energy that might fulfil all planetary needs. And this forever, just so long as there is nature, and just so long as nature and her elementals have our recognition and *heartfelt respect*. And perhaps we should see this much fuller and deeply meaningful reverence for nature as one further bridge that must for this and other reasons, eventually be crossed. So for Earth, this wonderful clean energy-form requires that we cast aside old, erroneous, destructive ideology and cross three highly significant bridges; another big thought!

Bonniol continued: ~ ***"There are other forms of energy of course, that could be developed, but this is the one we are now using for power in machines."***

Sarah: "Do you use nuclear power at all?"

~ ***"We are not familiar with this one. It seems unnecessary for our world."***

George: "If you have alternative energies, I am sure you have made wise decision."

~ ***"Thank you."***

Graham: "Do you pay the elementals for the work that they do for you?"

~ ***"They do not charge anything, but we nevertheless bring them offerings in the form of presents, gifts and our love."***

Graham: "Are you physically aware of the elementals? Do you see them and speak with them?"

~ ***"We see them in a sense, but not physically. They are different from us—not quite physical. But we are able to see their light—their energies—beautiful energies."***

Graham: "Extraordinary! That must be amazing! Your entire industry is powered by this energy?"

~ ***"All our machines use this power now."***

Sarah: "What sort of gifts do you bring them apart from love?"

~ ***"We bring them food, but they don't eat. We bring them pictures, artefacts and crafts. They are not of any real use to them. It is only our thought—we are wanting to give them something."***

Graham "As an acknowledgement—"

Sarah: "So could you not just give them your thought and not give the actual presents?"

George: "Perhaps the present is a *focus* for thought?"

~ ***"Some like to give something material but it is not really necessary. The thought is the important thing."***

Graham: "If you live in balance with your planet, and you have automobiles, machinery and your houses, then for balance of your planet, you must have recycling, so that you no longer take from the planet—"

~ ***"It may seem like our planet is perfect, but it is not."***

This again provoked laughter, and perhaps it also showed some degree of relief from fixing on the idea of ourselves as cosmic underdogs!

~ ***"We have our problems. There is never complete harmony."***

George: "What about lighting? Does the energy find use there?"

~ ***"Yes, it provides the lighting in our homes and buildings."***

Sarah: "So that's the only form you have, is it?"

~ ***"It's the only form we have now, yes."***

We asked if they used other energies before.

~ ***"We have had different forms, yes. At one time we burned fossil fuels like you have. And that was before we were able to use the earth one with the elementals."***

Graham: "That's very interesting. The population of our planet is six billions. What is the population of yours?"

~ ***"We have many billions. There are many of us—billions and billions."***

Sarah: "Is that overcrowded?"

~ ***"We have had to move some of our people to our nearest moon."***

Sarah: "So how long does it take to get to your nearest moon?"

There was discussion about travel time and speed, but the figures did not connect too well and Bonniol conceded that he found calculations confusing. He estimated speed to be 7 – 800 mph and observed it to be not fast, but fast enough. But we felt there might easily be a nought missing!

Sarah: "So when did you start taking people out to the moon?"

~ ***"We began 400 years ago, but it has taken a long time to build up."***

George: "Does your moon have an atmosphere?"

~ ***"It's getting MORE 'atmospheric'—that was a joke!"***

We laughed at the cosmic joke.

~ ***"Yes, there IS an atmosphere. It's quite dense, but not as dense as our planet."***

Sarah: "So do people visit?"

~ ***"There is much traffic, yes."***

Sarah: "After 400-years, I was going to say, has language changed much? But if you are visiting all the time, it probably hasn't."

~ ***"We do have different languages but we also communicate with thought."***

Sarah then made an observation that I feel on reflection, has a deeper implication than one might at first suppose, revealing advantages of a more basic lifestyle: "You don't have a very expensive life do you? You don't have a telephone because you communicate with thought, and you don't have to pay electricity charges. You do quite well really!"

~ ***"It's um—it's quite different, yes."***

Sarah: "And you only really eat food you get from the earth—you don't manufacture?"

~ ***"We blend the different foods of the earth into different mixtures. Is that what you mean?"***

Sarah: "I was just thinking, we tend to eat a lot of processed foods—"

George: "Do you cook food, or do you have a preference for raw food?"

~ ***"We do eat food which is cooked and also raw food, like you."***

The reader may well be thinking: why lightly skip along from topic to topic, without more often getting down to fundamental issues. One answer to that is: it *feels* right, and it is producing interesting facts and an easy flow of words, the latter of course being all-important at this early stage. I nevertheless tried introducing a little chemistry at this point, but element recognition was too difficult, so we will try again later. Perhaps it is still too early to dig deeply. But one of us thought: it has to be a good time to refer back to a previous matter that got shelved.

Sarah: "You did talk to us last time about the sexes. You have male and female and one other. Are you going to tell us any more about that?"

~ ***"I wish I had not—"***

Laughter!

~ "***—got into that!***"

More laughter!

~ ***"It's still a problem for us to explain the difference in our genders. We have several you see. It's not just male and female. There is a third, which is neither one nor the other of course, and is not for breeding (asexual). And there is a fourth, which is able to breed but which does not need either of the others (hermaphrodite, as with our earthworms). There is another, which is able to breed but may require another at some point to begin with. Anyway, we do have these approximate male-female ones, which approximate to yours I suppose, but they are quite—I can't think of the word again—they are 'androgynous' as well as being male and female—they are neither one nor the other really. They are both. The distinctions are less prevalent."***

George: "We appreciate what you are saying because we have different systems in our animal kingdom and some of our insects—the bees have an extraordinary system of not exactly males and females. So yes, we can understand what you are saying."

~ ***"We have been trying to find an example in your world, and we did look at bees. Perhaps they are something like, in that the bee is able to change."***

George: "Are the various genders natural or have they been developed in some way?"

~ ***"They are natural, but of course, we can influence ourselves naturally."***

Sarah: "These people—do they all look alike—or can you tell the difference? And would they produce a male or female, or would they produce their own kind?"

~ ***"They would produce their own kind."***

Sarah: "And do they look like male and female?"

~ ***"They look very similar but there is a slight difference."***

This was interesting and Sarah, leaned forward: "Oh?"

~ ***"They have a protuberance on their—"***

We waited through the pause as Bonniol searched for the best word: ~ ***"heads—a small node."***

Sarah: "Do you live all together, or in separate groups?"

~ ***"We choose to live where we wish to—to share the group and to share the solitude."***

Sarah: "You can live all mixed together? There is no segregation?"

~ ***"No segregation—we are all active in that sense."***

Thinking a return to the topic of 'knowledge' might possibly pave the way for a joke to lighten proceedings, I asked: "Do you have within your society, those who specialise where knowledge is concerned?"

~ ***"We have our experts, yes. But not as many as you, I think. You have many different areas of expertise that we simply do not need in our world. You are more complex."***

A much less complex society is certainly the picture that seems to be building. I tried the joke: "It is said that there are two extremes in knowledge. One can specialise until one knows more and more—everything there is to know about nothing at all (chuckles). Or there is the other extreme, where one knows nothing at all about everything!" There followed a few half-suppressed gurgles, but Bonniol remained silent.

Sarah came to the rescue: "And do you have a ruler on your planet, a government or whatever?"

~ ***"We do have a government, yes. It is a problem sometimes—our government—like yours (laughs). We have choices. There are those who are not so keen on the elementals, for example, who wish to be not so interdependent. There are differences of opinion."***

Graham: "Do you have a need for controlling your society—police and laws and things like that? Do you have a police force?"

~ ***"We have a police force, yes. We have less need of them. They are also used for other things, like rescues and emergencies of all kinds."***

Graham: "Yes. Do you have courts for people who break the law, and prisons or consequences within your society for wrongdoers?"

~ ***"We have a detention centre, yes, for holding people who are dangerous—dangerous to others or themselves, yes."***

Sarah: "We have quite a problem with drug-taking. Do you have drugs on Aerah?"

~ ***"There are plants that are used for recreational purposes, so they can be abused."***

Graham: "Your planet it seems, like ours, is a planet of learning, and you are a lot further down the road than we are—"

~ ***"I think we have taken different roads, but the ultimate destination is the same—the routes we have, are different. And your journey will provide you with much that ours will not. So the different routes are equally valid."***

Now that is an interesting philosophical point. But there was more to be said on the issue of drugs: "So you have some plants that you regard as recreational, and these are allowed in moderation, but some people might overdo it. Is that what you are saying?"

~ ***"We allow some of them. There are some that are not allowed. And this is like your drug problem, I think."***

George: "And not allowed, presumably because they would be dangerous—"

~ ***"They can be dangerous to the people themselves, or to others. So they are discouraged, yes. But the young people, they like to experiment."***

George: "Yes, just like here."

I must admit to feeling that the Earth drugs scene has wayward, bizarre and often damaging aspects, but it seems we do not stand alone in the need for policing. It is interesting that others also find this little conundrum along their pathway forward.

Sarah: "You said previously that you have webbed feet, and you kick the air to disperse it, to make it easier to move around. Does that mean that you don't wear shoes?"

~ ***"We wear shoes sometimes. They are bigger of course. But we don't NEED shoes. We normally do not wear them."***

There was further discussion on this, indicating that wearing shoes is much more the norm here than with Aerans. Following that, Bonniol departed with the fondest of farewells.

This was becoming a magnificent project yielding so much about Aerah, a planet with so many Earthly comparisons. She has her cities and countryside, and there is some degree of crime, the familiar drugs scene and a police force, perhaps with more extended roles. There is much to think on in regard to the many possibilities that lie open to us for shaping an Earthly future; this in the more general sense, and more specifically, if only we could believe in elementals! If only! That could then lead to an ongoing clean fuel economy! That is a spectacular vision that would firmly knock on the head our mega-problems of nuclear waste and escalating pollutions! Aerah has her nature-agriculture centred regime, a corner-stone of comparatively uncluttered lifestyle; perhaps an enviable lifestyle? Our world was in some small measure towards that before the industrial revolution. Even in my own lifetime, I was brought up on a 100-acre Hampshire farm in the 1930s. I well remember it employed six through the winter months and twelve through haymaking and harvest. So even then, a mere 70-years ago, there was a more widespread adherence to agriculture and to nature and her gentle ways. The memory of that now fades as scientific disciplines, technology, finance controls and pursuit of material exuberance take over. Today, there is realisation of the rueful consequences in moving away from that pastoral idyll. We see sadly diminished bird populations, loss of wild flowers, less beauty in landscape, a depleted spiritual awareness and poorer health; the latter largely through increased stress and less wholesome foods. Perhaps we are just beginning to re-evaluate our love of nature so that once again we move towards her.

There cannot be perfection. Perhaps nothing is perfect, except for the overall divine plan. It is nevertheless good to see how things are on a different, relatively uncluttered planet of learning; one with which we may compare notes. And the one area where Aerah is *more* complex than Earth appears to be in sex and gender! There is a reason for this and there will be more to say on that later. But as the link becomes stronger, our discussions can go deeper, can encompass so much; such matters as life's principles, the many mysteries of Earth's past and how mind remains paramount in all matters within this universe.

CHAPTER: 9

More on Mind – Rescues – Building Blocks … 6th June 2005

SALUMET NOW HAD much more to say on mind and just salient points are briefly given: ~ **"There are many forms of energy of which you would not be aware. What I want you to focus upon is not so much the information given to you about another planet, but to focus upon the *mind projection*. It is something that, later, you could contemplate for yourselves. It is possible whilst (you are) upon this planet—in focusing on *mind projection*, you will most certainly grow."**

Paul speculated that *Mind projection* is different from *thought projection*: ~ **"Mind projection belongs to the spirit. Thought can be projected from the *conscious* part of the thinking, but mind projection *has* to be done from the *spirit*, if it is to work successfully. Always remember that difference. Thought is connected to the consciousness of the body, and to the spiritual mind. The brain belongs to the physical, the *mind* is spiritual. The mind is not something that you can see or feel. It is a part of your whole being. It is that greater part of your spirit that will continue to grow and will continue to exist through all levels of spirit. IT BELONGS TO SOUL. In showing you that mind projection is working, we bring it to you with information of interest. You do not have to go into the silence (of meditation) to send out a *thought*. This you realise, but mind projection entails rather more."**

It helped sort our confused thinking, enabling physical intellect to come to terms. Mind as spirit, belonging to soul, will grow in its forward pathway through successive incarnations and it is this *spiritual mind* that travels. We have since learned that a fragment of mind attaches to physical brain as *subconscious*. It is only this fragment that becomes involved in hypnotism and self-hypnosis. So let us not be confused where *subconscious* is concerned. That is a different, smaller part of mind. *Spiritual mind* is a much, much wider issue, and mind projection is an attribute of spirit having truly universal application.

Before Bonniol's visit this time, there were three 'rescues'. Each individual had become 'stuck' in transition from Earth life.

[The nature of 'Rescues': When a physical being dies, there are guides who watch over the departing spirit in case assistance is needed. Help would likely be required when there is no belief in the life hereafter. The one in transition will still feel alive and therefore will refuse to accept that they have died—yet something is odd. The situation may become an impasse. One solution is for a guide to bring them to a channelling group, where they can speak through a medium and receive counselling from one such as Lilian, so that they can accept the reality of life in spirit. A fuller description of rescue work will be found on www.salumet.com or www.salumetandfriends.org .]

It is amazing how, at time of death, a disbelief in the hereafter can result in becoming 'stuck', and it is our experience that disbelief is the most common causal factor. These matters would be referred to.

Lilian explained about puzzled spirits not realising they have died and who just need a helping hand.

~ ***"It can be interesting work."***

Lilian: "Do you do something similar?"

~ ***"We do have something similar, but it's not very common. There is usually a smoother crossing. Occasionally we have to do our counselling as well, to help them over."***

We ambled on, bringing into the conversation Salumet and his teaching.

~ ***"You have learned much from your teacher—"***

Lilian: "Much, yes," and as we laughed "lots!"

~ ***"And there is so much more to learn!"***.

This seemed a convenient moment to say: "Yes and there is much we would like to learn about *mind projection*. We have been thinking about this. Mind, we understand is part of spirit. There also seems to be this *vehicle* aspect to mind. Mind has an ability to travel, and mind seems to be a little different from our thoughts. Our thoughts can be projected, but not in quite the same way. Is there anything further you can say about that?"

~ ***"Yes, your thoughts are something else—other than your mind—but they are very similar in that they are also energy that is alive in itself. They work in similar ways, but your mind of course is your spirit SELF, which is part of YOU. Thoughts become separated from you when you have sent them."***

Now that helps—thoughts separate—while mind is and remains spirit-self. But we sought more: "Yes, thoughts—would I be right in saying: thoughts contribute to individual consciousness and also contribute to collective consciousness? Would that be a fair statement?"

~ ***"I would say there are different types of thought. Some would join with other thoughts—perhaps like your collectives. Some thoughts will disintegrate, some will grow. They are like babies. You create them—then send the thoughts into the ether. Your mind, however, it is yourself, and that is a different thing again. You don't send it forth as such."***

It had been a difficult subject for us, but now we were getting there with help from both Salumet and Bonniol. And I have to keep telling myself that neither is of this planet! We are doing our best to gain understanding from other and higher intelligences—one who is physical and one a pure energy light-being! And we are so fortunate to have such opportunity! The next question: "You are able to speak to us through what we call mind projection, but ordinarily, we would not be receiving your thoughts. In order to receive your thoughts, mind is necessary. Does that make sense?"

~ ***"Mind is EVERYTHING in some ways, it is the mind that has all the—mind has—I am not connecting so well tonight."***

Lilian: "It's probably a lack of energy in the room—"

~ ***"Projecting the mind, is like sending YOURSELF out, rather than a thought."***

George: "Yes!"

~ ***"You decide where or who you wish to visit—"***

George: "Yes—*that* (deciding) is the thought—"

~ *"And then you—send yourself. It is impossible to say how it all works. It's an incredible ability, and it's something you can do."*

Lilian: "Do you have a helper from spirit while this is happening to you?"

~ *"There are beings who help to make it happen."*

Lilian: "Yes, who take care of the spirit side—"

~ *"Yes, there are always beings in the background."*

George: "It is difficult (for us) to visualise that mind and spirit have no time or space, yet there are these beings—one feels, although there is no time or space, there is something else, that enables the various beings to be 'contained'. It's something beyond our perception!"

There was a substantial pause at this point and I could not help but wonder if this was too difficult for our friend who was trying his best to explain—and Lilian was saying: "I think the majority of people on our planet, if we told them that we listen to you, from a galaxy that we don't even know, they would mostly not believe."

I had time to think to myself: 'How very true, and why should they?' And then Bonniol returned from his pause with a deeply philosophical pronouncement: **~ *"We have the idea that there IS space and time, but for the mind, it is IRRELEVANT."***

George: "Ah yes! I follow! There *is* space and time, but mind is something apart. Mind does not connect. Perhaps that is a way of looking at it—"

~ *"Yes, space and time work well up to a point, and then you go forward without needing them. They are like building blocks, which are useful stages. But, when you begin to use your mind projection, they are not necessary."*

George: "Yes, that's a great help!"

Lilian: "Are there any others who travel, to other parts of this planet? Or are there not many who do this?"

~ *"Travelling to other planets is limited to only a few."*

Lilian: "I see, and it's got to be for the right reasons."

~ *"Yes. This is one of the most complicated and exciting areas, and we feel very honoured to be able to do it."*

Lilian: "We feel the same."

George: "We feel very privileged to be in contact with you."

Lilian: "So, how many are with you tonight?"

There's the usual gathering of my family and friends, about 60 or 70."

The number took us just a little by surprise. This, by our standards, was a large group!

Bonniol returned us to mind by referring to our attempts to make bricks go lighter and he offered some useful tips. This led to the question: "When you make blocks of stone lighter for ease of construction, is the stone, in its state of lightness, easier to work—easier to shape?"

~ ***"There are methods for lightening the blocks. There are also methods for helping to shape them. They are different methods. One thing does not make the other thing happen. We can MAKE THEM MORE PLIABLE. When you dematerialise the block of stone, it is possible to re-materialise it in any shape or form, if you have clarity of thought. You can manipulate or change anything with thought, if your thoughts are strong and clear enough."***

George: "Yes, thank you. That's interesting."

~ ***"There are no boundaries!"***

So it is all down to power and clarity of thought, and its application from deep within the spirit self. There has been talk about how, in ancient times, huge stone blocks could have been worked and set in precise, often elevated positions, in South America and elsewhere. Salumet had already confirmed for us, that thought-power was the elevating tool. Now Bonniol was again confirming and adding that shaping might also follow. Many have wondered how the ancients managed to get their massive blocks to fit with such precision. Clearly they were sufficiently *pliable* at time of placement to 'settle' into the space available, before returning to normal rigid form! It was applied mind power. We have instinctive feelings and scraps of legend handed down, and now confirmation from extraterrestrial minds.

[As to legend: the world had laughed when Heinrich Schliemann set out in search of Troy, the Troy of Homer, long seen as mere legend. He excavated in 1870, while the laughter continued. But then the Mound of Hissarlik had *yielded* the legend and it was time to become serious. Legends are so often rooted in firm pre-historic fact, and it is simply a matter of time before the fact surfaces to be recognised as such.]

Continuing the 'building' theme, we enquired if trees were grown and felled for timber: ~ ***"We used to use wood, but now we use other materials."***

And on enquiring if the other materials are better: ~ ***"Other materials are better than the wood for most things, but there are still things made from wood. They are mostly older things. We do not need to use timber now."***

Sarah returned at this stage, having been 'away' providing extra power: "The material that you use—is that something you make yourselves?"

~ ***"There are many different materials for different purposes. We make our buildings from brick—a kind of stone really."***

George: "So your bricks are manufactured?"

~ ***"Our bricks are 'produced', you could say. But not in the way you would do it here."***

George: "No? We use clay that is baked at a high temperature to make our bricks. You have a better process?"

~ ***"We are able to produce them with our minds."***

George: "Ah! That is a better process! Yes!"

So, by application of thought-power, it is possible to make bricks go lighter, to re-shape, and to create them in the first place. Incredible! (But to speak of bricks may have been a simplification for our understanding. We shall return to this.)

Before departing, Bonniol gave tips for practising mind projection. He suggests working in pairs sending simple mind pictures to each other. Clear mind focus is needed with no extraneous thoughts, so that daily meditation is a prerequisite. He added that there would be help in our endeavours from spirit.

CHAPTER: **10**

Principles and Other Worlds ... 20th June 2005

THIS MID-SUMMER MEETING began with a control speaking through Sarah who assured us of help in what we do. She carefully described it as an 'influence' that would not infringe free will in any way. It was a touching declaration following Bonniol's closing remark of two weeks earlier. All begins to knit together wonderfully well!

Following usual greetings, there was a substantial pause: ~ ***"I am having a few problems, but it is getting better with practise. Shall we perhaps have some of your questions, or shall I ask YOU some questions?"***

Lilian: "Yes, that would be a change."

~ ***"I've been wanting to find out a little more about the PRINCIPLES of your lives, that you live by. That is something that is of interest to us"***

Now here was a big question. Where should we begin? And of course, there is considerable variation across the whole planet. We ambled into a reply of sorts, with obvious uncertainty.

Lilian: "I think they vary from person to person—"

~ ***"Yes—"***

George: "As a planet, we are very varied and confused where our principles and our living are concerned."

Bonniol attempted to get us headed into a useful direction, saying: ~ ***"Do you have many principles or just a few?"***

I offered a few words on work and commerce, pointing to a need to work to earn money to buy food and necessities; then indicating a confusion of principles that issue from religious beliefs.

~ "Maybe we should talk about your OWN principles then—leaving the religions aside—and the things that you have to do in order to live."

Sarah: "We have laws that we have to abide by, and there are many things that we have to do to keep peace—"

~ "And it's a structure from outside?"

Sarah: "Yes."

~ "—and what about your OWN principles?"

Now we were homing in onto our friend's particular target of interest, not so much the constraints imposed from outside but what makes each of us tick at an individual level. What rules do we set for *ourselves*? I began again: "We have a principle of honesty that I think I'd be right in saying the majority of the population regard. But there are those who do not believe in the principle of honesty, which can make life a little difficult sometimes."

Lilian: "And we try to help one another—those who are in difficulties. I think the majority would agree to that.

Sarah pointed out that some of our principles are changing with time.

~ "Some principles should last longer than others."

Sara: "Yes, the principles of love and non-judgement stand the test of time. We try to be loving in our behaviour and thoughts—an ever-evolving situation, because our definition of love changes, as we mature we see more clearly—so the principle of loving ever grows."

Sarah: "I feel that in the past, the family was very important. People didn't really travel much, so the family stayed close, and children had a lot to do with grandparents. A lot of people today go out to work, and perhaps haven't got much time for their families."

Sara: "The principles are still there but maybe they are harder to live up to with modern living—"

Graham elaborated: "Our society at the moment is going through a period of materialism, as something that is thrust upon us. We are evolving forward all the time and we would like to adjust and cope with materialism and put it in its place. At the moment materialism is having an adverse effect on people's lives."

Sara: "People need to learn that they can't live life too materially. It is a lesson that is currently being learned by many. There are different levels of materialism, but it is definitely a problem for our society."

The two Sara(h)s had nicely brought into the picture the more spiritual issues and yes, there has been some smothering of this vital area, by rampant material growth.

~ ***"Yes, the principles are many and some are higher than others, and that is natural. And you all strive for the higher ones, as you leave the lower ones gradually. I think it is the natural progression."***

So one might say that the higher principles of 'mutual love' and of 'recognising spiritual life' lie at the heart of our society as they should, but the cloak of materialism and conditions arising from its smothering shadow may dim awareness. One might of course, see many of the said lower principles, enmeshed within the mêlée of material growth. They will include such things as locking cars, locking houses, coping with litter and observing ever-increasing legal requirements. These should all become less of a problem and less time consuming as we become more devoted to the higher principles of living. And the key to this change has to be a moderation of excessive zeal in personal material gain. Our discussion seemed pointed in this direction, but all is connected, so quoting one more: the chicken-and-egg principle; it must surely operate between so many base motivations. We might ask ourselves: which is the prime mover in law breaking; is it *burglar's greed* or might it be *wanton self-aggrandizement of the burgled*? Both surely make their contribution. The debate continued: "There's the principle of right and wrong, a black-and-white principle taught to children that might later be seen as cause and effect—the principle of giving to society, for example books by thinkers and writers and those who make discovery."

~ ***"Yes, you are learning as you go, and may that always continue. I wish you all—most profoundly—that you bring your principles with you—ALWAYS—in your lives, and then you will never go far wrong."***

Sarah: "How do our principles compare with yours?"

~ ***"We believe in 'loving our neighbours' too. That is an important one. And to leave them—let them be—not to interfere or to judge***

them. There are baser principles too—the higher and the lower ones. There are ones that are more for the benefit of the society, to keep the system running smoothly, because there is no real right or wrong in some things. The system principles are fine, but the higher ones are the real important ones."

There was some further exchange on helping each other, whereupon Bonniol said: ~ ***"Helping is always an act of love, helping is being at one with the other."***

We spoke of *greed* within our own society and accumulation of great wealth by those who seek it, and enquired if they were similar.

~ ***"We have people who want to be better than others, and they think they are better somehow if they have more power—a higher position—but fortunately now they are a minority."***

Lilian suggested they are not happy people.

~ ***"They are never happy, because they are looking in the wrong places."***

I suggested: "You are more advanced than us, because we still have quite a number who seek wealth rather than the good way forward."

~ ***"As your world evolves, before long, people like yourselves will become the norm, not the minority."***

Sarah: "There is quite a problem with drugs. People take drugs that change their character. And there's the greed with the people that sell the drugs. They make lots of money. And there are problems related to that—burglaries, muggings and killing."

~ ***"I think it will always be a problem, until their minds change and they move away from their greedy ideas."***

George: "But as you say—and I think we all feel—things are changing for the good *fairly* rapidly."

~ ***"Yes, it CANNOT happen too quickly—"***

But then Bonniol received a prompt, from a guide again, and he quickly altered course; an interesting reminder to us of spirit protocol and how these exchanges are 'overseen': ~ ***"I am being told—it is for reasons I don't understand yet—it's moving up—okay!***

The obvious aside got us laughing again as Bonniol continued: ~ ***"It's moving, and you are very much part of that movement."***

Wonderful! This reiterated a Salumet teaching. He has spoken often of Earth's upsurge and how we are moving forward at this time, and the reminder came in such an intriguing way.

Lilian observed: "We are beginning to take it for granted that you come all this distance. It's just a normal thing really, isn't it—almost?"

~ ***"I am pleased that you are now thinking it NORMAL. It's a NATURAL thing."***

George: "There are a few things that really, really impress us, and this is becoming seemingly *more* normal. But it still really impresses us that this is happening!"

Laughter endorsed our general agreement.

~ ***"That is always the way with a new thing—it always starts like that, and then after a time YOU will be doing it—in your sleep!"***

We took it to be Bonniol's wit. That was fine, but I think Bonniol knew secretly how he was also being serious, and we now realise how he must have been amused. We remained ignorant at the time, of any link between mind projection and sleep state. This would come later. Lilian concluded: "Let us say you're beginning to be like an old friend," but the session was not yet ended.

More was said about vain attempts to 'brow-beat' bricks into getting lighter. But we were close to temporarily putting this particular pursuit on the back burner in favour of 'mind projection for communicating'. This would have a more spiritual value and I think Bonniol agrees: ~ ***"Mind projection is so important—if you can learn that, then other things become so much easier. You can do all kinds of things once you've learned to project YOURSELVES when you need to, or when you wish to communicate with another maybe—in this world, or in spirit, or on another planet. To be able to do that can open so many doors, and it's within your grasp."***

We sought more information on visualising the target person.

~ ***"You should visualise them in your mind. You should also 'feel' them a little as you visualise them. It may bring a memory of them into your mind. And you may then proceed with your intention to project towards them."***

That was another useful tip. Next we spoke of other planets that Bonniol had prospected: ~ ***"Yes, there is much we can tell you about***

the others—the seven other worlds. It is almost impossible to know where to begin. Each one is unique in its own way, and special. We feel that the information would be of little use to you at this time, but, for your enjoyment, you may find it interesting to hear a little about the planets. There is one, which is by far the most beautiful of all our worlds. It is a planet of ice. And the inhabitants are beings of—are not physical—that inhabit that planet. I am beginning to feel an unusual energy, when I talk about this world—"

George: "Is this a problem?"

~ ***"I think it becomes weaker when I speak about other places—other planets. It is almost like my own mind begins to wander out of focus."***

George: "Yes, so perhaps it is good not to pursue—"

~ ***"But one day, you could visit them yourselves. But little steps at first are due, while you are here in this world."***

We explained that our interest was merely to gain some idea of the diversity of life. This might easily wait. Following mention of the 'ice world' there was general talk of the beauty of crystals and it became evident that Bonniol sees more than just their physical appearance: ~ ***"Crystals have the appearance of—the pattern of the energies—spiritual energies that form like an imprint. And it is this that you become more familiar with as you develop—the pattern of the energies that surround."***

Our friend appears to be aura-sighted where crystals are concerned and this must enhance their beauty. And with this further piece of information it was again time to depart.

CHAPTER: **11**

Timing – Space Exploration – Natural Disasters ... 27th June 2005

~ ***"EACH TIME I come I think it is a little clearer and easier, and I hope you are beginning to feel a little more connected, with creation—with all of creation."***

Excellent opening words! There can be nothing to quite match chatting across the universe, and we certainly felt more connected to that universal prevalence, an integrated belonging.

~ ***"Are there any questions that you would like to ask, or shall we ask the questions?"***

We settled for some of each. Graham had been wondering about the timing of between-world connections: "There must be helpers who are working on 'timing' because your meetings synchronise with ours. Do you have an explanation as to how this process can occur?"

~ ***"We have to choose our moments. Because we are physical, we are governed by time."***

Graham: "Does that mean that you have to have *your* meetings at strange times of *your* day?"

~ ***"We do have to have our meetings at peculiar times sometimes, in order to coincide with other worlds or other people."***

Graham: "And on those occasions when you don't come through, is that because you oversleep?"

Midst our muted laughter, Bonniol continued: ~ ***"We are usually available, but there are not always the right conditions or there are other plans."***

George: "Of course, and there have been occasions when you have arrived a little early. On one occasion at least, you arrived early and heard Salumet."

~ ***"Yes, and I was very happy to hear that one."***

Lilian: "Perhaps you could put a question to him sometime—that would be interesting."

~ ***"It would be an unusual experiment!"***

George: "I imagine that would be possible?"

Sarah: "I don't see why not, but you would have to come early!"

~ ***"I will consult my watch!"***

We laughed, this time at Bonniol's Earth-styled banter and Graham got back to his question: "So you must sense when we are meeting—how do you do this?"

~ ***"We have our ways of knowing, at the right time, and it is mainly through our feelings—yes—which are impressed on us of course, by our guides. We are told sometimes if it is not possible."***

More was said on the idea of Bonniol sitting in on a Salumet session, he adding:

~ ***"And it is always interesting to try new things. We always like to experiment, even if it doesn't work out so well, we can find out something from it."***

Returning to contacting other planets, we enquired if there is any sense of direction.

~ ***"There is no sense of direction when it comes to mind projection."***

George: "Or distance either?"

~ ***"You don't need to know WHERE. You only need to know WHO."***

Eileen: "Do you use mind projection mostly or do you space-travel as well?"

~ ***"We have vehicles, but we HAVE TO use our (material form) vehicles. There are other ways to travel, but we cannot do it—only with our minds or our limited vehicles."***

So Aerans have the choice of physical space-ships or unlimited mind projection. They have not mastered a de-materialisation procedure that could very much accelerate physical travel. We enquired if their ships go beyond the moons: ~ ***"We can go quite a lot further than the moons, but there are no important reasons for us to at the moment. There is no great benefit in using the vehicles to explore space."***

Lilian: "Because it's better to mind travel—"

~ ***"Partly, yes."***

Lilian spoke of our unmanned space probes.

~ ***"Your space ships are bringing you information as you explore your galaxy, yes. At some point you may be able to go a little further, but it might not be of that much benefit to you, because it is exploring the MATERIAL universe."***

Quite so, and we went on to explain how satellites are launched into orbit for the purpose of reflecting radio and TV signals; suggesting that perhaps Aerah does not need this, but Bonniol again surprised us: ~ ***"There are satellites where we come from too, because we have something like your radio and television. The satellites of my world are used for purposes of navigation—navigation—pinpointing areas, and for pilot's radios. We bounce signals from them as you do."***

Much the same as Earth! Eileen then asked about passing to spirit, putting it to our friend that Aerans are spiritually more advanced.

~ ***"We do not like to say that we are more advanced in ALL ways. BUT MIND PROJECTION AND OUR LEARNING THROUGH MANY AEONS OF TIME, HAS TAUGHT US TO LIVE PEACEFULLY WITH NATURE AND ELEMENTALS, AND IN THESE WAYS THEREFORE, OUR CROSSINGS OVER TO SPIRIT ARE LESS TRAUMATIC AND GENERALLY SMOOTHER THAN YOURS. We can skip some of the stages that you have to go through, but like all planets, we are a mixture of levels. There are ones like masters and younger souls too. It is a planet of learning like yours."***

The statement says much. Mind projection ability plus Aerah's accumulated learning clearly provide an understanding of planetary life's complete involvement with the spiritual existence; yielding an easier and a *pre-known* transition, at time of death. A second important factor is of course that Aerans live peacefully with nature and her elementals. Earth is so different here, there being near total disbelief in elementals (fairy tales being seen as having fictional origin by most adults). Therefore, Bonniol has spoken well and it is worth reflecting on this clear, informative statement that comes from afar.

The next question came from Pia, a welcome visitor from Helsinki University, Finland. It is quite often the case with visitors that questions are asked that have already come up in earlier sessions. This matters not, since it serves as a check on consistency of information, and if similar answers are given, it reassures that what we are hearing is repeatable data.

Pia: "Are you in communication with many planets or just ours?"

~ ***"We have eight planets now that we are in communication—with you. We are hoping for another—that is, we are hoping for many more, but we have been told about one other."***

Lilian: "Would it be farther away from you, this one?"

~ ***"It is further I believe, but distance of course is irrelevant."***

George: "How do you know that it is further? Is this a spiritual communication?"

~ ***"Yes, we do not know where you are except for information gathered from our guides."***

Graham: "I think I would assume that life is extremely rare in space, apart from a few planets such as yours and ours. Have you any information on that?"

~ ***"We have come to believe that there is more out there than we realised. Some planets that look barren may have life on them, even like your planet has elementals on it, though for the most part, you are unaware of them. But LEARNING PLANETS are rarer I think."***

George: "Yes, and one thing about learning planets—or about *our* learning planet—we do have terrible disasters from time to time, in the shape of volcanic eruptions and floods and that sort of thing. Do you have disasters?"

~ ***"There are always natural disasters, yes, as our planet is also alive, and ages and changes. Change is part of that beautiful movement of life."***

George: "Since you have not had wars on your planet for many, many years, and you have a better relationship with nature and the elementals, I could not help but wonder if that leads to fewer disasters? There obviously has to be planetary evolution. Do you still have disasters to the same sort of frequency as in the past?"

~ "There are times when you seem to get a run of them and then it calms down. These are natural ebbs and flows. But if we are in danger, then I think we would know."

We suggested that the knowing would make disasters easier to handle.

~ "You can also pick up I believe, if you are 'open', that a disaster is about to happen."

Lilian: "Yes, I think the animals of this planet are probably better at it than we are."

~ "When you are in tune with nature, then these things are nothing more than part of a song. I can't think of the word, (but) they are like exclamations."

Several important matters were broached here, not least space exploration. On Earth, its cost using rocketry has met with ongoing controversy. Now, it is made clear that this technique merely brings back data on the least interesting, material, part of our galaxy, and only an extremely local part at that. But mind work by comparison is low-budget and much more revealing, so surely space-rockets must eventually phase out in favour of mind projection! And there followed the matter of premonition of natural disaster. So we might well tune into nature and develop this sense more. Another truly thought provoking evening!

CHAPTER: 12

Love Thy Neighbour - Floor Sweepers - Bonniol Sings! ... 4th July 2005

OUR FRIEND CAME through strongly:

~ ***"I am beginning to feel more at home here each time—like another home from home. When I first came, it was all very strange. Now, I think we are all feeling more at peace with this kind of link between our worlds."***

A grand start; and Lilian assured we were all delighted with the link.

~ ***"And now if you would like, we shall answer any questions—or shall we ask some?"***

Well, firstly there was just one to return to: "We were talking about 'principles', and it may be of interest to *you* to know, or you may know already but—"

~ ***"I've been thinking about your answers, and they appear to be about the same as ours in our world, but you have more rules I think, a lot more rules and laws. And it is so confusing for your mind, because with your laws, you are not really making YOUR OWN principles. That I think was the main difference."***

An excellent summing up! I continued: "—what I was going to say about that—it would be about 3,200 years ago—there was one on the Earth called Moses. And he received from spirit what has been written down as 'The Ten Commandments'. Those commandments are based very much on the principles of 'love' and 'peace' and 'loving your neighbour'. So *those* principles have a very firm place in our history, and they have been written down as part of one of our major religions. I thought that might be of interest."

~ ***"Yes, the principle of 'loving your neighbour', is the root of our principles, I think. Because you then feel 'at oneness' with your***

people, and there is no boundary between you. And this is what—Moses was it?—tried to bring to you."

George: "Yes, he received the principles from spirit—from God—it is written."

~ ***"And now you can understand them more fully, I imagine—"***

George: "Yes. And those principles have been a great influence to large numbers of people on the Earth over the last 3,000 years."

So, neighbourly love is a shared fundamental principle and that is something to reflect on.

We next discussed our relatively busy lives; this in connection with finding time to practise mind projection.

~ ***"Your lives are far more complicated, yes—you have many—you have more activities during your days. We are simpler in our daily routines. We have been able to balance our lives between what we wish to do and what we NEED to do, a bit more evenly I would say."***

As Sarah declared that to be interesting, Bonniol received a prompt, I think from a knowing guide: ~ ***"I am being told: you CAN find the time if you really try!"***

Sarah: "I think it's true. I think we do sometimes get a bit caught up in things that we probably don't *need* to do."

I suggested it has become fashionable in a way to do various things that are simply not needed, to which several said: "Yes!"

~ ***"It's bewildering I would think—what all your possibilities are."***

And Parkinson's Laws came to mind, about work expanding to fill the time and space available. Humanity is perhaps in danger of getting swamped with daily busy attitudes, games, the pub, TV, habitual repetitiveness and such, to frustrate pursuit of life's richness of spirit. Then, just as we were beginning to wonder where this backwater of menial chat might lead, it took off in an unexpected direction. We enquired if there are daily chores on Aerah, for example: dust getting into the home and need for cleaning.

~ ***"We have dust, yes—another similarity between our worlds!"***

We laughed, partly I think, with relief to have uncovered a shared nuisance, continuing: "We have vacuum cleaners for going about the house and collecting the dust."

~ ***"Yes, I've been looking at these machines of yours."***

Lilian: "It all creates rather a lot of noise—"

~ ***"We have animals that help us clean our houses."***

Well! So these wonderfully advanced Aerans, who can colonise a moon, organise a near miraculous fuel economy and mind project across the universe, get animals in to do their housework! We were—I think the best word is—flabbergasted!

Lilian: "Would they be called pets?"

~ ***"They are our pets."***

Lilian: "What kind of animal?"

~ ***"They are a bit like your—badgers. These animals help us clean the floors. They brush it with their tails."***

Sara: "What a good idea!"

The next section of the recording is jumbled with diverse comments and laughter.

Lilian: "We have dogs that help people that are blind, and those who are deaf."

~ ***"We still have to clean of course. They cannot clean the high surfaces, but they do keep our floors clean."***

Lilian: "You've got them very well trained."

~ ***"And they help keep our house safe."***

Several: "Guard it?"

~ ***"They make noises, yes."***

Lilian explained our similar dependence on dogs.

Sarah: "Do these animals have fur, and does the fur not come out on the floor?"

~ ***"They have fur, yes, and sometimes it does come out, and we—tick them off!"***

The hesitation followed by colloquial expression got us all going again, and Bonniol added:

~ ***"They sweep their own fluff up too!"***

We asked how this had come about.

~ ***"It is something they do naturally, but we train them a little further."***

There was more general talk of animals leading to an opportunity to speak of our dairy industry: "Are you aware of our cows?"

~ ***"I am only aware of them from this one's memories, yes."***

I explained: "We are extremely quaint in the way we milk cows *and drink the milk of another species*. And we have huge industries based on milk and milk products. Does this seem strange to you?"

A substantial pause followed, and I suspect Bonniol was again choosing words carefully: ~ ***"It is peculiar to YOUR species, this cow. But the idea of milking is not that unusual for me to comprehend."***

George: "Would I be right in thinking that you do not do this yourselves, but you have come across the idea, on other planets perhaps?"

~ ***"We have been milking plants of course (for energy), so we understand the term. There are no animals that we can or would wish to milk, I think."***

Well, I have to say, I have long felt that imbibing the suckling fluid of other animals is a bizarre practice, peculiar perhaps only to humanity. Aerans would not wish to do it, and still we know of no others in the universe that do. Perhaps we are unique in this; a rather yucky side to we Earthlings!

Sara: "Going back to the animals in your homes—what about body functions?"

~ ***"They are very clean with their—"***

There was an awkward pause as Bonniol hesitated.

~ ***"I'm looking for the right term—"***

George: "Yes, we have dogs. They do tend to pooh on the pavement, which can be a nuisance."

We were past the little difficulty with a few titters.

~ ***"Our badgers have special places which they use every time."***

Sarah: "What do these badgers eat?"

~ ***"They are vegetarian."***

Lilian: "Are most of your animals vegetarian, or do you have some that are not?"

~ ***"We have some that are carnivorous, but the badgers eat only plants and fruit."***

Pia then saw an opportunity, and asked if Bonniol felt we might have animals on *this* planet that could help with the housework.

Perhaps she visualised a 'Bushy-tails Cleaning Service' back in Finland!

~ ***"I am not sure—we will have to try out different animals—it is possible."***

George: "So far we've only tried out humans—"

Sara: "I think we've had enough of that though!"

Graham went on to generalise on reasons for keeping pets.

~ ***"We have special pets, yes, like our badgers. Some people prefer them to other people—like on your planet."***

Sarah: "And they do say, that for people in hospital, or old people, it is therapeutic to have an animal to stroke. Do you have the same thing in your world?"

~ ***"We have animals which are very sensitive, and can help us with certain illnesses like depression—where they need lightening up and to be looking after—something vulnerable—it can be of benefit to them, to work with animals. But we are very—I'm looking for the right word again—people play with animals, and even when they are adults, they spend much time playing with them. They are a big part in our world."***

Pia: "Can you communicate by mind projection to the animals?"

~ ***"Animals pick up our emotions, they pick up our feelings and our thoughts. I am unable to mind project because they do not have that rational mind, that thinking power that we have. Theirs is a more—um—innate, instinctive mind. They do not probe the world for answers."***

The statement aligns to the view that there are the two kinds of knowledge (innate and empirical), and animals have just the one kind. So this particular difference between animals and humans may be simply stated.

George: "I think I would be right in saying that the *thoughts* that they receive are *wordless thoughts* so that language doesn't come into it—"

~ ***"They do not have language like us, because they are not seeking things to understand life like we are. They would receive thoughts—simple thoughts—thoughts of an emotional type, I think."***

Pia: "They are able to *experience* emotional thoughts also?"

~ ***"They most certainly do, yes."***

Lilian: "I would guess that most animals are creatures of habit—I mean, if we have a dog, it seems to know the time to go for a walk or the time for food."

~ ***"Sometimes they appear to be quite clever, yes. They are picking up signals from us or from our thoughts, and they understand them in a way. But they are understanding them in a more simple way. That is a nice way to be I think."***

Lilian: "It is really."

Graham next described our Third World countries and their need for aid to relieve famine and disease.

~ ***"We have had famines and problems with diseases on a large scale. And there are natural disasters, but these things pass with time. It is possible to free yourselves from poverty of course, and this will happen."***

Graham: "Does your world have lots of countries or have you organised yourselves as one domain?"

~ ***"Our planet has changed over time, we have had more borders—boundaries, now there are less. There are seven major countries. These are very large and were once divided into much smaller and numerous countries."***

George: "Would these be continents, or large landmasses within your oceans?"

~ ***"They would be more like continents, yes."***

George: "Yes, I think we are moving towards that."

Sarah: "To change the subject again, last week with Salumet—he was talking to us about music, and he preferred to call it 'vibrations of love'. It would be interesting if you could give us an example of some of *your* music."

I turned to Sarah: "Are you asking Bonniol to sing us a song?"

Midst good-natured chuckles at the thought, Bonniol again surprised us: ~ ***"I would be very happy to sing for you, if I can."***

Sarah: "Oh thank you!"

~ ***"I will try, ♪♫♪♫—I'm practising.***

Several: "That's good! That's good!"

Bonniol's song then followed, taking the form of a series of long notes; a strange sound. Our applause and verbal appreciation followed.

~ ***"I think it will be better in the future. The problem is—the words. I cannot sing one of MY songs with THESE words. They don't fit."***

Sarah: "Can you sing it with *your* language?"

~ ***"I could sing in my own language. I would prefer it."***

George: "Would there be a problem with that?"

Sarah: "Yes please—"

~ ***"I am not sure if it can be done at this moment. The link is still fragile, and we have found that speaking in our own language is a problem for the mind of this one, yes."***

George: "Perhaps that is something for us to look forward to in the future—"

Sarah: "Or you could just try if you like. If it doesn't work, it doesn't matter."

I must confess to being a little apprehensive during the pause that followed; a pause pregnant with many thoughts. Was Bonniol about to give it a try? Or was he just thinking? What if the attempt fails? How might that affect Paul? I guessed it would just mean a fragmentation of the link so that this session would terminate. We could live with that, just so long as—but next, we were treated to a series of vocal utterances from Bonniol that might easily and simply be described as 'UNEARTHLY', which of course it was; long phrases with some semblance of Gregorian chant but interwoven with what I can only think of as an 'unfalsettoed Swiss yodel', if it is possible to imagine that! After a further pause, there was vigorous applause and cries of 'excellent!' Again I was apprehensive. Would the volume of our appreciation disturb the link? It did not. It was an amazing conclusion to the evening. And in describing Bonniol's song as 'UNEARTHLY', I nearly said 'UNWORLDLY', forgetting for the moment that Aerah, like our own planet, is also a world.

I declared: "We have nothing quite like that on our planet!"

~ ***"It went better than I actually thought."***

And there was much agreeing to that!

~ ***"The throat is different you see, and the tongue."***

Compliments continued.

Sarah: "What do the words mean?"

~ ***"It was a poem really, about love and light, and the bright purity of them."***

Sarah: "Right."

~ ***"We are feeling it is time to say 'goodbye' once more."***

George: "You have given us an example of your language and of your music, and that is very nice to sign off with—a wonderful evening again! Thank you Bonniol, and thank you team!"

As we played back the recording afterwards, Paul declared that he would not find it possible to produce such a sound of his own volition. He also spoke of how he had been conscious of strange, induced throat movements. The captured, truly extraordinary sound, perhaps underlines the reality of these encounters.

Salumet, during his visit two weeks later, added the next statement: ~ **"What has transpired before you is meant to make you think more deeply, not only about mind projection, not only about the information given, but to your connection to the whole of existence, and just how unique that is."**

Then he invited questions and I began saying that Bonniol had listened to his teaching when he accidentally arrived a little early—

~ **"Let me stop you. There has been no accident!"**

All laughed heartily, and we all know by now from our many exchanges, that in spirit communication, *there are no accidents* although we are still apt to slip up occasionally and forget. All is by design. But when the design mechanism is not understood, it is an Earthly simplification to think of it as just an accident or a curious coincidence! Well anyway, Salumet is perfectly correct of course, what has transpired has certainly made us think more deeply on our '*connection to the whole of existence*'. We enquired: if Bonniol were to deliberately arrive sufficiently early, could he 'sit in' on a teaching session? To this Salumet replied: ~ **"If he so desires, of course that is possible. If the gentleman who offers his voice for his use** (Paul) **is willing, then of course he may sit and listen to my words."**

It had occurred to us that to have Bonniol *and* our much-loved master, *both* sitting with us; that should make a most interesting evening. There are just so many wonderful possibilities that we may look forward to, while this inter-galactic doorway continues.

CHAPTER: 13

Wonderful World – Dancing Waters – Industrial Devolution ... 1st August 2005

Lilian enquired if Bonniol had chanced to hear the previous speaker.

~ ***"I was not able to come so early this time."***

Lilian: "It was about the energy needed for these meetings."

In fact, one had spoken through Sarah, who has had the responsibility for transmuting energy to assist the sessions.

~ ***"Yes, you have many helpers."***

Lilian: "Yes, we are becoming more aware of all the help that is needed."

~ ***"As you delve deeper, you will see that there are many workers behind the scenes."***

Bonniol's song was still fresh in our minds from last time and it seemed appropriate to offer to play a recorded piece of *our* music for him that he could experience through Paul's ears.

~ ***"I would be very happy to hear something, yes."***

We had thought carefully. It should be something popular and meaningful, and copyright of course does not come into the equation since that formality would certainly not extend beyond the galaxy. We settled for Louis Armstrong's: *What a Wonderful World,* feeling it to carry just the right message. The piece was played, and so L A's music is now known on Aerah.

Graham: "A famous piece of music. Just about everybody on the planet probably knows that!"

~ ***"It was a lovely sound for these ears, very sensitive ears I think."***

It was explained that he played trumpet, and we felt the idea of 'wonderful world' to fit rather nicely with the communications, adding: "And he spoke of the 'rainbow'. I wonder if you have appreciation of the rainbows that we get here, and how the sunlight is split into its primary colours, by the moisture in our atmosphere. Do you have rainbows on your planet?"

~ ***"This is something that is peculiar to your planet I think. A rainbow—it is a beautiful way to see your colours. We have other natural lights, but this rainbow is something your Earth has that makes it special I think."***

George: "I guess it's the nature of the output of light from the sun and the way the moisture drops disperse in our atmosphere."

~ ***"You have different atmosphere to ours, and your weather conditions are also different, yes."***

Graham: "Do you get rain as we do?"

~ ***"We do get rain but the density is different, as I believe I mentioned once before. Water is somehow 'thicker' on our planet, and it flows in a less 'up-and-down' way. It goes in other directions, not always straight to the earth. It can be pulled sideways at times."***

The water of Aerah sounds distinctly different from ours, and so we asked questions in an attempt to understand why.

~ ***"It is to do with densities and the sizes of everything."***

George: "You have rivers that flow down to your oceans. Do these ever freeze—go solid, where there are low temperatures in your world?"

This question got shelved as Bonniol received guidance from another:

~ ***"I am being told you are not familiar with the way our waters change shape, and they 'dance', in a way like your fire. It is natural to us of course. It flows sideways and out—inwards—a bit like your flames."***

Sarah: "How do you explain a river that goes sideways?"

~ ***"The rivers—they move as one—and yet each droplet is alive and independent and moves on its own pathway as well. Something like a flock of birds, always moving together and yet each one can change slightly and change course."***

This was getting complicated and I asked: "Do you know the reason for the dancing of your rivers?"

~ ***"It is all energy that is alive, and somehow it manages to show its aliveness, perhaps more so in our world. Your water is also alive."***

It sounds a little like what we know as 'Brownian movement', the random movement of small particles (seen under a microscope); and this might well be more pronounced in a world of lower densities. I thought about the further scientific implications, but felt it best to keep the exchange simple: "It sounds as if your water is more alive than ours—"

~ ***"It's a phenomenon in our world that is quite different to some of the other worlds—more closely similar to that you will find in spirit. You have been told about the water you find in spirit?"***

We had in fact learned of the Astral Plane waters that are different from the denser waters of Earth.

~ ***"These waters are more clearly energy that is alive, and we can observe it as alive—watching our own waters."***

Sarah spoke of the power a body of water can have.

~ ***"We have powerful movement of water, yes."***

George: "Just to recap a little—you can swim in your water. Do you get wet? Are you dry when you come out of it?"

~ ***"Our water is dry, yes—it is probably easier to imagine our waters as those in spirit—as flows of pure energy."***

By now we were all beginning to picture the water of Aerah as *a less material water,* and much more energetic than ours.

Sarah: "Our bodies are made up of a high percentage of water and we need to drink water. Do you drink water?"

~ ***"We also drink this water, yes. And it makes up a large proportion of our bodies too."***

Sarah: "And it is dry?"

~ ***"It is dry. It does not leave any residue on our skin."***

Sarah's son Ben, on a visit from Australia, asked: "Our planet surface is made up of large areas of water. Does the surface of your planet also have large areas of water?"

~ ***"The water, yes, it makes up over half our world."***

Graham extended the water theme, speaking of volcanic activity and how solids, liquids and gases are all brought to the surface, pointing out that Earth would have dried out long ago but for water surfacing from the depths.

~ ***"Yes, our planet is also alive and constantly changing. There is always movement from deep within to the surface."***

Graham: "So you have volcanoes?"

~ ***"We have had volcanoes. At the moment there is not much activity. But there is always some interaction of the elements, and of course, at some point, our world will cease to be habitable, but that is not for a long time, we have been told."***

Graham: "And your sun like our sun, will probably become stronger as it becomes older, and in time will become too hot—"

~ ***"Everything is in constant flux—nothing stays the same forever. But we are talking many aeons of time."***

Graham: "Yes, about a billion years from now, life on this planet will probably be impossible."

~ ***"And by then, do you think mankind will still need this world?"***

George: "Well hopefully, we will have moved on beyond the material form!"

Sarah: "Salumet told us that in the end, we shall no longer need it."

~ ***"Things are designed incredibly well—to last as long as they are needed."***

All agreed and I added: "We have been told that *the plan is perfect.* I think what we have been discussing, falls within that plan's perfection."

A fresh topic was needed and we moved on to mining and metals industries.

~ ***"We have had in the past but of course now we do not make or generate materials in this way."***

So the question became retrospective, but worth continuing: "Yes, I was going to ask if you have an iron or steel industry, and a funny little thing about iron is that it can be used for making magnets, which can attract or repel. And I just wondered out of interest, if this came into your technology at all—the use of iron for making magnets?"

~ ***"We have a metal, which attracts and repels like your magnets, yes."***

George: "I see, so do you have to act on it in some way, to make it have this property, or is it natural?"

~ ***"We can make it more magnetic but it appears to have a natural attraction to metals."***

George: "I see—oh!—to *other* metals!"

~ ***"Yes, but not all metals."***

George: "I see. It sounds like it is something different from our iron that just acts on itself."

~ ***"There are many things that would be a little different when comparing, and there will be things that are completely different. But this magnetic metal, I feel is comparable to the one on your planet."***

Now that is sensible comment, and that iron exists on Aerah with nearly but not *quite* the same properties, feels right—some progress in comparative chemistry! And here was the opportunity to check another element, so I ventured: "Yes, right! Going back to volcanoes, something that we get from our volcanoes is 'sulphur', a yellow element that gives rise to terrible smells of sulphurous gases. Do you have that yellow element: sulphur, associated with your volcanoes?"

~ ***"We are familiar with many bad smells."***

As a fresh spate of titters broke out, Bonniol continued: ~ ***"This sulphur one is probably the same chemical—yes—because we do have something, which causes the smell around volcanic areas."***

I suggested this to be a piece of chemistry that our planets share.

~ ***"It is not yellow, but I think that is due to our atmosphere being different. The colours may appear different with our different lighting."***

A pattern of chemical similarity was emerging. It is a fair certainty that both planets have iron and sulphur, albeit not quite of identical form. The compound water also is very similarly distributed, but its character differs. We asked about a paper industry, stating how we make writing paper from plant fibres and how this has been our practise for hundreds of years. But Aerah, it seems, has moved beyond that development.

~ ***"Again, it is something that we have done in the past. It is no longer necessary to make things in our world, when you have thought projection abilities."***

George: "No need to write things down on paper when you can communicate in this way?"

~ ***"We still like to write but we don't need to make the paper in the way you are describing. If we wish to have paper, we can produce it with our minds. We can materialise objects."***

George: "So the thought process has really replaced industry to a large degree—"

~ ***"There are still some industries. But, in that sense, yes, it has replaced them to a large degree. Once you start down that road, industries no longer need to exist. It is a lot of activity and it can produce all kinds of problems environmentally."***

George: "Yes indeed, as we know! Yes, thinking things into existence—it occurs to me that this is the very *creation process*! You seem to use the *creation process* in your daily lives! Would that be a fair statement?"

Bonniol was careful to qualify: ~ ***"It is not really creating life. It is creating objects that we need. But this is not the same as creating something unique."***

George: "Not the same as creating a planet or creating a universe, but you are creating objects for your daily needs—"

~ ***"Yes. And these objects are simple objects. They are not objects involving complex mechanisms. We still have limits in our thought / mind activities. We cannot materialise everything we wish for. There are limits, just as in your world, but simple objects like paper, like building blocks, items of furniture and simple tools—anything that is uncomplicated we can easily materialise. The more complicated the object the more difficult it becomes."***

George: "And I think you said earlier that you are able to make things change shape, as with your building blocks?"

~ ***"Yes, we can manipulate the form of objects. It is not something that we can ALL do well. But it is common in our world. And it***

is something that we practise, and this is one of the ways we are progressing—with these abilities."

We asked about making a piece of furniture: ~ ***"You would imagine the piece in your mind, and you would breathe it into existence, in a sense."***

George: "So you would imagine it and it would become the material form of your imagination—"

~ ***"If the thought is strong enough, yes."***

Graham: "How long does it take for you to do this?"

~ ***"It requires a deep state of meditation—concentration. But it can be done quickly. For some it can take a lot of practise. Provided the clarity of thought is there, it would be quick. But this is something that has developed over much time in our world."***

George, hesitatingly: "No—this is something that we could not aspire to, but it is very interesting to hear of *your* ways."

Another prompt from guides: ~ ***"I am being told that there ARE people who can materialise objects, on your world. So already the abilities are coming to your planet."***

George: "Yes, we have a word: 'apport', in our language and I think this is making things appear through an energy transmutation. I'm not sure if this would be the same process—"

~ ***"If they are materialising objects, then they are practising the same basic procedure."***

George: "Well, you are correct that there are just a few people in our world who can do that. I think they represent a very small percentage of our population, but yes, they do exist."

~ ***"In our world, it was the same at one time. Only a few could do these things, but they showed others, and others practised. And now it is common for everyone to be able to do it to some degree."***

We moved on to the necessity for meditation and how it should be deep.

~ ***"Your meditation, is the key to so many things. It will sharpen your mind—help you in so many ways. So yes, meditations are enormously valuable to you. We would not have developed these gifts without it. Meditation is like the growing phase."***

More was said on this, and part of the growing has to be strengthening soul bond, with access to the 'inner being' of wondrous abilities. As the session drew to a close, we checked if further musical interludes would be welcomed, and our friend was happy at the prospect.

CHAPTER: 14
Love – Evolution – Energy Density ... 8th August 2005

THE NEXT MEETING began with three rescues. All three visitors guided to us had been held back through their disbelief in continued life after physical death. As Lilian talked with each in turn, they became aware of the spiritual light and were then able to move on into that light. One said he had been aware of it for some time without knowing what it was, and it had bothered him! Rescues continue to be an important part of our work, and in addition to helping those in need, they add to our own awareness of the many facets of spiritual existence.

Bonniol was saying: ~ ***"Now that we have become more intimate, there is more knowledge about ourselves."***

Lilian: "Yes, a deeper friendship."

~ ***"We have found that it takes time, whenever you begin to bring two worlds together. There are so many differences that you may find it confusing at first. But now I think there is the beginning of understanding between us."***

We enthusiastically agreed, at the same time acknowledging our ignorance and expressing happiness for Bonniol to continue doing the 'spadework'. And as to the differences between our cultures, well I just continue to be enthralled by so many *similarities* that keep cropping up.

~ ***"As another world once came to us and helped with OUR understanding, now maybe, we are able to help with yours a little, as well as helping with our own understanding of the universe."***

George: "Yes, you certainly stimulate a few thought processes with us, and yes, we are beginning to have thoughts that just didn't occur before." (Fresh in my mind was: thought-powered-manufacture to replace industries, and the notion that chemical elements do not share quite the same properties across the universe.)

~ ***"Then it truly is a mind-expanding experience for us all."***

Lilian: "Yes it is."

Sarah: "Salumet says it is a two-way exercise. It helps him and it helps us. And it's probably the same with you..."

~ ***"It is part of the perfection I think, the perfection of the universe. There is always this interaction, it is never one way. You have been helping people this evening, but you have also gained much pleasure in it—and because of this, more knowledge and wisdom."***

George: "It's very nice to feel that those people, who had problems in going forward, are now on their way."

Several: "Yes."

Following a pause, music was offered.

~ ***"I was hoping you would play some more of your Earth music!"***

A helping of 'The Beatles' awaited. The popularity of groups with guitars and drums of 40-years ago was explained, and this group was popular! Songs were usually about some aspect of love and now our little gathering became permeated with: 'She loves you, yeah, yeah, yeah—'. I think we all wondered what Bonniol would make of a Beatles era offering.

Lilian commented: "They are all young people."

~ ***"A very pleasant feeling—that sound, it makes me feel good to be alive!"***

And there was general agreement to that.

Eileen: "May we ask how you interpret 'love'?"

~ ***"Love is the very essence of our existence, everything we do, we do for love."***

Eileen: "Would you use that word in your world?"

~ ***"Words are always never quite the same when translated, but this word 'love' is one that we all know deep down I think."***

Eileen: "Instinctively—"

~ ***"Yes, and there are many levels to it, many purities. And it is what we aim for—that pure love, which is really merging with the***

purest energies. And we are almost, no longer contaminated with less pure energies. We've cleansed our selves."

George: "By less pure energies, you mean 'fear', 'hate' and such things?"

~ ***"Yes, yes, and it takes many lifetimes, and we never seem to get there. It is nevertheless always the most profound motivation for us, at whatever level we're on, whichever world we are with, everybody feels the same—drawn towards it. This is the thing that we aim for—the purest form of love, which is creation in its purest form, purest energy. LOVE IS CREATION."***

A profound statement, on which Sarah reflected then ventured: "So there isn't really any trouble on your planet? Everybody is—" She was not allowed to finish.

Bonniol very quickly declared: ~ ***"We haven't got THAT far!"*** to which there was hearty and understanding laughter.

Eileen asked if Aerans receive teachers from spirit.

~ ***"We occasionally channel a teacher. But with our mind projection, we can more easily communicate with our (spirit) guides."***

Eileen: "And it's mind-to-mind directly?"

~ ***"We can do it directly, yes."***

Sarah asked if it is possible on a group basis.

~ ***"We can link up with the same person. It has no limits when you are working with the mind."***

We enquired of spirit values on the other planets visited.

~ ***"Everyone is at a slightly different stage—yes."***

We recalled it has been suggested that Earth is near the bottom of the league table, whereupon Bonniol joked, saying: they probably say that to everyone to make them work harder! Hearty laughter had followed, but one cannot quite say that Earth is the least developed planet, and both Bonniol and Salumet have stated that one cannot judge these things. It must be accepted however, that we have a long way to go, a lengthy road to travel and bridges to cross; leading to peace, trust and to beyond-Earth communications. 'Out of the Silent Planet' was a book by C. S. Lewis, and I think the implication of his title was that Earth remained silent within the vaults of the heavens. No word emerged. Its author, in his time, was of course a man of deeper spiritual perception. Now, thanks to Salumet and Bonniol, and of course others; also to our own striving, Earth has the opportunity to no longer wear a cloak of silence. Already, the first steps are being taken to explore the wider vista of creation.

It was now time for the topic of *energy density*. It was suggested to Bonniol that the properties of water and chemical elements differ between our planets due to their underlying energies being less dense.

~ ***"Yes, the 'density' is a good way to describe the differences here. Your water IS more dense than our water. That is what brings its slightly different qualities."***

George: "And your iron too—our iron attracts itself when in magnetic form, but your iron I understand, attracts several different metals. I suspect that you have much the same chemical elements and compounds on your planet, but their properties are rather different because of this energy-density difference."

~ ***"Yes, the energy-density is the main difference, and this is the key. But each world has its own forms and structures, which will be different too, based on whatever happens to have been put there, and how it is integrated into that world. The denser it is, the slower it is, as you know. The less dense worlds vibrate faster, yes. But that is—wait a minute—"***

We waited as Bonniol clearly received advice. As suspected, we were onto an important issue here that was receiving further input. Excellent!

~ ***"There is another piece to the puzzle, and that is the 'plan' for the planet—yes—if I can explain it that way. There are plans for each planet on how things will develop with shapes and forms—independent, or a little bit so. Yes—I am getting into a muddle I think."***

George: "Well, it's a difficult area—"

~ ***"It is. But the densities are CHANGING—following the plans—"***

George: "Yes!"

~ ***"And the progression of each planet—and as your planet progresses—"***

George: "The energy-density will change with progression!"

~ ***"Your world—has already changed actually, and you will notice further changes."***

George: "This is a point I've wondered about. Does the basic energy-density of everything on your planet, change with advancing spirituality?"

~ ***"IT CHANGES WITH ADVANCING SPIRITUALITY. But remember the planet itself is (also) a spiritual being, and this being will be progressing at its own rate—and there will be interaction—your own progression and the planet's progression, interact. But the characteristics of your world will change as the densities change."***

As we thanked our friend for this revelation, Sarah added: "That *does* make sense."

It most certainly does. There are huge, huge implications. When we speak of energy density, we mean the very essence of created matter. Our science has long understood Earth and all life to be comprised of small units called molecules and atoms, in turn made up of even smaller sub-atomic particles; and at this level, all is energy in motion. The basis of all matter is the restless energy, and this ultimate stuff of being is the focus of our debate. There is nothing more fundamental than this essence apart from its creator: the Creative Principle—God. Bonniol is saying that as spirituality advances, the energy-density decreases. Some might prefer to see it written differently: as we get nearer to God, the lightness of spirit prevails—something more to think on.

Lilian invited questions from Bonniol.

~ ***"I've got some questions about your evolution, yes. And I understand that you have evolved from the primates, yes? But you have not been linked with other animals?"***

We explained our evolution as best we could; how *Homo erectus* had appeared around two million years ago, leading to modern man for the past 100,000 years. In response to Bonniol's questions we described changes that had occurred (head shape, hair distribution, stance etc) and the reasons for becoming upright. We finally got onto our four human roots having different skin colours, and Bonniol contributed much towards how this factor may have come about: ~ ***"This adaptation is more than a question of the powers of nature, if you like, or amount of sunshine—there will be the nature spirits who***

will be influencing the way things grow. So it's interesting to think about how and why it is these people have grown in particular ways. The genetics are a physical structure, and yet there is an interaction with the nature spirits and the environment, and these things are all relevant in your evolution. So what is produced, tells a lot about the nature spirits and the conditions of your world."

A major point is that there are the elementals to be considered that hitherto have not formed part of standard scientific debate! More and more we are being led to think spiritually as well as physically; both being necessary in understanding ourselves and charting the way forward.

Eileen returned us to mind work: "Most beings in this world do not know when it's their time to go to spirit. With your ability to mind project, can you prepare?"

~ ***"Yes, we have that information. It is available if we wish to know it. We do not fear death, and so most of us—I would say, nearly all of us—will be curious enough to have that question answered before we die, as to when our time will be up. But we may not wish to know the PRECISE times."***

Eileen: "So it's not automatic knowing—"

~ ***"I know that I still have a fairly long time, but I do not wish to know EXACTLY when my time is up, until I get that—tap on the shoulder."***

We continue to marvel at Bonniol's choice of expressions.

Eileen: "Can you explain why you don't want to know?"

~ ***"It's not an important thing for me at the moment. I feel it could be a distraction to know the time and place of my death. I am happy at the moment to leave that. When the time is nearer you feel it anyway."***

George: "Can I just say, we are pleased to know you will be with us a bit longer!"

Midst agreement and laughs, Bonniol added: ~ ***"Then again, there is always free will!"***

Sarah: "I don't know if we've asked you, and maybe it would be rude to ask, but how old are you in our years?"

~ ***"I am about 47 of your Earthly years—nearly half of my expected life."***

Sarah: "Well, that makes you the baby amongst us all."

We explained that most on Earth have little idea of departure time.

[In fact, just a few have known, for example, the Irish mystic and healer Saint Malachy, accurately foretold his own time and place of death on All Souls' Day, November 1148 at Clairvaux, France, where he was laid to rest, his skull later being transferred to the cathedral at Troyes as a relic.]

Returning to evolution, there was some talk of our dependence on fossil record and it seems that fossils are also available to Aerans.

~ ***"Our development was a bit more complicated in that we evolved from two different species, yes. So there was an animal, which quite by chance bred with quite a different animal, and we evolved from this, which is why there are more differences, I would say, amongst our population than yours."***

George: "So, in your distant past, you would have developed from what we might call a 'hybrid'?"

~ ***"Yes, this is correct, and the one animal, we took on more completely than the other. So we resemble one a little bit more closely."***

Sarah: "And they are both extinct now?"

~ ***"They are both extinct. Our past has been by no means perfect, and we have been through many dark times in our history."***

Sarah: "It is all part of the learning curve isn't it? We're here to learn. If everything went smoothly all the way, we wouldn't learn anything would we?"

~ ***"This is what I was about to say! It is all within the evolutionary pattern, as we go from the darkness into the light."***

We gave brief account of our recent interference with nature through genetic modification and asked if Aerans had tried this.

~ ***"We have not—we are being told—"***, and again Bonniol appeared to receive information from guides.

~ ***"—that the way that you are interfering, is quite different from the way we interfered in the past, though we did have a time when we tried to manipulate our natural world, but I think the difference was, you are trying it with completely different species***

now. We have had many problems in the past through interfering with nature, which is like interfering with creation itself."

Sarah: "So it's not a good idea—"

~ ***"We have learnt the hard way that it will rebound, and this is something you are learning too, I think."***

George: "Yes, when it first began to happen, we spoke of it to Salumet and he described it as *an unnecessary step*. Then we spoke of it again some years later, after that step had been taken and he said: well, we are now travelling down that road and *some* good will come of it, and we must not judge. Let it happen."

~ ***"These are wise words."***

We referred to imbalance in nature and the possible need to control locust plagues. They would it seems be organised by the nature spirits.

~ ***"Yes, if only you could communicate with your nature spirits, they would gladly help you with so many of these problems of balance. They do so love to be acknowledged. They are the carers of the trees and the plants and the animals. It is their work."***

George: "So if there were a plague of locusts, would I be right in thinking that either the elementals think it necessary or the angelic beings who oversee might think it necessary, for whatever reason?"

~ ***"When you begin to think about why would there be a plague of locusts, then you might find there is a good reason for it."***

It was suggested that crop destruction might signal an opportunity for people on Earth to exercise compassion and help one another.

~ ***"It is not for me to say why these things happen. It's simply that THERE WILL BE GOOD REASONS."***

Perhaps it was fitting conclusion to this exchange. Spiritual advancement, goes hand-in-hand with commitment to spiritual thinking; thus bringing elementals, angelic beings and people interactions, all into the equation of life. DDT kills locusts, but we all know by now that this heavy-handed approach creates other devastating problems in its wake. It simply does not work in the wider scheme, and there is always that underlying feeling that nature must be allowed proper balance.

Eileen picked up on the angelic beings and was interested to know how Aerans *see* them.

~ ***"Well, we see the lights, and there IS form. But we understand the form is changeable. The form could be any living creature really. We often just see a face or a shimmering glow. It is a living energy, conscious, living, aware energy, pulsating in front of us."***

Sarah reminded that Salumet had said that we are all of us energy and this led to a final statement from Bonniol: ~ ***"Yes, and this is something that we will be more aware of when we are no longer physical. These physical bodies teach us a lot, but they also inhibit us a lot as well. That is the purpose of them, to provide a certain focus, a certain set of challenges—I am beginning to—I think it's time to be off again."***

CHAPTER: 15

Elements and Elementals – Environmental Beauty ... 15th August 2005

We asked if, when we play music, Bonniol's friends back home get the full benefit of hearing it through the human ear.

~ ***"They share with me that experience, yes."***

George: "Oh good! That's nice."

~ ***"So we are all looking forward to a little more Earth music at this time."***

It was explained that so far we had played 'popular' pieces but there are also the 'classical' works, and something was said on these. We played a passage from 'The Marriage of Figaro' sung by two Italian lady sopranos.

"Thank you! That was very beautiful, to hear the voices, like dancing with each other!"

Now, voices 'dancing with each other', we felt to be most apt description.

~ ***"Yes, we are enjoying your Earth music. It has a distinctive sound to it. Each planet has its own music of course."***

Our friend was asked about the music of other planets.

~ ***"We have not experienced much, but we have listened to some of the music from each planet, yes. And it is always interesting to listen to such different sounds. But at first it is quite confusing, because the instruments are different. The voices are different too, and when you listen with different ears, then you need time to adjust—to make sense of their noises—if you can understand that."***

We moved on to discuss how different sounds are generated by instruments, and it of course all depends upon vibrating parts. And the pitch of the voice for Aerans, we understand, depends very much on the size of the person (and corresponding size of tubes within), so that large ones would have low voices and children high voices.

We next took that important matter of 'changing energy-density' just a little further, Bonniol being asked if they had actually monitored it over the years.

~ ***"We have monitored this a little bit, and we are able to detect changes in the densities of our planetary elements, yes. But they are very gradual over large periods of time."***

We expressed interest and Bonniol continued:

~ ***"It is perhaps less clear because our own densities have changed as well, so everything is changing including our selves. So it's not always easy to tell that the water is becoming less dense, while we also are becoming less dense. Our elements HAVE become less dense. But this has taken thousands of years. I am sure it is always changing from as far back as you can go, but the changes are very subtle, so they are not something that you would notice readily."***

I pointed out that I had examined two sets of atomic weight tables for our elements spaced 20-years apart and there is no or virtually no difference, so perhaps we need to wait 100-years or so before looking at our revised tables. Bonniol replied: ~ ***"Yes, I was going to say, best not to hold your breath—you might be waiting a long time!"***

And that was another opportunity for laughter!

We moved on from 'elements' to 'elementals' and those two words are similar only because of the multiple meaning of the word 'element'. Perhaps this should be clarified since the terms embrace important issues. Originally, Earth's elements were seen as four: earth, air, fire and water, and the elementals are the four kinds of ether-being that live and work within the ether of each. But the elements of modern science are simple substances such as copper, iron, sulphur and oxygen that cannot be split by chemical means into simpler substance. There are more than one hundred elements including a few that have been synthesised in trace amount, and atomic weight tables define them.

A searching question next came from Bonniol, inspired by some wonderful pictures in Paul's mind from his travels.

~ ***"I was looking at some pictures in the mind of this one, and they are incredible pictures of places far away. And I was thinking of the many different environments in your world—yes, I'm searching for the phrase at the moment—I think it's the term you use for packaging your products. Yes, your 'natural' environment is the most beautiful 'aspect' of your world. Would you agree?"***

All came alive at once with cries of 'yes', 'the natural environment', 'trees', 'rivers', 'and the animals'; then adding: 'As opposed to townships and the repetitiveness of agriculture's fields.'

~ ***"And when you wish to produce something of beauty in your world, the source of the beauty is your nature, is it not?"***

This sparked some discussion about perception of beauty and how artists might see it.

~ ***"Yes, I was saying that in the search for beauty, we sometimes wish to package it up, when perhaps we would want to (or it would be best to), take the packaging away. The natural world has the most outstanding beauty."***

George: "Yes, and in a way, a painting of that natural world is rather spoiled by putting it in a frame, the frame becomes the packaging. Is that the sort of thing that you were implying?"

~ ***"Yes, we wondered what your reasons are for some of the 'packaging', if I could use that word that you do to nature—some of your gardens—some of your houses. It is like you are not wanting nature to show itself in its full glory."***

Richard: "Are you referring to keeping things under control, like potted plants and neat gardens?"

~ ***"Yes, the word 'control' seems to be an important one."***

We explained about garden plots and how we *control* in order to grow vegetables and not weeds. But the truly beautiful areas are the wild parts—on the mountains, along riverbanks and unspoiled woodlands.

~ ***"And a lot of these places have no packaging at all. They have been allowed to develop independently."***

Eileen: "And they would be governed by the elementals."

~ ***"Yes!"***

Eileen: "When you say they are just wild, there must be some kind of structure, some kind of order—"

~ ***"—Elementals will enhance a place in their own way."***

Eileen: "So perhaps that's why we are inclined to say it is always so much more beautiful, when it's been left wild."

~ ***"Yes, the elementals have an ability to enhance the places, the plants, the flowers, in such a way that there is a balance, which is difficult to explain."***

Eileen: "Well, there's no interference from us!"

~ ***"They are able to balance the different elements (components), yes, so that there is a maximum of life within that area. They will try to make as many things thrive as possible—as many different things."***

Richard referred to our attempts to reclaim green areas following spoilage.

~ ***"Yes, that sounds like POSITIVE packaging, which you understand. I think for this time, we should say 'goodbye' once more. And I look forward to our next meeting."***

The debate on 'beauty' produced interesting ideas, not least that 'unspoiled nature' is its true source. Our knowledge of how elementals enhance nature has been extended. And perhaps the term 'wild' really means 'freely organised by elementals'—a new definition for our dictionaries.

CHAPTER: **16**

An Unexpected Extra Guest ... 22nd August 2005

A CONTROL CAME through Sarah with a lengthy, amazing and at first confusing message. In a nutshell, it amounted to: our permission was sought for a being from another planet to join with Bonniol and Bonniol would speak for him; as well as speaking for himself, all via Paul.

~ ***"Hello, I am pleased to come to you again."***

Lilian: "Thank you."

~ ***"As you have been hearing, this evening we may be able to help to bring another world closer to yours."***

Lilian: "That would be wonderful!"

~ ***"I am happy to play my part in this. I will speak for this other visitor, yes."***

Lilian: "I see."

~ ***"He will communicate with you via me."***

George: "So we shall just receive the one voice, your voice?"

~ ***"That is correct, yes—I am AWARE of this person. They are one of the worlds which we communicate with, and they have been given SOME information about you, and they would like to say: 'Hello'."***

Lilian: "We would like to say 'Hello' back."

George: "Yes, we would like to say, 'hello and welcome' to both of you, this time."

~ ***"They are saying that they would love to be here, but they cannot at this time, project themselves adequately. They are learning, and in time they will I'm sure, forge their own link with you, as our universe begins to bring itself together."***

We spoke of how communication and travel had made Earth seem a smaller place, and that process was now at work shrinking the universe.

~ "Yes, and this is the natural progression is it not?"

George: "It is certainly a most wonderful and very interesting progression so far as we are concerned."

~ "They—my friend—would like to explain a little about HIS world."

And there were general sounds of agreement and enthusiasm to that.

~ "He is saying that his world is much smaller than yours he believes, and his physical appearance is quite different. They are NOT like anything that we have noticed from this one's memories. They are—I don't know how to explain it—they are more like vegetables, and that may seem very strange to you."

George: "Is this the *physical* side of things?"

~ "Yes, they grow in the ground like your vegetables, like trees, yes. Like your trees, they are rooted in the ground."

George: "I see, so they do not move around—"

~ "That is correct."

Sarah, equally astonished: "So they can't travel physically—"

~ "They cannot travel physically, but they communicate with each other by thought projection."

Our exclamations embraced surprise, astonishment, wonder, and admiration. I mentioned John Wyndham's fictional *triffids*, so that in fictional writing we have the 'idea' of the developed vegetable.

Sarah: "And now we have the reality!"

I repeated: "And now we have the reality!"

~ "And these beings are very beautiful beings, I must add. But they obviously have developed along vastly different lines of evolution to your selves, and indeed us. They have a method of mind projection, which is a little different, and this is why they are unable to communicate directly with you at this point."

Lilian: "Please tell your friend we are very pleased to have made contact."

~ "Thank you. They have a good warm sense of humour and fun, and they are so connected with their planet. It is incredible for

us to have a species of vegetable, which is also as aware as they are. It gives us tremendous insight into planetary awareness."

George: "Might I ask if there are animals on the planet, or is it entirely a vegetable and spirit planet?"

~ ***"They do have animals, yes. But the animals are perhaps more similar to the animals on our planet, in that these animals have not developed the same reasoning, awareness and communication abilities that we have."***

Sarah: "If they don't move and they don't make contact, how do they—do they have families? Do they live in groups?"

~ ***"Yes, they have their own clans. They form circles of their own, so they can propagate of course, with other circles. And this is how they grow."***

George: "We have some vegetable species that grow in a circle, the 'mushrooms'. Do they develop in a circle in that way?"

~ ***"They develop in a slightly different way to your mushrooms, but they have a little bit in common with them. They are something similar in shape to the mushrooms. But they are made from something different, yes, something a bit harder—they are not so soft."***

George: "Yes, we understand that. So they are obviously a well-developed vegetable, principally. And we describe things as being 'woody' when they are a hard vegetable composition, as with our trees."

~ ***"Your trees also have spirits of course."***

We commented how wonderful to hear of a vegetable species developed in this way.

~ ***"But you are probably wondering HOW they develop, what they do with themselves, if they are aware of themselves to this extent—what makes them tick!"***

We asked if it is all *spiritual* communication between them.

~ ***"They sleep, and during their dream-states, they are able to venture into the spirit realms and journey into many different realms of existence. And when they are not dreaming, they are able to contemplate from their own standpoint, physical standpoint, the different spiritual realms. There are so many realms, so many***

worlds within worlds, that to have a fixed place to return to can be very useful as a focal point."

Sarah: "So they travel, probably much further than we do, but in their sleep state—"

"Yes, when they are sleeping, they explore, and this is why they do not require movement. They can journey together in their sleep state."

Sarah: "Right, so the contact they would make with each other would be when they are awake?"

~ ***"When they are awake, they are asleep almost. When they are awake, they are within their circles. They are able to reflect on their journeys and compare what they have discovered with others. But when they are asleep, that is really when they begin to do their work."***

Sarah: "Right, so they don't need physical contact."

George: "Do they have a physical language?"

~ ***"Yes, when they are awake, they are certainly able to communicate with each other."***

I think at this stage, we were finding it hard to *imagine* this new reality, and so we moved on to enquire about their size in relation to the animals.

~ ***"They are as big as a mushroom or larger, probably larger—again, it is difficult to compare sizes."***

Sarah: "So what happens if an animal were to tread on one and injure it—how would it react?"

~ ***"They are telling me that they do not suffer if they are destroyed. It is a simple transition to a life in spirit, not so different from their physical existence. The animals would not be able to damage them normally. They are a similar size but the mushroom shape is harder. They have larger ones, larger than them and others are smaller."***

Sarah: "Right—and how long do these mushroom beings live for?"

~ ***"They have a long life span. They probably live as long as some of your trees, they are telling me."***

We asked if they reincarnate on a personalised basis.

~ ***"They CAN reincarnate. This is an option available to them, and it is common. But it is not a rule. It is a choice."***

Sarah: "During their long lives, they must learn a tremendous amount."

~ ***"They probably know more about the many realms than any of us do."***

Sarah: "Would you say they are more advanced than we are, or just different?"

~ ***"I would say they are most advanced in that they seem to know about everything and more. But I think in the spiritual sense, it is very difficult to gauge this, but they are full of knowledge."***

We sought some clarification as to the many realms.

~ ***"Yes, there are so many different worlds, I don't think any of us would believe it possible. Even in your 'nature spirit existences', each element (earth, air, fire, water) has its own world, and you could spend time in each, a lifetime in each. But there are, even on your Earth, there is so much to explore. There are spiritual energies, which we know nothing about. But these are worlds within worlds. There are numerous beings throughout existence and our knowledge is very scanty. They are able to explore many of them."***

George: "Yes, I think we are *beginning* to realise just *how* scanty our knowledge is!"

~ ***"And they would like to offer you a little blessing for your planet."***

Sarah: "That would be gratefully received."

~ ***"They are very interested in your trees of course, and your plants, and would like you all to feel the bond between you and the plants of your Earth. You are all a part of the planet, and you and the plants are sharing the same space. You are interacting with them in ways that you don't fully understand."***

We spoke of the little we know of plant intelligence, communication and response, and how this is sadly not widespread knowledge on Earth. (People are still laughed at when they play music to tomatoes but there is undeniable experimental proof [17, 20] that the melodic vibrations speed growth.) And it may be true that those in eastern countries following the Buddhist teaching have greater respect for all life forms.

~ ***"Yes, it's another way of becoming part of the universe, to accept everything as having its place and everything as a friend.***

Everything is there for your benefit and you will therefore be 'benefit-ers' of everything else."

Sarah: "It's a two-way thing."

~ ***"There is much love out there waiting to be tapped."***

Sarah: "Your friend—in their dream-state—have they met with plants on this planet?"

~ ***"They have visited your world many times, yes, in their dream-state. And they are more familiar than WE are with your plants and trees, your animals and all your nature."***

George: "Have they become interested in humans? Have they developed *special* interests?"

~ ***"When they first visit a world, they say they begin by looking at nature, attempting to communicate with the plant species, clearly because they are interested to meet with other plant species with an awareness similar to theirs. But they have not met one yet similar to their own. And they are aware obviously of the humans and animals and all who live on this Earth, but they have less interest in humans who are not part of the nature. They look for the areas in your world, where there is less separation, where there is unison."***

George: "They would perhaps be more interested in the North American Indians, who have a greater connection with nature."

~ ***"They want to see worlds where all the inhabitants are connecting, rather than worlds where there is much segregation."***

Sarah: "I'm afraid this world has a lot of that. We have a long way to go."

~ ***"But they are happy that many of you are growing in your awareness."***

Sarah: "When you say that they visit our plants, do they actually visit the plant or the nature spirit with the plant?"

~ ***"They visit the plant, and they feel the plant's energies, if you like."***

George: "Have they been able to communicate with any species?"

~ ***"They have not been able to communicate in the way you mean, with other plant life on your Earth. But they are also aware of your nature spirits of course. And there are other living beings on your Earth that they have communicated with. They are talking***

about your—finding the name for—your 'elephants'. Your elephants have some degree of awareness, which can be interacted with, yes."

George: "Yes, the elephants are sensitive, are trainable and have good memory."

~ ***"They have an awareness that might surprise you. They are able to use their thoughts to a small degree. But they do not have the awareness of a human of course."***

George: "Mark who has sat with this group—he has tried thought-communication with an elephant. And he felt there was a connection because a tear appeared in the elephant's eye. Yes, we do feel that they are sensitive beings."

~ ***"Yes, they have a fondness for your elephants, and of course, they are one of many that they have explored."***

And in reply to questions concerning their planetary conditions:
~ ***"Their world is much hotter than your world, but they do need a certain amount of moisture to survive. Their roots go deep into the earth, so they are able to get at the moisture. It rains rarely, but it can rain. But this is something that has not happened for a long time."***

Sarah: "So it's rather like our deserts is it?"

~ ***"It is more like your deserts, yes."***

Sarah: "So are they the *only* plant species?"

~ ***"There are other species of plant, but of course with nothing like their awareness."***

Sarah: "And the other plant species just provide food for the animals, do they?"

~ ***"Yes, and other things, but plant species are always, or nearly always, possessed of a different awareness. This is the important thing, and a very unusual thing, about this world that we bring to you this evening. It is unusual to find a world with something from the vegetable kingdom with this awareness."***

This has to be seen as a definitive statement concerning a truly amazing species that is in no way humanoid, yet possesses a spirit of adventure, enquiry, vast knowledge and sensitivity that leaves one almost speechless. We asked about names; they do in fact have names but Bonniol was unable to devise a meaningful expression for us.

George: "So clearly, they have elementals on their planet, and they would recognise and have communication, would they?"

~ ***"They certainly do, yes—um—I'm being told that it's time that we should be leaving. So we have to leave at this point. And my friend is delighted that they have at last communicated with you."***

Sarah: "We're delighted too."

George: "Yes, wonderful! Thank you Bonniol, and thank you, friend-from-the-other-planet, and your support team—and we give you our warmest love, and I hope you will be able to bring your friend again."

~ ***"I'm sure he would like that very much too. It's a lot for you to—"***

George: "Take on board?"

~ ***"Ah yes—"***

George: "But we do, we do! We are eager to learn and we realise that we have a long way to go."

~ ***"And we do not wish to rush these things. We do not want to open your minds to too many new ideas. We were told it would be okay, so we have brought this to you."***

Our friends left with our heartfelt appreciation.

[As to that 'vegetable awareness', many will be unfamiliar with this notion, this only because it is not an overt part of our science. Cleve Backster, in the mid 20th-century, conducted experiments using a polygraph connected to various plant species. His work leaves no doubt that plants do indeed possess a consciousness that is influenced by humans. It is not only actions that can have instant dramatic effect, but thoughts prior to those actions. Plants perceive! Backster's work has since been confirmed, followed up and much extended by others.]

CHAPTER: 17

Double Debriefing – Others – Mathematics ... 5th September 2005

As Salumet joined us, Lilian referred to our 'mushroom visitor', saying we had simply not imagined the possibility of 'immobile travellers'.

~ **"Again you see my dear friends, that so much your human ego affects your thinking. Think of creation on a much larger scale. Do not be surprised by anything that you hear. I do not say accept it without deep thinking, but that which you can accept, take aboard and think about it deeply, that which you wish to reject, then please reject it, because it means that you are not ready for that knowledge. But what you are trying to achieve now, is to open your hearts and minds to much deeper and greater things."**

We recalled our teacher's earlier words: "**All things are possible.**"

~ **"Yes, you are beginning to know the ground rules, as you would say in your world,"** adding with humorous nuance: ~ **"You are quite a long way from 'all-knowledge'!"**

Our unrestrained laughter followed that!

~ **"But at the same time, I can tell you how much your minds have opened to the way of spirit and, after all, as sparks of divinity, you must have that all-knowledge knowledge within, otherwise how could we make sense of it all?"**

Quite so, it is just that all-knowledge is difficult for us to access, yet there are the feelings that arise and these are important.

Salumet withdrew and Bonniol declared:

~ ***"I have been listening to your communication a little, and I am pleased that you had an interesting listening to my friend from the other world."***

A gross understatement!

Lilian added: "It shows how different all the planets are."

~ *"Yes, when you begin to experience these other planets, you realise that there are no rules really in creation. Anything is possible."*

George: "Yes, the words of our master: *all things are possible.*"

~ *"But it would seem that all of creation is created with such love and a kind of beauty in it, that though anything is possible, it would seem that creation creates very wisely. Yes, there is always such harmony and balance whenever creation is at work. I am happy to bring others if you wish—"*

This was greeted with instant, general enthusiasm, Sarah adding: "We'd love that!"

~ *"Yes, we can hopefully bring others to you, if you are happy. I feel that it is a natural way forward, to gradually bring more to you, of this universe that we share, and the most direct route available to us at the moment, is perhaps to bring others to you like we did last time."*

Sarah: "That would be good."

~ *"I will see if I can arrange this. It would have been difficult earlier, but now that the connection is improving we can bring more."*

There was some discussion of this method of exploration compared to rocketry, the latter having so many disadvantages, not least the time it takes.

~ *"There would be far more problems than doing it this way! You CAN physically, yes. All things ARE possible, and there are ways around these problems. And at some time, you will no doubt have visitors from other worlds—physically too."*

George: "Yes, I'm sure, I think we already have."

~ *"We have had some visitors from other worlds, physically, yes. We are able to use our minds of course, and with some worlds, this would be the only method available to us. But there are OTHER worlds that are able to visit US physically."*

Sarah: "And are they very different from you, physically?"

~ *"We are all individuals you could say. All worlds have their own distinctness, yes. But nevertheless, there are some similarities.*

And more and more we find we look for similarities rather than differences."

In fact, we are surprised that Aerans and humans are as similar as they appear to be, and we spoke of this.

~ ***"There are often similarities with other races. The friend I brought last time was unusual. Normally there are more similarities than differences, I would say, though not always."***

George: "I would imagine beings with arms and legs have certain efficiency as a result of developing into that form."

~ ***"Yes, when you are evolving, you need some form of movement, whether it be legs or some other method, but there is nearly always a few limbs involved. They require them for moving and for doing things. The form of these limbs may vary, but we can still see them as limbs. When it comes to the senses, then there is usually at least one eye and there is at least one ear."***

Graham: "We find that having two eyes and two ears, gives us direction."

~ ***"Yes, I would agree. One is the minimum. To have more than one would seem an advantage. We also find that most beings have mouths for speech, and this is not always the case, as with our friend last time."***

Lilian: "You said that these beings are very beautiful. Are they colourful or do they shine? "

~ ***"They have a shine to them, yes. They have a wonderful—their physical colouring is a pearly white, and they look very elegant to our eyes. But the main thing is the auric glow that surrounds them. Yes, these beings have a beautiful energy about them, and they have much knowledge as we mentioned last time. They are the true explorers—we feel that."***

Lilian: "Do they vary in size?"

~ ***"They have some variance, but not a great deal."***

George: "We are very fortunate. It was a wonderful experience for us."

A natural pause followed, so it was a suitable break for music, this time 'relaxation music' including sounds of the seashore and dolphins: '♪♪♫'.

~ "Thank you. There were many sounds included in that one I have not heard before. I can understand why you find it relaxing. I am hoping this will continue."

George: "We shall be delighted. I think it sensible if we give you as varied a collection of musical items as we can present."

~ "Thank you. It will be most interesting for us. We are learning more each time we listen."

Moving on, we spoke of disciplines, recalling mention of chemistry, music and poetry, and clearly these are shared. Now we came to mathematics.

~ "Yes, I understand your subject of mathematics is one of your areas of science is it?"

We explained about counting and measuring distances across the universe, and how we are concerned with describing shapes.

~ "We have also developed along these lines with our sciences and the 'mathematical language' if that is the right word."

George: "Yes, and those philosophers who have thought on this, they feel that this is something that goes right through the universe. I was just wondering if you have any knowledge on that from your contacts."

~ "Yes, when you are working to try to understand the physical universe, then the language of mathematics in some form, appears to be utilised on most planets we are familiar with."

The relationship to music was briefly discussed and communication of music and these we understand would be common to many worlds.

~ "It is something that we have encountered in the other worlds, and we have used it ourselves. There are certain subjects that will always appear."

George: "How about mechanics and engineering that we would use for example, for constructing bridges across rivers?"

~ "Again this is something that we in the physical worlds will always have a need of, so again, it is one of the subjects that is always necessary."

George: "We are beginning to see just how much common ground there is between us all."

~ ***"In terms of the physical laws, if you like—the physical side to existence—there are many common grounds, yes."***

George: "And how about chefs, cooking food and study of diet? Is that another area that is common to us all?"

~ ***"When there is need of food, there are always those who are better able to cook it, yes."***

George: "And there are scientists I expect, who study diet and what is good in diet and what is not good in food?"

~ ***"Yes, again we are able to agree on that one. It is another necessity, I think, of the physical world."***

So it has become quite clear just how much physicality of being dictates lifestyle and interests in the different worlds. The disciplines named are all fairly obvious ones but where do we stand regarding more obscure disciplines? Would 'kinesiology' be known to Bonniol? I needed to place the question with some care: "We have an area of science that we call 'kinesiology'. It's a kind of body-interrogation, and you get answers through muscle response. It began with two people working together, and one holds up an arm, and a small container of a chemical is held against the body. And if that substance is good for the body, the muscle in the arm remains strong, and if it is not good, the muscle goes weak and the arm drops. So this is the basis of addressing the body and getting an answer in terms of muscle response. That's its simplest form, but it does go on to become a more complicated science. Have you anything like that?"

~ ***"We have had something which you could have used for that kind of medicine. But we no longer use that method of finding out about illness. I think if you can learn to mind project, you will no longer need to use your muscle response."***

George: "Ah yes, of course! So this is a rather clumsy method that you simply don't need because you mind project instead!"

~ ***"Yes, it is perhaps a clever way, without having to use the mind projection."***

This was most elegantly put. Kinesiology and its quantitative development are certainly clever by Earthly standards, but of course clumsy compared to mind projection.

We explained that kinesiology is not generally acknowledged on *our* planet, so it is good to have confirmation of its genuine value, even if it is destined to be eventually outmoded. As Bonniol departed we thanked him and his team for another wonderful evening. And just think, had we blasted off by rocket ten years earlier to a nearby solar system planet, we might now, if lucky, just about be arriving midst its microbes and uncertainties! This kind of thought now recurs quite often!

CHAPTER: 18

Mind – Music – Expanding Universe – Infinity ... 12th September 2005

As the conversation picked up we asked about Bonniol's team, so that we might picture them.

~ ***"We are all in my house sitting, yes."***

We referred to his previous mention of a gathering of 60: ~ ***"That's correct yes, there are 60 here tonight. We like to work in large groups, or rather a lot of us enjoy this work so, if there is room, they come."***

Sarah: "You must have a big house."

~ ***"It's not that big, but somehow we manage 60."***

George: "And are you all in one large room?"

~ ***"Yes, the seats are close together in a circle, a large circle."***

(We have since learned that the houses themselves are on a circular base and the living space is the first floor. If our friends are a little wider than us, then the room circumference would be roughly 60 X 2.5 = 150 feet, or 48 feet diameter = 15 metres.)

George: "Are your colleagues all conscious or are they in trance?"

~ ***"We are conscious, yes. But we are in a state of relaxation, which you could call a trance maybe."***

George: "Not a deep trance—"

~ ***"It is a familiar state to us. It may be that it is deep, but to us it is a common state, so we would not necessarily say it is deep though perhaps for you, this word would describe it better."***

Sarah: "So when you are relaying the information back to your friends, do you have to speak or are they just picking it up?"

~ ***"We are able to link together as one, so what I hear and perceive, we all hear and perceive together. That is why they come.***

They wish to hear the Earth music, and they wish to be a part of this communion."

George: "Yes, so is that a good cue to have a piece of music?"

~ ***"Well it sounds like it is. Thank you for your sharing of more Earth music."***

George: "This is a classical piece, played by an orchestra. An orchestra consists of many musicians playing different instruments and the composer is from Finland, his name is Sibelius, and it is said that his music is inspired by the countryside. And this is called The Karelia Suite. Karelia is a province on the border of Finland. It is lengthy, but there's a short piece called: The Intermezzo—a short connecting piece of music and that is what we are going to play for you." ♫♫♫.

~ ***"Thank you! That was very different from the others!"***

There was general agreement to that, and Sarah asked if Bonniol was able to hear it all right.

~ ***"I could—thank you, yes. It was more complex. There were many instruments!"***

George: "Many instruments, and a conductor who waves a baton and keeps it all together."

~ ***"I was quite mesmerised by it—many things to take in!"***

Sarah: "So that's very unlike any of your music, is it?"

~ ***"VERY unlike, yes. We do not have anything quite like this. It seems very organised and many things going on. But it had a certain beauty to it—a very organised beauty, if I can put it like that."***

George: "That's a very good description. Yes, classical music in general—it is complex and organised—quite different from the popular songs and lyrics of today. But these were often by composers who lived perhaps one or two hundred years ago and life was a little different then."

~ ***"Ah yes, maybe this accounts for the feeling behind the music."***

We chatted on about changing times and how music has evolved through those times, and how people tend to either like pop or classical. Sarah spoke of the spectacle of an orchestra playing—the formal dress, the gleaming instruments, which our friends were of course unable to observe. Graham asked if Aeran music evolves.

~ ***"Our music changes, yes—as I believe it does on all the planets. As the planet changes and the people change, the music somehow reflects this like a language."***

This led to some discussion of nature's musical sounds, and we had with us several minutes of birdsong also to play; early morning dawn chorus from Hampshire woodlands.

~ ***"A very beautiful type of music—so many sounds! They have such lovely voices, your birds I think."***

Sarah asked about the birds of Aerah.

~ ***"We have birds. They also sing, but it is a song which is perhaps distinctive to our planet and yours is distinctive to yours."***

We explained about birdsong of different regions.

~ ***"Even within your planet there is that variation, so throughout the universe there is even more—so much more variation, and this is one of the things which makes our work so interesting, because we never know what we will find when we meet another world."***

Sarah: "So your birds, they fly?"

~ ***"Yes, they are able to fly. There are a few that we have problems defining, whether they are birds or not. They fly, but they are something between a bird and another mammal really."***

We mentioned our bats that are flying mammals with skin wings and fur.

~ ***"Yes, we have several types of flying animal. There is a group which resemble your birds in that they have a kind of feather, but they are quite different in other ways."***

We explained also about flightless birds, such as penguins.

~ ***"The birds on our planet would be able to fly; if they cannot fly we do not call them birds. But the bird population and other flying animals, they are—perhaps it's not the correct way to describe them. I think they are more like your insects than birds. They have something like fur, but it's not really feathers. So I would say: your birds are something unique to your planet."***

Sarah: "Would your flying insects be like our moths and butterflies?"

~ ***"Yes, perhaps that's closer."***

We made the point that in times past Earth had some *very large* flying insects.

~ ***"Yes, it's always a problem categorising your animals and deciding how to compare them, from one planet to another. There will always be something that is the closest match, but it is unlikely to be a perfect match."***

Our exchange again took a philosophical turn as we asked if it was possible to move forwards and backwards in time, during mind projection.

~ ***"Ah, that is a deep question and the answer is: no. We cannot travel backwards in time with our minds. This is not—'available', I think is the word. It's not that it's necessarily impossible, but we have not found a way to do it, whilst physically encumbered."***

Sarah made the point that we are all of us on our respective planets to learn, and if we accessed too much of past and future it could interfere with that learning.

~ ***"There are always reasons for having abilities and not having them. There would seem to be no great advantage in going backwards in time."***

I pointed out that the reason for the question relates to the military scientific remote viewing program, and the claim that they can do this.

~ ***"Yes, what they may have been doing is—perhaps they were going backwards in their OWN time. I wonder if they were actually going backwards in time itself, because that is something that would require an enormous ability I think."***

I indicated our understanding that they were observers, not participants in what was happening.

~ ***"Well, I am not able to comment on that, but I am being told that this is perhaps a misunderstanding. WE don't go backwards or forwards."***

I thanked Bonniol and moved on to the next subject: "Our observations in the universe indicate that it is an expanding universe, expanding from all points within its self. It is reasoned that it had a beginning, and a popular description in our science is that that beginning is a *singularity* and that the physical universe arose from a *big bang,* and a tremendous expansion, and it's still expanding. Have you any thought on that?"

But firstly, Bonniol had a further thought on that matter of time: ~ ***"Yes, before I say something about that, if I could go back to the 'time' question. I think, for our people, we are mainly concerned with the present and being in the present is when you maximise your awareness. When you are in the—truly in the present, you are also a little bit in the past and the future You are not going to the past or the future, but being in the present gives you an awareness of what's gone before and what is to come. It would be almost an illusion, to go into a past but not be able to interact in that past, or to go into a future but not be able to be a part of it. It would be an illusion—it would not really be the past and it would not really be the future."***

Lilian: "No benefits at all."

~ ***"It may have some value, but it would not be—to us, it would not be the truth. The truth is now. This is reality. Everything else is a shadow, a picture, perhaps a memory or guesswork. But it is whatever you enter into in a time-travel situation—(it) is only a possibility. It becomes less factual I think."***

More was said on our understanding of the future. Graham made the point that our science indicates that if we were to physically travel fast enough, we would move into the future, but there would be problems in this.

~ ***"And would you really be able to survive if you travelled into the future?"***

George: "Well, we've been talking physically of course. We also have seers and prophets, and they can go into trance and see in the way of spirit, where time is not linear."

~ ***"They are given visions?"***

George: "Yes, a small number of people have that gift. They are able to *see* in the way of spirit where time is as one."

~ ***"They are given glimpses of what COULD become the future—"***

George: "Well, it's my understanding that the future is largely ordained, and to the extent that there would be a 98% chance of that being the true future that they have glimpsed."

~ *"The future is certainly ordained as you say. But the ROAD to the future is not."*

George: "Ah! That is a very wise statement!"

This was an illuminating statement. Long have mystics and teachers held that the future is ordained, apart from that *free will factor,* and this must have its small effect. Bonniol has a slightly different way of expressing it, with free will acting on the *road* to ordained future. There is both agreement and clarity of perception here.

~ *"And when you get given a vision of the future, it is just a glimpse, because the future is of course endless as well. There is no future in a sense because the future is endless. But if you get a glimpse of something IN the future, that is given to you to help you in the right direction—we find it difficult to talk in definite futures—but some things are certain and the visions given are there to encourage and help us find our way—to maximise the best possible future. But the route is always through the present. You won't get there by travelling into it, only by 'living in the present'. We haven't found a way to travel in this way. Part of that maybe is: we do not wish to pursue that line of enquiry. But whether it is possible or not—perhaps it is—but (it is) not something we at present would find any use in."*

Our friend's reply was lengthy and carefully put. We indicated our understanding and he was duly thanked. He continued: ~ ***"And then your question of the expanding universe and the singularity—you—this is something which has—I'm having to—I am waiting to be told—ah yes! Your question was about whether we have a similar—"***

Bonniol was fragmenting a little and I felt it might be helpful to elaborate a little. It was a deep question that could become even more so: "Yes, I placed the question because it's a very popular and strong theory in our science; that the physical universe began as a *singularity* or *point source,* and has expanded from that, and is still expanding. And there are various astronomical observations leading to this conclusion that the universe continues to expand. This could lead to other interesting things, so I wondered if you had made any such observation and developed any similar theory yourselves?"

~ *"Yes, we have also observed that the bodies in the universe appear to be moving away, and this would imply expansion, yes. We*

feel that there is also contraction, but the evidence for contraction is less available. But at this point (in time) it appears that everything is expanding outwards, does it not?"

George: "Yes, that is in line with our theories, and the possibility of contraction at some stage has also featured in our theories."

~ ***"But you do not believe it is contracting at this moment?"***

George: "No. What we call *red shift* and various other factors seem to indicate that it is expanding at the present time."

Graham: "Interestingly, scientists are of the opinion that it's accelerating in its expansion at the moment. Have you come across this—acceleration of expansion?"

~ ***"We also have noticed this, yes—that it appears to expand even more quickly."***

George: "The limit of our observation, across the universe, is to that point where the universe appears to be receding at the speed of light. We cannot see beyond that boundary."

~ ***"So this is a very deep subject is it not?"***

There was our general agreement to that!

~ ***"Where is it going?"***

George: "I was going to say: our Master who comes to us, he has several times indicated that *spirit has always been,* which we of course accept, and it is also indicated that spirit has no space or time, and that is why our dialogues are instantaneous. So instead of thinking physically and looking to a *singularity* origin of the universe, we can simply look at the problem spiritually and think: well, the physical universe has been created from spirit, which (equally) has no space or time. This is a different way of looking at it, and this is what I was coming to, to see if this seems reasonable and rational to *your* selves. I think Salumet agrees that way of thinking is reasonable."

~ ***"So you are of the opinion that the movement in the universe is not purely physical, that somehow it could be linked to more spiritual dimensions, which (also) allows for the limitlessness of it?"***

Now we were getting to the nub of the issue, and Bonniol had added an interesting connection by bringing in 'limitlessness' that I must admit I failed to latch onto immediately. And I continued: "I'm thinking there could have been a single point source as the beginning of the physical universe. But that is only because we're thinking about it and looking at it with physical eyes. If we were thinking spiritually, then it would be much easier to think: Ah! The physical universe has been created from the realm of spirit! But if we're thinking too physically, we can only see that as a point source, because only a point source would have no space or time. That is thinking physically. But the alternative view, the spiritual view, is that all has been created from spirit."

~ "I think this has to come into the equation, yes ... WHEN YOU OBSERVE PHYSICAL THINGS BEHAVING IN WAYS WHICH APPEAR TO BE LIMITLESS, THEN YOU HAVE TO BEGIN TO THINK IT IS TIED INTO ITS SPIRITUAL NATURE."

George: "Yes, so I'm really putting the idea that our scientists are in error for thinking this through in entirely physical terms. It doesn't work like that!"

~ "You will never understand it if you think only physically. When you have spiritual knowledge, then all becomes possible. IT WOULD SEEM THAT THE PHYSICAL UNIVERSE HAS BEEN ENDOWED WITH SPIRITUAL ATTRIBUTES, WHICH ALLOW IT TO HAVE UNLIMITED POSSIBILITIES."

Graham: "That's a nice way of wording it."

George: "Yes, indeed. It's a difficult area to think through."

~ "We are living on little planets, which have been designed with simple rules. But the universe and even the planets as well, are actually outside of those physical rules. In fact we all are outside of the physical rules, once we begin to consider spirit and the interconnectedness of all things."

George: "Yes, I think we have to see it as the physical and the spiritual, being entwined. They are all much together and yet we can think and perceive entirely physically, and we can operate also at an entirely spiritual level. And in *mind projection, we are operating at a spiritual level and just making the physical connections.* Would that be a reasonable way of putting it?"

~ "Yes, I can see that you have thought long and hard about these things."

George: "Yes, and because it operates at a spiritual level, space and time do not come into it, and therefore there are no time delays in our dialogue. All is instantaneous."

~ ***"Yes, we have another example of—we are physical beings and yet we are able to bypass all these physical laws, are we not?"***

And there was general agreement to that!

~ ***"And this is another example of how we cannot explain using PHYSICAL laws, because we are SPIRITUAL and so these limits do not apply."***

George: "Yes, so although my initial question seemed rather obscure, it's brought us right back, I think, to a better understanding of mind projection work, in the end."

~ ***"Yes, I think it's a very good idea to explore all these things around us and the universe, with all the stars and planets. Space is a wonderful example is it not, of the limitlessness of the true nature of life. It's staring at us all the time—this 'unlimitedness'."***

Graham: "We do find it very humbling."

~ ***"We also find it humbling, and if we feel that life weighs us down, to look up to the skies and the limitlessness around us, humbles us, yes."***

Graham: "We realise there's so much more beyond our little world."

We spoke in addition of how much better our view of the stars would be without streetlights.

~ ***"And know that you have friends out there in space!"***

Graham: "We shall wave to you next time."

~ ***"Thank you. And our thoughts will be sent to you."***

Lilian: "Before you came, Salumet, he did say: in our prayers, remember our brothers who live on other planets. And soon after, you came to talk to us—pretty amazing!"

Perhaps 'pretty amazing' sums it all up rather well. One of Leslie's favoured words was 'stupendous'. That too would be apt description. Bonniol was then saying: ~ ***"I feel I have perhaps stayed long enough this time."***

George: "I hope we are not wearing you down with too much deep philosophy?"

~ ***"It is always a joy to exchange these deep areas with another world."***

George: “It’s nice for us to know how others are thinking—how our cosmic friends are thinking, and whether they think along similar lines.”

~ ***“We all try to piece things together.”***

It is indeed a joy to exchange thoughts on the deeper issues; also a rare privilege. In our world, much theory has been propounded upon the creation and on the notion of infinity. Much good sense has been debated; also of course some non-sense. In mathematics, that the same infinity results from dividing any number, no matter how large or small, by zero, does not sit comfortably within our physical brains. Even simple arithmetic, has its strange backwaters of numbers that are viewed with suspicion by enquiring intellect. Those numbers that mathematicians call ‘imaginary’—based on the square root of minus one which simply cannot be, for example, and Bonniol views what we call ‘infinity’ as ‘limitlessness’. It is good description. Neither imaginary numbers nor limitlessness fit comfortably into the pattern of physical laws that apply to everyday living. Sometimes it is necessary to observe that the system prevailing is not just simply physical with unyielding boundary markers. We are always first and foremost spiritual beings and all factors within the universe have their spirit connection. Even mathematics must yield to this truth. Perhaps limitlessness in its pure state abounds only in spirit—the true domain of the ‘Infinite’.

Within that infinity, the physical universe expands. This is not just an Earthly notion that may or may not be correct. It is, we now know, an observation shared by others out there across the heavens. Perhaps all existence expands to one shared future that is to some degree ordained. But of course, such a future is likely to be unfixed in time and of infinite duration. One thing is certain, such a construct lies well beyond the present comprehension of our intellect. But there are individual planetary futures that appear to be ordained, either steered by past events on those planets or by divine plan or both, and anyway, influence from past events would likely be a working component of any master plan; a part of its internal detail. But *pathways* to planetary futures are clearly slightly fluid, allowing free will to play its part. This view reflects inspired teaching that has been received on both Earth and Aerah.

CHAPTER: 19
Death – War – Fireworks – Family Matters ... 19th September 2005

AT THE START of this meeting, there were happenings that became connected. As always, we began by giving names for healing and for those in need. Concern was voiced for one approaching death, that appeared not to believe in the continued life in spirit, and it was suggested perhaps a vision might help. (To suggest this was very unusual, but it just felt right in this instance.) One spoke through Sarah next, representing a group in spirit called 'The Monday Group'. They apparently, frequently join with us when we meet on Monday evenings, and she told us they each had no belief in afterlife until they passed over. This was a problem but they were helped. Now they help others who have that same problem. Prior to this we had a general awareness of help teams in spirit, but it was so nice, as well as timely, that this particular group should now make itself known. There followed a 'rescue', also via Sarah. An elderly gentleman had died at a bus stop somewhere up north. Lilian explained to him that he had been brought to her home in Hampshire and he became confused; at first thinking he must have caught the wrong bus! That little misunderstanding was soon sorted. His problem had been: no belief in afterlife, and of course, it is necessary to know and to *have* that belief. As soon as all was explained, he understood, and was able to see his loved ones waiting in the light. He was then able to move on and was of course wonderfully happy. Bonniol's visit followed on from these events.

~ ***"Hello."***

Lilian: "Have you been listening to the rescue that we've just had?"

~ ***"I was aware of it, yes."***

Lilian: "The gentleman didn't realise what had happened."

~ "It is a wonderful job that you do."

Lilian: "It's very satisfying."

George: "Yes, it's nice to be able to help them on their way."

~ "And they must then feel happy when they are home safely."

George: "Yes, it's always so pleasant when they see their loved ones and identify them. It's always a very good point in these transitions."

Rescues may well begin with stress and confusion, and maybe Lilian would be roughly told to 'go away!' But when the true nature of physical death is finally made clear and accepted, and the awaiting loved-ones become visible in the light, it is then just awe and happiness that prevail.

~ "They just need that bit of encouragement and to feel safe."

Lilian: "Yes."

Sarah: "Do most of the beings on your planet believe in an afterlife?"

~ "I am sure, yes, they believe it and accept it. There were times I'm sure, when this was not understood as clearly as it is now, because always it becomes clearer—your understanding."

George: "Yes, we appreciate that you are further along that road than we are, and I did wonder at one stage—we talked about 'futures' recently—and I just wondered if your future might be more ordained than ours, because we are not so far along that *development road*?"

~ "I am not sure if future is any less ordained. I can't imagine it would be any less in our world. It would be the same I would have thought, in all the worlds. But we are not the ones to know all. We are learning as well."

Lilian: "This may seem an odd question, but do you have burial grounds for the bodies when you have finished with them? We have burial grounds where they are laid in the earth; also there are places where they are cremated."

~ "We have another way of disposing of the bodies. We give them back to nature and they are absorbed back, as with the natural creatures of the Earth."

Lilian: "I see."

George: "So are they buried *in* the earth?"

~ ***"They are not buried, but they are laid on top of the ground in places of nature—isolated places. There would be creatures that take what they can, and the body disappears quite quickly."***

George: "And this is done in an organised way? Do you have special locations?"

~ ***"We have special locations, yes, away from many people."***

Lilian: "Yes, it's a good way. What made me think of it was the lady across the way. She thought of her relations as being in the churchyard, and that made me think to ask you what you do."

~ ***"Yes, it's always a problem what to do with them. We have been doing it this way for a long time now."***

Lilian: "I see."

Sarah: "Do you have any place where you can remember them? Do you have a headstone or a plaque that commemorates?"

~ ***"We do not have these graveyards as such. It is not very important because of our mind projection."***

Sarah: "Yes of course! It wouldn't be important."

~ ***"It's mainly a matter of finding a way of disposing of the body, and giving it back to nature."***

Graham: "Do you have any ceremony? We have a ceremony when we thank God for the life of the person, and thoughts of love from all the people. Do you have anything like that?"

~ ***"We sometimes have get-togethers, with friends and families, yes."***

Lilian then realised the full import of what was being said, and ventured: "Of course, with mind projection, you can be in contact anyway!"

~ ***"The main difference I think is, with mind projection abilities, we do not grieve as much as you."***

Lilian: "No, I can see. There would be no point—"

~ ***"There is still some sadness."***

George: "Sadness, yes."

~ ***"—because they are no longer physically part of our lives."***

George: "So, with mind projection, do you keep in touch for a time, after the event?"

~ ***"We keep in touch for as long as we wish to, and often, that is quite a long time."***

Sarah: "So, do they give you much information as to how it is on the other side?"

~ ***"They are able to answer our questions, yes. But they are not allowed to tell us everything. They are often overruled—blocked by our guides, who have the final say on what can be said. We have to accept that some things are better left unknown, and it makes life more exciting—life would not be the challenge that it is."***

Lilian: "That's interesting."

Graham: "Are there beings on your planet that are aware of the fact that they've reached the point where they don't need to incarnate anymore? Are there beings in that position?"

~ ***"Yes, we have people who are aware that they no longer need to return, and they are aware that they will probably not return. But they could still return if they wish, for reasons of teaching and not learning. It's the same with yours I believe."***

George: "That's right! We've been told that, yes!"

~ ***"Yes, the spiritual side—the rules, or the laws—the spiritual ways are the same, I think. When we are talking of these—I don't like the word 'rules', but—"***

George: "Yes, we imagine that to be so, and it's very nice to have that confirmed."

~ ***"Yes."***

It is noteworthy that links between Astral Planes and those living planetary lives are so alike. Earth and Aerah are so very similar. But Aerans are clearly much more aware of their transition from the physical life than here on Earth, and with their more developed minds, communication freely continues. Here, there are also exchanges of course, but frequently these are via sensitive intermediaries such as psychics and Spiritual Church, and there is the splendid detailed account of direct mind link with one in spirit by Helen Greaves[4].

Having reached a brief pause in the flow of conversation, it was a good time to offer a musical interlude. We explained how World War II had been such an emotive period in our history and played a little of *Lili Marlene,* one verse in English and one in German. It seemed appropriate, because in the North African desert, it mattered not whose language or whose radio station, all listened to the voice of Marlene Dietrich, many being reminded of a girl back home.

The song transcended the strife of conflict. We followed up with Vera Lynn singing: *We'll Meet Again.* This of course was a wartime favourite that has since lived on, being sung at so many reunions. We explained that most of the countries of our world were involved in this war, 60 years ago, and expressed the hope that there would be nothing like it ever again: ♪♪♫♫.

Sarah: "They were singing songs to cheer the troops, I guess."

~ ***"Yes, they have that feeling of raising spirits—cheering songs. And it is such a wonderful medium—music—to do that with, when perhaps words cannot. The music seems to be able to perforate or get through into dark areas."***

Lilian: "Something that everyone understands."

George: "Someone once defined song as something produced when words are not enough."

~ ***"Yes, it seems to have an almost magical cleansing effect on dark energies."***

George: "That last lady, she visited a number of the battle zones. She was well-noted for that."

~ ***"Yes, it's like a healing, a form of healing."***

Lilian: "That's true."

~ ***"I think it's really another example of the richness of your music, and I am sure that you have enormous amounts of rich music for purpose of raising your spirits."***

Sarah added: "Perhaps that's why it's been developed so much, because we have so many problems that we *need* to raise our spirits, whereas in your world—"

~ ***"I think we still also need our music at times. There is nothing better than music to find your balance sometimes."***

Lilian: "So, do you have people singing love songs, songs that mean something to you?"

~ ***"We have many different types of music, but probably mostly, our music is closest to your 'relaxation music'. It has many different types, but it is almost always to produce the mood of relaxation."***

But we had not yet done with the subject of *war.* Sarah brought us back to that with mention of a rather different type of musical expression, the military marching band, adding: "Of course, you don't need *that* anymore."

George: "Many of the songs of *that* particular period were songs of love, and songs of looking to the time when there would be no—"

Margaret: "No more war, yes!"

George: "Many had that character."

~ *"Yes, you still have these scars of war in your world, do you?"*

Lilian: "I'm afraid we still have."

Sarah: "There are wars going on at the moment, somewhere in the world."

~ *"Yes, it is another example of the misunderstanding in the world."*

Sarah: "And misunderstanding of religion—wars have been created in the name of religions, which really is—"

George: "Well, we have misunderstandings of religion, misunderstandings between people and nations, and the other one is, a misunderstanding of what warfare *means.* If people had a much better understanding of—*when two nations go to war, neither wins*—that would do much to end it! But it is interesting and valuable to talk about these things. There are several reasons why there will not be a third 'world war'. One is the *physical* reason that weapons have been developed so much that humankind cannot possible sustain another and survive. Another reason is spirituality—we have moved further forward now."

~ *"Yes, it is not an area that I am able to give much help with, only to say: STOP IT!"*

Bonniol's words, delivered with a terse economy, brought hearty and spontaneous laughter. I responded as the laughter continued: "Those are two wise words!"

Sarah: "And what about the other planets? Are they as we are, or are they more peaceful?"

~ *"They are on the whole peaceful planets, but that would give a wrong impression, I think. All of these planets are learning planets. They will all have their struggles and changes."*

George: "But many were warring in the distant past I imagine—"

~ *"They will not be fighting each other physically. Perhaps this is a difference. But they will be fighting in other ways on occasions.*

There is struggle on all of our worlds, I would say, in one way or another."

Lilian: "Would you call it a *power struggle*?"

~ ***"Yes."***

George: "We have power struggles and commercial struggles."

~ ***"There are many ways to struggle."***

George: "—and financial struggles."

~ ***"Being too greedy."***

Sarah: "Do these other planets have variations in religion as we do or are they more like you, and understand the spiritual side better?"

~ ***"Each is a little different of course, (compared) to the next—they all have their own religions, and there will be similarities. I would say that several of the worlds are living more peacefully than your world at this time, and that means living peacefully with nature as well as each other. There are one or two that have problems with their natural world, and have not found, perhaps, that right balance yet."***

We agreed to failing where nature is concerned, but feel there are signs that some understanding is beginning.

~ ***"The nature unfortunately, may be the thing that comes later, but it is coming I am sure."***

We turned from competition with nature to competition in sport, enquiring if this might be a common interest.

~ ***"Yes, we like to play games, sport, yes—it helps the young people."***

George: "Do you have ball games?"

~ ***"We have ball games, yes. There are many different games, and the children clearly need to play these different games."***

George: "Well, I bet you don't have cricket!"

(Bonniol may have details of this from Paul's memory data.)

~ ***"We don't have quite the same games as you."***

Sarah: "It (cricket) would be more difficult, for you have webbed feet and your atmosphere is thicker!"

~ ***"Yes, we have to adapt to the conditions of our world, but this is something that all worlds do. You will always find games, especially amongst the children, on all of the worlds, I think."***

Sarah: "So, how do you play your ball games?"

~ ***"One of the most popular ones—I think it involves eight balls, and the idea is to obtain all of the balls, by chasing after the one who has a ball, and taking it and bringing it back to your team. When you collect all eight you win the game. There are rules of how you take the ball. But it is a skilful game and very energetic."***

Sarah: "And do you play on a special court—an enclosed area?"

~ ***"We have circular areas, yes."***

Graham next outlined our professional sports structure, with large salaries paid to players, gate admission fees and then the way professionals may have world ranking status.

~ ***"We do have teams that are related to our townships, yes, and they play each other. It is not a profession as such. There is no money as such involved, but there are prizes. And it is of popularity to watch these events. So yes, sport is something that we share I think."***

Sarah then wondered if spectators sing songs, as at our rugby and football matches. There was a pause before Bonniol's reply came with a further presentation of humour:

~ ***"Some would call it singing, others would not! They are noisy events—sporting events. But they are part of our world, yes."***

Sarah: "In addition to sports, we have gymnastics where we swing on ropes and bars. Do you do things like that?"

~ ***"We have a kind of swing yes, but I feel it is not such a sport as it is on your world. As I say, many of these things happen for the children. But we do have adult teams as well."***

George: "Some of us would prefer to go to the theatre. Do you have theatre, where plays are performed by actors and actresses?"

~ ***"We have a variety of entertaining events, which perhaps correspond to your theatres. Sometimes they would involve an enactment of—"***

George: "A story with a message perhaps?"

~ ***"Yes, they can be enacted stories, or they can be events that demonstrate abilities of the mind."***

George: "Of the mind—"

~ ***"Projections of the mind, like an exhibition or demonstration of an ability."***

There were 'mms and ahs' to this, and we were becoming more and more aware of the impact within Bonniol's society of the developed mind.

Sarah: "When do you start to use mind projection, when you are very young?"

~ ***"At an early age—we begin to instruct the children as soon as they are able to communicate, and often they are able to communicate even before they are born."***

This was an unexpected answer!

~ ***"Yes, they are already able to communicate with their minds, though they still need to practise, because as their physical bodies develop, there can be interference with their mind projection ability—there are distractions of the physical body, which need to be keyed up."***

Whilst talking to the unborn child has been the recognised norm in certain Earthly societies, it has been slow to catch on in western culture but happily that is fast changing. In the past, medical services probed the unborn with ultrasound or instruments for physical data, and for many, that was the extent of communication. Graham, the most experienced teacher in our group, was more interested in who takes responsibility for child education.

~ ***"We've organised our society so that the young are brought up with other young children in houses (that are) quite large. They are able to be with families on occasions, but most of the time they live in—I think we used the word 'kibbutz'."***

George: "Yes. Do they have toys, as our children have?"

~ ***"Yes, we have toys for the children—toys, games, yes."***

Much may of course be said in favour of a kibbutz system, and one of us has actually lived on an Israeli kibbutz. The system may well especially suit where very large families prevail, and we shall shortly see how this applies to Aerah. But I was anxious at this point to return to public events and take that discussion a step further: "Going back to the 'events'—we have one particular, bizarre thing that we do, and I'm curious to know if you do this. We have *fireworks displays.* Using chemicals, we produce light effects in the sky—starbursts, colours and rockets. Do you have fireworks displays at all?"

~ "Yes, I understand. We used to have some displays, using these chemicals to create lights. This is something that we did in the past—I think you would say."

George: "And you've grown out of it!"

~ "We—"

Lilian: "I wish we had!"

George: "Yes, and one feels that this is something that we shall eventually grow out of, as you already *have*. That's very interesting!"

~ "But we do enjoy other displays that I mentioned earlier—theatrical displays, using mind techniques to influence and create certain effects, that we have developed."

Lilian then returned us to the important matter of families: "Do the families vary on your planet? Here, some people only have one child; some have two, four, six, it varies. Does it vary on your planet?"

There was hesitation in Bonniol's reply. This could be a sensitive issue: ~ ***"It, yes—um—not so many of us HAVE children. But if we do, I think I've said before, we produce a large number."***

Lilian: "And you said *you* have a large family—"

~ "Yes."

Lilian: "And I wondered if everyone did."

In retrospect, I can well understand our friend's hesitation. He would have quite a clear idea by now, how things are on Earth, and there has to be a right time for delivering the details of the contrasting family situation of Aerah. Now, was the time for fuller revelation, and Bonniol continued: ~ ***"No, not so many—so, yes, I have many children, yes—eighty-five—yes."***

Several exclaimed 'ooh!', and good-humoured chuckles followed.

~ "—and they all have names. I may have said that incorrectly—no, eighty—eighty-five, yes. That is correct."

Lilian: "That is such a lot!"

Graham: "And they were all born at the same time?"

~ "Um—yes, they were born together. It is a slightly strange thing to describe it. It is a different way—"

Lilian: "Different altogether!"

~ ***"Very different, and this is why few of us actually do have children. When we do have them, we have large numbers. So it is quite different to where most of you produce a few, whereas a few of us produce a lot, yes."***

Graham: "So you have large numbers of people who decide that they will not have children. So that is their decision, or is that just the way it is?"

~ ***"It is in keeping with the opportunity. The opportunity is not always there for everyone. It is (that) the compatibilities are less, because we come from two different species."***

George: "Oh yes and you told us about the different genders."

Lilian: "Oh yes, of course."

~ ***"And we have—that's right—several different genders. And it's much more—the probabilities are less that you will produce children, yes."***

Graham: "And as you said before, your children spend a little time with their families, but there are so many children, and you use the resources of the community as a whole, to look after the children."

~ ***"That's quite right, not everyone, in fact most people, don't have children. But they nevertheless like to share in a way, with the children. So it is a shared responsibility. It is not always the parent that is most important for the child. This is again something that may seem strange to other worlds."***

Lilian: "It's different."

~ ***"It's often—yes it is different—it is often the way with the breeding habits, and the family units vary much more when you view other worlds. But it's an area that one has to accept—that there are many, many ways to raise your population.***

Lilian: "Yes, it's very interesting. Thank you for all that!"

We had learned more about Aeran families and now felt privy to sensitive information. We could have sought more explicit details, but it seemed right to not probe further, at this stage at least.

We asked if Bonniol had any question he would like to put to us, but the session had been quite lengthy and he felt the time had come to depart. As always, there were fond farewells and our friend expressed the hope that we were all benefiting from the exchanges. We replied that what he and his team are doing is of immense value not just for ourselves and whosoever reads these texts but for the entire universe. Information exchange can only benefit the entire creation. And that is one grand thought to ponder.

CHAPTER: 20

Beyond the Light – Political Issues – A Turning Point ... 26th September 2005

LILIAN: "HELLO."

~ ***"Good evening, we are very happy to be connecting with your world again."***

Lilian: "We are still getting over the shock of talking with someone from another world," and this was a thought still shared by us all, despite the wonderful progress made.

~ ***"Yes, it's an incredible thing for us even now, though we have been doing it for a long time. We always feel such a sense of wonder, to be able to reach out to other worlds to say: 'hello'."***

Lilian: "Is this the furthest you have travelled?"

~ ***"I am told this is about as far as any of the other planets, yes. We are able of course—we are able to go as far as we like with mind projection. But the distance, we are told, is almost unimaginable."***

George: "Yes, we have our feelings for the physical universe that we have talked about before—the expanding physical universe. And we know the limit of our observation is at the distance where the physical universe is receding at the speed of light. Obviously we cannot see beyond that. But I imagine, by mind projection, that is no limit?"

~ ***"Yes exactly, there IS no limit, because it is spirit."***

George: "So we can communicate further than our astronomy can see!"

~ ***"Yes, there are no physical laws when it comes to mind projection."***

Graham: "Scientists think that we can only see galaxies as far back as the edge of the universe. And scientists think the big bang occurred 12 – 15 billion years ago, so it is not possible for us to see more. And that area that we *can* see is known as our *observable universe.* Is your planet beyond what we would call the observable universe?"

~ *"Yes, and again, it is not something that we would be able to answer, but we are told that IT IS BEYOND YOUR OBSERVABLE UNIVERSE, yes."*

This is of course another astonishing realisation, that our friend who speaks as if in the room with us—his material being is sitting somewhere beyond any star or galaxy that can be detected by Earth's most advanced telescopes! Wow!

George: "That would be information from your spirit guides?"

~ *"Yes."*

Graham: "So it would be physically impossible to travel even a tiny fraction of the distance towards your planet—"

~ *"It would be impossible, yes, as far as we are aware."*

Sarah quickly added: "So you can rest assured you are not going to be invaded by us!" And Bonniol's reply came midst laughter: ~ ***"Thank you! But of course, if you could, we would welcome you!"***

Sarah: "Thank you for that!"

George: "And we would *certainly* welcome *you,* as we do in your mind projection."

Graham: "You have a sense of humour. Do you laugh in the same way as we do, about funny things?"

~ *"Humour is very important in our world and in all the other worlds too—and it is a universal—ah—what's the word for it?"*

George: "Well, as humour can uplift the spirit, I can easily accept that it runs right through the universe."

~ *"We all have our own ways of laughing, yes. And it is a little different of course, because we have different equipment, if you like, for making our sounds, yes."*

Graham: "Yes, even amongst ourselves, our laughter varies hugely. So I imagine your laughter would be very different from ours."

Sarah: "Is your body made up internally, more or less in the same way as ours?"

~ *"Not the same, there are many differences I think internally, as there are externally, and this is to be expected."*

Sarah: "Yes. I believe you have a different voice, so you don't have the same vocal cords, or the way you breathe—"

~ ***"We have vocal cords and we breathe, so there are similarities."***

George: "And since, as we do, you have limbs and hands and feet, you have a comparable skeleton to support it all?"

Sarah: "And blood. Do you have blood that goes around your body?"

~ ***"Well yes, we have a fluid, which would be comparable to your blood, yes."***

We indicated at this stage, that there are sometimes accidents; hence our hospitals have 'blood banks'. It was further explained about blood grouping and the need for stocks of different types.

~ ***"Yes, we have a similar system in our hospitals, yes. There are stores of this blood that can be given to others who need it."***

George: "I expect you have all the same problems, having people of different blood groupings, so that they have to be matched?"

~ ***"Well actually, this is less complicated with our species. We only require three types of our fluid, even though we have several types of our being. There are only three different groups in terms of the blood."***

We were openly surprised at this in view of the several gender types and hybrid origin of the species, expressing the thought that it is good that it is not a more complicated matter.

Sarah: "When you store this blood, do you freeze it, or how do you preserve it?"

~ ***"It is kept in vacuum, yes, and this seems to store it satisfactorily. It cannot be frozen apparently. It cannot survive freezing. This is where it differs from your blood. So it has qualities about it which are different."***

Lilian: "If you lost an arm in an accident, are you able to grow another one?"

~ ***"We have learnt to, yes. It is something that has become available to us through much work. At some point in our history, we were made aware of this possibility, and we practise much like the practise with your thought projections—you are able to re-grow parts of your bodies."***

Again, there was surprise. This was a clear example of mind over matter control!

Sarah: "So you would each repair your own bodies, not someone else's?"

~ *"There are those that require help, but there is no reason why an individual should not be able to repair much of his own body."*

George: "This sounds like an extension to 'self heal'—"

~ *"Yes, it is another aspect of your power of thought."*

Sarah: "And do you have teeth?"

~ *"We have a kind of bone that is used as your teeth, yes. It is more like a bone, but it does have a serrated edge to it, so it is something like your teeth."*

Sarah: "So, when you smile, is that attractive?"

There were chuckles at Sarah's probing question that broke into laughter as Bonniol replied pointedly: **~ *"WE think so!"***

Sarah: "And that is an example of your humour!"

George: "And would some more music make you smile?"

~ *"Yes, it will always make us smile. Thank you."*

George: "I hope you like this piece. About 300-years ago there was Johann Sebastian Bach. He is regarded as a musical genius and he composed much. This is the third movement of the Brandenburg Concerto, described as Baroque Counterpoint, and this means that it is exuberant in its style."

The piece was played and I think we all rather enjoyed it, and someone said, 'wonderful'.

~ *"Thank you! We've had another lovely piece."*

George: "Yes, it's quite a lengthy piece, but it seemed a pity not to play all of it."

~ *"Yes, sometimes it's better to let it finish."*

George: "Yes, he was one of our greatest classical composers."

~ *"Well, we are really beginning to get a feel for your different music now."*

Lilian: "The variation—"

~ *"Yes, certainly you have so much you can express with your music."*

Lilian then invited a question from Bonniol, and that was a signal for moving on to more gritty matters. There was hesitation at first.

~ ***"I—we wondered about your system of government, yes."***

George: "Yes, *we* wonder about this—", and on the recording, uproarious laughter and a jumble of comments followed these opening words. But it was of course a serious question that we went on to answer as best we could.

~ ***"You have a group of people who make a lot of decisions for you—who you have appointed into this role—"***

Sarah: "Yes, we appoint just one leader."

George: "It does vary from country to country, but our system in this country is—we hold elections in which political parties are voted for, by the people. And there is always a governing party voted in. And there is always a party in opposition, so there is always a certain amount of competition in our Houses of Parliament, where decisions are made."

~ ***"Yes, we can understand that, and we do understand that things are meant to be debated properly. But what we find puzzling is, why you appoint such a small group of people to make so many decisions. Within OUR WORLD, these choices are put to MANY people, and we all decide together how to deal with each situation."***

We countered: "So it is more a government by the people—"

~ ***"Yes, we come together and listen to the debates, and then we give our vote, if you like, on the big decisions that are made."***

Graham: "We do actually do something equivalent to that, over very, very big decisions, and we call it a 'referendum'—all in the nation get a vote. They are very rare, our last was at least 10-years ago."

~ ***"I think this is the right word, yes (referendum), but because our world is set up differently, we have these referendums more frequently."***

Graham: "Do you mind project your votes, or do you use pieces of paper as we do?"

~ ***"We have another system. Using our electronic system, a little bit like your computer system—so we are able to listen to the debates through our 'computer system', and then vote accordingly. This keeps everyone in touch and is a part of these big decisions that are made."***

The idea came to mind of how the Internet or TV might be used as a device for regular political referendum. Well, that might be possible, but how would such a voting system connect to a party control?

Graham: "Do you actually have parties as we have?"

~ ***"We do not have parties as such. We have individuals, but we do have groups of individuals—we could almost call them a party, but they are not strictly speaking forming one party, but they are of a similar mind when it comes to certain issues. But as 'individuals', that is how they stand. And these are given the chance to become speakers—to debate the issues."***

Graham: "How are they chosen to represent?"

~ ***"We have a number of pathways, but they generally would need to have achieved something."***

George: "I would imagine some of these pathways would involve experts in particular fields—"

~ ***"They would need to have some experience in areas of life, yes. It could be nature or farming."***

George: "We sometimes have groups within or affiliated to government that we refer to as a 'think tank', sometimes to debate what would be a good pathway."

~ ***"Yes, they need to have an ability with words, and this is something that not everyone is good at—because the spoken word is important during these debates."***

Graham: "Yes, we call that 'rhetoric'."

~ ***"Yes, that is an apt word."***

Graham: "Would someone be *chosen* for the responsibility of being in government, or would they put themselves forward to be considered?"

~ ***"Some are chosen, and for some it seems to be a calling, and it comes from within themselves."***

Graham: "Your original question was: why do we have so few people representing us? I think many would find it difficult to understand the complexity of the issues being discussed, so the people that *are* in government are usually intelligent, and they have background and skills and are able to make decisions. We don't have the ability to have national voting systems for issues, so we bring the small group of people we have chosen for a period of time—five years. If we like the way they make their decisions, then we vote them in for another five years. If we don't, then they move out and another party becomes the principle power. The good thing about it is, those elected have the time to think about these issues."

~ ***"Your world is far more complicated."***

Graham: "You've said that before, yes. Are your people paid a salary for what they do?"

~ ***"They are paid, yes. It is not a big salary. But this is not the reason that they do the work."***

George: "It may be that we pay ours a little too much, so that becomes the reason, or part of the reason that they do the work."

Lilian got us a step further forward, saying: "I think you are much more aware on the whole, of the spirit world around you, so you just don't need all the rules that we have here."

~ ***"Yes, I think that's a big factor, yes, which is the reason for making life so complicated. Because you are not aware of the spirit side of life so much, you have created a very physical structure of laws and organisation that you cater for."***

Lilian: "We are rather materialistic."

~ ***"Many of the things that spirit would—ah—"***

I felt it may help Bonniol through his hesitation to say: "I think I can say that, all here would agree that we have made our system *far too* complicated."

~ ***"I was going to say that many of the things are dealt with, when the spirit would do these things for you, because perhaps you have not taken advantage of the spiritual links available."***

George: "I'm sure we have all tried to tackle this for ourselves."

All: "Yes."

Lilian: "It's a shame."

Sarah: "Yes, Salumet is constantly telling us that we make life difficult for ourselves—too complicated."

~ ***"Yes, it becomes a—you are rushing around like busy bees."***

Sarah: "Rushing around unnecessarily."

~ ***"Yes, you are rushing around for all these complicated activities, which could be done in other ways, allowing spirit to come to the fore."***

George: "You are absolutely right! We were looking at the physical items of our civilisation—we all of us here agree I am sure—we have *far too many* streetlamps, we travel around in cars *far too much*, we import and export *far too many* goods, and it's all got rather out of hand. And it would be good I think to slow down our economy."

~ ***"YES!"***

George: "And I'm sure we could use the media to encourage people to live simpler lives. I'm sure that would be possible."

The idea of deliberately slowing down our economy would I think meet with resistance at the outset, simply because it means reduced profits for business, reduced taxation funds and less money in the pocket. But the values of cash and profits have to be weighed against quality of life, and life is of course *the most valuable physical commodity*. What value has cash profit without life? Economic slowdown has to be seen as the key to simpler lifestyle, and a route that eventually leads to happier more fulfilled LIFE.

~ ***"Yes, and I'm sure you will go down this road."***

[We were unaware of course that in just 3-years from now the 'crunch' would begin a worldwide economic slow-down.]

Graham latched onto 'road' and considered the amount of time we spend actually on the roads: "Do you travel as much as we do? Most of us spend so much of our time travelling—"

~ ***"I don't think we need to travel as much as you. We still have to make journeys, but the mind projection gives us a much easier alternative."***

So we asked if Aerans take holiday breaks: ~ ***"We have holidays, oh yes, we certainly do!"***

Sarah then gave us the opportunity to laugh again by enquiring if they work at all, and Bonniol's reply came in similar jocular vein: ~ ***"We have been known to, yes! I think I have said, our lives are far simpler, and the work is mostly in relation to nature and farming—one of the aspects of nature. And it does not revolve around business journeys (or) to places where you do lots of shopping."***

George: "Yes, I am aware that we do far too much shopping."

~ ***"But we do have holidays."***

George: "Do you travel to locations for your holidays?"

~ ***"We travel to many different places on our planet, as well as the nearby moon, and we have explored a little further afield as well."***

George: "Do you use public transport and also personal transport?"

~ ***"Yes, we have public transport, as well as our own smaller vehicles."***

George: "And of course, all powered by the clean energy system."

~ ***"Yes, we have developed very clean vehicles for travelling."***

Graham: "How do your vehicles travel? Do they have wheels or do they fly through the air?"

~ ***"They fly, yes, through the air."***

George: "Your *personal* vehicles fly?"

~ ***"Yes. We have roads, but mostly we fly, if at all possible. Occasionally, we do need to use the roads."***

George: "I imagine the flying is an easier proposition for you, because your atmosphere is thicker—"

~ ***"We have travelled by road, along the ground, but it is much faster to fly."***

Sarah: "Do you fly on power waves, or what is the system? How do you not crash? What is the system that you fly by?"

~ ***"No, we navigate our own journeys. There are guidelines too—if another vehicle is approaching we have a certain rule whereby one will fly over the other, in the (same) general direction."***

Sarah: "Do you have speed limits?"

~ ***"We have limits, yes. We are not allowed to go fast through the more crowded areas."***

Sarah: "And do you have a runway to take off, or do you go up straight away?"

~ ***"Yes, we come up straight away. They are very manoeuvrable."***

Sarah: "Are they in any way like our helicopters?"

~ ***"They do not have any moving propellers. They are streamlined and they are lightweight."***

George: "Fixed wings?"

~ ***"They have small wings."***

Graham: "Do your vehicles float in the atmosphere, like our boats float on the sea—some kind of anti-gravity device?"

~ ***"They are powered by an engine—we are told is not exactly like your jet engine, but is a different design."***

Sarah: "So how do they come straight up off the ground?"

~ ***"The force is able to be directed from a number of areas on the vehicle."***

George: "I imagine it is a bit like our 'jump jet'—"

Graham: "Is there much noise emission?"

~ ***"They are quiet, much quieter than they were in the past."***

Sarah: "So what is the fuel that they run on?"

~ ***"The fuel is the one we mentioned before. It is energy of the plant kingdom. It is utilised to create propulsion."***

George: "May I ask if your vehicles wear out? Do you have to scrap them and buy another at times?"

~ ***"All things eventually wear out, but our vehicles last as long as they are needed in general, and it is more often that they are improved upon than that they are changed."***

Sarah: "You said they are lightweight, so they are not made of metal?"

~ ***"They are made of metal, yes."***

Sarah: "Right, a lightweight metal."

~ ***"It is a strong metal, but a light one."***

We discussed a little, the fact that Earth also has its light metals and alloys, and then Graham enquired about accidents: ~ ***"We have had collisions in the past, but we (now) have warning systems, which should inform us, and the vehicles themselves should automatically avoid colliding with another."***

Sarah: "Do most people have a vehicle, or can just those who have more money afford them?"

~ ***"Not most, but many people have their own vehicle—it is common to share a vehicle within the family. We don't make as many journeys as you, so we don't all need to have a vehicle."***

Sarah: "And do you find your vehicles get stolen?"

~ ***"We have had thieves, but it is not a common occurrence in our world anymore."***

Graham: "We have to lock our houses, lock our cars and lock everything. We would like to live in a world where we didn't have to do this, but there is a proportion of the population who are thieves, and they cause a lot of trouble for all of us. It's one of the things that make lives complicated."

Sarah: "It's one thing that's got worse recently."

~ ***"Again, your complicated rules in life—(they are) not working, and it seems that the more complicated you make it, the less well it works."***

George: "You're right."

Graham: "That makes sense. A lot of people are convinced that *materialism is in fact causing many problems.* People think: I would like that but can't afford it so I shall take it! Greed—desire—in the old days, there were not that many material objects, but today—"

Sarah: It's not just (personal) greed, the governments in some countries are also greedy, and that causes tremendous suffering."

George: "There are many problems."

Lilian: "This is not our spiritual side."

George: "Yes, we need to raise awareness and be more spiritual."

~ ***"Yes, we all at times make the mistake of not using the tremendous help that is available to us. And of course, we aren't fully aware of the tremendous help."***

Sarah: "Salumet has told us that we should not judge, and I was just thinking that things aren't good, but maybe this is meant to be. In times of trouble you turn to spirit, and this is what is needed at the moment. A little bit of trouble helps people go in the right direction."

~ ***"Yes, that is often the case, and I am being told that you are certainly at the stage where much is being given—SO YOU ARE AT A TURNING POINT."***

George: "Yes, we are at a turning point!"

~ ***"And you ones I am told, will help to set the new example to your fellows."***

George: "Although we are a small group here, we are conscious of receiving so much help and guidance, and it is our job and aim to make the information as widely available as we can, so that others may take advantage for *their* guidance."

~ ***"And one of the great steps will be your own knowing to mind project, and how many doors that will open to you! And you will also be able to explain it to others, and that will create much benefit I'm sure."***

George: "Yes, we are always looking to ways of presenting the material that we receive. We write articles, we publish books and it is our aim to have a website. The electronic media will help. That will be an important step. Have similar processes happened in the past on your planet—that you have had spiritual instruction that you have then placed before many other people?"

~ ***"There is so much that we could tell you about our past, and I'm sure that you could also tell us. But I don't know how useful that would be—to listen to our histories and our learning, and where we went wrong and where we went right. Perhaps some if it would be of value to you."***

George: "One thing I can say about our distant past: I know that we have had visitors from other planets in the *remote* past, and these have left their mark, in terms of myth and legend, a few skills in moving huge rocks, that have been lost again…"

~ ***"Mind projection skills!"***

Several: "Yes! / Yes! / Yes!"

There is the clear evidence that mind projection skills have been known on our planet in ancient times. Previous civilisations have left their massive constructions, myth and legend; much of it since corroborated through spirit communication.

George: "Do you have a mythical past on your planet, where you have some evidence left by visitors?"

~ ***"There is less myth now of course, because we are able to verify the truth from spirit, as to what occurred in our histories. We have had visitors from other worlds, who have come and taught us and influenced us, as have you."***

George: "Yes, I imagine this to have been a general pattern throughout the universe."

~ ***"This is common, as I understand it, yes. And you will have other visitors, and hopefully they will influence YOU, so that it will be a great time ahead for your planet."***

Sarah: "Salumet has told us that others would visit us when we are ready, but at the moment, I think we are not quite ready—"

Bearing in mind the hard facts central to UFO sightings with their crop circle connections (often poorly reported), I added: "—and the process has begun."

~ ***"When you're ready—"***

Sarah: "Well, *we're* ready, but some of the others—"

As Sarah's voice tailed away, we had to laugh—a knowing laughter. There has been so much well-versed and well-rehearsed propaganda designed to counter the many passionate eye-witness accounts of UFOs, crop circle formations and the light signs. This is the start. The process has begun, of that there can be no doubt, even if not widely accepted, even if many make of them objects of ridicule. I reflected: "Yes, communication—not *just* communication, but communication-with-acceptance has to come into the equation."

And Lilian added: "Life on other planets is certainly talked about much more."

~ ***"Yes, I think you are able to look back into your past, and see how much you've moved on. So who knows what is round the corner for you in the next few years? And that is an exciting note, maybe to finish with for tonight."***

We were left once again with many thoughts. The message is now loud and clear about our living such 'cluttered' lives and this derives from excessive materialism. It has become obvious that if we are to connect more positively with the spirit within, then we must make moves to simplify the living. The political scene is important, and could help steer us, but it means extensive economic slow-down and drastically reduced infrastructures. Systems currently run to excess; too much detail, too much abuse, too much upkeep and not nearly enough nature. And all those streetlamps so much obscure the true glory of the heavens, and all those starry vistas are lost—out of sight is out of mind—and all the time, we see mind as more and more important in our living. Mind is fundamental to existence. Mind is our all, and mind is drawn to natural beauty!

It has been said, that rules and regulations have steadily increased to replace personal thinking. Thought of course is of the mind, of spirit, and there is the danger in our daily living that spirit will be swamped by excess legislation. This also must be addressed. Just as too many road signs can divert attention from what really matters, equally, minds may become just too over-cluttered with material paraphernalia. But Earth has reached a turning point! We have learned much from our dalliance with the material diversion, and it seems fitting that there should now be steady withdrawal from it—an industrial devolution! How could our cluttered material world possibly continue in the direction of yet more complexity? The turning point has arrived—a turning towards freedom of the inner being and towards a united brotherhood, and that united brotherhood shall extend beyond any petty Earthly sub-division to embrace an entire universe.

CHAPTER: 21
The Link – Masters and Religions – Dancing … 3rd October … 7th Nov 2005

THE FOLLOWING WEEK as Salumet addressed us, the same theme continued: ~ **"It is almost like an explosion of truth in your world at this present time. No longer are people being kept quiet about what they know to be the truth. The people of today on your planet are recognising that each one is an individual with a *mind* and thinking of their own. Have you any questions?"**

We quickly referred to our debate of last week and how rules and regulations so often compete with *personal thinking* here on Earth, in contrast to Planet Aerah.

~ **"Yes of course, I have told you previously that this planet is such a young planet as far as spiritual growth goes. And yes, your connection with that mind projector, which was after all meant for your own spiritual growth—(Aerah) is a planet which is much different from your own."**

George: "The comparisons help us in a way, to see ourselves more clearly, I feel."

~ **"Yes, that is a good point. It is something that you should study well. You should learn from the information which is being given to you, but at the same time it is not only information which we seek to give to you, but we wish to *teach* you of the experience that you are ultimately capable of, and which I am pleased to see you are trying now to put into some kind of action."**

We spoke of our continuing efforts. Salumet was indicating the duality of function of the Bonniol experience: that we should accept the information given, and that we should practise its method of delivery. Both aspects are clearly important. Whilst on the subject of Planet Aerah information, it seemed a good time to check on that important subject of *changing matter-density* that had come up earlier. So I put it to our teacher that the matter-density of a planet decreases with increasing spirituality, pointing out that the water of Aerah sounds similar to the water described for Earth's Astral Planes (a very much lighter form of matter).

~ **"You are quite correct in that assumption. After all, if you grow spiritually you are leaving behind that heaviness, that *density* as you call it, and you become much lighter beings—so too does that have an effect on the planet within which you live. In the same way as you human beings give out thoughts of love to many on your planet—when those thoughts are received and help is given by all involved, there are areas within your planet, which also become much lighter, much purer. So can you imagine the lightness of a planet whose spirituality is far above your own?"**

We could indeed, and I went on to suggest that eventually, this will be quite a realisation for our scientists, and especially chemists, who's first thought has to be that matter is much the same throughout the universe. Salumet went on:

~ **"It does have to have some effect. It is the love element, which alters matter and structure and people. Always remember this, and you will not go wrong in your thinking."**

So love conquers all—extends into the very chemistry and substance of the creation. It is good to tidy up one's thinking from time to time, and it was helpful to have these two very important factors embellished prior to Bonniol's next visit, and that came one month later. The interval was mainly on account of Paul being away in Thailand in the interim.

~ ***"Hello again—"***

In reply to Bonniol's greeting there was an especially enthusiastic welcome from all.

~ ***"Lovely to be here again."***

Lilian: "It's been six-weeks in our time since our last meeting."

~ ***"Yes, I've been looking forward to returning."***

George: "We've missed you. Did you know from spirit guides that we've missed a few meetings?"

~ ***"Yes, we were aware that there would be a small break. These things are well known to us."***

George: "Ah! So you understand. Good!"

~ ***"And we were very happy anyway. Nevertheless, it is always good to return to our new friends across the universe."***

Graham: "It's still very difficult for us to understand how you do it—unbelievable! But I am sure it *is* happening!"

George: "I've been trying to think of it as two separate universes—the one *physical* universe, and the *spiritual* universe, and the two unite together. But the physical universe has space and time, and the speed of light as a 'speed limit', but the spiritual universe of course, does not. And yet it connects with all the elements of the physical universe, so it's kind of 'expansive', yet has no space. That is difficult for us to get our heads around!"

~ ***"Yes, it's a mind-boggling thing—the physical and spiritual entwinement."***

George: "Yes, we can accept, but it is difficult to understand."

~ ***"They work well together. It is a remarkable feat that they are able to weave themselves together so naturally, but the mechanics of it are beyond our understanding."***

George: "Beyond *your* understanding, as it is totally beyond *our* understanding."

Eileen: "I don't know if this has been asked before, forgive me if it has. How were you chosen to be the one to make the communication with us? Was there an election? Can you explain to us?"

~ ***"Yes, we have been doing this for a long time now—communicating with other worlds. And I was chosen for my abilities, to form this link with your world. There are many of us who would be able to project ourselves in this way. It was decided that I would be given the privilege, because my experience with other worlds that I have had over the years has given me some training. I have worked with those in my world who connect with the other planets, and I have been a part of communication with those, though I have***

not led them. It was decided that I would be allowed to lead this communication."

Eileen: "Could I ask who approached you? Because we all feel so very honoured that we have been selected for this communication, but I am curious as to how it all happened with *you*. Were you approached, or is it something you just knew?"

~ ***"We have the advantage of our clearer connections with our guides. They make us aware of many things, including the matter of your planet being 'ready' to receive this communication. It was told to us quite a long time ago, that preparations were under way, and more recently we were told that it was time to communicate with you, so I was given the task. And it was decided that I would be leading the communication, though there are many of us who are listening as I speak to you."***

George: "We've been aware that this planet is in the process of taking a step forward, and I think I understand that your guides would have been aware of this, and that explains part of the timing."

Lilian: "So would your guides have anything to do with choosing the channel that you are using?"

~ ***"Well, my own guide would be more concerned with my own development, I suppose. But they would link up with guides from your world, who are concerned with YOUR development, and they would then set this up. It is as with all things—everything is set up in spirit, before it develops in the physical."***

Eileen: "Coming from the same guides?"

~ ***"Yes, we don't know how many there are behind the scenes, setting all these things up. We could probably find out, but it may be so complicated, to fully understand it."***

We enquired if the guides would be associated with the Astral Planes, spiritually close to the planet.

~ ***"The guides would be concerned with whichever planes are their domain at the time. Some guides are concerned with different planes of existence. But the guides concerned with this matter would mainly be concerned with the physical planes for this bringing together of the worlds."***

We acknowledged this statement, feeling that 'physical planes' would carry similar meaning to 'Astral Planes' (but seen from beyond

Earth). Bonniol spoke further on the interconnectedness of planes, but concluded with: ~ ***"Your master would explain that better."***

George: "Yes, I think of our master as one who comes from what I think of as 'deeper spirit'. I don't know if that is a proper way to think about it—"

Graham: "Do you have any masters in the present or past, that have visited *your* planet?"

~ ***"We also have masters, yes, whose knowledge is far greater than ours. This is always the way as far as we know. There are always those who have greater knowledge and greater purity of energy."***

Graham: "Have you ever had any masters who have incarnated on your planet, like Jesus? Have you had any famous incarnations of masters that have helped your planet at strategic times?"

~ ***"Yes, they are famous on our planet, yes. There have been many as there have been on yours."***

George: "Yes, and religions have developed based on some, and I guess it might be similar on your planet?"

~ ***"And one day, YOU may all be masters."***

We laughed at that proposition, as Bonniol continued: ~ ***"That is the way of things, we start at the bottom and we work our way up."***

Perhaps we should ponder for a moment this important and often unconsidered picture. Masters who come to us from that 'deeper spirit' bring with them so much greater knowledge. Our Earthly religions have built around that knowledge (delivered at different times and in different regions, through history according to the abilities and consciousness of people). The religions are temporary stepping stones of our own adaptation, based upon and including the teachings received. Jesus, Krishna, Buddha, the Divine Pymander and others, are lovingly well-remembered on Earth by generations that follow. But Earth is not alone in this. Equally, other names remain 'famous' on Aerah, for the word brought to that planet is from that very same 'deeper spirit'. The same pattern is common throughout creation. The essential factor in all this is of course THE WORD itself. It is of the Creative Principle—God—permeating the entire universe, and available to all planets.

The dialogue moved on. Graham mentioned the difficulty of imagining the expanse of time that lies before us, and we declared how we value Bonniol's words.

~ ***"I wish we could be of more help. We have things that we are allowed to help you with. There are always rules about these communications."***

George: "Yes, I appreciate there is knowledge for which we are not yet ready. That has to be recognised."

~ ***"But we can help each other in lots of ways. We cannot give you technological help."***

This is something that is known or sensed anyway, but it is good nevertheless to actually voice the thought. And it was at this point that Eileen, sitting opposite Paul, noticed the light.

Eileen: "As I am sitting speaking to you, I am aware of a very bright light on Paul. It would be between his eyes in the centre of his forehead. Does that show on you, in your own body form? Does the light emanate from your head?"

~ ***"I understand. Yes, this light that you see is a spiritual aspect of us."***

Eileen: "So it's actually shining through from you?"

~ ***"Yes, it is not part of our physical bodies, but it is perceived by us, like a chakra point."***

Eileen: "Which makes communication easier between you?"

~ ***"It is part of my energy system, which does deal with communication, yes. I am pleased that you can see it."***

Eileen: "Well, it's not there all the time, but I've seen it quite a number of times this evening."

The conversation moved on to the more general spread of planets and how each has its own evolutionary path that cannot really be compared to another. Graham referred to one Salumet had spoken of, inhabited by angelic beings. Now that was different.

~ ***"We have heard of this, yes. But we have never been able to communicate with this planet, but would love to. There is so much out there—so many wonderful planets and beings. Perhaps that's one of the things we can get across to you—the diversity, and wonderful beings that roam this universe."***

George: "It's very nice to have confirmation that there are these inhabited planets with advanced cultures, which we've imagined and thought about—it's nice to have our thoughts confirmed."

~ ***"And for us, YOU are wonderful beings."***

I think several gulps and coughs followed, and it seemed a good time to pause and offer a little music. We explained about Glen Miller's *Moonlight Serenade* and the saxophone sound, and the ongoing popularity through more than half a century. As the music faded, we spoke of it being a dance number and how many people would dance in pairs."

~ ***"It had a nice rhythm to it, a gentle rhythm. I can see that this would be good for dancing slowly."***

George: "And do you do that sort of thing on your planet?"

~ ***"We enjoy dancing very much. We have much music for dancing, yes. It is something that helps us to connect with other people."***

George: "Would you dance in pairs or in groups?"

~ ***"Yes, we can dance with pairs or groups, or alone."***

We observed that dancing to music is something else shared, and I must confess to just not having dreamt that cultures across the universe might go bopping around dance floors, that we could all be so very similar in habits and lifestyle. This really was getting to be like chatting with a neighbour over the garden fence!

~ ***"We usually dance to slow music. We like that one—its rhythm. This we find the best for the type of dancing we like to do—allowing our minds to be calm."***

I suggested perhaps we should play a Strauss waltz next time, adding that it was so good to have Bonniol's comments.

Lilian added: "Something in common."

Graham then decided to pursue the light entertainment theme a little further: "Do you have television or anything like that?"

~ ***"We DO have something similar to your television. It is useful for learning lots of things, and it helps us to know what is happening everywhere."***

Amazing! They watch TV too! This was becoming just more and more incredible, but I felt Graham was really pushing his luck with the next question: "Do you have anything like 'soap operas'? Soap operas are awful—"

The next few seconds of recording were impossible to decipher, being largely an unintelligible confusion of laughter and backchat. Then Graham was able to go on: "We've all got our favourites but don't like to admit it—"

There was more laughter and shouts of 'how true!'

Graham: "It's enjoyable because you can learn something from the drama of other people's lives, even though it is fiction, and you can get something from it."

Feeling that we must be getting a little too off track, I added: "Do you understand from Paul's mind, what a soap opera is?"

~ ***"We—have been working our way through various files in his mind. We HAVE come across the soap opera item, of yours. We have something similar on our planet, which may surprise you."***

Well, surprise, yes. But I think 'flabbergasted' is the word that rests more comfortably. Bonniol continued: ~ ***"We also enjoy following the fortunes of people (portrayed) in a fictional manner. It is—um—probably mainly entertainment, but especially for the younger ones. There is some role-modelling and some useful information in these programs as well."***

I added that we also have 'adventure movies', in which a story is depicted that is rather more adventurous than most of us would care to be in true life.

~ ***"Yes, we've been experiencing some of these from this one's memories too. They are certainly fast moving, and sometimes quite violent."***

George: "Yes. That perhaps is a problem area. Some fiction writers have presented violence because it seems an attractive thing to do—it catches the attention—while at the same time, such presentation has been criticised. It is felt that it would encourage violence in real life. Have you experienced any such thing, or do you have any thoughts on the matter?"

~ ***"Yes, it would be a little—not light-hearted enough for our taste. For most of us, entertainment is more designed to add lightness and creativity. We need a little adventure also, but it is of a less violent nature I think."***

We suggested it seems right that some of us see *violence presentation* as a problem area, and we asked if our friends had humour programs, adventure and wildlife.

~ ***"We do not have that many choices, but there are daily programs involving those things. There are those dealing with more of an artistic nature."***

Moving on to period pieces with storylines, in which life is depicted as it was hundreds of years ago: ~ ***"Yes, and with the added historical interest as well—we also have these films and documentaries. Again, it's particularly for the younger ones. It helps them understand where we have all come from."***

Graham: "And then there are prehistoric times, going back a few *thousand* years. There was no mechanism at that time to record events in such a way that they would have been preserved. How far back does *your* history go, for events to be known? How far back do you have to go before you get to prehistory?"

~ ***"We can go back as far as we like, using our minds of course—"***

Graham: "Yes, of course!"

~ ***"—and our links with our guides. We can get a lot of information, and we can review the past using our projections."***

Graham: "So you can access your own past lives in this way?"

~ ***"Yes, we can look back at past lives."***

Now this is an interesting way to examine history, free from misinterpretation and cover-up. It was pointed out that we have had much-revered seers on Earth that have peeped into the future and made predictions. They have applied their talent more to foretell as opposed to looking in the other direction to view history.

Graham continued: "So you are able to access events that occurred a million years ago?"

~ ***"We would not be able to access events beyond our own mind's experience. But if we wished to know of (such) events, we can get information from our guides. We don't have to study the rocks and fossils!"***

There were general sounds to indicate that this was seen as a considerable short cut. There are all kinds of advantages it seems from recognising, understanding and strengthening spirit connection.

~ "I do not want to continue too late. Maybe it would be a good time to say 'bye bye' for this time. And I look forward to seeing you again."

And so, it was again the time of fond farewells. Another momentous evening, this time with such diversity—input from Salumet—the planning of the Bonniol link—dance bands and light entertainment—the universal process of advancing spirit and how Earth's religions fit into that wide-screen view. Can such a pace continue?

CHAPTER: 22

Mind-Link Blueprint – History Books – Life's Problems ... 21st November 2005

THE WEATHER WAS turning cold and our evening began quietly. Numbers were down, and indeed it was my turn to be away on holiday, once again enjoying with friends, the snows of the French Alps. The meeting began with a child-rescue via Sarah. Then Bonniol was welcomed, Lilian adding: "Very few at our meeting tonight."

~ ***"Yes, but that does not matter."***

Lilian: "No, they'll all get to know what we've talked about."

~ ***"Yes."***

Sarah had been receiving clairvoyance and spoke of it: "I was getting some very strong pictures of flowers. I don't know if that has anything to do with you?"

~ ***"I have not brought any with me, but they may be to do with our world. What are they like?"***

Sarah: "Mainly roses and something similar to chrysanthemums—and now I'm getting much smaller flowers, like little daisies."

~ ***"I think they are from YOUR world."***

Sarah: "It's not your birthday today, is it?"

~ ***"No, it sounds like somebody's giving YOU flowers."***

Sarah: "O well, 'Thank you' whoever's giving them to me. It's not my birthday either."

~ ***"But you did a very good job, didn't you, just now?"***

Sarah: "Oh! Yes!"

Lilian: "We just did a rescue of a child!"

~ ***"Yes."***

Sarah: "O well, thank you for the flowers then!"

So they were flowers from those in spirit for services rendered. How very nice!

Lilian: "Have you got a large gathering where you are tonight?"

~ ***"We have a large group, yes. It is perhaps easier for us with less busy lives, than (for) you."***

There followed a little chat about our cold weather, the norm for late November; then Eileen was explaining about our attempts at mind projection that were not showing too much progress, and she enquired if Bonniol could give useful tips or suggestions. This was to lead to a most helpful exchange, almost one might say, a blueprint for the art: ~ ***"Yes, I'm being told that you are practising with each other, and you have had a small amount of success."***

Eileen: "Yes, very limited."

~ ***"You are sending each other images of an object usually, yes?"***

It was agreed this was so, visualising the object with eyes closed and in relaxed, almost meditative mood. At the same time, one would be aware of the intention to project to a target person.

~ ***"And that object is an everyday simple one?"***

This was so.

~ ***"I would continue to send these objects, but change them more frequently, so that each day you send a different one. You may need to write down each day what you receive. The point is, the focus on the object needs to be fresh and clear and if it is a new one each time, it will benefit from, a certain sharpness in your mind. SEE that object, in as much detail as you can—three-dimensionally if possible. See it, feel it and send it to your target. You feel it, see it, and send it on its way."***

Sarah: "Do we need to focus on who we are sending it to, by seeing them also in 3-D, or is it just the focus on the object and *knowing* who you are sending to?"

~ ***"The target is less important at the moment, because the people that you are sending to, are well-known to you and these are clear enough."***

Sarah: "And they're aware that they are going to be receiving something—"

~ ***"So the link is strong in that area. The objects need to be a little stronger though."***

Eileen: "Would it help if you actually held it in your hands? It's not always easy to 'feel'. I don't think we find that easy."

~ "That may refresh your memory—BEFORE—you mentally visualise it."

Eileen: "It would be easier to visualise, if you were feeling it?"

~ "Yes, if you study it first, look at it, and consider it for a time. That can be useful."

Sarah: "Not actually hold it at the time you are mind projecting?"

~ "It is not necessary. You still have to focus mentally. The actual object is not so important—THE MENTAL CLARITY IS THE MAIN IMPORTANT THING—your mental picture of the object. But it helps to involve the other senses. So when you're sending something, like a chair, you may picture the chair, but also 'feel' the chair in your mind—what this chair feels like to you. All objects, remember, have their own energy, their own spirit. And a chair will have its own energy, and it will feel a certain way. So this is the first step—to really 'feel' your object, and then you can send it to your target."

To put it in a slightly different way: it is important to firstly get to know the object by handling it. This will then help in getting a clear mind image to *feel mentally*. Then it can be sent.

Sarah: "So could we say that you are sending the energy of the object to the others? Or am I barking up the wrong tree there?"

~ "You are not actually sending the energy. But in the thought that you are sending, it contains an aspect of it, yes. But it is a different kind of energy—more abstract."

Sarah: "Thank you."

Lilian: "Would it be better to stick to a certain time of day, or does time not matter?"

~ "Yes, I would stick to your timing at the moment. This will help, and especially to begin with, receiving the thought—it would be an advantage to know that a new one is being sent at a certain time. When you are receiving, you should open your mind to the person, if you know that this person is sending. Then, you can, open to their energy, if you like, and you may find that that helps. But it takes practise."

Eileen: "I had a strong feeling this week, that it would be useful, rather than send objects, to send colours. After all, we *are* colours. And I wondered if it would be easier to pick up colours to begin with."

~ ***"I think colour is a very good thing to work with, yes."***

Eileen: "It's easier to visualise I think, which may make it easier to project."

~ ***"Yes, colours—"***

Eileen: "Would it not connect with our own aura's colour and make it easier to pick up?"

But Bonniol wanted us to keep the main objective in sight, and so he went on: ~ ***"You need to develop this mind projection in order to communicate. As you develop, you will need to learn to send more complicated messages. To begin with, an object or a colour would be a good starting point."***

Sarah pointed out the much greater complexity of an object compared to just a colour.

~ ***"I would try to develop both. The objects are very useful in one way. Colour is important too. You may find it easier sometimes, to choose an object with a strong colour. If you just begin with colour, you may become successful at that very quickly, but then you would need to move on—to objects. But it is very good to hear that you are practising, because it's not an easy thing to learn to start with. But once you get going, you will be surprised how it develops. But getting started is often the hardest stage."***

Eileen: "What's the difference between mind projection and telepathy? Is there a slight difference, or not really? Only, I'm thinking, with telepathy you don't have to visualise do you? It's an instantaneous thought? Is there a difference?"

~ ***"With telepathy—I am using this one's (Paul's) definitions for these words—but it would seem telepathy would be a little bit unconscious, like a clairvoyant being impressed with thoughts. Telepathy seems to be more receiving the information. But to be able to communicate telepathically, would INVOLVE mind projection. So, perhaps it is another word for the same thing. Mind projection perhaps is a more—"***

Eileen: "Is it just a newer word? It's only been in the last few years that 'mind projection' has been used. Is it just a new name for telepathy?"

~ ***"It could be. It's difficult from another planet, to decide on the newness!"***

Everyone fairly hooted at the thought. Our meetings at times appear on the surface to be casual and we are apt to overlook the fact that these are exceptional interplanetary exchanges, and one can so easily get carried away. We'll be expecting Bonniol to serve tea at the end of the evening next!

~ ***"But I'm feeling that—yes, it is a new name. But I'm (also) feeling that it is not QUITE the same."***

Eileen: "I'm just wondering if telepathy seems simpler, why we really need to focus. I just wonder what it is that's different—"

~ ***"Telepathy is perhaps the same mechanism involved, but maybe calling it 'mind projection', is a way of helping us focus on what needs to be concentrated on."***

Eileen: "I wonder if with mind projection, the thought is travelling further. 'Telepathy' is usually happening in *this* world, whereas mind projection can happen from planet to planet. Perhaps that's the difference."

Lilian: "Yes, I see what you mean."

Eileen: "Sorry if I'm being awkward, but these thoughts are coming into my head."

There was a little laughter at this, and Bonniol continued: ~ ***"Yes, it's good that it is being talked about. I cannot isolate the difference if there is one. But I don't know why you shouldn't use the word 'telepathic' with the same meaning. Often there's more than one word to describe something."***

The wordiness of language is of course a human failing or foible, and often several words mean the same thing!

It was a valiant effort by Bonniol, but it is of course quite unfair to expect a detailed critique of Earthly word-definition from one living on a distant planet, especially concerning terms that are unclear even to the majority of Earth-dwellers! And as like as not, also unclear to spirit guides who observe our often curious ways. But this is nonetheless an important matter that deserves elaborating further, and since I was not there myself on the evening in question, I can deal with the matter with all the unashamed advantages of both hindsight and sifting through the copious literature that relates. And it really amounts to this:

TELEPATHY: What used to be called 'thought transference' is now known as telepathy. That is a newness factor. The word 'telepathy' is derived from two Greek words meaning: *distant* and *feeling*. As a branch of ESP it has been investigated by members of the Society for Psychical Research from 1886, and I refer to a book by Sir Oliver Lodge: The Survival of Man [7], 1909. A number of interesting experiments are accounted and I am very taken with the description of one in particular, involving a silver paper cut-out of a teapot-shape. The author describes how Dr H and Miss R knew and were thinking of the shape, while the percipient Miss E attempted to perceive its form from their minds. Miss E declared it to be *something oval* and like *a silver duck*. It was indeed rather oval and silver, but a teapot. So it was an incorrect result—or was it? Afterwards, Dr H stated that: *he had been thinking all the time how like a duck the original teapot was, and, in fact, had been thinking more of ducks than teapots*. In identifying a thought of course, it must be conceded that it is the thought that counts! In this work, the thought is really more fundamental than the picture on which the thought is based! So well done Miss E! Further into the same book I found a significant statement that a previous reader had underlined in red crayon: *The message is conveyed etherially, not by matter at all—though it is sent and received and interpreted by matter;* quite so, brains are indeed matter whilst the transmission medium between them is not. A further term used, alternative to telepathy is 'mental radio'. This suits quite well and follows the book of that same title: Mental Radio [8], by Upton Sinclair, 1930 with foreword by Albert Einstein.

MIND PROJECTION: Although mind projection also concerns the propagation of thought, it differs slightly from telepathy, and it is worth mentioning that it could also quite easily be confused with 'astral projection', which is again, slightly different. (My understanding of astral projection is that it involves both mind and astral body and can occur in either sleep or trance state. It can also connect to out-of-body-experience (OBE), during which one might observe the physical body from a distance; then return to it.) Mind projection is not quite the same and has different purpose. It is as stated, just the projection of mind (spirit). Conscious mind connecting with targeted mind is used as a means of communicating, which can, in the physical consideration, occur across huge distance. It is ideal for interplanetary work since all transpires within spirit domain, which itself has no space-time, so that physical distance is simply not involved. Mind projection quite simply does not involve the fabric of space-time. It follows that there are no delays in any ensuing dialogue. A second important factor where the mind-to-mind connection is concerned is the automatic language facility provided by brain for incoming thought. Amazingly, even for cultures living on different planets, there is no language barrier. There are also further requirements in successful mind projection work: the involvement and good offices of spirit guides and physical support groups for both projector and receiver. Mind projection communication therefore has qualitative differences as well as a difference of purpose when compared to telepathy and astral projection. These matters are accounted quite well and freely on the Internet, and I note that the 'India Daily' publication's technical team has on occasion actually referred to *use of mind projection by extraterrestrials*; also to extensive current use of 'remote viewing' by RAW (India's equivalent of CIA) for political and anti-terrorism purpose.

Lilian's next question moved us gently towards accounting history: "I'm fairly sure we've mentioned this before, but I was talking to a friend, and she's interested in your visits to us, and she said: on your planet, are there different countries? I believe you said there were."

~ ***"Yes, I did say that there were countries, but not as many as you have now. But in the past we had more borders, but gradually, there is a natural coming together. This is the way of things in all planets. You can tell a lot about a planet by how many borders it has."***

Sarah: "And we've got a lot!"

Lilian: "And it was one language I believe, wasn't it?"

~ ***"We have one language, but we have had many, and there are still others spoken, yes."***

Sarah pointed out that in our own history, languages have slowly disappeared, with tongues such as Cornish and Breton giving way to appropriate lingua franca, and Lilian declared we still have far to go.

~ ***"I've been thinking about your history—why you have had such a problem with your recording of history—because, much of your history is confused I think."***

Eileen: "That's because we're human!"

Sarah: "Which bit of history were you thinking of in particular?"

~ ***"Well, you have your religious history."***

Sarah: "That's in a good muddle, yes!"

~ ***"—which I understand has been deliberately manipulated."***

There was agreement to this, and Eileen reminded Bonniol that we are a learning planet and this is likely to have been a valid part of our evolution. Well, she has a point. Sarah went on: "Salumet has told us that, in the future, we will all be harmonious, all have one belief and all love each other. And when that happens, that'll be the end of this planet, because we won't need it anymore!"

~ ***"—just when it was getting better!"***

Laughter again took over, and it is nice that we can occasionally turn to periods of lighter mood and levity. Sarah qualified by saying our spiritual progression beyond further requirement of the planet is a long, long way ahead, with myriad incarnations yet to follow, and Lilian reflected: "As a race of people on this planet, we tend to—in the history books especially—put down the wars and more dreadful things, forgetting that the majority of people are perfectly good kind people, just caught up in these things."

~ ***"And they often write the books from a particular point of view."***

Sarah: "That's right, depending which side they're on!"

~ ***"It seems rare to write books from a neutral point of view."***

Lilian: "Do you have many history books on your planet?"

~ ***"We have many books yes, and of course, we can check the reliability of them. But those that write do not try to cover things up, I think. They simply write about the history from—or as they understand it. I think it is a detachment from the material. There is no interest in making it one way or the other. But there is still of***

course much love in it, in the way it is written, in the little details of the accounts—the smaller parts, which would perhaps get lost too easily if they were not recorded."

Sarah: "Of course, in this world, if someone is writing a history, they cannot be in all places all of the time, so they have to rely on other people, which makes it difficult; whereas, if you could mind project, you could get the exact information from wherever."

Eileen: "I presume that, as you can mind project, you can also go back in time, can you?"

~ ***"We can go backwards in our minds, yes. We are revisiting the MEMORY of the past."***

Eileen: "Yes, whereas we rely on books, you can actually sense and feel what happened, which obviously would be much better."

~ ***"Yes, this is the reason that books are less important nowadays on our planet. People wish to (prefer to?) journey back in their minds, but the books are still important overviews of the past and all the different aspects of the past. So they will always be here, I think, as written records."***

Sarah explained the difference between hieroglyphs and phonetic language and enquired the form of writing on Aerah.

~ ***"All writings change, and all writings begin as pictures, and gradually these pictures get shortened, and this is how our language has developed, as has yours I believe. Ours has come from pictures, yes. But it no longer resembles the pictures."***

It was time for a fresh topic. Lilian was saying: "Over time, on your planet, has the climate changed?"

~ ***"Oh yes, it always changes, as does life. Everything changes, nothing stops."***

Eileen: "Is there any one issue on your planet that's very important? For example, here, we are all very concerned about 'global warming.'"

~ ***"Yes, we have a number of issues. One of our biggest is what to do with our population expanding. We have many people now, and we all need a degree of space, and we cannot continue to live together forever on our world, which is why we have begun to develop one of our moons. But it is not easy to spread out in this way, and it is a problem which will continue I think. But this is one***

of the areas which you will say: 'worries us'. We have I think, a very good system of energy now, so our lives are easier in that way. We still get diseases, and occasionally have problems with people not getting on, shall we say."

Sarah: "But you don't have wars—"

~ ***"We have not had wars for many, many—a very long time. There are smaller struggles, if you like, between people, and sometimes it is more to do with the space, a lack of space."***

Sarah: "So if you haven't got much space, what do you do with all your waste—your household waste and all that, because that's one of the problems that we've got?"

~ ***"We live a more—we are sustained by the plants more I think, than on your world—so what we eat is more natural. We don't use the plastics and glass, as you do."***

Sarah: "So if you buy anything, it will be in natural containers—biodegradable containers, will it?"

~ ***"We would have our shopping delivered to us, and we would re-use the containers that it comes in. So the food would not be wrapped up in plastic that produces rubbish."***

Sarah: "So if you had some grain or flour or whatever, it would come loose and it would be put into your own container, would it?"

~ ***"It would come in a container, and it could be transferred to another container when it arrives, or it might be swapped."***

Lilian: "Going back a hundred years to my grandparent's days, it just wouldn't have happened—all this packaging."

Sarah: "Everything is packaged, often double-wrapped."

Lilian: "We are beginning to recycle though, which is a good thing."

Sarah: "But then you need so much energy to transport—"

Eileen: "If you're eating very healthily, what causes the diseases amongst people? Is it the mind?"

It is of course a part of the Salumet teaching and of Source teaching in general, that the seat of disease lies within mind and the thinking. And it was perhaps no surprise that Bonniol quickly aligned to this: ~ ***"Yes, disease starts in the mind."***

Eileen, reflecting on the more generally prevailing Earthly belief: "Yes, we are a long way from that way of thinking on this planet, but we (as a group) *do know* that it is a big cause of disease (the way we think). But you readily accept that that's the cause do you?"

~ ***"We have accepted this for a long time, that the mind produces the body, and that if the body becomes ill, it is the mind that is wrong, yes."***

The reader will have noticed by now that our extraterrestrial friend often adds a 'yes' to the end of a sentence. It is clear I think from the sound file, that he seeks to emphasise or affirm the statement made. In this instance, I would certainly take it to be strong affirmation of the statement.

Sarah: "But we do have things called viruses. I don't think that's to do with the mind is it Eileen?"

Eileen: "Mind set could attract the virus. I suppose that would explain why some people get it and others don't."

Sarah: "I obviously haven't been thinking very well recently—mm." (Sarah had a cold the week before).

~ ***"It seems to be one of the results of being physical, and they are little reminders that we have somehow lapsed in our thinking. I think it is true that if you are always thinking in the right ways, you will not get ill."***

Eileen: "Perhaps we should change one of our sayings from: 'You are what you eat'. Perhaps we should say: 'You are what you think'. Perhaps that would be more apt."

~ ***"Yes, but the eating IS important."***

Eileen: "But not the main thing, otherwise you would not have people who have abused their bodies, on this planet, and yet they remain healthy. So it has to be something more than food."

Sarah: "But then, if you don't eat properly, you *do* get ill."

~ ***"Not necessarily."***

Eileen: "That's what I'm saying—you have people who eat supposedly all the wrong things, all of their life, and they live to a ripe old age."

~ ***"And you can get people eating well, but they still get ill."***

Eileen: "Yes, exactly."

~ ***"But EATING WELL on our planet has become THE MOST SENSIBLE WAY TO GROW OUR FOOD, PREPARE IT AND EAT IT. It all fits together."***

Eileen: "It is all part of the way you've evolved, which hopefully we'll do one day."

Sarah: "Which is another reason why you need some space—to grow your own food."

~ *"Yes. But yes, we've all got our own problems."*

Sarah: "I'm sure we've asked this before, but do you have seasons?"

~ *"Yes, we have these different periods of change."*

Sarah: "What period are you in at the moment?"

~ *"We have a stormy period. It is very windy. We do not say it is cold, it is not the coldest time, but it is the windiest time."*

Lilian: "But that would vary—it wouldn't be the same all over the planet."

~ *"No, where I live it follows a pattern of being windy, followed by a much hotter time, and this leads to a period of a—"*

The speech faded at this point. Then Bonniol was saying: ~ ***"We will have to try that question again some time. I can't think it through at the moment, in your terms."***

Sarah: "Would you say that your seasons are changing as ours are, or have they been static for a while?"

~ *"They are never static for too long."*

Lilian: "When you started colonising your moon, as you were saying, was there any other physical life there?"

~ *"There was no physical life on the moon. We were the first physical forms, I believe, there."*

Lilian: "It must have been exciting."

Sarah: "And have you had any other interesting contacts with other planets recently?"

~ *"We are still communicating with the others."*

Sarah: "The 'mushroom' people—"

~ *"They are very well."*

Sarah: "Yes, do send them our best wishes when you next speak to them."

Lilian: "Yes, I must say it's broadened our horizons a lot since you've been coming."

Eileen: "I haven't looked at a mushroom in the same way since!"

Laughter again took over, and then Sarah was enquiring as to the nature of other beings encountered, to which Bonniol replied: ~ ***"Each is very different—hopefully we can bring one of the others soon. Yes, we will try to bring you one of the others, who can tell you a little about THEIR world. The connection needs a little bit of work still, but we will persevere. I should leave it for this time though."***

There were thanks for another memorable visit, concluding with such a most amiable freewheeling chat, and of course there was much enthusiasm at the prospect of another visitor. And Eileen had a parting request: "Perhaps you could leave us with one of your thoughts? We can try to pick it up—"

~ ***"I will send something, and you may be able to tell me now—"***

Eileen: "Are you sending it now?"

~ ***"Yes."***

Eileen: "Is there a colour?"

~ ***"There is a colour involved."***

Eileen: "I keep thinking of yellow. Is it the sun?"

~ ***"Yes."***

Progress! It had been another intriguing evening, coming at a time when the media were reminiscing on World War I. That had been 90 years ago. Nine still live who fought and to this day, survive. One recounted the last moment of a dying comrade—how his face had lit up as he cried out: 'Mother!' His spirit was clearly met as he departed that life. And surely, this is the calibre of material that would make good reading in *our* history books? The human and beyond-human factors can sometimes say so much more than biased, intellectual, political diatribe. But 20th-century Earth has so often favoured the latter, a trait that Bonniol finds puzzling! Other important issues were touched upon in this session, not least packaging. On Aerah, there is no need to recycle because they avoid producing such awful rubbish in the first place, and you do not have to be a Sherlock Holmes to work that one through! Is all the packaging that we use really necessary? No! I remember my own childhood in the 1930s when milk was delivered and dispensed into the household jug, just like on another planet of our recent acquaintance! Maybe it would be prudent to begin a process of change, by at least legislating against more that a single layer of wrapping on goods. If we can go back to square one and avoid manufacturing potential garbage, just think of the energy and recycling hassle that would save!

CHAPTER: 23

Other Planetary Ways and Christmas ... 12th December ... 17th December 2005

EARTHLY PREPARATIONS FOR Christmas were in place. Bonniol, the essential Bonniol, his mind that is, was with us and as usual the conversation began casually, before drifting into topics of a more compulsive interest.

Lilian explained: "We have two visitors with us this evening."

~ ***"That is a very good thing—to involve more people—the more that know this universe is full of all kinds of other life forms, the better it is."***

Lilian: "It makes us realise just how much there is to know."

~ ***"Yes. We are always learning new things as we travel—as we go through life."***

George: "It's wonderful to have you with us again. We've missed you these last three-weeks."

Lilian added lightly: "We thought you must be on holiday!"

~ ***"We are often busy with our work in various ways, but we always try to find the time to reach out to other worlds."***

Lilian: "Have you included any other planets since we spoke last?"

~ ***"We are still working towards a ninth planet, but we have not been able to contact them properly yet. It takes time."***

It was suggested at this stage that there must be much information accumulated, and perhaps at some stage we could learn of other planets and beings from Bonniol's travels.

~ ***"There is a lot of information, which may be of little value to you. But there is always SOMETHING of interest I feel. I could tell you about the seventh planet that we contacted—before you."***

Lilian: "That would be nice."

~ ***"This is also a fairly recent communication—it is a world where people are especially able to speak the language of the earth—the elementals—of the trees and plants. These people have worked with them for such a long time. They are able to communicate very easily, and this helps us with OUR communication with THEM."***

Our interest was clearly apparent and Bonniol continued: ~ ***"They are a—what you might call a primitive culture, because they have not considered it necessary to develop the material things in their world."***

George: "So they haven't developed technology—"

~ ***"They have not. They feel no need to. They get ALL their needs from nature."***

Lilian: "Obviously they are aware of the spiritual side of themselves—"

~ ***"Yes, I think the natural world encourages this from people. The more 'developed' you become, the more closed your mind can become."***

George: "Yes, I'm beginning to get the feeling that one can develop the material sense, or develop spiritually. There are the two roads that one may travel. And I am also getting the impression that *so many more doorways open* travelling that spiritual road."

~ ***"There are planets that are able to balance the material and the spiritual, and we have to a degree, managed this I think. But the material world becomes dominant at times."***

George: "Yes, I think unfortunately, we have become rather 'dominant' ourselves, but hopefully we are beginning to change."

~ ***"Yes, it will gradually be realised that the way forward—is to go backwards."***

Lilian: "It is for us—I understand what you are saying."

~ ***"But not ALL the way back!—there ARE technologies which will make things better for you."***

We pointed out that Aerah was interesting to us *because* she had achieved more balance, with much of her material development centred on nature and agriculture.

~ ***"Yes, most of our jobs are in agriculture, yes. This is the main activity of production—working with nature to provide our foods and our energy. It all comes from the natural world—nature. But***

it's more than that. It's the place we go when we want to find our balance—find some beauty."

Exploring this theme a little further, it seems that the countryside of Aerah is substantially open to its public.

George: "Your one problem that you spoke on briefly is the lack of space, living space for your large population. So you must be very carefully trying to strike this balance between sufficient *living*-space for your population, and sufficient *open*-space for your agriculture—"

~ ***"There is always room to mix the two. We try to live within our nature in natural dwellings these days."***

George: "Ah yes! So you don't build high-rise flats as we do."

~ ***"We prefer to be closer to the ground."***

So despite a space problem, those on Aerah resist the 'block of flats' solution and opt for spreading into the countryside, where they feel comfortable.

~ ***"But you are right, there is not enough room for us, or as much room as we will need in the future as our population grows. But we have plans for other areas such as our moon."***

George: "Yes. We have areas that we have actually reclaimed from the sea. Do you do anything like that?"

~ ***"This is something that we could have tried in the past, but now these things are not considered correct, unless we have—um—some clear advice on this from spirit. The whole of the land is very well managed by the elementals and various beings, and to impose our wills on it to that degree—"***

We indicated a measure of understanding of the relationship with elementals, and after all, their work is the source of clean fuel as well as Aerah's agricultural output. It would weaken the relationship to impose technology or hamper their land management through unilateral decision.

~ ***"But we have in the past created new areas, and we don't rule out doing it again, but it will always be from now on, a consultation with all of the beings involved."***

Clearly, whatever ensues, it will result from democratic decision involving all life forms, and this will chart the good way forward—a true democracy extending beyond just physical beings!

~ ***"And there is always a solution to all of these things when one looks hard enough."***

On Earth, awareness of our spiritual connections is increasing and we made this point; but also that it remains at this time, a minority perception. On Aerah, the connections are of course, *generally* recognised. This is the difference.

~ ***"It is very helpful to have a clearer communication with spirit, but I understand that you are also working on this, and YOU will also get the guidance through to you more clearly."***

George: "Yes, groups such as this are becoming more aware, and this information is being passed to others, and so it spreads."

We moved on to point out that this time of year is a special time when we celebrate Christmas, and asked if Bonniol had information on this from Paul.

~ ***"Yes, we have looked at this in the memories, yes."***

George: "This concerns one of those whom we call 'Master'—Jesus, who was on this Earth. And this is the time when we celebrate his birth. What I was leading to is, we have music associated with this, and can we play you another piece of music?"

~ ***"That would be very good."***

Brief explanation was given of the traditional snowy scenes of Christmastide and the popularity of Bing Crosby. Then the drifting notes of 'White Christmas' filled the room.

~ ***"Thank you! Another interesting song, with a pleasant feeling about it."***

Lilian: "Yes, there *is* actually."

~ ***"I can feel something of your Christmas spirit with that music!"***

George: "Yes, the music does convey a little of that. As I say, Christmas celebrates the time when Jesus was born onto this planet. Do you have anything like that on your planet—the celebration of past masters?"

~ ***"We have special days in our calendar for remembering special people or special times, and I think it is something similar, yes. And these are sometimes excellent days for FEELING THE GOODNESS OF CREATION."***

George: "Yes, nicely expressed!"

It was then time for Bonniol to depart, but he promised to return soon. 'Feeling the goodness of creation' was an excellent note on which to end the session.

But another treat was in store for this evening. Leslie's dear wife Ruth dropped by, speaking through Eileen. She brought Leslie's good wishes, and had learned from him about the Salumet evenings that we now receive. Ruth was 'around' it seems, listening with pleasure to the strains of White Christmas; an old favourite whilst she was on the Earth.

Bonniol, true to his word, returned the following Monday to continue the Christmas theme. This time the room had just a little more light than usual from a small decorated tree in the corner; this for the benefit of a group of young children who visit from spirit each year at this time. They had chatted with enthusiasm about their lives and schooling that continues where they are. Then, after a few words from their teacher and guardian, that doorway closed and Bonniol was able to resume the Christmas dialogue.

~ ***"I'm delighted to be here at this time. It's a beautiful time for you is it not? You celebrate with lots of lights and colours."***

All: "Yes."

~ ***"This is a wise thing to do I think."***

Sarah: "Oh right—"

George: "It is a time of year that many of us enjoy, especially, I think, the children."

~ ***"And it makes you feel more alive does it not?—with all the colours and lights being lit."***

Sarah: "Also, it's a very dull time of year—winter—with no leaves on the trees, and not many flowers, so it makes things a bit jolly."

~ ***"Yes, I am happy that you are feeling jolly."***

We went on to present Bonniol with the pros and cons of this festive period: how it is enjoyed, how it is religious, how it is too commercial, how it can be exhausting, and how it has been influenced from much earlier pre-Christian times. It all must have sounded rather confusing.

~ ***"Well it's something that has maybe given you hope, through your dark periods. Even if the purpose for it is a bit confused by people, the overall flavour of it is positive."***

All agreed, with the feeling that our friend actually understood the complexity of our Christmas. Amazing!

~ ***"So, it's a good festival I would think."***

Sarah: "And people are thinking of other people—even in the buying of presents that we give, even in the giving of a card.

~ ***"There are some festivals that do not have a positive feel to them—this one does!"***

Sarah: "Were you thinking of *our* festivals when you say that, or were you thinking of other planets?"

~ ***"I was mainly thinking of YOUR festivals that I have acquainted myself with."***

Bonniol may well have had in mind Guy Fawkes or the way we celebrate Halloween, for example. These we must concede have negative overtones.

George: "Yes, although this festival has its commercial side, there is also a great depth of feeling and tradition associated with it."

~ ***"Yes, the history of it is important I suppose, but the main thing is the thoughts that are generated from it today, and how it provides a focus for us all to be as one—even if it's for only one day, that's a bit of progress."***

All: "Yes!

Sarah: "And one nice thing, you can go for a walk and it's often free of traffic."

~ ***"It gives people a chance to—"***

Lilian: "To wind down."

~ ***"Yes!"***

Sarah: "I think that even burglars—they don't work on Christmas Day!"

As we laughed, Bonniol added:

~ ***"Breaking all barriers!"***

Eileen: "Do you have a main festival that *you* celebrate?"

~ ***"We have quite a few days of our calendar—um—there are about seven main festivals in our year, but they have all become similar now, though in the past, they were associated with different things. But now, our festivals all have a similar theme to them—that of CELEBRATING LIFE. We've learnt that the power of thought is the important thing. So whereas in the past, some of the festivals***

were 'tainted' with struggles and in some ways negative thoughts, we've changed them—made them into CELEBRATIONS OF LIFE, so that the festivals become generators of thought, like a prayer."

It was suggested that Earth might usefully follow that example, since many of our holidays are simply time-off-from-work or 'freedom days'. Perhaps it would be good to inject more feelings about celebrating life.

~ ***"But it feels as if you have already made these links. They just need reinforcement."***

It was elegantly put and seemed to wind up the discussion rather well. Next, we asked a question, about Bonniol's senses, pointing out that he has been able to use Paul's ears: "Can you also see with Paul's eyes?"

~ ***"I COULD do, yes. We prefer to keep them closed initially, because it could be a distraction. They COULD be opened."***

George: "So it would be possible to observe the little tree with its lights in the corner of the room. This is something that we do at Christmas time. Most houses have a little tree with decorations and lights."

~ ***"Yes, I've been looking at it through the memories of this one—I understand."***

George: "Yes, I appreciate your chosen method of viewing it via the memories. But I just wondered if it was possible with the eyes, and you've answered my question. That's interesting. Thank you."

~ ***"It would be nice to open them. I feel it is still a little early to experiment with another sense."***

George: "Yes, I understand."

~ ***"Each sense is another thing to adjust to—to get used to, and we are still finding plenty of adjustments to be made with other senses."***

This was interesting, and begins to illustrate how Bonniol operates. Perhaps it is for him a little like watching recorded film as opposed to live theatre. He sees it all, but indirectly.

We declared at this point that it is wonderful to be asking questions of Bonniol as we do, but does he have questions for us?

~ ***"We always have questions—if I can find the words this time. You have your astronauts, I understand?"***

Sarah: "Yes, we do."

~ ***"And they have explored your moon, but they are unable to go as far as your other planets. We feel that your astronauts are not bringing you the full picture of space."***

Now that was interesting because Salumet had said something similar. That had been ten years earlier, during our meeting of 3rd April 1995. His words on that occasion were: ~ **"Your space travellers have much knowledge that has been kept under wraps—their knowledge is much more extended—fuller—than has been permitted to the ordinary people."**

Well, that was clearly stated. Bonniol now carefully explained the nature of that withheld information: ~ ***"When you fly from one planet to another or to the moon, there are some wonderful lights, well not quite lights, layers—layers?—around the planet."***

I asked: "Would 'aura' be a good word?"

~ ***"Yes, that is a word we could use here, yes. But its character would have these layers, more easily visible when you are flying away from them or towards them. They should be visible with the naked eye from your spaceships, and they would not perhaps be photographed. We are surprised that this one (Paul), does not have information on this (in his memory)—the auric patterns around your Earth, that your spacemen have or may have observed."***

Such data might well have been withheld and I explained: "We are aware that we have silly politics at times. And we are aware that a number of items would be called 'classified information'. That means that it becomes a closely guarded secret, guarded by a political faction. We are all aware that this happens. We all of us in this group would agree with you wholeheartedly, that it is surprising that such information is not made readily available. It sounds from your description that it is, or would be for us, joyful knowledge to have."

~ ***"It is one of the most beautiful parts of journeying, to see the colours unfold around each planet, and it gives you a sense that these planets are ALIVE."***

We asked: "Are you able to say anything about the significance of the layered light around the planets? Is that part of their 'spiritual light' or part of their natural make-up?"

~ ***"Yes, it is part of their spiritual light, but it is so strong that, unlike the aura of the people, it is more visible. It is on a much larger scale."***

George: "I see. Something that has been mentioned in our Salumet evenings has been the 'spiritual light of the sun'. As the sun gives out much physical light as well, I imagine that it would be nothing like as visible as for the planets?"

~ ***"The sun's auric field would also be a magnificent arrangement of colours, and we are also able to observe these stars from our spaceships, though when we are too close to them, we are disturbed by the physical light."***

George: "And that would obscure the spiritual light—"

~ ***"Yes, our physical eyes would be unable to look."***

George: "Are you saying that the spiritual light is more visible from a great distance?"

~ ***"From a great distance it is still possible to observe the spiritual light, yes, and the further you are away, the fainter it becomes. So there is an ideal distance, when the physical is not obscuring the spiritual light."***

Eileen: "Are you able to pick up through Paul, *our* individual auric colours, or is that not possible at the moment?"

~ ***"If I were to open my eyes—Paul's eyes—I would see through his physical system, which would NOT detect your auric colours."***

George: "You would see exactly as Paul would see."

Eileen: "Could you not use the spiritual eye to see?"

~ ***"I would not be able to use spiritual eyes. I would be able to see with MY spiritual eyes, but this would be a little more complicated than it sounds. I would have to momentarily disconnect from this one. It could disrupt the connection."***

Eileen: "Well we wouldn't want you to do that!"

~ ***"But when we improve, I am hoping to be able to do more than I can at this time."***

George: "Going back to the astronauts—I have read some material, and I know that at least one on the mission, found it a deeply moving experience, that has changed his life. He has become a more spiritually-orientated person, which may well connect with what you have just told us."

Lilian: "Maybe he saw the lights or something else—"

~ ***"It would be very strange if the astronauts had not been touched."***

Lilian: "I think they all were in different ways, from what I have read."

~ ***"Perhaps if they send more into space you will get a better picture."***

George: "I'm beginning to feel that perhaps there is some useful outcome from mechanical space exploration after all!"

Eileen: "Or perhaps we should all mind travel—"

George: "It's so much more productive!" and all had to agree that!

After the pause that followed, it seemed a good time to again offer music, which Bonniol welcomed. A story was attached, and there had already been reference to politics: "Going back 56 years, there were some very silly politics—the Cold War between Eastern- and Western-Blocs. Early in the Cold War period, Paul Robeson had sung a number of songs at the now legendary Moscow Concert, Tchaikovsky Hall; 14th June 1949. The event should have improved East-West relations, but sadly it just became another political issue. Robeson was an interesting figure with world-acclaimed rich bass voice, born of plantation slave stock, had parts in films, and now he became a political dissident with confiscated passport. A concert recording was not known in the West until a tape turned up 46-years later." We now played 'Ol' Man River' from a copy of that tape that had finally come to light. The ovation he received was also on the tape. It went on for quite some time, and we faded out part of that.

~ ***"It sounded like a very popular song!"***

Eileen: "A very meaningful song at the time I think."

~ ***"Certainly a voice that is very different from what I have heard. I am probably not hearing it as YOU would, because these things take time tuning, but it was an INTERESTING one, and I understand a little of what you mean by the politics."***

It was explained that the concert had been appreciated by many people at that time who wanted a more peaceful, overt world, in which East and West would have cultural exchange and could move closer together.

~ ***"And sometimes these messages are best given through music. It can certainly reach many people."***

Lilian: "All people."

~ ***"Yes, it is a favoured method of the spiritual realms I think. But they work with musicians when they find politicians a bit blocked—but they try all avenues. That I am sure you know from (the) teachings here."***

George: "Yes and there's many a good message in the music and the songs that are written."

~ ***"Yes, and the music also lifts us to great heights—even when we don't understand the message. So it really is a powerful art. We are anxious not to be too long, so if it is a good time to finish then perhaps we should, and leave it to next time."***

Bonniol was assured that we are very happy to be guided by him in this and we said how much we had enjoyed his visit as we always do.

~ ***"And I hope you are encouraged by your mind projection practice and I'm sure you will make progress."***

George: "We all hope so and thank you again Bonniol, and thank you support team, we so enjoy your visits."

There were general heartfelt thanks and Bonniol declared it to be wonderful for them to visit.

This communication brings us to the year end, closing in a way this first phase of a fantastic adventure. The Christmas period is embraced and regardless of our confused motivations for this festival, it is as stated, a wonderful time for 'Celebration of Life'; also as has been stated, we are at a turning point in the affairs of this planet. It will doubtless be easier to see this later in retrospect. New energies will begin to prevail as our friend returns in the New Year and Earthly life patterns change.

CHAPTER: 24

In Perspective – What Does It All Mean? – And What Next?

We have been experiencing a journey into the unknown using the only mode of travel available for such a journey. We have benefited from our dear friend's capability to mind-link and what we have experienced is clearly not a journey in the ordinary world-view sense. Yet it still has that kind of feel about it. Perhaps we might compare the adventurous mind to a seagoing vessel. In earlier times, ships played their key role in exploring this planet, navigating and charting its vast oceans. Pioneering ones who sailed had the support of others in the dockyards, at naval command, financiers, king and country and more. Many helped in so many ways. Discoveries of new lands followed and the fresh ports of call multiplied whilst, at the conclusion of each voyage, ship and crew sought home and safe harbour. There was on occasion the added interest of passengers picked up along the way. These were exciting and illuminating times. There was soon an accumulation of news and new facts; always important, and so much more so, compared to any material commodities brought back. The increasing knowledge ever grew and flourished. Its growth continued throughout the old millennium and always held a certain fascination for the seeking mind. Now, in a new phase of exploration, we chart the universe.

Mind travel, mind projection across the cosmos, is equally a voyage of discovery bearing some semblance to those earlier maritime ventures. As to ports of call, the planetary possibilities are quite numerous. News and new knowledge remain prime merchandise for those who seek. As with charting an ocean, mind travellers have support teams in attendance. There are many helpers. These are important and remain a necessary feature. Passengers too, may be picked up along the way to be introduced and speak their histories. Each mind-voyage is concluded by return to safe harbour—of the physical being whence it came. In general principle there is so much to compare with those earlier ocean voyages.

Huge differences of detail there must also be of course, on account of mind being not of this material realm, but of spirit; the ocean sailed is both timeless and trackless, yet embracing all bounds and backwaters of the physical creation, even beyond what may be observed by astronomers. This is hard to take in. But spirit is like an ocean in that it adjoins each and every planet and those who dwell thereon, and all connections are by instant mind thought. Thought is truly universal both in scope and in the knowing; void of language, instantaneous and limitless in reach. It utilises precious connections. Physical brain is the incredible converter of universal thought to appropriate word language that can then be uttered, and that brain process with word selection might then just take a second or so.

It is most fortunate for 21st-century humanity that, firstly Salumet should choose this time to teach the fundamentals of existence, and secondly that he should arrange the Bonniol link to bring home to us awareness of our connection to the further reaches of creation. As I write (2008-9), I am happy to report that the visits of both Salumet and Bonniol continue. In fact, much more has already transpired, so that 'Part Two' of 'The Chronicles' builds fast. Part Two includes new facts on space-travel, UFOs, black holes and wormholes; and data on other planetary beings and how one culture in particular has visited Earth in our prehistory leaving petro-glyphic record in the Nevada Desert, and there have been astounding clairvoyant presentations of Aeran scenes to two of our team. There is lengthy description of the subtle nature of the orientated pyramid shape, how it is understood by others and utilised; and fascinating details on the origin of those first pyramids in Egypt. There are facts pertaining to the origin of Halloween and that festival's connection to Earth energy. And so, it has become clearly evident that as we learn more of the universe around us we cannot but help acquire a more complete understanding of our own planet. But these details are of course dwarfed by the fuller realisation of the immensity of all existence, that wider universal picture and our place within the boundless heavens. As we navigate this current TURNING POINT of Earthly progress, it is inevitable that humanity becomes much more aware of its place within all that surrounds.

PART TWO: *Masters, Religions, Space-travel, Pyramids, Cosmic Visits, Clairvoyant Scenes, Creation and the Immensity of All Existence*

To see a World in a grain of sand,
And a Heaven in a wild flower,
Hold Infinity in the palm of your hand,
And Eternity in an hour—

William Blake 1757 - 1827

[Bonniol is about to return in the New Year of 2006, a time that marks a turning point in Earthly affairs. There will soon be profound changes in our living and in the way we regard our planetary home; already to some degree apparent by the time these words are read. It is the advice of both Salumet and Bonniol that we practise *meditation* and *mind projection* amongst ourselves, and with even small success, individual endeavours will open doorways to enhance the spirit. There is much to reflect on as we await the return of our dear friend.]

CHAPTER: 25

A New Year Hiccup – Mind Projection & Materialisation … 2nd … 16th Jan 2006

WE WERE DELIGHTED, also a little surprised as well as apprehensive, to hear Bonniol's cheery 'hello' so soon. This was only the second evening of the New Year. Salumet usually resumes around the middle of the month and not without good reason. Our dear friend declared:

~ ***"Yes, I am waiting just a little time while I make some adjustments—I'm having a few problems again—"***

Lilian: "We can hear you quite clearly."

~ ***"The link is a little different—your world—is a little different this time. There is an atmosphere pervading your world, which clouds things a little for us. But we are adjusting to it."***

George: "Yes, I can imagine that to be so. Please take plenty of time."

In fact, we know that our world's collective consciousness shows marked variation at this time. In recent years this has been demonstrated scientifically and is now well acknowledged. It is one area where experimental results in science, the observations of spirit communicators and the teaching of masters all agree wholeheartedly. And it is wonderful when such widely differing sources of information are in unison. Particular times that show marked changes in the energy of Earth's collective consciousness have been, not surprisingly, the 9 /11 atrocity when worldwide, so many were appalled, and then there have been the end-of-year celebrations, separately registered for each time zone around our planet. These facts are very well accounted in the accepted scientific literature. We explained to Bonniol that there would likely be strange mixtures of both joy as well as depression at this time, all feeding into the system, and this may be creating problems. Following due consideration, our dear friend finally announced: ~ ***"Since the beginning of the communications, we've been developing quite nicely. I think this evening we will depart, because it would be a pity to struggle on—"***

So this first session of the New Year was a hiccup that ended in Bonniol's hasty withdrawal midst two-way interplanetary apologies. And we reiterated that it is both amazing and wonderful that this sequence of dialogue is happening at all. But bearing in mind the known 'festivities factor', we were not surprised and remained confident that Bonniol would return again once stable conditions were restored.

Two weeks later Lilian was saying: "Hello, let's hope you can stay a little longer this time."

~ ***"Hello, yes, I feel the connection is better again this time."***

Lilian: "Yes, there's a nice lot of us here this evening (eleven nicely fills the room), not as many as on your side, but a nice gathering."

~ ***"That's a good beginning for your New Year then—more people."***

George: "Yes indeed. It's good that you have returned again, and that the connection is good. We are very pleased to have you with us. Would you have any feelings about the difficulties last time? Would that have related to the consciousness around our planet?"

~ ***"Yes, it was the vibrations that had changed, because of your holiday time, we were told, yes. But it has returned to a similar vibration as before."***

George: "It is interesting that this happens—interesting that it makes such a difference."

~ ***"Yes, as I have said before, we could have adjusted our link, but it would have been complicated to re-adjust it, when USUALLY your vibration is not changing so much."***

We understood, and clearly Bonniol is a shrewd operator who employs wise strategy. But what happened is especially interesting in view of its fitting so well into the pattern of results from Earth's scientific community, also the teaching received from Salumet. All should of course be in perfect accord where truth prevails, and it certainly is where these known facts of planetary collective consciousness are concerned. It is one area where science and spirituality meet, and any who seek scientific proof of spirit would do well to study the rapidly developing field that issues from random number generator (RNG) and linked-RNG work.

Having dealt with that little matter, there was discussion of our feeble attempts at mind projection. In one series, I had attempted to project images to the group, a different item at 7.30 pm each evening, with little success, but nevertheless *something* was happening. I had sent out round objects on two evenings that Eileen had correctly noted on those two evenings without more specifically identifying either. Another evening, Paul correctly described a shape as a cylinder-with-a-sphere-on-top, without further description to say it was a Russian doll. And on a fourth evening I had projected a living furry cat that was in a friend's house where I happened to be staying. Lilian had correctly described the cat but on the wrong evening! In addition to these items, Bonniol had projected an object *to us from Aerah*.

He explained: ~ ***"I chose a small coin."***

Lilian: "Oh! I got a coin this week, but not last."

~ ***"It was a little of your money, yes."***

Lilian: "Well it came to me rather late!"

~ ***"It was a round, brown coloured coin, a penny I believe—not very much."***

George: "I got something brown, but it was square, so mine was the wrong shape.

Lilian: "Can they stay around so that we pick them up later, much later?"

~ ***"Yes, the thought can remain, in the ether if you like, for a long time. But it depends on how powerful the thought is."***

Lilian: "There you are George! And this has happened before—we have got the object, but not on the day sent. So perhaps we are just a little better than we thought."

So, midst our misses and near-misses, Lilian's cat was a winner and a surprise item since we do not have one at home. We conceded that perhaps there was just a glimmer of something beginning to happen.

~ ***"And if you continue, you will find more than a glimmer. But the projection needs to be clear, and as clear as the real thing, if you like, or even clearer if that's possible. So the thought becomes such a reality in your mind that it is as material, if you like, as a physical thing."***

That sparked a thought in Richard's mind: "Mm, Bonniol—"

~ ***"Yes?"***

Richard: "If you are mind projecting something with extreme clarity, would you be able to *materialise* that object?"

~ ***"We are able to materialise simple objects, yes."***

Richard: "In that way?"

~ ***"In that way, yes—they are visualised, and brought into being through our imagination. The thought is—it becomes a reality in front of our eyes. It begins to appear as we put energy into it. We create the image and we intensify the image, with our energy, until it is intense enough to take form. This intensity develops naturally. As you begin to practise, you may find already, that your visualisations have become a little more intense."***

George: "So materialising—I would see that as a 'stage two'—intensifying the energy that goes into the original picture."

~ ***"It's true that some find it more difficult than the normal thought projection, and not everyone is able to do it."***

George: "When you do this, do you get the precise material that you seek? I mean, do you get a metal or a plastic—a specific metal such as brass or gold? Are you able to materialise particular materials?"

~ ***"The material—well, the object that is visualised becomes what you put into it. If the material is of a certain kind, then that is what develops. That is what takes form. There are more complicated materials, which are harder."***

George: "Suppose you were materialising a piece of furniture and you wanted wood, would you actually have a piece of furniture of wood with the cellular structure that wood has?"

~ ***"We can materialise wood. Wood is an uncomplicated material for us, if you like. The patterns on the wood—the grains—they are something which I think you would say: they are never the same."***

George: "That's right."

~ ***"You will also find that, when you visualise and materialise a piece of wood—strangely, it will always vary in its grain."***

George: "Just like the natural thing!"

~ ***"I think our imaginations understand that variance in nature, and follow it. It is a complicated subject, but it is a—energy transformation."***

Graham: "The amount of energy involved must be enormous. Our scientists have the equation $E = mc^2$, where the energy is equal to mass-times-the-speed-of-light-squared. And just a kilogram of material (quite a small piece of furniture), would require a fantastic amount of energy, and the fact that you are able to materialise the thing in front of your eyes—"

George: "I suppose the universe just has an *enormous* amount of energy—"

~ ***"And it all comes down to your thoughts having an unlimited amount—well they are limited to all of us—and yet we understand that there IS no limit."***

George: "That is what our teacher is always telling us (that thought is immensely powerful)."

Graham: "When you manifest an object, does it gradually appear, or does it just suddenly appear?"

~ ***"It is not quite instant. It can take form quickly. Again, it would be as far as the thought process of the person getting the energy in—how quickly they manage to intensify their thoughts to the right degree."***

Richard: "The energy that's put into materialising the object, is that drawn from the person doing it or from a different source?"

~ ***"It is an energy that comes THROUGH us. It does not deplete us."***

George: "Uh—it is the universal energy that you are organising. Would that be correct?"

~ ***"It's a spiritual energy—the energy of thought, which is not limited like our physical bodies."***

Richard: "Are you able to materialise in a different place, other than in front of you?"

~ ***"WE cannot materialise things in other places, but it is possible. There are other planets where they would have the ability to do this. I am able to materialise objects in front of me. To materialise them elsewhere would confuse me too much. It would involve two sets of images and merging them together."***

Richard: "Would the link be strong enough to materialise something here?"

~ ***"I have anticipated that question! IT WOULD BE POSSIBLE, AND I WOULD LIKE TO TRY!"***

To the exclamations of surprise and wonder that followed, I simply added: "The mind boggles!"

~ ***"I am being instructed to tell you that the time will come when they will permit me to try."***

So the guides would in due course allow an attempted materialisation! Now this could be interesting. If an object foreign to our world were materialised, it might just convince a sceptic or two of the reality of these communications. The thought was voiced and Bonniol replied: ~ ***"You will never convince people unless they WANT to be convinced."***

George: "Yes, I imagine that's very true."

~ ***"This would be something that we could do, or try to do, it would not be of huge benefit to anyone here, because to see someone else do it—(it) will give you added validity of it—but will not help you unless you practise yourselves. That is the point. We come together to help each other, and for you to know that this is possible."***

George: "Yes, that must be our aim. That is the first thing that you said: that we help each other. We also have a second motivation—to put whatever we manage to learn, before other people in this world, so that they in turn have the opportunity to understand. And I was just thinking that, if an object that is alien to our thinking were produced, it might possibly start people thinking more seriously. But, as you say, the first thing is that we should help each other in our understanding."

There followed a brief pause, then Jan, who had missed some earlier sessions ventured: "I can't help wondering why, if you are able to project thought, why you are not able to pick up our thoughts instantly—"

~ ***"Yes, I've mentioned before, that I am communicating to you now, through this one's (Paul's) senses. I am hearing you through these ears, which are linking with my own senses."***

In fact, what follows had been explained briefly in an earlier meeting, but now there is further embellishment. A little repetition can be useful: firstly it verifies what has gone before, and secondly, it may result in extra details being given, as in this instance.

George: "It's all via Paul, and this is the connection to us all."

Jan: "This is the connection—Paul. So if Paul were to pick up something while he was being controlled, are you then able to pick up Paul's thoughts?"

~ ***"I can pick up all the memories—the thoughts that HAVE occurred. I cannot pick up anything that is not yet in memory."***

Jan: "Why?"

~ ***"We do not have a direct link to your thoughts."***

Lilian: "That wouldn't be permitted would it?"

Jan: "So your connection would be via spirit—"

~ ***"It (a direct link to thought) is not something that we have available. So the only way we can communicate at this time, is through projecting to one of your people and using it (the link) to communicate."***

Lilian: "So whatever you do is controlled mainly by spirit—"

~ ***"We are governed by spiritual laws—spiritual guidance."***

At this point the link suddenly terminated, again we were reminded of the fragility of connection that has to depend on so many factors; not least the consciousness surrounding Earth. This might well still have a gremlin or two left behind from the festivities. But nevertheless, the session had run along quite smoothly to this point, the exchanges had progressed a little further and we were so grateful.

CHAPTER: 26

More on Music and Materialisation ... 23rd January 2006

BONNIOL WAS WITH us again the following Monday: ~ ***"Hello again—I am glad to be here again. I apologise for the last time. The link—communication—broke suddenly did it not?"***

George: "It did, yes, and we're delighted to see you again, and we realise that, of course, these things will sometimes happen. And we apologise too, that we were unable to say our proper 'goodbyes'. But it was a very good session that we had."

~ ***"There is still some improvement to make in the communication, but it is all coming along well, I think."***

Lilian: "I think we're all still rather amazed by everything."

~ ***"The process should not amaze you so much now, I think."***

How true! It was becoming more familiar all the time, and we were so much more accepting that this exchange happens within our midst. It was real, not just some weird echo from a substrate of consciousness. Too many terrestrially-unthinkable ideas, too many astounding surprises, and altogether too many bridges crossed, for this to be linked to any stratum of own personality. A wonderful reality this most certainly was, still is, and continues to be, at every twist and unexpected turn.

~ ***"You have had much information about the POWER OF THOUGHT, I understand—"***

We explained a little of Salumet's teaching on this and how his words had often been repeated for emphasis. It was a central pillar of the teaching as received.

~ ***"And this is only one of many ways that you can use your thoughts. They are as your master says: the most important things you have."***

George: "Yes indeed. I think we can say, they are our reality—our ongoing reality."

~ ***"There will be hopefully, much (many) more chances for you to practise with your mind projection. And I am sure you will make progress, yes."***

George: "Well, this is certainly something that we shall continue."

Sarah: "Yes, we have been—"

Sarah explained that instead of projecting to each other last week, we had been projecting an object to Bonniol, and wondered if he had got it. Our friend seemed thrown by this, and there followed a lengthy pause, and then with some hesitation: ~ ***"You sent a thought to me—"***

As the pause lengthened, I began to work things through: "I think the thought would have to be picked up by Paul, and then in turn, *if* he has picked it up, then I would think *you* would have to find it in his memory. I think it would work like that. Please correct me if—"

~ ***"Your thoughts, if they were directed to Paul, they MAY BE in his memory. This is not so straightforward for me to work through."***

I realised we had made a boo-boo. Hunting through memory banks for a trivial thought that might only possibly be there would be rather like failing to find the proverbial needle in a haystack! This was not a good idea! Bonniol went on: ~ ***"If you direct your thoughts to me, then we can see how well you are forming them. You will need to think of me rather than the instrument. I will 'turn my ear'—that is probably not the right way to say it. I will be waiting."***

(Equally, it would be wrong to say: put an ear to the ground. That would not work! Perhaps a new expression is needed for interplanetary work: putting ear to ether?)

Graham: "In trying to project our thoughts to you, should we think of your name, Bonniol, and just project our thoughts towards your name?"

~ ***"You can to start with, yes, but try to think of ME a little bit in connection with that name."***

Lilian: "Would it help if we picture a different planet?"

~ "You don't need to visualise. You can FEEL with your mind what you understand by the word 'Bonniol'. And remember, there are many who are helping to direct your thoughts, as your postman directs your mail. As long as your address is clear, it should make its delivery."

Sarah: "TO BONNIOL – PLANET AERAH!"

Our laughter concluded that topic, and it was time for a fresh one. Bonniol had spoken previously of his group, consisting of family and friends, and we asked if it included some of his children.

~ "Yes, we have several generations with us usually."

George: "Yes, that's as it is with us. Your instrument Paul is my son, and the second to your left is Sara who is Paul's sister. And the next one is Natalie who is with us tonight, and she is my granddaughter. So there are three generations."

~ "Yes, I said I think once before, we have MUCH in common."

George: "We certainly have! And another thing that is on my mind—we haven't played you any music on the last two occasions. Would you like a piece now?"

~ "Of course—yes, I would!"

It was a surprise item—a track from one of Sara's home-produced CDs, with Sara singing, playing keyboard, and she composed it too. I had not fixed it with Sara, so there were a few surprise giggles from that corner! It was a new piece, and there were nice comments all round.

~ "Thank you! I LIKED that one!"

George: "'This is Your Life' it was."

~ "The vibration was good—A LOVELY song!"

Sara: "I'm glad you enjoyed it."

~ "This music of your Earth has much to it I think. We have plenty of music on our world. Somehow I feel we take it for granted a little bit now. There is lovely music on our planet, but I've become more interested in yours of late."

Again we had to smile as Lilian said: "We sometimes get used to the sound of music and forget to listen."

George: "One can get mentally lost with it sometimes. Is the music on your planet carefully composed, with repetition in the process, or is it more spontaneous with you?"

~ ***"Some prefer to be spontaneous, and others prefer to compose it gradually piece by piece, and work on it that way. It depends on the individual."***

Sarah: "Do your composers write down the piece? Do they write? Or is there some other way?"

~ ***"There are those who like to develop it slowly and usually write it, yes. Others prefer to let the music flow through them, more spontaneously."***

Sarah: "Do you have paper, or what do you write on?"

~ ***"We have something a little different, more like a block of plastic—something like that—which records the words and can be rubbed off or saved. It does not involve wastage—something like a computer, but it is more easy to use. It is convenient for scribbling down information."***

In reply to further questions, Bonniol elaborated: ~ ***"You need a writing pen, yes. It is like a pen and a book, but the book is electronic, and it records the scribbles or words, and can be used again and again."***

Lilian: "Do your animals make musical sounds?"

~ ***"Each of our animals has its own sound, yes."***

We went on to speak of purring cats and birdsong, and the way parrots can mimic.

~ ***"We have birds and another group of animals, which produce fabulous sounds. They may be like your flamingos, with long necks. They are long and thin, but they make a beautiful song, yes."***

There was more on sounds and our dawn chorus—and we moved on to enquire about instruments: ~ ***"I think the instruments are not so different. We have blowing ones and the stringed ones. They all vibrate in different ways."***

We agreed that it is all, of course, vibration.

~ ***"And the singing is very popular. It is a shame we cannot share OUR music."***

All: "Yes!"

~ ***"It is a difficult thing to try to—um—explain our music, when the easiest way would be to play it for you. But at this point we cannot share it in that way. It would be much better if we could***

bring some of our musicians through, but unfortunately we are not at that stage."

To materialise a CD came as an attractive idea, but we were quickly assured that approach would not work. But this led to a further thought on materialisation, and we asked if Aerah has a monetary system with coins as we have.

~ ***"No, we HAVE had coins but not now."***

George: "No, so they would be museum pieces now, would they?"

~ ***"Yes."***

Sarah: "So what system do you use?"

~ ***"It is all via—um—cards, yes. There is no currency."***

George: "Yes, of course, we often use plastic credit cards as well, so that's another similarity that we have."

I went on to enquire if it might be possible to materialise for us, one of Aerah's old coins, and then, would that coin have the energy density of Aerah or Earth?

~ ***"The coin would be of MY planet, yes."***

It was explained that this might be interesting, and we could ask some scientists to do a spectrographic analysis. If the metal did not agree with Earthly atomic weight tables, this would at first be viewed as impossible, but where might this then lead? It would almost certainly result in some raised eyebrows and hard thinking on the matter.

~ ***"It would have some peculiar aspects to it, for THIS planet. And it may be interesting to have it analysed. But there are always people who would dismiss it."***

Perhaps Bonniol was beginning to sense that trait of human nature that tends to dismiss all things supernatural or not fitting into accepted natural pattern. I ventured that it would be very nice to have two coins so that one could go for analysis and the other we keep for reference. There were a few titters and Bonniol said: ~ ***"I will try to do this for you."***

I replied that perhaps this would have to be later when the link becomes stronger.

~ ***"It is partly the link and partly timing. Everything has to be done according to when we are told the time is right. We are***

not absolutely sure that we will be successful, but the possibility (prospect) is good, and one way of sharing our world with yours. But there are things that I cannot share."

There was further discussion on information exchange and how it has to be within the limits set by spirit protocol. Earth and Aerah are both learning planets after all, and much learning potential would simply be lost if every answer to every problem were freely exchanged. There obviously must be some limitation, and in any event, none would wish to infringe spirit formality. Then Bonniol was saying:.~ ***"Hopefully much more can be given. I will leave now, and say 'goodbye' properly!"***

And this time we all said our proper goodbyes and thanked Bonniol, his team and family.

CHAPTER: 27

A Realisation of togetherness – Spaceless Minds ... 30th Jan – 27th Feb 2006

UNCERTAINTIES REMAINED, THE link stayed fragile into February. Two visits terminated with only brief exchange, with time to discuss our poor attempts to mind project simple objects for Bonniol to identify. There were two main problems: firstly our inability to visualise clear, sharp images and secondly Bonniol's doubtful recognition of Earthly fruit. Yes, we tried sending him fruit! But he correctly declared an orange that we sent, to be a fruit. It was a ripe 'orange-coloured' orange but it apparently arrived 'green'. This led to an interesting short exchange on colour perception and Graham asked if Aerans see the same colours as we do.

~ ***"You have seven main colours, yes?"***

Graham: "Yes, that's right."

~ ***"Yes, we have the same—seven."***

There were exclamations of surprise.

~ ***"There will be variations I think. But the seven main colours are usually the ones that we physical beings are able to perceive. There are other colours of course, but these are far more difficult to see, with these physical eyes."***

There was more on infra red and ultra violet and how some Earthly creatures can see into these regions but then followed a sudden loss of connection.

The next time, a useful exchange developed on the nature of mind in mind projection. Bonniol was reiterating useful tips for enhancing image clarity and was saying that our minds would become more proficient. I added: "When we project our mind, would I be right in saying that what we call 'the subconscious', is just a small part of mind that stays with our brain. But when we project mind, I imagine there is a major part that gets projected—but a little bit gets left behind? Would you have anything to say on that?"

Bonniol corrected my thinking in an interesting and forthright way: ~ ***"Yes, the projection is not really through space. Our minds stay where they are. And yet they are projected in a sense. BUT IT IS NOT A PHYSICAL PROJECTION. This (projection) is a word, but it is not used in that way."***

George: "In a way, it is more of a connection than a projection—"

~ ***"Yes, that would be nearer. The mind links with another mind but there is no travelling involved, which is why it is instant. The link cannot have any physical space to travel through."***

It is such a simple bold statement that nevertheless says all. One of our problems is of course that we are so conditioned into physical thought pattern, but mind is not physical. Hence our dilemma—we are tempted to think physically but there is no physical space separating minds. Bonniol continued: ~ ***"Yes, it is mind-to-mind. And we are even closer than you realise when we cut through the physical aspect."***

Sarah: "The trouble is we think physically, and we *need* to think spiritually."

It occurred to me at this point that there is exactly the same problem in the way most of us see the 'big bang' idea. It was a clumsy question to put into words, but I felt it would be good to seek our friend's opinion on that particular fundamental issue. So I ventured: "Our scientists have deduced that it (the universe) began with a singularity or point source. I appreciate that spirit has no time or space—and a singularity has no time or space. But it's just begun to dawn I think, that minds that connect, are not involved with space. And it seems very like the singularity that has been deduced. So perhaps our scientists were not so far wrong in making that deduction. For 'singularity' we should read simply 'spirit', which also has no time or space, and in a way, is like a point source. Does that make any sense?"

I hoped Bonniol would not be thrown by such an involved and poorly presented question. He was not. And after some deliberation, replied: ~ ***"Yes, I believe you are thinking in the right way."***

Sarah: "And Salumet has just been saying the experience is instantaneous when you've got your mind projection friend."

~ ***"Yes, the spiritual communication needs all the mind. It has shown you are all together in one place regardless of distance—just as if you are with us at all times, regardless of where we are. And we have to almost ignore our physical surroundings and realise that we are never far away from anyone."***

We just about understood and acknowledged, and there followed a brief pause, then Bonniol was saying: ~ ***"I think, for this time, I will withdraw. But I have been very pleased to have been here again."***

We were likewise pleased—no, that was an understatement! And there remained time for fond farewells. The session had again been brief but nevertheless had produced a wonderfully significant realisation. It is one thing to give lip service to the idea that spirit has no space dimensions. But the plain truth is: we are mind, and mind is indeed spirit, and so, we are all of us 'together'. In mind projection there is no space to travel. There is no space for mind to project across. It follows that 'mind projection' is really a misnomer, just a term we use. It is a very physical expression that we have derived from human physical reason. This session has brought home to us this reality. 'Projection' is just a word, as Bonniol says (as also is 'singularity'). One more thought must be added: if the creation began with a singularity, then that space-less singularity continues and all our minds are within it! But of course, there is and has to be some form of separation of entities within that spirit or singularity or whatever we choose to call it. All we have to get our heads around is that it is not a 'spatial' separation, and if we think about it, even in the material world there are alternative separators to 'space'. Television transmissions for example, are able to coexist within themselves on account of their different frequencies. Different frequencies stay individual even if they occupy the same space. So it should be clear to 21st-century humanity that space is in no way essential as a means of separating. Perhaps we should see this as a fundamental principle that has come to our notice in recent years. And this should help us to understand that space is not a mandatory factor where other dimensions are concerned.

The following week we met and sat in silence for half an hour while nothing seemed to happen. This was unusual in the extreme. But one cannot make predictions where séance evenings are concerned; even so, such a long silence in Lilian's room is most unusual. Paul appeared to be 'away', and so Lilian approached.

~ ***"Hello."***

Lilian: "Hello."

~ ***"I have been here a while, but I wasn't planning to speak much this time."***

Lilian: "I see."

~ ***"It has been a useful period to build up the connection—I'm still working on improving things and it has helped to sit quietly this time."***

George: "Yes, we've had a quiet evening so far, which is unusual."

~ ***"Sometimes the quiet moments are when the main things happen."***

George: "Yes. Are you happy to speak now, or do you wish to continue working?"

~ ***"Yes, I would like to continue quietly."***

We indicated that we understood and thanked our friend who continued in silence with Paul.

More minutes passed and a control came through Sarah who spoke of 'conditions' being difficult this evening. We know from experience that this happens. (A physical equivalent of adverse conditions might be the way electric storms sometimes make radio communication difficult or impossible.) Salumet arrived later and greeted us with the words: ~ **"As always my dear friends, there is a purpose and a reason behind all that occurs within this room. This evening has had its purpose. It has had a purpose, not only for your selves but for those in our world. As we come into this silence together, so many expectations await you, not only from this side of life but from yours, and without each other these meetings would not occur. It is I feel, most apt for you all to learn that we**

from our world cannot be summoned at will—that sometimes 'conditions', as you have been told, are more difficult."

Salumet went on to remind us that love is an essential factor in these exchanges, and assured that this remains in plentiful supply. But the learning to be had from this unusual evening with its silent periods is the recognition that we cannot take for granted, those who join with us from spirit—that we must always observe. In conclusion, I am delighted to report that adverse conditions cleared, and Bonniol's efforts working in silence, indeed built up the connection. Both he and Salumet were able to join with us for full sessions the following week.

CHAPTER: 28

An Evolving Universal Pattern – Salumet Explains … 6th March 2006

SALUMET CAME THROUGH at the start of our meeting; as always, with topics of great interest, but he also referred back to last time when he spoke at the end, saying how he had been amused that we should have recognised the evening as 'unusual'. But he hoped we had thought on the information given.

Now, as is more 'usual', Bonniol followed Salumet. Lilian now enquired of Bonniol how his 'journey' was this time: ~ ***"It was better, thank you."***

And there were general appreciative sounds as Bonniol continued:

~ ***"I had a very easy entry."***

Graham: "Is that because conditions have returned to what they were, or have you managed to adjust?"

~ ***"I believe conditions have returned, and we are also improving our links all the time."***

Lilian: "I'm sure you do."

~ ***"It's always a beautiful experience for us."***

Lilian: "And for us!"

George: "Mm—yes!"

Lilian: "And you are much more used to it than we are!"

Our friend hesitated a little before replying: ~ ***"It is something that we never really get used to."***

And one instinctively knows that to be a good honest answer. There followed brief mention of our meagre attempts at mind projection. Our friend had received only unidentifiable shadowy forms, and being foreign as well as fuzzy made it doubly difficult. We left it that he will say if he notices a clear image one day. It is good that our friend has patience. And Rod had tried sending a watering can, which threw up the piece of information that they too use them. But happily, dialogue continued smoothly.

Sarah: "It seems to be a very good connection this time Bonniol. Do you feel it is better?"

~ ***"Yes, I have had a little bit of quiet time with this one and I think it has helped this time—improving the link. We are improving each time, and it should become more varied. The communications may become more interesting as we get the sort of link we are hoping for. It is always hard to talk about more unusual things at the beginning. We have had to be patient, and discuss things that we are familiar with. Hopefully we will be able to broaden our communications."***

George: "Well, so far we've had a wonderful mixture, of science and philosophy, music and poetry—an incredible mixture, of living things and industry, legal system—quite fascinating!"

~ ***"Yes, these are all topics which are familiar to you. We also have much that will not be familiar, and we hope to share a little of that."***

Graham indicated that that would be most welcome and I attempted to outline a general picture that had emerged thus far from our exchanges: "Spirit—mind of God—however one wishes to define it—extends throughout the universe, and is an influence throughout the entire universe, so that both our planets are subject to the influence of this all-pervading spirit / mind. So it is not surprising really that there are so many similarities within our cultures. There are the joys of understanding music, literature and theatre. It seems so natural that we have such similarities—"

Sarah added: "It is understandable, but if you think about the 'mushroom people'—they would I expect be quite different."

~ ***"Yes."***

George: "But they might be similar in the things that connect to spirit."

And Lilian observed: "Yes, I see what you mean George."

~ ***"Yes, the—(pause)—the word eludes me for the moment—but the way of spirit defines itself in the various worlds of matter—um—there is always the truth that comes to the surface in all worlds. But***

the patterns, if you like, are incredibly varied. It's the various ways of getting to that truth that defies the imagination."

George: "I think that evolution comes into it. We evolve in different directions or with emphasis on different things as we evolve. So perhaps, where we have differences, it arises out of the ways in which we evolve."

~ ***"Yes, the evolving is your pathway, the road that you take to your final destination."***

I reflected with a hint of sadness: "In recent years, we've evolved in the direction of materialism, whereas you have evolved on your planet much more in the direction of nature, recognition of nature spirits and—"

~ ***"When you become aware of them, it becomes natural to work with them."***

Sarah: "Has your planet gone through a period where it was materialistic like us?"

~ ***"It was once very materialistic, in a slightly different way of course to the way yours has grown. Each person is different, and each planet is equally different, in the way it displays its material nature. It would seem strange probably, to talk about how we display our material natures. But when you look at your past civilisations, they also displayed it in different ways to today, did they not?"***

George: "Yes. Just looking back 100-years, we were closer to nature and farming economy then, and in the UK, one small farm might have had ten people working on it, whereas today, that same small farm would have only one person organising a lot of machinery to actually do the work. So in that sense, we have moved away from agriculture and nature."

~ ***"Yes, machines have in some ways—cut you off from the land experience."***

Sarah: "Yes, and in cooking, you used to use your hands a lot more to make things—we now use machines, so that contact with the raw materials is again taken away."

George: "And we are not preparing the food with love in quite the same way—"

This was the moment when Lilian looked across and noticed Eileen's hand movements. It was clear that Salumet remained with us and now wished to speak. And I think we had all forgotten that Salumet still worked quietly with Eileen on this occasion. So Lilian asked: "Can I just see if Salumet wishes to say anything?"

There was a brief pause and Salumet spoke: ~ **"Thank you. I apologise for this intrusion."**

Now there is no established etiquette to meet the occasion of a 'light-being master' joining an interplanetary dialogue; it is unusual!!! A few words seemed necessary and I found myself inadequately saying: "You are most welcome!"

~ **"I wish to say just one thing—and Bonniol does not have the knowledge which can tell you about the connection between all planets and spirit. There is a simple explanation, and I will put it to you thus: the unifying bond between spirit and all matter, no matter what that form of matter is, is LOVE and PERFECTION. That is what every planet strives for and that is the unifying bond."**

Lilian: "It seems simple when you say it."

~ **"Bonniol was struggling to define that question, so I do apologise to him. But I felt it was a point to be clarified."**

George: "Wonderful!"

~ **"I will now leave you once more."**

George: "Could I just suggest that that bond then leads to or is responsible for there being many similarities between cultures on different planets?"

~ **"The love consciousness is what connects you no matter what, whether you be human form, vegetable form or whatever. And it shows in the vegetable form as perfection in the way that it tries to grow and demonstrate itself. Do you understand?"**

Lilian: "Yes."

George: "Thank you so much for that."

~ **"But every planet is striving towards the same goal."**

And Bonniol added his thanks as Salumet withdrew:

~ ***"Thank you! That clarifies it for me too!"***

Lilian said quietly: "It's very simple."

I think it would be correct to say that we were awed by this event and spoke rather quietly for some considerable time. We had in an earlier session voiced the thought that it would be nice for Bonniol to visit when Salumet was with us. Now we had experienced exactly that, and Bonniol summed up with:

~ ***"Three ways—a truly very interesting evening!"***

I was later saying: "So where do we go from here? Are there any questions you'd like to ask us, or would you like us to ask you questions?"

There was a pause as Bonniol considered previous dialogue. He wished to come clean on a small point: ~ ***"I would like to be a little more—frank—about some of our—um—peoples. I think you have an idea that our world is perfection in many ways. And I have told you that we have different problems—of overpopulation and disagreements over how we work with the elementals, for examples."***

We acknowledged memory of this.

~ ***"We do not have wars or fighting, but we do have unrest from time to time, and this may (also) apply to you, but we have had—'assassination'—I think that's the word."***

There were responses of 'oh!', 'ah!', 'yes!' to this.

~ ***"So there are political groups struggling for their points of view."***

We of course understood, indicating our own problems in this regard; such names in recent memory as President John F Kennedy, Lord Louis Mountbatten and Mahatma Gandhi coming to mind. The Earthly record of political assassination is a sad one.

~ ***"It is not common but we have had it. And so it is something that cannot be dismissed."***

George: "But nevertheless, people have the collective good sense not to go to war over disputes or over annoyances—"

~ ***"There is enough love from the majority of us, to not allow war."***

George: "Ah! So again 'love' is the key to that matter."

~ ***"But there are those that are prepared to take life, if they feel it helps their cause."***

Rod: "Do you have armies that fight or protect people, one against the other?"

~ ***"We have something that has evolved from armies, but it no longer functions like that. They are like a group who rescue people—***

deal with natural disasters—are available for many different activities, depending on what is needed at the time."

Rod: "Almost like a United Nations—"

~ ***"Yes, they understand medical as well as natural disasters. They understand how to fight, but it is not a main part of their training."***

Sarah: "What would happen to the assassin if they catch him?"

~ ***"If this person is caught, they would be placed in confinement for a time."***

Sarah: "Do you have prisons as we do? Do you need them?"

~ ***"We have something like a prison in the sense that it separates them from the world, but it is not meant as a punishment place."***

George: "And are they left to their own thinking or would they be subject to what might be considered helpful learning for them?"

~ ***"They will have many who will try to help them. They are not so many to deal with. It is less common in our world. But there are always those who, for some reason, are unhappy with the way things are, and are prepared to act without regard for another. They need to be watched over carefully, and if possible, finding out why they have chosen that pathway, and if they can be encouraged out of it in this lifetime, as opposed to waiting for the disappointment when they move on."***

I think we all saw the logic of that—better to change direction now than have to acknowledge a failed lifetime once in spirit.

Sarah: "Salumet has told us that you should never take a life, so all of you must be aware of that—"

~ ***"It is something that we hope everyone is aware of, but when you have massive populations, it seems there are always some individuals who choose another course other than the one that is reckoned."***

Sarah: "Maybe it's partly due to the overcrowding on your planet do you think?"

~ ***"There are many possible reasons. That is one that has been voiced."***

Rod: "Reading between the lines, you seem to know how many people we've got in prison here—"

~ ***"I have looked through the memories of this one and I do not know the numbers."***

Graham: "It's about one in 800 in England at the moment."

~ ***"I am aware of your problems with prisons and the scale of it. It would seem to be a problem that has not been settled very imaginatively, can I say?"***

George: "Yes, I agree."

Graham: "I think we are trying to find alternative methods, allowing people to reform outside prison—giving them opportunities, which I think is a step in the right direction."

George: "Yes, we're trying. We still have a long way to go. Would you like a break? Would you like a piece of music at this stage?"

~ ***"That sounds a good idea, yes."***

George: "I think we mentioned the theatre before. We have 'musical' shows, and these are often centred on a story. It can be any sort of story. Occasionally it is taken out of politics. There was one musical in fairly recent times called 'Evita', and it concerned the government of Argentina—one of our countries. Juan Peron was its president and his wife Evita was First Lady and she assisted with running the country. She was in charge of social welfare and she was much loved by the people. She departed this life before her husband, and 'Don't Cry for Me Argentina' was her song: ♪♫♫."

~ ***"It's a little easier now, to listen, with these ears, and that one was able to sound the words a little more easily than in some of the (earlier) songs."***

The voice of Julie Covington in the recording was certainly beautifully clear, hence Bonniol's comment.

Sarah: "When you say it's easier for you to listen to, is it easier for you to relay back to your audience, for them to pick up?"

~ ***"It's not that I relay exactly. They experience it with me. We share the experience. I'm sure they enjoyed it too, yes."***

George: "Is it as if they were here with us?"

~ ***"It is for them as it is for me, yes. They would be listening with me."***

Sarah: "And also with your words?"

~ "I speak for myself, but when YOU speak, they are able to listen. We all listen together. So it makes it even more a meeting of worlds."

At this point I think we felt as goldfish in a bowl and a little out of our depth, while sixty or so wonderful beings watched us blow bubbles. But we were doing our best, and now another question: "Could I ask, have you all listened to a master who has visited another planet—have you experienced what was experienced tonight, before in your travels? Or is it a first?"

~ "It is a first for me. I would imagine it has been done before, but it has been a first for me, and something very special. I have listened to your master before, but to have him come into the discussion is something I will cherish."

George: "We are delighted that this has happened, and we shall equally cherish this evening for this reason."

Indeed, we all felt and knew that this evening had been 'something special'. Bonniol had on occasions arrived early and had been able to listen to Salumet, but this had been different. And when Salumet next visited he observed: **~ "It only goes to show, does it not, how much connection and communication is possible between all, when it is needed."**

So it was once again time for farewells and we were as ever left to reflect on the evening's exchanges; not least how an army might evolve into a valuable task force that could actually *help* people in their times of need. The skills developed could be put to such good constructive use, and a children's TV series quickly comes to mind in which the idea of an international rescue force has already been presented—Thunderbirds Are Go!

CHAPTER: 29

Disease – Beyond Inflation – Wants Versus Needs – See Bonniol? ... 13th Mar 2006

AT THE START Bonniol was saying: ~ ***"I am pleased to continue our meetings, and as we become more acquainted with each other, it feels more and more like a gathering of friends."***

Lilian: "Definitely, yes."

George: "Yes, I think we all feel this."

Lilian: "We almost forget where you're from."

~ ***"You have no idea! It is just a stone's throw within thought! This time it feels a particularly small distance."***

Sarah: "Good, it becomes more and more easy compared to earlier?"

~ ***"The old barriers or problems are fading now, I have been having a few problems with the channel, but the more we use him, the easier it will be."***

Sarah: "Practise makes perfect."

Eileen then led us into a useful question-and-answer dialogue: "Bonniol, here we call ourselves 'human beings'. Do you have a name for your own race?"

~ ***"Yes, we have our own name. We call ourselves a name which is to do with our planet's name. So like the name Aerah, we are like saying: 'Aerans'."***

George: "In writing about this, I have in fact used the term 'Aeran'."

~ ***"You were right! This is like your 'Earthlings'. We have no similar word like 'human'."***

Useful information! The subject of illness had already been broached, but I felt we might expand on this a little: "There is one thing we have that we call 'the common cold', that is not at all serious. Are you familiar with that from Paul's memory?"

~ ***"I have been asked this before. Yes, we have germs that would be similar to your cold."***

George: "I see. Do you have the snivels and runny noses as we do on these occasions?"

~ ***"We have symptoms which can affect our breathing. Our airways become clogged up—congested."***

George: "Very much as we have here. We have failed to find the complete answer. We have remedies that relieve the symptoms to some degree. Do I understand that on your planet also, you have not found the complete answer?"

~ ***"We are still searching for a cure for many illnesses."***

Eileen: "What is the main illness that would cause you to pass to spirit?"

~ ***"The main cause of death in our world is a disease that is like a virus; it can be like your—um—you have encephalitis, a viral infection of the brain. I think this is the closest disease to compare, and there are occasional outbreaks of this."***

Eileen: "I was just wondering—you are so advanced in the way you can use thought. Do you use it for self-healing?"

~ ***"We of course use our thoughts for self-healing, yes. And we do not have SO much illness. But there remains for some this problem, which is not really a problem when you look at it spiritually of course. It is another avenue of learning."***

This brings us back to the mind connection to illness, and of course there can be much spiritual benefit from whatever ill prevails. Illness, mind-play and the way forward in spirit all go hand-in-hand, although it may be difficult sometimes to understand. But even on spiritually-more-advanced Aerah, it appears that illness has a place despite applied self-healing. Sarah recalled that Salumet had mentioned the ocean shark as being immune from disease and asked a question about this, to which Bonniol responded: ~ ***"We have***

various animals which rarely become ill, but I am not certain that they would never ever be ill. I would have to research, but it sounds unusual."

Sarah: "I'm not sure that any on Earth were aware of that."

~ ***"Yes, your master has such knowledge. We are all benefiting from it now!"***

George: "Yes, it was a lovely meeting last time when he came through and participated."

Sarah: "We are very pleased to pass the word around on Earth, and we're even happier if it's reaching other galaxies!"

~ ***"It certainly is, and makes the link even more special!"***

There followed some talk about animals and how carnivores form a part of the balance in evolution. Then it was time for another topic. Here on Earth, we spiral into inflation. Costs and salaries increase as monetary value decreases. Greed has to be the driving force and so, in a more advanced society, one might expect a more static condition. So we enquired about the Aeran economy: ~ ***"Yes of course, we have been down the road of money and how it changes its value, and how it has been far too important in people's lives. We still use it, but now it has become more in line with other aspects of existence. It is simply a way of moderating and providing for everybody instead of being a power object for people."***

George: "Yes, for people. We have certainly focussed our attention far too much on money and finance, I feel. Has it for you become of more constant value in recent years?"

~ ***"Yes, it has not changed for a long time now. It becomes more like a credit, which is used to exchange—as a token would be exchanged for an object. And a token is worth whatever the object is worth, so it does not change."***

It is implied that value lies in actual worldly goods as opposed to the money equivalent. Its power object status accordingly fades until it is regarded as mere token. When questioned further, our friend added: ~ ***"Our needs have become far less complicated—this is one of the ways in which we have grown—by accepting our NEEDS as opposed to our WANTS."***

Now we had reached a nub where nests a basic wisdom. While 'needs' are the relatively simple things required to sustain meaningful and progressive lifestyle, 'wants' are something apart that relate to advertising, TV imagery and aspects of brainwashing such as keeping up with the Joneses. A 'want' can so easily equate to irrational desire. And the good salesman can sell you what you simply do not need! So 'needs' versus 'wants' is a thought-provoking concept. The society that observes modest needs can truly advance, while the one that succumbs to induced wants has all the complications that arise from debt, long hours of hard work, worries, stress and the hang-ups of rampant materialism. There is much to think on here.

We moved on to other matters as Eileen posed a searching question about how the various planetary beings might exist when in spirit domain: "Bonniol—when we have contact with spirits, most people (in spirit) retain some identity of human form. As far as I know, there has not been a mention of any other beings from other planets. Are you aware in your communications, of anyone mentioning other beings, or are they separated in some way?"

~ ***"I think in your world, you have been largely unaware of other worlds—other physical beings. And this is perhaps why it is not mentioned often in spirit communications."***

Eileen: "But would knowledge not be greater once in spirit?"

~ ***"The knowledge is there, the knowledge is always there, but unless you have the desire for that knowledge it may not come to you."***

George: "So, in *your* planetary Astral Planes, there would be the knowledge and there would also be the desire. So there would be the awareness of other beings. Is that true?"

~ ***"Yes. We have links with other worlds. It is a natural thing for us. So it would be strange for it not to continue in spirit."***

Eileen: "Yes, but would you have that counterpart of form in spirit?"

I suspect Eileen was wondering at this point if beings having identities that relate to different planets would happily *co-exist* in spirit.

Lilian: "It might be a question for Salumet—"

Eileen: "It's given me something to think about."

Lilian: "I was just thinking: we can't see you, but it would be nice if we could meet in spirit."

~ ***"Of course, when in spirit, you will, if the desire is there, be able to meet people from many worlds."***

Lilian: "Yes."

Eileen: "But only in thought form—"

~ ***"Yes, as you will take on another appearance yourself, so will those from other worlds. So you will—"***

Several were now quick to complete the sentence: "See Bonniol—right!"

~ ***"Yes, we all have to have our own overcoats."***

Eileen: "That makes me wonder why it's never been mentioned. There must be those in spirit who are more aware, and I just wonder why that communication's never been made."

George: "I guess the answer might be that they've got to have practical experience of such a meeting."

~ ***"I think it might be one of those avenues, opening up to you at this time."***

Several: "Yes!"

Sarah: "Salumet has said that once a contact has been made it is never lost Bonniol, so you're not going to get rid of us that easily!"

There was a pause as Bonniol noted the flippancy, then replied: ~ ***"That's good! We do feel there is much that can be gained from these links. They are highly sophisticated and yet an extremely good way of finding out many things. I didn't explain that very well—in your words."***

George: "But we understand. Well, I have a thought about that—this way of communicating, it beats rocketry—no contest!"

Lilian: "—which takes rather a long time!"

There followed some talk about how it would take years to reach another galaxy and then more years for the return, and that brought us to the time for Bonniol's departure. It had been another informative evening. The idea of replacing 'wants' with 'needs', to make a less cluttered society, remained with us. It lingered long, and this could surely be a key to the kind of mind-growth within a society, required for substantial enrichment of spirit.

CHAPTER: 30

Memory Lane Downloaded – Brain the Processor: Links Spirit? … 3rd Apr 2006

Bonniol began by speaking on how much more the connection had improved; pointing out that it will extend the possibilities that now lay before us. And he queried if we were happy to continue or are we getting tired of these exchanges? We responded that what had been achieved so far was already wildly beyond any expectation that we may have had, and no way did we wish to close the lid on this Pandora's Box of wondrous opportunity. We were more than happy—delighted to continue. Our friend went on to say: ~ ***"We would like to tell you of the other planets, which you are now a part of—"***

George: "A part of the *collection*, yes!"

~ ***"We would really like to bring the representatives of these planets to tell you a little more of themselves."***

Needless to say, we were jubilant at the prospect.

~ ***"I did try to describe them a little for you but found it a slight problem, and perhaps the connection would allow this more now. I'm sure we can arrange others to talk to you as the one did before."***

This would most certainly be a development to look forward to. We asked, in the meantime if Bonniol had questions he wished to ask of us, to which he replied: ~ ***"We are happy now that we have—um—'downloaded' you could say—a good amount of data from this one's memories, which is giving us plenty of food for thought."***

A few chuckles went around as we mused on the sort of stuff that might be found—not just in Paul's memories—but *any* of us would possess such an assortment of pickings that an advanced being could perchance find fascinating, perplexing, appalling or just plain bizarre. But Bonniol holds our trust and a bond of mutual respect has built, all within the cloak of spiritual oversee.

~ ***"Questions will arise, but we feel very happy in the knowledge we now have."***

Graham: "Do you access this knowledge only during these meetings or whenever you—"

~ ***"Once we have downloaded it, we can examine it at any time."***

Graham: "So you already have all the information on your planet?"

~ ***"We have a good deal of information, yes."***

George: "When you say 'download', do you have a replica—a recording on an instrument?"

~ ***"Yes, this is another avenue (scientific pursuit) for you. But there are ways of downloading thoughts / memories, and enclosing them in an energy device which preserves them, I think. It is like your computers, but it is an energy configuration which we have learned to use in this way. Thought forms can be sent out as messages, but there is so much more you can do with them, and this is one other—um—exercise in thought, which you can—um—or which we have been able to do. We can put thoughts into an energy field, which preserves them there, rather than sending them on to another."***

Graham: "Is it a physical device that you've made?"

~ ***"It is not physical in that way, no. It is an energy field, which ENCLOSES thoughts that we do not wish to send forth, but which we wish to store."***

Graham: "Good heavens! Is this something that you have learnt to do yourselves, or has this been given from spirit, or—"

~ ***"It is something that has come to us from spirit, as have all things, and we have been using it now for some time. It is mainly used to store VAST amounts of thought energy, which would (otherwise) overwhelm us."***

Graham: "Is it the entire collection of Paul's thinking?"

~ ***"It is by no means the entire collection. It is a small amount, but it is still far too great an amount of data for us to process quickly."***

George: "So, is this a general method that works for the various planets?"

~ ***"Nothing is so general when it comes to these processes. Each planet has different abilities. We are able to digest information in this way, and we have our other planets who deal with it in different ways. It is a—a—"***

Lilian: "A library?"

~ ***"That would be a good description of it."***

Graham: "Would this information be subconscious, that you're accessing, that even Paul himself would not be able to access easily?"

~ ***"It would be memories that he WOULD be able to access."***

George: "It would, I expect, relate to the conscious mind—"

~ ***"Yes—um—I believe you sometimes have difficulty in remembering details, but you remember—"***

Graham: "Main events."

~ ***"—the main events, yes."***

Graham: "Is that true of you? Do you have difficulty remembering details?"

~ ***"I think we would say our memories are a little clearer. They are not always perfect. When we wish to remember something, we can mentally put it into a place where it WILL be remembered. We have a few, tricks if you like, which help us. But we have said before how busy your days are, and probably this is the reason you do not always remember so well."***

Graham next explained about how we know that only a small proportion of the human brain actually finds use, the rest being dormant, and this got us onto another *very* interesting tack.

~ ***"We would say that much of the brain is—yes, it is underused, but the biggest (more important) thing, is to link it to your spiritual mind. That is the main reason you have your incredible brains."***

I suggested that if we link better with the spiritual mind, then we could access so much more. And Sara made the point that it empowers all that we do, so that we would then be open to so much more inspiration.

~ ***"You have the machinery to connect very well with spirit."***

George: "I think what you are saying is that if we connect much more satisfactorily with spirit, then there is a potential for much more of our brain being used. So we have a brain-use-potential that will become realised when we make that spiritual connection better. Does that make sense?"

~ ***"Yes, the brain is all about finding or linking with spirit. The thinking that you do is not your brain but your spiritual mind. Your brain is interpreting the messages it is getting, but it is not 'thinking'. It is processing."***

Graham: "An interesting thought."

~ ***"It is being fed the thoughts from your spiritual mind. It is the 'receiving aspect' of your brain which it would help to be developed more."***

There was some attempt to further the discussion by introducing the idea of 'intellect' as our physical interpretation, while 'innate knowledge' we know comes to us from spirit. A potential for the latter to increase should come from *enhancing our spirit connection*. But Bonniol responded neatly with: ~ ***"Maybe—um—it is time for us to disconnect,"*** and that concluded both that topic and the evening with another good laugh.

After farewells, we were left feeling this session had opened doorways to reveal so much. Firstly, Aerans have an understanding of thought and mind with a clarity far beyond Earthly perception. This we would expect. But this has led them on to an ability to actually download thought-memories and hold a thought-library contained within an energy device, perhaps in some measure akin to mind or brain itself. Going on from that astounding revelation, there is the matter of our so much *underused* brains. But this shortfall in brain usage comes about with good reason, and appears to relate to a potential for much more development of spirit connection. The lid to *this* Pandora's Box has been raised just a little bit, sufficient to permit a glimpse of what might be forthcoming. And when Bonniol declared it to be time to disconnect, well maybe those who were overseeing had awareness that the lid should not be opened further, and that to suit our own Earthly striving.

More and more it seems we must see the physical human brain as a 'processor' that has huge potential to link human form with spirit domains and to the limitless universal energies and knowledge. As evidence of just one single aspect of this, we have the Bonniol communications themselves, *processed* by brain into current English language! These facts extend well beyond the bounds of present day Earthly scientific ability or understanding. Perhaps we have to regard 'science' as pursuing painstakingly and methodically, a blinkered view of creation that can never catch up. This is not to say that the scientific method has no place in our world. It has, and makes valuable contribution to our way forward. But science has largely been built from bastions of *physical* reasoning, so that instead of uniting harmoniously with spirit encounter, it is seen to falter and shy away. As has already been said, it is now 125-years since formation of The Society for Psychical Research, and truly vast amounts of published data have followed, yet still there remains a stoical scepticism for the intangible. Mankind has for too long labelled that which appears to be above and beyond nature as simply 'supernatural' and that label has remained; meaning not of tested and acceptable standard for our science. Perhaps we should finally quote Salumet on this. His earlier words from 10th March 1997 refer to sometime in our more distant future: ~ **"No longer will there be the fear and the distrust, shall I say, over all things termed 'supernatural'. They will become known and natural to mankind."**

CHAPTER: 31

More Salumet – Alcohol – Mice and Elementals – A Song ... 17th April 2006

THE CONNECTION HAD really come on a pace, with Bonniol describing his visit as: ~ ***"Just popping in to see my friends."***

I replied: "Just popping in from the other side of the universe!"

~ ***"Just a few galaxies down the road and we are here!"***

Sarah: "And without getting tired!"

~ ***"Yes, it saves a lot of time. Even in our world travelling from one place to another takes time and effort. This is by far the easiest and by far the most comfortable way to visit our friends."***

Sarah: "It's certainly very easy for us anyway, we just sit here."

~ ***"You have had a good evening tonight already haven't you?"***

Knowing light laughter went around the room as Lilian said: "Yes we have!"

George: "You were here were you?"

~ ***"I was around, yes."***

Our friend had been listening and he was right, and oh how right! It had been especially splendid and it had been a *lengthy* session with Salumet. The energy was exceptional, the dialogue chatty, and it flowed like a millstream, and we all remained on cloud nine. At one point during the discourse, Sarah had been saying: "You were thanking us Salumet, for passing on the word, but I can only say that it's your inspiration and those in spirit, that has inspired us to *want* to pass it on. It seems the natural thing."

In his reply, our teacher had referred briefly to earlier missions from deeper spirit that had encountered stony ground or had in some way fallen short of intended value: ~ **"Thank you for those words my dear friend. On many, many occasions have we tried to inspire amongst humankind, elements of truth, which somehow**

have been corrupted and changed. But I am sure, not only from what I say, but from your own recognition of humankind, that you also can (now) see a quickening and awareness throughout your world. It is there for all to see. But our object is to try to spread the truth even further at this time, and much is being done."

George: "Yes and perhaps we should not overlook the development with Bonniol, which *in itself* I feel, is a further help to us in spreading the truth, and presenting a particular slant of interest to people."

~ "Yes."

George: "It is so nice that we are able to compare our own progress as physical beings on a physical planet, with another group of physical beings on another planet."

~ "Yes."

George: "It seems somehow to reinforce everything, in making those comparisons."

~ "Yes, you have very aptly led me into the introduction of my next words, to say, why as a group, you have been introduced to such knowledge. Because, my dear friends, you *have* been ready to receive, you *have* been ready to accept, and you *are* now ready to give forth that knowledge also. And I am sure in some way you will find (encounter) disbelief. But it matters not, because as I have told you on many occasions, if only the seeds are sown, then you have achieved, and we cannot ask more."

Sarah: "Are there many other groups having visits from other planets?"

~ "There are many groups throughout your world, who have contact with other beings, who can speak as you do, with a certainty and knowledge. The way *I* have introduced you is slightly different, in as much as *your* visitor comes through another, whereas with lots of groups it is 'trance' work."

Sarah and Paul both picked up on 'trance' and sought some clarification.

~ "Yes they receive information in that way. But of course, we had been speaking much on 'mind projection'. So, as it is not easy for each here to project mind, we felt it was a very good exercise to combine both things (extraterrestrial knowledge and mind

projection). But to answer your question: yes, many people would clarify knowledge of other (extraterrestrial) life."

Sarah: "That's good."

George: "It's interesting too that it comes to us by this other method of communication, which apart from anything else, helps us to understand the nature of 'mind', which by and large on this planet, is rather poorly understood."

~ **"And still is! Yes, you will never fully understand the workings of the mind, because after all the mind is spirit. Therefore there must be limitations in your understanding."**

Sarah: "So, only when we return to spirit will we fully understand?"

~ **"Fully understand—but of course, as we continue forward in our knowledge, your understanding will become a little greater—of course it will. But to *fully* understand the mind, you must belong to spirit. And even then I would have to say, it would take some considerable time, because you see it is a natural part of your spirit to use the mind without fully understanding the mechanics of it."**

George: "Yes, at least we are becoming more and more aware that mind is so much exterior to the physical brain."

~ **"Oh, of course it is—I would say almost SEPARATE! There is a union of course, but the mind exists on its own merits. It does not need a physical body (in order) to function."**

George: "I know that in the past, many have credited the physical brain with far too much."

~ **"Yes of course, but it is their lack of knowledge which brings forth these words. They do not understand. They only see a physical being and nothing else, so of course their thinking is dulled."**

So, just two weeks following the conclusions of the previous chapter, Salumet firmly endorses the separateness and virtual independence of mind. Mind is our true being, assisted by brain the physical processor. Mind is paramount. To *acknowledge* that mind has this autonomy, with ability to function in its own right, is such an important step. Mind has to be the keystone of the metaphoric bridge connecting science and spirit. Deny the keystone and our understanding crumbles into disarray!

Sarah now addressed Bonniol suggesting that if ever he wished a question to be placed to Salumet, we would be pleased to arrange that.

~ ***"Thank you! That would be a great honour. I am also able to ask questions by projection."***

Sarah: "Yes, of course!"

~ ***"But voicing them would be an honour."***

Sarah: "Oh right. We keep forgetting how much more advanced you are with mind projection. We're a bit behind you there as far as intelligence goes!"

~ ***"I think it is not as clear-cut as that. We are all experiencing different learning curves."***

There was general agreement to that, and I went on to describe one of the things that we on Earth have for quite some time been rather good at: "With the various civilisations that we've had, one of the first things that people seem to do is set up a brewing industry—ferment things to make alcohol—which seems to be a favoured drink—which lightens the mood of people. I was wondering if perhaps you have an alcohol industry, or brewing, or wine industry, on Aerah."

~ ***"Yes, we understand. The drinks that contain this chemical have been of use to us at different stages of our development. Now we prefer to avoid them. They cloud our minds."***

George: "Yes, I can understand that. I would say that here, it clouds *some* people's minds rather too much!"

As our gentle chokes and chuckles subsided, Bonniol continued:

~ ***"But in the past we have had different ways of—'losing ourselves', if you like. Now, we try to 'find ourselves' more fully. And we work towards clarity rather than confusion."***

George: "So does that mean that you don't have any alcoholic drinks on Aerah now, at the present time?"

~ ***"We don't have any that I know about. It is possible that it is still used, but it is not something you can buy in a shop."***

George: "That's very interesting. Alcohol it would seem, disappears from the scene with spiritual advancement, shall we say?"

~ ***"We have our pleasures, but they change as we change. There are certain medicinal herbs that we can use, but I think the chemical you are talking about, is no longer a part of our lives."***

Well that was certainly all very interesting, and left the impression that alcohol has been passed over in favour of certain herbal drugs that are less befuddling. And whatever herbs Aerans have selected for use, they will doubtless *find* as opposed to *lose* the subtleties of mind. On Earth, the drugs scene is chaotic with the majority being *manufactured*. Just a few will doubtless be *finding* as opposed to *losing* category, and *finding* would doubtless prevail where shamanic practices with herbs have been concerned. But as to alcohol, it certainly has its troublesome consequences in today's world—addiction, toxicity, road accidents, poverty and an assortment of crime connections. There can be no doubt that in excess it is indeed a 'mind loser'. And it would appear to be a trait that an advancing world can and should grow beyond.

Another troublesome matter was next discussed—'mice'. Mice in the home can be destroyers and a great nuisance, and we wondered if there might be an equivalent rogue-animal on Aerah.

~ ***"We—I'm sorry, I have to use the word again—we HAVE had. Now we have learned to communicate with our animals."***

Well I suppose one might have expected that answer, and it is true that just a few of us here have tried communicating, with a modicum of success in moving moles off the lawn and to other locations, but mice, well they can be very persistent. Bonniol continued: ~ ***"Yes and also involving the nature spirits who take care of these animals. When you learn to love nature and all the animals, and the nature spirits, and communicate your wishes—if they are governed with love, the nature spirits will help the animals to re-locate to new places."***

Lilian: "Yes, we've some way to go before we get *there*."

~ ***"It's a natural thing once you accept that the nature spirits are working with the animals. Then you can begin to become part of the plan. If you become involved in the plans that the nature spirits are working on, they will take on board what you say and use their influences. It is very possible to have that harmony with your cohabitants. They all have their reasons for being here."***

Lilian: "Of course they have."

Sarah: "We're not always sure what their purpose is—"

~ ***"We have all had to learn about communicating with our fellows, and finding out what they are about, and learning to live in harmony with them."***

Now, that I see as a definitive statement. It is surely incumbent upon physical beings living on physical planets, whether Earth, Aerah or some other, to eventually learn to communicate and seek harmony. This has to be seen as a necessary step in successful planetary life. Harmonious living should be consistent with such values as species survival, mutual trust, a 'green' sustainable environment and spiritual progression. All such factors will contribute towards a world that is harmonised, and here on Earth I think we are just beginning to take some account. Earlier evolution will have involved the survival of self, dominance over competing life forms, killing for food—perhaps unaccompanied by compassion, exploitation of others and open warfare. It has been a lengthy road to where we stand now. To finally achieve harmony means leaving behind old aggressions. This of necessity takes time, but all advancing cultures must at some point come of age, dispense with base motives and look to higher principles.

George: "The actual communication is really with the elementals rather than with the animals. Is that correct?"

~ ***"Yes the communication of your ideas and intentions, is with the elementals, but your feelings can be directed to the animals."***

Eileen had just about returned from trance once more and now contributed a question: "Could I ask you what form your elementals take?"

~ ***"We see them as light beings."***

Eileen: "Just as beings of light—"

~ ***"They have taken other forms for us, but most of us see them as beings of light. They can of course, take on different forms."***

Eileen: "Thank you—the same as ours."

George: "Yes, and they make themselves larger or smaller to suit the situation—"

~ ***"I think they are an energy that is conscious of its self, and unlike us, not clothed in a physical body as such. They can appear and disappear, and they can appear in different forms. But most commonly we see the energy or the light of these beings."***

Sarah: "You don't see form, just the light?"

~ ***"Without a physical form, yes."***

Sarah: "And would different animals have different intensities of light?"

~ ***"The animals have physical overcoats."***

Sarah: "I mean the elementals—"

~ ***"The elementals would have different lights, yes."***

Sarah: "Different lights without a shape—"

~ ***"Yes they would be formless to us."***

Having sorted out the subject of elemental light, Bonniol took us completely by surprise by suggesting he sing another song. Wonderful! He explained that we had given much Earth music and they were sad that Aeran music could not be shared in the same way. We also wondered if we might possibly have overdone the music a little. Apparently not, but of course as Bonniol pointed out, they also can now get it from Paul's memories! Anyway, we felt it might be time to have a break from physical-ear-music, especially since they can now get it from the down-loads.

Lilian: "I believe you said that the friends and family sitting with you, can listen to the music as well. Am I right?"

~ ***"Yes. They also can dip into the memories of this one, as it is happening now or later on when we are finished."***

Lilian: "That's interesting."

~ ***"The song is called, in your words: 'The Passage of Time'."***

Bonniol's song came in three verses, each of approximately one minute duration. There was much wavering, use of slur and long 'ooh' sounds. I can quite easily think of it as the voice of a variable wind. The song ended and there was a pause before we responded, just in case another verse might be coming, then our responses: "Wow! / Wonderful! / Very, very nice! / Thank you!"

And Lilian reminded that we can listen to it again because it is recorded.

~ ***"I was beginning to feel that it was coming through better."***

George: "Yes, there was a drifting of the note, which was interesting."

~ ***"Lips were more useful this time in doing the song, it was a better connection for it."***

Sarah: "It was almost like an instrument producing the sound."

~ ***"Yes, we are more 'instrumental' with our mouths I think, in our music."***

We talked some more about 'drifting slurs', comparing electric guitar sounds and the music of some of our Oriental countries.

~ ***"It is probably more pronounced when we do it. I was not quite able to use the vocal equipment to give its full message. There was another half, but I felt it was still early days to do it fully. It could become quite close to the original with practise, but it was more fluid than it would have been in earlier days when we started. We are happy with that experiment."***

Perhaps this serves to illustrate the progress that has been made. And it was a good note on which to end the evening. There were fond farewells as ever, while Bonniol's parting words were:

~ ***"And Planet Aerah sends its love as we leave you this time."***

CHAPTER: 32

Space Travel – UFOs – Wormhole Travel ... 8th May 2006

AGAIN WE ENJOYED the luxury of a Salumet discourse followed by a Bonniol visit, and as our teacher withdrew there was much to think on. The subject had been healing prayers and angels of healing, and of course, as with the current mind projection work, the receipt of prayer and the connections are all instantaneous. Salumet had explained: ~ **"As human beings you think much of space, when in fact in our world there is no such thing. I want you to dwell upon those words just for a second. As you speak their name, so our angelic healing beings, have them (prayers) in their midst."**

We have to keep reminding ourselves, that space belongs to the physical creation, while spirit although entwined with it has no space. It follows that all connections within spirit are instantaneous. It is perhaps understandable that as Lilian welcomed Bonniol, she mentioned that we had been left deep in thought.

Graham: "Did you hear any of that?"

~ ***"I was able to hear from the beginning, yes."***

It was clear that he was not connected with Paul earlier because Paul had been voicing questions, so I enquired in what capacity he was present.

~ ***"I was, in the room if you like—I was not using Paul at that time. We are able to—"***

Lilian: "Hover?"

~ ***"Yes, that is a reasonable word, I think."***

Lilian: "And you need Paul for speech, obviously."

~ ***"We need Paul to communicate. Yes that is correct."***

Sarah: "If Paul hadn't been here, would you be able to join the meeting?"

~ "I would be able to find this room. It would be possible to find another to try to speak through, but this takes time."

The exchange ambled on concerning the variety of influences and visits that we receive from spirit and how there are gatekeepers who exert a measure of control and keep things orderly. Then Sarah got us onto *physical* travel by pointing out that we have physical visitors using spacecraft (UFOs) that make circles and patterns in the cornfields. She went on to ask if Aerans ever visit other planets physically, and this enquiry blossomed into a fruitful discussion.

~ "We only travel 'great' distances in this way. We prefer this (mind link) way, rather than using our craft to visit other planets."

Sarah: "But you could if you wanted to?"

~ "We could visit some, but we are not able to visit ALL planets, no."

Sarah: "And would these be the same sort of craft as you use to get to your moon?"

~ "We have a number of different ones, but something similar to that one, yes."

Bonniol began to say more but then hesitated: ***~ "Your visitors that make the patterns in the crops—"***

Lilian: "It has been said that lights have been seen when they make the crop circles."

Now we had entered a tricky area and I felt Bonniol needed to know how much we already knew. Our knowledge within the group, I can simply say: I believe to be far ahead of what has been widely popularised. So I volunteered a statement for the benefit of Bonniol and overseeing guides (in the interest of opening the doorway on this sensitive topic as fully as possible). So here goes: "There are connections with what we call UFOs—unidentified flying objects, which are often seen as lights travelling in the sky, and we think the crop circles are a means of communicating that we haven't entirely fathomed yet."

Sarah: "You were going to say something Bonniol?"

~ "I was pondering my words carefully. These ships are very hard to see, because they are made of different substances and are not always physical as such."

George: "I believe they can be material form or de-materialised form."

~ ***"Yes, but they are there for you to observe and you WILL see more. That is what we understand."***

Graham: "Have they visited *your* planet?"

~ ***"The ones you are observing have never been to our planet. We are—we are—"***

Lilian: "Too far away?"

~ ***"Yes, that is one issue. Another is, there are certain beings you would find it harder to meet with, for different reasons. Some have such a different energy pattern it can be difficult to even NOTICE them."***

We have some understanding of that little difficulty. If energy densities are too diverse then one material being will scarcely notice another, and then there is also de-materialised form. It is for these very reasons that some of us are able to perceive extraterrestrials and their ships while others simply cannot. And likewise, what proportion of Earth-dwellers can see our own auras or the elementals? But Bonniol had more to say: ~ ***"Some worlds find it easier than others—we have been communicating with your visitors—some of your visitors."***

Lilian: "Really—"

~ ***"The link is not of the same—"***

Lilian: "Form?"

~ ***"Yes, but it is a link which is still very unclear to US."***

George: "Yes, we have spoken to visitors through séance on rare occasions, and I did once put a question: do you have a material body? And the answer was: 'if I wish it'. Well, that makes a lot of sense if they are using de-materialised form."

Richard: "I am assuming that they come from somewhere close to our planet, if great distances are a problem. Have you any idea where?"

~ ***"We do know which part of the galaxy they are from, yes. It is a part which is more easily connected with your region of space. With the kind of craft that we have, we cannot at this time make that journey."***

Richard: "Is it somewhere that we would be able to see, or have knowledge of? Is it somewhere that we are aware of?"

~ ***"You would find it in your night sky, yes."***

George: "Would I be right in thinking that, using the principle of de-materialisation, one can travel very much faster through space, but even with *that* procedure, one would still be restricted to travelling within a galaxy?"

~ ***"It is not so much the ability to hop from one galaxy to another. This is possible through certain—'holes', if you like. But these holes only run from certain places."***

This came as music to my ears and very, very exciting! Within those present on this particular evening, I think I was alone in having read a little of our Earthly scientific theory on such matters—theory that remains as theory—untested. And here was one from another planet actually introducing the untested subject! Bonniol continued:
~ ***"It is not possible to use them for every part—every place—"***

George: "This is I think what we call 'wormholes.'"

~ ***"And you need to use them at certain times. Yes, they are not always open."***

Sarah: "What causes them to close?"

~ ***"They are governed by certain laws I believe. They are in one direction at certain times and then they switch. So you have to wait for them to be going in the right way."***

Richard: "I would assume the reason for that is part of the universe is shifting—in the same way as our solar system is, around the sun. So you could probably plot it by calendar."

~ ***"Yes if you use them much then you know how they operate. You wouldn't need to look at a map. You would remember because they follow very precise patterns."***

Graham: "Are they very common?"

~ ***"Yes, there are many of them."***

Graham: "So, all you have to do is enter one and you pop out the other end. That's all you have to do—get into it?"

~ ***"Yes, they are almost instantaneous."***

Sarah: "So you would travel in what form?"

~ ***"This would be in your craft, these are for when you are visiting with your physical body."***

Sarah: "And what is the craft powered by?"

~ ***"The craft that WE use, as we have said, are powered by energy from our plants, but other worlds have different forms of energy. We would tell you more about your visitors, but there is a certain feeling that it is better to—"***

George: "Make the discoveries for ourselves?"

~ ***"Learn from them, yes."***

Jan: "So there's a protocol that we need to abide by—"

~ ***"Yes, we are not supposed to give you ALL the information. It has to be—um—"***

As Bonniol's sentence faded, we continued; bringing world governments into the general picture, explaining how they withhold information. This has become plainly obvious. A recent program on TV had attempted to dispose of 'lights in the sky' as atmospheric effects. But of course atmospheric phenomena do not fly in triangulated formation or perform intricate manoeuvres! Even so, one has to observe the plausibility of de-materialised form appearing to some at times very like an atmospheric glow. Our media currently present a mixture of photographs, ridicule, ludicrous tales, hype and little in the way of sensible investigation. So the impressions received by Earth's population are mixed-up and confused. Understanding is generally in disarray, with only a minority able to apply Ockham's razor logic; discarding untruth, to work things through for themselves. Our dear friend continued with understandable hesitation: ~ ***"Yes—yes. This is—um—why this meeting of your visitors—the timing of it is so important. Every step has to be carefully taken before, so that everything is ready for that time."***

Jan: "Bonniol, with due respect, why would you choose a group such as ourselves? Why would you choose to give us information if we are not, as a planet, ready to accept?"

Richard: "We asked for it, didn't we?"

Lilian: "I think it was to tell us more about thought and mind—"

~ ***"Yes, I think these preliminary trips, if you like, usually take place with smaller groups who ARE prepared to listen."***

We made it clear that there are groups around this world, known to us, who do know about UFOs and crop patterns. These have got to know by various means and now readily accept. But there still remains an ocean of scepticism. Finally I was saying: "It's very nice for us to have our beliefs confirmed in this way by talking with Bonniol. And we are left in a stronger position to talk about this to other people. I think this is an important factor here."

~ ***"Yes, and in time you will explore much more fully. And I am sure that will take place at the right time, whenever that time happens to be."***

Sarah recalled that Salumet had in fact made a very similar statement. The timing must be right or there will be much difficulty. I would add that humanity has to rise above such primitive, reactionary qualities as fear, panic, hysteria and flagrant warring. These must be seen as relics of our growing up, that should now be firmly locked away in the cupboard of our yesterdays, before we can meet well-intentioned neighbours of the universe in peaceful acceptance. As has been said, the timing must be right. And for this time that concluded the exchanges prior to farewells and Bonniol's withdrawal.

Returning to our dear friend's mention of 'wormholes', I think the full significance of this only becomes apparent on very briefly describing how Earth came to this important realisation concerning space. The salient steps are:

1915: Albert Einstein publishes his General Theory of Relativity (that many still cannot get their heads around).

1916: Karl Schwartzchild solves field equations of the theory for non-rotating black holes and Ludwig Flamm suggests the possibility of a tunnel through space-time, connecting black holes.

1933: Einstein and Nathan Rosen solve equations leading to the Einstein-Rosen Bridge. This is the first mathematically proven 'wormhole' (not yet named as such), and a connection between different regions of space-time. It is consistent with space being warped by huge mass and the space-warp bridging distant galaxies.

1960s: John Wheeler coins the term 'wormhole', a conversational term for Einstein –Rosen Bridge.

1985: Kip Thorne and colleagues suggest in a paper that *traversable* wormholes could exist, considering the wormhole mouth to be of rotating black hole form.

The Present Position: So far as the Earth is concerned it is still just theory, albeit extremely well constructed theory; all following from Einstein's inspired relativity concept. Still articles are being published stating that no one actually knows if wormholes really exist. There is talk of black holes spinning at the speed of light so that the mouth stays open. There is talk of an exotic matter alternative. But our theories have not yet reached the stage of seeing them as periodic switching devices that keep to calendar schedule. Bonniol confirms their existence as a natural part of space and he has knowledge of their actual use for space-travel. It is an extension to our present theory. This is exciting and spectacular fact, and Star Trek and fiction writers have been astute to seize upon the idea of 'wormhole travel' to incorporate into plausible storylines.

CHAPTER: 33

Black Holes – To See or Not to See – Suwaxians … 22 May 2006

PRIOR TO BONNIOL's visit it had this time once again been a busy evening. A clearly spoken control came via Sarah and welcomed Jim who joined us for the first time; a reminder of how those 'above' take note of changing details. One we know as Yasmin came through; she had last visited 12-years earlier; this time to arrange the 'rescue' of two traumatised children, brother and sister. They were with Sue and Sarah. It was a memorable rescue in which the children / mediums finally held hands as the children moved towards the light together and were warmly met by one they recognised.

~ ***"Hello…"***

There was hesitation on both sides at first, followed by welcoming 'hellos' from everyone, with Bonniol adding: ~ ***"We weren't quite sure if there would be any more."***

We acknowledged and checked if he had been listening again.

~ ***"Yes, I was around, watching and listening."***

Lilian: "You probably don't have that problem with your children if they pass to spirit."

~ ***"There are occasionally those who seem reluctant to move on, though in our world, everyone is taught the principles of life more openly. So they are aware that the physical body is just on loan for a short time."***

Lilian: "That's a good way to look at it!"

~ ***"So just occasionally they forget that it is a 'short term loan' and they need a little nudge, but normally this is not needed."***

That got the conversation running nicely, and I was then able to refer back to last time and say how very interesting the wormhole discussion had been, pointing out that whilst he had spoken on wormhole-use-in-space-travel, Earth had at least deduced from theory their existence, so that his words had been readily understood.

~ ***"Yes, I am pleased that these things have occurred to your world. They are very much a part of the cosmos."***

George: "I think I would be right in saying that the connecting parts of the cosmos are what we term 'black holes.'"

Apparently, I had got it wrong and there is no connection between black holes and wormholes, but it then became clear that Bonniol knows all about black holes too: ~ ***"Black holes—um—you refer to black holes as collapsed stars do you not?"***

George: "Yes, regions that light no longer escapes from. Regions of enormous gravity, that could result from collapsed stars, yes."

~ ***"We have our own terms for these and they are different from the wormholes. They have another function."***

George: "Are you saying they are not connected to the wormholes?"

~ ***"Everything is connected but they are distinct from them. They are places where, as you say, there is no light. There is of course other elements to them, but they are not as yet—um—known to you."***

George: "Elements not known—yes, I understand."

~ ***"You call them BLACK holes, but they are not black to all races in other worlds. It is a point of view. They also have energy that can be seen very brightly, but much escapes the physical eyes where energy is concerned."***

Sarah: "What colour do you see them?"

~ ***"We see the energy of them as—um—the words escape me, but we see a dazzling energy around them. We would not give it a colour. It is a—'fluorescence'—mainly of a purple fluorescence, yes."***

George: "We understand fluorescence, yes. Thank you."

~ ***"These black holes will continue to puzzle you for some time, we are told."***

Graham: "Right. We are led to believe that they would be very dangerous to go near. There are gravitational fields so strong that the forces would be too great for astronauts to go anywhere near them. I was wondering if it is possible to travel through or into one. Has that ever been done?"

~ ***"It is physically possible, but where would you go in one? They would not lead you anywhere physical."***

Graham: "We are led to believe that, inside one, matter is reduced to a singularity with no space—an infinite density."

~ ***"We are able to probe them of course with our minds—study them in that way."***

George: "Another use for mind projection."

~ ***"It has so many advantages. The projections however, cannot always be interpreted in ways that are understandable to us. There are those who investigate such things, but for most of us these black holes are (just) part of the necessary makeup of the cosmos. But they are not of any particular use to physical beings."***

Graham went on to speak of concentrations of black holes believed to be at galactic centres, but Bonniol was perhaps 'under orders' not to divulge further and there was knowing laughter as he said: ~ ***"We cannot tell you too much right now. Your master may give you more details. I am happy to point you in the right directions when I can."***

George: "Yes, this is appreciated. I think we understand that."

There followed a little chat about our efforts to receive mind pictures sent by Bonniol. Most of us were off target but there were two interesting near-misses. Graham was sent an orange that he thought was a lemon, and Sarah thought she received a gold ring as opposed to a gold-coloured £1 coin. Bonniol explained that he had been feeling generous! We continue to practise.

I reminded Bonniol that also last time, he had spoken of differing energy patterns making some beings scarcely noticeable. I enquired if we might also see this as an energy *density* difference.

~ ***"Yes, so you would find it easier to observe those of a similar density."***

George: "Yes, I assume that follows."

~ ***"Yes, the physical eye is not good at picking up the higher vibrations—the lower densities, so these will often not be visible to the physical eye."***

George: "So if we were to meet, we might have difficulty in seeing yourselves—your physical selves."

~ ***"Well, this wouldn't happen, for the reason that we are so far—"***

George: "No, I appreciate it wouldn't happen. It is a hypothetical thought."

~ ***"But if we WERE to travel physically, we would have to adjust in some way to your environment. We could not remain as we are. Our physical makeup would not last long in your atmosphere."***

Sarah pursued the line of question from another direction: "In your world, do you have a problem with seeing visitors?"

~ ***"With our physical eyes, yes, we have a certain range, which you also have."***

Sarah: "Has your planet experienced visitors? Are there people there that have actually seen visitors who might not be the same density as you?"

~ ***"We have had visitors yes, from other worlds. We are able to see them physically and interact with them, because they are similar to us in that respect. Physically we are of similar densities."***

Sarah: "And do these visitors not come from far? Is that why they are of similar densities?"

~ ***"No, this is not the factor—um—they are from far away."***

Sarah: "Oh right!"

~ ***"But they are able to reach us through one of the wormholes, and they are similar to us enough so that we can perceive each other physically."***

Sarah: "So are they more intelligent than you?"

Now this was tricky ground and there was a pause, so I ventured: "How would you measure that?"

We all had to laugh, and then Sarah was saying: "Well I was thinking, they've visited you but have you visited them?"

~ ***"We have not visited them, because our ships are not built to travel such distances. They have developed in some ways more than us. We would not—um—say that they are more advanced in all ways."***

Sarah: "Just in space travel—"

~ ***"They have the better technology in THIS respect."***

Sarah: "And are they prepared to teach you?"

~ ***"They are very happy for us to benefit from their ships, yes."***

We acknowledged the admirable accord. Then Lilian asked: "Can they mind travel as you do?"

~ ***"They have some ability, yes, but it is not as developed as on our world."***

Lilian: "So probably, somewhere on a planet, there are beings that look similar to … humans?"

~ ***"We are not similar to these others in 'appearance'."***

Lilian: "Oh, I see."

~ ***"But we are on a similar vibration to them so that we can physically see each other."***

Sarah: "Could you briefly tell us what they look like?"

~ ***"They have very long ears, as your hares, but they are not hairy. They have a skeleton structure on their outer-side. So they look a little bit like your insects, you could say. They are quite small compared to us."***

George: "For reference purposes, has their planet got a name that you can tell us?"

~ ***"We would pronounce them as 'SUWAXIANS' from 'SUWAX'. This is highly—not clearly pronounced of course, for reasons you could imagine."***

Lilian: "That's quite good enough for us."

Sarah: "—Something that we can pronounce. Going back to these people—you say they are smaller—"

~ ***"They are about a quarter the size of us."***

Well, it is good that we now know just a little of the diversity of intelligent life form that exists. Many have developed skills and technologies that far exceed our own, but the universe is not a racetrack on which to compete. It has no timekeeper. It is of course infinite, and infinite in respect of its possibilities with endless enchantment, so that we can simply enjoy the exploration on offer. And we cannot help but learn something on the way. The last ten minutes of the evening were given to an experiment suggested by our friend. It was an attempt to materialise something of Aerah within our midst while we remained silent with eyes closed. The attempt did not succeed but Bonniol concluded: ~ ***"Mm—that was a useful attempt. We can see***

some of the—um—possibilities, in making the attempt. It will need a bit more work."

We voiced appreciation to Bonniol and his team for their efforts, and perhaps this was a building block that might lead eventually towards another mega-leap in interplanetary exchange. Time will tell. And once again it was time to say 'goodbye'.

It will have been noted that Bonniol has now named one culture with ability to travel a wormhole. Wow! He has also extended our present Earthly view of black holes. It may therefore be of interest to very briefly list a few notes from Earthly data on these mysterious objects:

Black Holes: In 1964, Roy Kerr predicted from theory the *rotating black hole* which may be closer to reality than the earlier Schwartzchild static model. Rotation confers non-spherical shape. The general black hole structure is a *singularity* (having infinite mass / gravity) at its centre, surrounded by an *event horizon* (from which no light escapes) and exterior to this, a *photon sphere* (possibly the part that is visible to Aerans). Kerr's mathematics relates to a wormhole connection *in theory*, but it is also stated that these *Kerr wormholes* are not actually expected to exist (in agreement with Bonniol's statement). Another type of black hole emission, reasoned by Stephen Hawking is *gamma ray bursts* arising from virtual-particle-pair separation, consistent with what is termed *black hole evaporation* (and possibly visible to some other life forms). Cosmologically, perhaps black holes could be seen as 'larders within the cosmos' where potential matter, in effect, gets tucked away. I suspect that in several ways they are a cosmic balancing mechanism, and after all, Bonniol says that *all* is connected. None of this is in disagreement with what has been communicated. The reader may wonder how much Paul knew at the time. He had, I can say, heard of both black holes and wormholes, but as with most of us he knew nothing of the theoretical details listed at the close of this and previous chapters.

CHAPTER: 34

Blue Blooded – The Point About These Dialogues … 29th May – 19th June 2006

ONE WEEK LATER, Salumet was again with us and I had reflected on how much our eyes had been opened by the knowledge of masters visiting other planets, and how religions had resulted. Earth is simply not alone in the way this happens. Our master had replied: ~ **"Yes, of course. Again it is always the wider picture that you strive to understand. In that way, you will open more fully to the truth. Man has so much to learn, but he cannot learn with a closed mind."**

George: "And it's good to look beyond this single planet within the creation—"

~ **"Yes—yes. It would be ill fortune indeed, for you to centre all of your thinking upon this one planet. Indeed, it would do much harm to your spiritual unfoldment, to be so closed in your minds."**

So we are encouraged to look to the wider, more universal picture in our thinking. The creation extends far beyond one single codex, far beyond any one set of planetary religions, far beyond Earth, far beyond this galaxy, and the creation is so much more than just one physical universe. There is no need to be of blinkered mind. The pea that stays in the pod can rest in a most comfortable situation, but its future lies beyond that place, and the parable of sowing seed applies to vista upon vista of stars in the heavens, far, far beyond this one single planet!

Three weeks later and two days before summer solstice we again received Salumet, followed by Bonniol.

~ ***"Hello!"***

Lilian: "Hello Bonniol, nice to have you with us again."

We enquired if he had been present during the Salumet session, which had been lengthy.

~ ***"I was in the room, yes. It is always fascinating for us to come early and listen."***

George: "We are pleased you manage to do it."

~ ***"And we enjoy the vibrations in this room—the colours, as you have been told, are beautiful."***

Lilian: "You can see those?"

~ ***"I am able to see them to some degree, yes. We can all see auric fields to some degree."***

Lilian: "*Some* people can here."

~ ***"There is so much colour in this room; so much movement."***

Jan: "When you say movement, do you see light bounce around—"

~ ***"We would see the energies flowing, moving as perhaps your oceans move."***

Jan: "Bonniol, does the Earth actually breathe?"

~ ***"You are asking whether your Earth is alive?"***

Jan: "I know it is alive. Can you describe how you may feel or see the Earth's breathing vibration?"

~ ***"The planets that we know of, work in a different way to the creatures, but they may be perceived as something similar. There are exchanges of energy going on, and this COULD be considered like your breathing, where you are exchanging are you not?"***

Jan: "That's the general pattern, yes."

Lilian then asked if body structures of Aerans are similar to ours.

~ ***"Yes, we have organs similar to yours. They are perhaps quite different to look at, at first, but they function in a reasonably similar way, yes."***

Lilian: "Well, we have blood flowing around our body and the colour of our blood is red. Is yours the same?"

~ *"Yes, we also have a fluid which circulates. It is more of a blue to our eyes—blue, yes. But it functions like your blood, yes."*

Jan: "George, am I right in saying that it is oxygen that makes our blood red?"

George, doing a quick think replied: "Well, it's an iron compound, haemoglobin, and oxygen plays a part. It's complicated chemistry."

Jim, also a retired chemist, added: "Oxy-haemoglobin is red, carboxy- (or de-oxygenated) haemoglobin is blue, I think."

Jan: "That's what I was getting at—"

Interesting, but I have to say that our names for chemical compounds mean little to Bonniol, who quickly sidestepped that issue with the suggestion that he try sending a mind projection of his own appearance to us, possibly during our sleep state.

There followed more discussion of wormholes and black holes that really just made the point that Bonniol's actual knowledge of these things and Earthly theory are in remarkable agreement. This brought a statement from our friend on the real point of these communications: ~ ***"The importance of these communications—we always like to say that the important things are not so much the understanding of the cosmos, as the belief or fact that we all coexist within the cosmos, and we are at this point, able to come together a little."***

George: "Yes, you're absolutely right about that and these meetings—these connections are so valuable. We are able to have ideas about other beings, and these ideas help us to see *ourselves* in a better light."

~ *"One of the most important things that we have found from our communications with other worlds, is that we are able to build up so much more of a picture of how this cosmos is put together, in terms of numbers of planets teeming with life, each at different stages of material progression and spiritual progression."*

George: "Yes, a term that has already been used this evening (with Salumet) is 'mind-boggling.'"

~ *"Yes, it helps to envisage some of the majesty or magic of creation, when you start to look in your night sky and ponder just some of the incredible life that is happening on each world at this time."*

Lilian: "You have certainly awakened our interest."

That interest now addresses the *entire* cosmos, all creation. As Bonniol says, we are all of us able to *come together a little*. And that was a majestic thought on which to close. As to the nature of blood and as Jim says, what we know as red blood corpuscles pick up oxygen in the lungs, and the oxygenated haemoglobin is the red colour. The fresh oxygen is transported to body cells and tissues, where the haemoglobin exchanges carbon dioxide and waste and returns to the heart. In this form it is blue. It is stated in our literature that every living (Earthly) organism needs a circulatory system to fuel its parts and to remove waste; a system clearly extending to other planets!

CHAPTER: 35

Pyramids are Important – Variable Atmosphere … 10th July 2006

In England we were experiencing a substantial period of drought. Just prior to Bonniol, one already known to us as 'Ond Kulla' spoke via Sarah. In Earth life he had been a 'head farmer' in Egypt at the time of the pharaoh and founder of the 19th dynasty, Ramasses I. He spoke on how to make little water go far—on the spiritual way of making the most of little water. He knew from his experience of such matters! As he left, Bonniol joined us.

Lilian: "Hello."

~ ***"Hello again!"***

Lilian: "I wonder if you know we've just had a visitor who lived on this planet a long time ago—"

~ ***"Yes, they are aware of what goes on in this room, I feel."***

We affirmed.

~ ***"This room has been a place for much teaching for some time, has it not?"***

Lilian: "It's been wonderful, yes."

~ ***"And everyone connected with it is aware of what is possible here."***

George: "Yes, when Salumet is not with us, on those occasions, others tend to come through, and some most interesting ones have been through at times."

Lilian: "And the Egyptians, as were others, were very much aware of the planets and the stars."

~ ***"Yes, sometimes these quiet times are very valuable. Your visitor gave you an important lesson there I feel."***

George: "About water and the energy therein—"

~ ***"Yes, you would be surprised at how far a little water could go."***

Lilian: "Yes, we do look at it rather differently. Were you aware of that energy in the water? You probably were—"

~ ***"We have been aware for some time. We can utilise the energy of our food and water, as much as the actual material food and drink. When you are constantly aware of the energy of these things, it helps your body and your gardens and everything to make the most of it."***

George: "Yes, we are becoming more and more aware of what I might call—the subtle energies."

~ ***"And if as well, when you look at the stars and your sun and all of those planets, the more that you are aware of the energies that they bring, the more you can receive them if you wish to."***

Sarah made the observation of how this might benefit people who are ill and have difficulty eating food and digesting, to which Bonniol responded:

~ ***"The body will receive these energies once it is told to open up to them. But they are your bodies to command or open as you will."***

Now, as it happens, here on Earth during this last decade, some extremely important work has been carried out on a particular form of subtle energy. I refer more specifically to the work of certain Russian scientists[9] who have investigated and published data on the properties of energy fields held within the pyramid shape. Pyramids are truly very special places. Details of this valuable work are listed at the end of this work in Appendix I. Referring briefly to this research, I enquired if Bonniol had knowledge of any similar pyramid experiments on Aerah.

~ ***"Yes, this is another subject which crosses the planetary divide, if you like. We also have found this benefits our—the energies that we wish to expand or use, can be helped by this shape."***

Sarah: "Do you have ancient pyramids as we have?"

~ ***"We do not have ancient pyramids like the ones you have, because our ancient ones were not built to last."***

George: "It just so happens that the gentleman who was with us earlier, from Egypt of several thousand years ago—that civilisation built large *stone* pyramids, and it's an interesting connection that he should have been here this evening. But we are finding with the modern experiments, that the energy of the pyramid shape is capable of doing a number of things. It can heal burns in flesh faster, and it can alter the structure of seeds so that the crops grown from those seeds give higher yield. There are all sorts of factors that arise from the energy stored in the pyramid."

~ ***"Yes—and now you should be able to understand a little more perhaps, why these shapes have these effects on things."***

George: "Yes and the nature of the energy, seems to be a little like sound energy—like a micro-sound that gets into things. It is interesting that you also are aware of these things."

Sarah: "Do you actually use your pyramids much today?"

~ ***"The pyramid shape is very much a part of our structure system, yes."***

Lilian: "So are any of your houses that you live in of similar shape?"

~ ***"Our houses are like your round—tents—like—um—"***

Sarah: "The Indians had?"

~ ***"Yes—ah—more like cones, yes."***

Sarah: "And does that shape produce energy as well?"

~ ***"The round shape is for us, we feel, a better LIVING structure. However, the pyramid shape is for us, found to be a USEFUL structure."***

Sarah: "You don't use it for your hospitals to heal people?"

~ ***"We have other structures that do specific jobs. The hospitals usually have round walls, because they sometimes involve people staying for a long time, and the round walls are better to live in. But the pyramid energy is, or the way it builds up energy, has other uses."***

George: "And do you find that in order to build up the energy in your pyramids, they need to be orientated to the rotation of your planet?"

~ ***"They must be orientated—um—to, yes, receive the flow of energy through their FLAT sides."***

George: "Yes—right So the build-up of energy really depends on the rotation of the planet."

~ ***"Yes, that is the main consideration—the way your energies flow, and the pyramid will then harness them better."***

It was nice to have that part of the Russian scientific work confirmed, which also of course explains the very precise orientation of the ancient Egyptian structures. (These have often been described as aligned to the Pole Star, but the real point is that one pair of sides is aligned east-west with planetary rotation.) Sarah went on to enquire what other shapes were utilised for buildings, and it would seem that the pentagon is used for meeting places and public buildings. Bonniol explained that, since that shape lies between pyramid and cone (the cone being an infinitely-sided pyramid), it has a mixture of values.

Rod: "So if we had a 'burns unit' within a pyramid, it would be more suitable—"

~ ***"Yes, it is a pity is it not, that this knowledge was forgotten?"***

Indeed, it is scarcely believable how things can sometimes get cloaked in superstition and then lost altogether. I added: "And it is only just coming back as far as we are concerned! I can see that the pyramid shape would be useful for, in the first place healing, as a storage area for prolonging the life of things, and as a storage area for *conditioning* things in a beneficial way. Is that similar with you?"

~ ***"Yes. We are able to use this shape in various ways and you will find that, though the pyramid shape is useful, it also has some disadvantages. But it is mainly the energy that is gathered in the shape—that is the important thing."***

We observed that one might use a pyramid to enhance meditation, but it might prove to be awkward living space.

~ ***"As a meditation site—the pyramid will allow your thoughts to move out of the Earthly realm more easily."***

Sarah: "This we can visualise. What are the disadvantages you have in mind?"

~ ***"Your meditations are at various times—it is not ALWAYS the best shape for when you are going within. It can help when you wish to elevate yourselves out of your physical shells."***

There was a pause and that concluded our discussion with Bonniol on this matter.

But in fact, we had already checked out the work of Professors Golod and Krasnoholovets and their 44-metres high constructions in Russia, with Salumet two weeks earlier. Some of their more striking results were mentioned: water failing to freeze at – 40 °C, and stored seeds having their crop yields increased by 20 – 100%. Salumet was confirming of their findings and made a number of comments to place the facts into historical perspective: ~ **"If you go back to the time of the ancient civilisations, they were much more aware of energies than you are at this present time. What is happening with your Russian friends and their pyramid experiments is not new knowledge, but is knowledge that has been regained and is now beginning to be understood by men of your time. The ancient Egyptians in your world in particular, had much more knowledge of energy and vibration and space travel."**

We know from other dialogue, that Salumet refers to the ancient Egypt of around 9,000 BC, the time of the building of the 'Great Pyramid'. He also made further comment as to the energy: ~ **"The shapes of many things have their own vibration—there are many people in your world now, who find benefit from being within the shape of pyramids, because of the energy which is created within. And if you think of the shape of the pyramid, you will begin to realise that all lines reach to a pinnacle, as if the energy is being drawn upwards to a higher vibration."**

I replied to this: "Yes, and I can say that radar does detect a column of some kind of energy reaching—I think the figure was 1,000 metres above the large pyramid."

~ **"And beyond—you will then find that the vibration becomes even finer, but that is something not to be understood at this time. It is important for your scientists in your world now, to recapture knowledge long lost."**

It is interesting that Salumet picked me up on the height of the column of energy, and correctly so. On checking the data next day, I found the figure given for radar detection is in fact to a height of 2-kilometres. As stated above, more information on this fascinating subject will be found in Appendix I.

The topic changed and we moved on to the thickness of the Aeran atmosphere, and on this Bonniol was saying: ~ ***"Yes, we have***

a technique for moving through our denser atmosphere. We can thin it by fanning it a little, or with our minds."

Sarah: "And as you said, you flap your legs like they have flippers."

~ ***"That's correct, yes—this is not always necessary, but at times the atmosphere can be thicker than normal."***

Rod: "If you raised yourself, as on a mountain, does it get less dense?"

~ ***"It would be less dense the higher, yes."***

George: "Could you tell me, in the vicinity of a pyramid, is it thinner there? Does the pyramid have an effect on your atmosphere?"

~ ***"It—um—there is an effect on the atmosphere. It breaks up the larger dense areas."***

George: "So, if you have several pyramids scattered around, it would have a general wide effect? Why I ask this is that we find that, in an area where there is an oil field, the viscosity of the oil is quite well reduced by the effect of pyramids in that area."

~ ***"Yes, it is able to thin the atmosphere, though it is necessary for the atmosphere to thicken, so we tend to get the thickness in other areas. They (thick zones) form away from the pyramids."***

Rod: "Would it be necessary in your hospitals to thin the atmosphere for some patients? Would they need a thinner atmosphere to benefit their health?"

~ ***"Yes, we would usually keep the atmosphere thin where people are ill. There is less energy needed in moving through thinner atmospheres."***

Rod: "When you are travelling in a car or bus, do you have a means in front to thin the atmosphere. Have you developed a system?"

~ ***"We can fan the atmosphere and there are vehicles that carry fans on the front. But when we are travelling large distances, we fly higher to avoid these dense patches. It is more a problem near the ground."***

I asked if the thick atmosphere had any advantages or is it just a nuisance.

~ ***"It is part of our world, like rain. We talk about it as (with) your weather."***

Rod: "Does it sometimes get thicker, more some days than others? And with rain, does the atmosphere thicken?"

~ ***"It does not relate to the rain. It is to do with the denseness of our planet and the energies that flow through our world being slightly different."***

Rod: Does it thicken at the poles?"

~ ***"They (the zones) thicken at around the midpoint—what you would call the equator line."***

George: "How about the flight of birds in relation to this? Do they find it easier to fly in the thicker atmosphere?"

~ ***"They are very good at avoiding it!"***

George: "Ah! So they prefer the thinner atmosphere—"

~ ***"Yes. There are animals that stay within it, but for birds it is very difficult."***

The thickness of the Aeran atmosphere seems a little strange and our dialogue gives some indication of its impact on life and how it can be controlled. Following that we got briefly onto the subject of plants; the flowering and seeding process being comparable with ours, and seeds are spread by insects, birds and animals as on Earth. But Bonniol comments that plants on Earth are more numerous. Following this there were a few general words on Aeran technology before the session closed, with Bonniol saying: ~ ***"We have developed technologically, not as far as some worlds, but we are able to live WITHOUT pollution now. And our technologies have improved so that we feel we are working WITH nature reasonably well. I should probably say 'goodbye' at this point."***

It was a brief statement, but to have advanced *without* pollution and *with* nature sounds wonderful; an excellent kind of future for mortals to aim for, and we now know a planet that has achieved precisely this! In our 'goodbyes' the pleasantries were particularly heartfelt this time, and Bonniol added: ~ ***"It would be good to be able to answer more fully some of your questions."***

But we are of course so wonderfully well pleased with it all, and made this clear to our friend. I can also say that there has developed a mutual understanding as regards spiritual protocol and order that must be observed at all times in these exchanges.

On reflection, this quite short chapter includes momentous issues. Our style of questioning has in general been a mixture of the deeply searching mixed with much lighter chat. All is contributing to a fascinating picture of Aerah, together with some important Earthly comparisons. Regarding spiritual protocol, it would be wrong to give or be given information that we should better discover for ourselves whilst charting our natural way forward, and guides will be overseeing this. But I believe it important that we continue to make clear how much we *do* know, especially when it is knowledge held by a small Earthly minority (examples of this kind of knowledge being *pyramid energy, UFOs* and *nature's elementals*). Bonniol is after all, a physical being like ourselves, and will not *fully* know the extent of our knowledge.

Pyramid energy is one issue that may reasonably be described as momentous at this time. On this, there are now agreeing statements from: the advanced physical being Bonniol, the light-being and master Salumet, and professors of the Russian Academy of Sciences. This is an impressive consensus. And in this context, the Michelson-Morley experiment of 1887 plus its later revisions were designed to demonstrate Earth's passage through the 'ether' by accurate measurement of the speed of light in two directions. No difference in light velocity was found. The conclusion drawn from the null result was that an ether medium does not exist. This conclusion can now clearly be seen as invalid. It has been a red herring seriously hampering Earth's proper understanding of the nature of space throughout the 20th-century. The accumulation of energy within a carefully orientated pyramid is proof of Earth's spin through the ether, and proof of ether existence per se.

Architects and town planners please note the importance of shape in design of buildings! Likewise, please consider hospital 'burns unit' design implications!

Aerah's variable atmosphere is at first glance curious. It may possibly be due to proximity and attraction between molecules under conditions of low energy density. This might explain the observations described. Planetary rotation also plays a part, so that there is a stretching and thinning at the poles with corresponding thickening at the equator. The thick regions sound almost 'gluey' which would explain why birds avoid them. Fanning would confer some movement into the mass so that some molecules 'un-stick' to make the system less viscous. As a general principle here on Earth, as temperature decreases, molecules of liquids and gases come closer together, so that viscosities increase—they get thicker. Most of us will have noticed this phenomenon with hot and cold cooking oil, treacle and such. Pressure increase has a similar effect. On Aerah, regions where molecules are close together will be denser, will in general gravitate to a lower level and will be spun towards the equator away from the poles. These considerations may help to explain the curious observations.

CHAPTER: 36
More on Buildings and Pyramids – The Lake People ... 17th July 2006

BONNIOL AGAIN FOLLOWED a lengthy Salumet session: ~ ***"Hello."***

Lilian: "Hello Bonniol! You're with us again..."

~ ***"I am with you again, yes. I can't keep away these days!"***

We laughed as I added: "We're not complaining!"

Lilian: "No! We wish we could visit *you*!"

~ ***"You will come someday somehow, I'm sure, and you will be able to see our world like we are able to see yours."***

Lilian: "Yes, that would be interesting."

~ ***"It is a lot easier to see it when you can actually go there. It's difficult to put into words and describe everything, but hopefully you are having a little understanding of what our world is like."***

George: "Yes, it was most interesting last time when you spoke on the shapes of various buildings. I wonder if we could continue that a little. You mentioned the round shapes—the buildings that you live in. Are these cone-shapes that go to a point at the top?"

~ ***"Yes."***

George: "You don't make use of flat roofs at all?"

~ ***"We very occasionally allow flat roofs, but we would not recommend it."***

George: "Your cone-shaped buildings would have an energy-enhancing effect I believe—"

~ ***"Yes, as you are becoming aware now."***

Earlier, we had been discussing vibrations within shapes with Salumet, so I asked if Bonniol had been listening in.

~ ***"I arrived some way into it, but yes."***

Sarah: "And were you aware that the reason you have it go to a point at the top is because of the energy?"

~ ***"We are aware that the shapes come into it. A point is useful—helps create the vibrations more clearly than if the shape was incomplete."***

George: "Might I ask if you have windows? Or is the material you use transparent?"

~ ***"We have windows, yes. We prefer not to live with completely see-through walls. But we have many windows."***

I explained that this was helping us to picture their living, and we were beginning to understand the value of energies within shapes.

~ ***"It is like—um—instruments of music, which increase the vibrations or make the vibrations amplified. But the building shapes are of course working with energies which are vibrating far higher."***

Lilian pointed out that it was also working with nature and allowing rain to run away.

~ ***"Yes, it is a more natural shape than the flat roofs which do not help in any way with vibration."***

George: "Within the cone, do you live on more than one level?"

~ ***"Yes, we have our bedrooms in the lowest floor and we use the higher floors for—"***

Lilian: "Living?"

~ ***"Um—we meditate in the higher levels."***

George: "Yes, the higher levels would be better for meditating and living generally … and you have a better view from your windows."

~ ***"Yes."***

Bonniol went on a little further, explaining that during sleep state, they like to be close to the planet that supports them. There would appear to be energy advantages to living within a cone shape and one can certainly feel it to be a stylish concept of living space. Jan enquired if they use marine energy at all.

~ ***"As we obtain enough energy from our plants, we do not need to use the energy of oceans. But there is huge energy there of course."***

We pointed out that in the near future, we are headed in the direction of energy from the seas, but the Aeran way of obtaining plant energy by liaison with elementals is really most attractive.

~ ***"There are so many ways and so much energy. I am sure there are many good alternatives."***

Staying with energy, we got back to pyramids. I put it to Bonniol that an orientated pyramid really works in two ways—it is a collector of energy by virtue of planetary spin and it is an enhancer of energy by virtue of shape.

~ ***"Yes, the shape itself and—um—the way it is positioned work to develop the energy, so you could say the energy always exists, but it is concentrated into one place, yes, concentrated within the walls of the pyramid."***

George: "So the pyramid is a collector of energy—"

~ ***"Yes, and then you have enough of it to accomplish certain things."***

George: "I think, in our ancient past, the Egyptians had structures within their pyramids to further enhance. They had layers—"

~ ***"When you understand the vibrations more fully, you can fine-tune your pyramids to perform better. The materials available will improve the performance of your pyramid and the vibrations will be a little different with different materials."***

George: "Yes, there's much we don't know and I think this is information we are relearning."

That took us just a little further. On reflection, it is obvious that all those intricate details of construction embodied in the Great Pyramid would be highly meaningful in regard to *its* fine-tuning.

Now it was our friend's turn to change the subject: ~ ***"I've been asked to—um—we have been approached by another world, and they are eager to visit as well."***

Various exclamations followed: Oh! Wow! Wonderful!

~ ***"We could with your permission do like we did with the others we brought."***

George: "Oh yes, certainly we would very much like to participate in that. They would be very welcome."

~ ***"So perhaps we could organise that for you soon."***

Sarah: "What sort of beings are they?"

~ ***"They are another race—um—"***

George: "Would they be the Suwaxians that you told us about?"

~ ***"No, they are yet another of our group of planets. They are from a world which is full of—lakes, yes."***

Jan: "Is it the water they live in?"

~ ***"No, they live on the land but their world has more lakes than most. And they use the lakes for much of their needs, but they are land dwellers. Their appearance would perhaps not surprise you as much as some from other worlds though—they have very long legs, yes. The legs are long but very useful for wading the lakes."***

George: "That's interesting. We have certain areas of our planet where we have many lakes, and there is one area where people's legs are long. They have evolved in that situation (I had in mind the Sudd wetlands region of southern Sudan)."

Sarah: "And is this world very far from you?"

~ ***"It is a long way from both of us, but we would guess they are nearer you. It is hard for us to calculate that. They would be incredibly far from both our worlds."***

Lilian: "Would they be able to mind travel?"

~ ***"Yes, they mind travel very easily. They have a good knowledge of spiritual matters."***

Jan: "Would they physically be able to travel at all?"

~ ***"They cannot travel physically as yet."***

George: "Do you have a name for them or their planet?"

~ ***"It would sound—um—in our tongue obviously not meaningful, but they are 'The Lake People'."***

Sarah: "How did they contact you? How did they get to know about you?"

~ ***"They have been involved in our exchanges for much time now. They have recently been made more aware of YOUR world and have asked to visit with us if this is possible."***

Sarah: "Mm, that would be lovely."

Jan, who had missed some earlier meetings, was puzzled as to how language disparity was got around in these exchanges and Bonniol added some further clarification to that: ~ ***"Well, we don't KNOW the language. We communicate with our thoughts. These thoughts are then translated for us."***

George: "Yes, this happens within the brain, I understand—"

~ ***"Yes, we would not be able to learn languages so quickly."***

George: "This seems to be one of the processes involved in mind projection."

Sarah: "Thought doesn't have a language."

~ ***"The thought carries ideas, which are then put into words—pause—I am having to—um—some of my thoughts don't get translated and this is—"***

George: "Is this because you are thinking of the other planet?"

~ ***"No, this is something that occurs when communicating in this way at times."***

Sarah: "Is it because some of the thoughts are not possible to translate?"

~ ***"I think it is to do with—because of our different worlds, some of our thought forms are not so easy to put into words, yes."***

Jan: "Am I right in thinking that also thoughts are filtered by spirit before they get here? So we aren't receiving those thoughts that are not appropriate?"

~ ***"You are receiving the thoughts as I send them. There are many helping with the sending. I would not say there is filtering as such. There is simply our awareness that we must not abuse this link."***

Jan questioned further the format of our exchanges to which Bonniol replied: ~ ***"I understand that you do not wish to force the conversation along YOUR lines, and that we should speak as we wish to. This is of course the proper way, and we are happy as it has turned out. There was much for you to ask at first, when we were unable to download more quickly, the information. It is natural that (then) you would be asking more questions."***

Sarah expressed a hope that if he found any of our questions to be irritating, he would tell us.

~ ***"It is not—it is never irritating for us to be communicating with another world! And all these questions are necessary."***

George: Well, we certainly appreciate being able to ask so many questions. Are there any further questions you would like to ask us?"

~ ***"I always have questions but I feel it is getting late for you."***

So again it was farewell time, and Jan suggested Bonniol ask questions on the next visit and our friend agreed to have some ready.

It is abundantly clear from numerous publications[10, 11] over the past three millennia as well as from exchanges with Bonniol and Salumet, that The Great Pyramid of Giza, presents a sharply poignant chapter in Earth's history. The wealth of publications that relate, of course are inevitably a mixture of both correct and incorrect views. This has to be the way of material thinking, but sooner or later these views must be critically examined and rationalised. A particular value therefore, of accurate extraterrestrial input, is to help us sort out the wheat from the chaff, produced from all that intellectual grist. The idea of adjusting energies within a shape is not unknown, and some of us will know of the Chinese Feng Shui approach. But how many are there who would think of fine-tuning nearly seven million tons of rock pyramid? Any such detail will of course have been incorporated into original design, and to this end several different kinds of rock have been used. Built off the bedrock of the Giza plateau, its core masonry blocks (major part) are coarse nummulitic limestone, quarried locally. Most of what is known as the King's Chamber, plus three plugging pieces in the lower Ascending Passage, are red granite from Aswân 500-miles to the south. The passage masonry consists of limestone blocks from the Moqattam Hills, 10-miles distant. The pyramid casing blocks are a polished, white, high-grade limestone, also quarried from the Moqattam Hills. Each of these materials has doubtless been carefully chosen for good reason. Next, we might consider a detail of shape. The layers of core blocks are not built to the flat-sided pyramid shape that one might have expected. Each side, from top to bottom has a concave crease, running to a maximum indent of one yard at the midpoint of each 250-yard base-course. But all the polished white casing blocks enclosing the core structure, have adjusted dimensions, such that the face finally presented is (or was) entirely flat. And it remains for us to decide if this is a funny little oddity that just happened, or is it a carefully arranged element of fine tuning installed by beings blessed with far superior intelligence and technical ability. I would say there is much here to support Bonniol's fine-tuning posit. But at this time of course, loss of original casing and other deteriorations work against the original plan. There must still be a significant energy presence within such a structure, but not quite to its original value.

CHAPTER: 37

To Teach the Child is Important ...
31st July 2006

GREETINGS DONE, IT was now time for Bonniol's awaited question: ~ ***"I have been thinking about your learning centres—your universities and places for the younger people to learn."***

Lilian explained our 'schools' for the pre-university younger ones.

~ ***"Yes. Have you any—um—particular way of teaching children your spiritual truths?"***

Ah! So this was it, and on this planet of ours, a tricky and muddled area one might say! We explained something of the general teaching system from nursery school to places of higher education.

~ ***"Yes, I have been looking at these places in the memory banks."***

This exacted an 'I say!' from Lilian; a response that somehow brought to mind the debonair 'Rattie' from 'Wind in the Willows'. Suddenly we were like the river bank animals looking up to wise Badger, all of us being much more familiar with the *river bank* than any *memory bank.*

~ ***"We are looking for how the young get their knowledge of spiritual—"***

This seemed to be the cue for all to sit up and say their piece.

Sara: "There isn't a great deal of thinking on this in my opinion. A lot of young children go to Sunday school, attached to an often Christian-based church, and they might go to a church service on a Sunday. They learn broadly about different religions in primary school, but it depends very much on the head teacher, and I think we could do much more for the children."

Lilian: "They don't talk about the *spiritual* side much, do they?"

Sara: "Not really, there's not very much knowledge—"

~ "Do you think children should be left for a time before they are instructed?"

Lilian: "If they could be influenced in simple ways—"

George: "I think, in nursery schools they pick up a certain amount of imagery, especially around Christmas and Easter times."

Sarah added that this would relate to formal religion as opposed to the living spirit connection, and if the word 'spiritualism' is used, this may be erroneously interpreted as an ill-defined witchcraft or extremism, through lack of understanding.

Sara: "My children at school often sing songs about love, kindness, sharing and growing. And I think that if children sing songs with good words, then that is helping. There are subtle ways of helping young children to have the right ideas. I think singing has it and can be taught whatever the religion."

We all suspect, I think, that the fundamental spirituality is not sufficiently well understood in many communities, for it to be taught effectively as a subject.

~ "It has been made confusing for the younger children—"

Sarah: "Yes. Have you any good ideas for teaching children?"

~ "We always tell our children the truths of spirit from as young as they are able to communicate. And we believe in—there is no need to wait and they are able to—um—find great comfort I think, and they understand with their young minds, the process of life. But I know there is still much battling to do with your religions, before the confusion—"

George: "Yes, it may be the children lack confidence that they have the 'correct story', so they probably don't derive quite the same comfort from knowledge of spirit."

~ "There must be great confusion for them when they are presented with spiritual truths, as opposed to the way your religions have chosen to present it."

Graham: "And to children it must seem that the religions around the world do cause conflict. There are wars raging at the moment on this planet in the name of religion, which is a shame!"

Perhaps we should also add that such wars are of course in flagrant violation of the original teachings of any master from spirit and contrary to any spontaneous spiritual awareness—a very, very sad spectacle.

Sara, referring to her own family: "*Our* children accept what *we* tell them but I think they are also aware that they are in the minority."

Lilian: "People *are beginning* to talk to their children about spirituality—"

~ ***"Yes, they will not be in the minority forever."***

Lilian voiced agreement and then went on to bring death into the discussion and how children really need to know that loved ones stay close after leaving Earthly life. And we brought in other matters. There have been times when input from family was greater but now much is left to school curriculum. In the UK we are familiar with how the Roman Empire has presented Christianity, also the Anglican version that our monarchy extracted from it, and then the monasteries (that were substantially destroyed in the 16th-century). All have helped shape present day society, together with influence from other denominations of smaller following. But perhaps we understand more of the history and human input than what remains visible of the *original teaching*. On becoming adult, some may forge their own spiritual journey, may become aware either by 'going within' or by reading the record, or both. All things considered we as a group were bound to admit that Bonniol had put his finger on an unresolved fundamental issue in our midst: spirituality is not being taught at all well and this reflects lack of understanding by a confused adult majority. Finally, Lilian was asking a lead question: "How old are *your* children when they start schooling?"

~ ***"They begin as soon as they are able to communicate and have reasonable mobility. The children are so important—such a wonderful time and a joyful time. It is the most impressionable time for spiritual matters."***

Lilian: "Very true."

I reminded that Aerans do not have the same family structure and schooling is more kibbutz style.

~ ***"Yes, they learn from ALL those around them. As you say, they spend much of their time in the company of their own age groups, which includes their eating and sleeping as well as learning."***

George: "And do they have a serious attitude to their schooling? Do you get a proportion that like to play and not be too serious?"

Bonniol got us all laughing and was smiling as he replied: ~ ***"There are always those who like to play ALL the time, and need a bit more coercing to get down to the practises that they are meant to do."***

Lilian: "Do you have late developers?"

~ ***"We have, yes. Each child is unique and (they) will develop at their own pace, yes."***

Sara: "And there is no pressure for those who need a bit longer?"

~ ***"There is no—we try not to pressure them. That is not the best way to develop."***

George: "Do you have a set of subjects to be studied at school, one of which is spirituality?"

~ ***"We teach them as much as, or whatever they are curious about. There is less structure. There is more 'intuitive teaching' I think you would call it."***

George: "Yes, less structure, so do you have examinations from time to time?"

~ ***"Yes, we need to test, to find out the stages and how much they have taken in, yes."***

Graham asked if teaching was by spoken word or mind projection. It seems that either is possible but speech is preferred for groups. And we enquired about teaching aids.

~ ***"We have big screens for writing on. There are several ways to present or display information. We can sometimes use our minds to materialise objects for display, but there are times when it is better to project pictures onto a screen. So it is often not so different from your places of teaching."***

Graham: "Do you have classrooms, groups and teachers?"

~ ***"Yes, there are classrooms. We usually have one main teacher for each, but there are other helps present."***

Graham: "Yes, very similar to us."

Sara: "Have your teachers passed formal examinations to teach or are they there for their natural gifts?"

~ ***"I think it is less that they are qualified. It is more their wish to teach, and they are given a chance, if they are capable."***

Seeking clarification on that point we suggested they might well have an aptitude for teaching a subject without necessarily having a qualification.

~ ***"Qualifications—um—can be misleading I believe."***

Sara: "People can study for qualifications, only to find that they have no interest in the job!"

~ ***"The only real way to know if someone has the right abilities, is to give them the chance."***

We asked if students go out into the countryside on field trips.

~ ***"Yes, we are in nature as much as possible."***

Sara: "Presumably, with less structure involved, your teachers are open to real inspiration. Does it work in that way?"

~ ***"Yes, the teacher is able to—they are guided."***

Sara: "Guided by inspiration—"

~ ***"That is correct, yes."***

That concluded a significant session and once again it was time to depart.

It is clear that Bonniol has highlighted with his question, a glaring weakness within our society—its inability to properly instruct children on the true nature of spiritual existence. It had puzzled him and understandably, he wanted to find out more, and in the process I think I can say it has helped to clarify things for us too. Recalling the assortment of terms used in my own school days and those of our children, they have included *comparative religion, bible study, religious studies* and *RK* connected to schoolwork and *Sunday school* and *confirmation class* connected to church. But the teaching under these headings is apt to omit the central and very important matter of life's natural immortality. Our spirit connection, the soul's ever-ongoing journey, the process of reincarnation and continued life in spirit for all, are factors embraced within that immortal truth (in fact, all this is in accord with the Nag Hamâdi writings of St Paul, written whilst with the Essene). Our departed loved ones still remain close by. These things have been so for millions upon millions of years, throughout the universe and for all human / humanoid cultures. The system is in place forever but something is changing. It is our consciousness, awareness and ability to comprehend, that changes all the time. The old dogmatised traditional religions have been cobbled together from the inspired teaching of masters, intended for human consciousness as it once was long ago. The 'parable teaching' of Jesus suited well in that earlier time. We should now be moving on. The deeper spirit remains much the same and contemporary masters continue to teach from that deeper spirit—to suit 21st-century consciousness. They are also aware that in today's world their words can be recorded, will stay pure and will likely be circulated on the Internet! We *have indeed moved on* in so many worthy ways.

The Great Pyramid and Great Sphinx; the two oldest structures on the Giza Plateau

The Great Pyramid with part of the Cairo metropolis seen in the distance

CHAPTER: 38

The Earliest Egyptian Pyramids – Salumet Speaks ... 7th August 2006

THERE WOULD NOW be a break of seven weeks before we again receive Bonniol. During this period Salumet devoted one whole evening to the Egyptian pyramids, those first few built on the Giza Plateau, beginning with the spectacular 'Great Pyramid'. It comes as a timely enlightenment following and explaining what has gone before, and it should now be reported here in some detail. As our teacher addressed us, it was felt to be an authoritative revelation that immediately galvanised attention: ~ **"I said that I would talk to you about the ancient civilisation known to you as Egypt and about energy in as much as you will understand. Much has been written and said about your ancient civilisations, much of which is incorrect. And I know to this day there is much puzzlement about the structures you call pyramids. We have spoken recently about the smaller versions of the pyramids and about the energies which they contain within."**

We had indeed had dialogue on the recent work of Russian scientists and Salumet had been confirming of their findings. He had also promised to speak further and I had in the meantime the opportunity to refresh my memory on certain details left for us by Herodotus and other noteworthy historians. Salumet continued: ~ **"But let us go back to that time when mankind had much knowledge, when that Egyptian race should have been leaders of their time in the way of 'spirituality', but of course, that word would not have been known to them."**

I asked if it would have been at the time of Osiris.

~ **"We go further back. We go further back in time when many from our world came to advise and to help this planet to become—I**

will use today's phrases for your understanding—to become more spiritual. The people of that time had much knowledge *within*. They understood much of the way of 'nature' in your world. They also had the abilities of spirit, in as much as they recognised the *transmutation of energies* and how energy could be used to benefit mankind. They understood what man has now lost. When first they began to build, and I say to you, the knowledge *came to them from within* from that innate understanding, but it also came to them from *other beings from other planets*. So you understand my dear friends, how much knowledge they had before them, as they began their structures, their building work. It was for the purpose of *travel* and *time* and to be in alignment with the sun and the planets. The structures were NOT for, as used in later days, as burial mounds for their pharaohs. That comes later. Within the structures that they built would be a chamber that would be used by all—man, woman, child and even the animals of that time. It was used like today's people would use your cathedrals; for upliftment, for healing and to gain knowledge. Within these structures there would be one who would be willing to teach, who had come to this planet for that very purpose. Therefore, these buildings were always in alignment to nature. And as we have spoken briefly, the energies within the pyramids is powerful. I will hesitate for any questions that you may have at this point."

So there was a real purpose and a power pertaining to these structures and the sources of knowledge as indicated, and we can say from having the benefit of earlier exchanges that the *travel* referred to is *space-travel*, and *transmutation of energies* includes *dematerialising matter*, one application of this being to aid space-travel. And I took up Salumet's invitation to place a question: "Regarding those who came from elsewhere, the names I have are 'Osiris' and his queen 'Isis', and there was a son 'Horus'. And it is my information that these were the last of that biological line from elsewhere."

~ **"Yes. That information is correct. That is why I said that we go further back, because they were indeed the last of that line."**

Thanking our teacher, I assured that we understood, adding: "And there is a connection that I wish to ask about. The Egyptian pharaohs that followed—there is one source which claims that they are reincarnations of Horus—"

~ **"Yes, we will discuss this. This is where problems begin to arise. From a race of great knowledge, mankind suddenly realises that he can have *status*, in that land at that time, because they had abundance of good earth, water, air and such, as well as limestone, granite and all of these material things—and which were indeed used for the later pyramids. But the pyramids of which I have spoken were constructed *both spiritually and manually*, whereas the later pyramids had mainly manual workers."**

We declared how wonderful it was for us to have that part confirmed. Those early edifices, the most spectacular that stand there in the desert today, have had the benefit of spiritual input—transmutation of physical weight and form to achieve perfect fit and placement of the huge and varied masonry blocks. This explains so much regarding the subtleties of the structures that have puzzled many for so long. And the reasons for such beyond-present-day precision that we observe are now laid bare. Paul asked if sound was used in their construction.

~ **"Sound of course was used, and the sounds were used in the hieroglyphics later used on all structure—the pyramids—on papyrus—on stone, in many ways. And I believe you probably will know that the coding on these drawings and word-pictures were to do with sound, connective sounds. I will explain as we go along. So we have reached a time when pharaohs decided that they were gods, and some I have to say *were reincarnations*, and you know about this subject, and will accept that some pharaohs *were* reincarnations of previous—what you like to term 'gods.'"**

So regarding the extraterrestrial beings as gods because of their far superior knowledge and believing that those 'gods' would reincarnate into the human frame, was a basis for later pharaohs seeing *themselves* as gods. The pharaohs and their scribes used the term 'gods' and this has been perpetuated into modern times by historians. We should really therefore in future, for 'ancient gods of Egypt' read 'extraterrestrials'. It seems that some pharaohs had the soul input of those extraterrestrial ones whilst of course being physically human flesh and blood. This is entirely plausible, and I enquired if it might be seen as a parallel with the fourteen Dalai Lamas seen as reincarnations of Buddha.

~ **"Yes, the same *kind* of situation, but with the Egyptian race it is a slightly different situation. Let me explain *this* to you—as time progressed, the pharaohs realised that they could amass great wealth, and it is shown on their drawings—that the more cattle they could have, the wealthier and more outstanding they became—*materialism started to creep into their lives.* But their downfall was that they began to think of themselves as infallible, and they themselves were godheads. And slowly, slowly this created many, many downfalls. Many pharaohs came to no good."**

Paul compared the loss of spiritual strength to similar decline in Atlantis (an earlier decline, now cross-referenced from several sources), and Salumet responded: ~ **"Of course, it is the same. It is greed of mankind. It is a denying of that inner knowledge."**

Lilian wondered if other civilisations on our planet had been similarly visited, having in mind no doubt that there are ancient pyramids in other countries. Not at this particular time it seems, and the space-travellers to Egypt were themselves instrumental in originating the Egyptian structures as their means of travel or part of it. Perhaps we could see the first pyramids as, in effect, space-ports linking to other star systems. Lilian then asked about the visitor's appearance which produced an interesting reply: ~ **"At that time, I would say, they would take the (humanoid) form so that recognition would not make the people fearful. And this is where we bring in 'energy'—and remember, it is not static, it is ever moving and energy can transmute itself into whatever (form), especially the higher energies—the higher vibrations. In the same way as I have told you about the angels. (They) can change shape to become whatever they wish. And this is indeed what happened at that time."**

Salumet then seemed to reflect on how all this might be regarded in today's world of different, much more intellectual logic, adding: ~ **"But I am sure, my dear friends, that this all sounds very fanciful to you in this day and age. But I want you to realise that that civilisation had great, great knowledge."**

I added that there was one Egyptian historian who referred to the visitors as 'gods' and was careful to differentiate them from the ordinary people.

~ **"Yes, because they had powers which surpassed, may I say, what the Egyptian civilisation recognised. And you must remember that, although they (the Egyptians) had great knowledge, this also became coupled with superstition, which became another part of their downfall."**

So this is where superstition came into the equation. At this point I felt that if we could return to energy, there might be a link with the Russian work and that would help to tie it all together rather well. So I referred to 'Rostau', which Salumet acknowledged as an old name for the Giza pyramid complex. 'And it means *shaft to the 'Duat'*, the Duat being the *sky map of stars.*' Again Salumet acknowledged, and I then asked if that shaft is the same energy shaft that we now know rises vertically from the apex of a pyramid.

~ **"Yes. It is that light energy which has been given those names. It is the spiritual energy which has been created within."**

Paul then sought further clarification asking if the spiritual energy just mentioned connects with the Earth's energy that concentrates within the pyramid.

~ **"Of course, but you must realise that the Earth energy is dense. It is the same energy but it is denser because it belongs to the Earth, in the same way that you as human beings are much denser than someone that exists in spirit. But it is all the same energy. It has to be because we are connected to all things."**

It may help to see energy as bipartite, the Earthly and the spiritual—just as *we each* have those same two parts, the Earthly and the spiritual—and equally just as there is a case for the existence of two universes, physical and spiritual co-existing throughout. A title given to Osiris was 'Lord of Rostau', which fits very nicely. I declared how wonderful it is to have this much confirmed, when the information available is overwhelming but so often seen as dubious, and it becomes a matter of deciding which evidence is correct and which is inept.

~ **"Yes, and you must use your inner feelings for this."**

I observed there is the Sirius connection mentioned in the literature, to which Salumet responded simply: ~ **"Yes. But of course the problem today in your world is that, as time continues the stars and the planets become a little—out of sync—that's how you would say it?"**

I said that was wonderfully expressed. And I think we all never cease to be amazed at how succinct in expression a light-being can be from that much, much higher vibration.

~ **"That also you have to take into consideration. But let me continue a little further—there came to that civilisation many pharaohs—good generally kind people but who became a little misguided about their purpose in life. And then the materialistic side of life came to be. And then, because of their great egos, they decided that they should have pyramids as pharaoh's resting places, which they so became. Some were built with manual labour, and also the help of spiritual knowledge."**

Salumet added that they had many resources including the waters of the Nile.

~ **"Everything was in their favour for these structures to be built—so that is, I would say about 9,000 years before Jesus the Christ."**

Now that date I have to say fits in very nicely with certain other records [10, 12] that we have.

~ **"It was around that time that the pharaohs decided that they should have special burial places, also that their cartouches should be specially made for them with the information for which they felt they had become great. There are many in existence today."**

That is of course correct, and Salumet went on to say more relating to the cartouche and the nature of hieroglyphs. It is understood that, during the period when much was written down, papyrus became expensive and this brought changes. More efficient procedures came into use to depict the picture-story. *Sound* entered the system, with use of the sounds 'oh', 'i' and 'pee' to shorten phrases. Here we have the phonetic form and distant mother of today's written language. We now know how modern versions have developed via hieroglyphs, demotic and Greek script, and how all three systems were found on the Rosetta stone (discovered 1799) making possible a translation between written forms. But as a race, the people of Egypt were at this point becoming filled with superstition and ways to please their gods and how to please their pharaohs. The power of the pharaohs became great and there was enormous wealth in the land. But sadly, their spiritual pathway faltered, they lost their understanding of the energies and of time and their ability to space-travel. A once great nation went into decline and the firm evidence of Egypt's past grandeur that still prevails, has presented a mystery to later generations; an enigma that has been much written about. And of course, the written languages used for this have all evolved from that first phonetic language of those early days.

We have digressed briefly from pyramids and their energy. But we are now able to close this account of a culture that rose to such accomplished heights of spiritual splendour, before becoming engrossed in materialism, greed and superstition which brought about their downward slide. Connection to spirit became obscured, and that is the key to our present understanding. An important outcome to be noted is that what has in the past been erroneously termed *Egyptian mythology* is not myth at all, but is a solid factual cornerstone of Earthly history. Osiris, Isis, Horus and others of that period were real beings of great knowledge that lived and prospered, and have left much for us to think on. Now, a small group on Earth has the link with Bonniol and his team on Aerah; a link arranged by Salumet and allowed by the light-beings and guides of spirit. I have no doubt that the resulting exchanges will help to raise awareness and focus on spirit for many. There may well have been similar arrangements set in place around 12,000 years ago. Precise details matter not, but nonetheless we in *this* day and age may count ourselves extremely fortunate in also having dialogue with beings of superior knowledge; as did those of Ancient Egypt. And one difference between then and now is that the early phonetic cartouche language has developed much, so that worldwide communication can now speed on its way via computers. *Superior Knowledge* is thus available to all—worldwide and beyond.

CHAPTER: 39

Homes – Political Symbol – Energy – Healing Thoughts ... 18th September 2006

FIRSTLY THERE WERE rescues counselled by Lilian, then, following the 7-week break, a cheery greeting from our friend: ~ ***"Hello!"***

I think we all responded together: "Hello! / Lovely! / It's been a long time! / Bonniol—yes, welcome!"

~ ***"Yes, I've been waiting to return. I am very happy to begin again."***

Lilian: "Ourselves too, to renew old acquaintances as we say."

~ ***"Yes. Thank you. You have been doing good work here, I believe."***

Lilian: "Yes."

George: "Perhaps you have been listening this evening—"

~ ***"I was around a little earlier, yes."***

Lilian: "Oh good! Do you have to join a queue?"

~ ***"It is—um—not a queue for us when we are just observing. But we do have a guide who tells us when we can attempt to come through—so your evenings are always well planned, are they not?"***

George: "Yes, planned from spirit and I guess it is the guides who organise things."

Lilian then explained the development since Bonniol's last visit, the information from Salumet on Egypt of past times, and how there has been that influence on Earth from other beings, most probably not as far distant as Aerah.

~ ***"Yes, you are beginning to realise that these things have happened."***

We said how helpful it had been to have key facts confirmed, because it has been a confused and controversial matter, and the majority of Earth-dwellers simply dismiss Egypt's past as insubstantial myth. Our teacher's statements have of course endorsed extraterrestrial participation in the pyramid work as the true reality. A pause followed, before we moved onto more mundane matters—details of Aerah's cone-shaped homes, and their windows: ~ ***"Our windows, yes, they are rounded."***

George: "Yes, I felt they would be, because that would be pleasing and look nice with the cone shape."

~ ***"They are usually of a similar roundness to the building itself."***

George: "So would they be oval rather than circular?"

~ ***"Yes, they are wider usually than they are tall."***

Sarah: "And what do you put in your windows? We put glass in ours."

~ ***"We also have a material which is hard and yet transparent."***

Sarah: "Do the harmful rays come through that material?"

~ ***"Yes, we have a small problem with dangerous rays, but it is smaller I think than yours, so we do not need to pay too much attention. We do appear to have a more protective (atmospheric) layer I believe, than you do at this time."***

When asked about the cone proportions, Bonniol replied: ~ ***"The height is perhaps three times the width, in most homes. We like to sleep below but meditate above."***

Sarah: "How many floors do you have?"

~ ***"Usually just two—yes, we have simpler homes. We do not need so many things."***

Rod: "We've usually got an attic with a lot of rubbish up there!"

There were some giggles at this but Bonniol explained: ~ ***"But it is easier for us to materialise things that we need, which alleviates the need to store so much."***

Well, that has to be more satisfactory than rummaging through an attic! We asked about garaging vehicles: ~ ***"They are parked under a roof, yes. Usually it is a simple roof with no strong curve, just enough to cover our vehicles."***

At this stage Sarah seemed to sense that these were very low structures and possibly scooped into the ground a little.

~ ***"Yes, they are indeed low, and close to the earth, yes. You have seen a glimpse then?"***

Sarah: "It felt like it."

Rod: "Do you heat your houses?"

~ ***"Heat is needed at times, yes and we have mentioned our energy system I think."***

We were again in need of a fresh subject. Perhaps Bonniol would oblige.

George: "We've jumped straight into asking you questions again. Is there anything you would like to ask us?"

Lilian added her encouragement and Bonniol produced another of his deeply searching questions: ~ ***"Yes—um—you have told us something of your political system. When you are unhappy with your leader's decisions, you are able to voice your concerns?"***

Sarah explained this happens in many countries but not all.

~ ***"So what do you think is the most favourable method of influencing your leaders?"***

We waded into this awkward and muddled area voicing various feelings, beginning with Salumet's teaching that thought is all-powerful so that merely having the thought will have *some* effect. But then there have been times of overt protest, with anti-nuclear campaigners carrying banners; at times 200,000 or more through a city. This approach concerns extreme issues. Sarah spoke of signed petitions and letters to the press, but when these go unpublished, it is ineffective and frustrating.

~ ***"Perhaps it would be interesting to find an example, for example, your war situations. How would you try to resolve these actions from your government, if you do not believe them to be good?"***

Now we were getting to the nub of the matter, and I reflected on how much I had admired the organised protest by schoolchildren in our capital city as the Iraq conflict came to a head. Those young minds *felt* from within, but the will of government had remained firm, and my own letters to the press had predictably, gone unpublished. It was a sadly frustrating time for many who sought non-violent solution as opposed to violent non-solution. Understandably, Sarah's answer to Bonniol's question was the cliché: "With difficulty!"

We voiced further feelings:

Rod: "It depends on what the opposition parties do in parliament as well."

Lilian: "At the moment the religions are causing quite a few problems."

Sarah: "If not religions themselves, it's the—but in the end religions, yes."

Sarah likely had in mind extremist terror groups falsely identifying with belief systems for pseudo credibility. It is a pitiful area of confusion. But now Bonniol cast aside confusion with a beautiful thought: ~ ***"We have in the past held effective protests—and normally we find a symbol to represent our thoughts. If you do not believe in war, maybe there is a symbol that you can focus on. People carry poppies do they not, which have become a symbol?"***

Lilian: "Yes, I see what you mean."

~ ***"When you have a symbol, a physical object, it can become a powerful tool."***

Rod: "A peaceful symbol like a dove—"

~ ***"Yes. If you are objecting, and have a particular symbol to wear, that demonstrates that objection."***

Rod: "We had one with the nuclear issue didn't we?"

~ ***"And these things can gain momentum."***

Sarah: "Yes, that's right. That would be good."

George: "So this is the approach that you have used at times in the past, on your planet?"

~ ***"Yes. If we begin to embody the symbol by wearing it, then it reminds everyone and they can either join in or not; also the action can spread to other forms, like your vehicles or your houses."***

We had to agree that widespread display of a white dove symbol would be an effective way to demonstrate feelings of peace—'people power confronting threat of war' one might say. Lilian added that it would bring people together, as Bonniol continued: ~ ***"It helps that these symbols are also uplifting in themselves, like your magnificent eagle for example."***

George: "I think you're right. It would be a better method than street demonstration."

Rod: "How many parties have you got in your government Bonniol?"

~ ***"We have candidates who have different ideas. I don't think they are quite as black-and-white, can I say. They are all perhaps closer than your political parties. WE have more say, so they mainly follow the common people's—"***

Rod: "Wishes?"

~ ***"Wishes, yes—thank you."***

Lilian: "On your planet, you are much more aware of your spiritual side aren't you? That must make a big difference."

~ ***"There is that awareness, yes. But you have had—um—there have been times, have there not, when you have HAD much awareness?"***

Lilian: "Yes—when we were visited from another planet!"

~ ***"It doesn't always mean you will not have problems. Awareness carries its own responsibilities and we must always act to the level of our awareness."***

This is true of course. We moved on to government funding and Bonniol reminded that we had spoken briefly on this. He reiterated regarding Aerah: ~ ***"There are ways of motivating people other than through monetary means. And there is sufficient food and basic requirements for everyone. So people who have skills, who have great skills, do not need any more money than anyone else."***

This is of course a vastly different paradigm to Earthly competitive pattern, and I was acutely aware having just completed my income tax returns! Our friend continued: ~ ***"We have an allowance which is sufficient, and if there are any circumstances where people need extra help, we have all that is required."***

Rod: "Who pays for the hospitals then Bonniol? Who pays the doctors and nurses?"

~ ***"The hospitals are built and maintained by those that have these skills. It is part of their work to do this. They receive the same—um—credits as everyone else."***

George: "I see. So the credits that people receive are fairly uniform within your society?"

~ ***"Yes, they are all able to obtain food and any of their needs and it is other people's jobs to provide the food. There is no need to tax people because there is no need to collect in this way."***

George: "So if a road needs to be built there is no special funding operation for it?"

~ ***"If everyone is being paid the same, then that (special fund) becomes a waste of your resources."***

We reflected on how this might compare to communist regime, but it is not really the same, and those in control always do well. Then Sarah returned us to hospitals, enquiring if healing is by thought, or would such procedures as acupuncture, injections or operations under anaesthetic be used.

~ ***"These different forms were once used—in the past we had many forms of healing, but now we are able to heal the body with the mind, yes."***

Sarah asked about success rate and if people were sometimes destined to die anyway.

~ ***"People are always dying of course, and there are accidents. But if they are incurable by our best healing doctors, then we don't think any other form of healing would have cured them either."***

George: "So all of your healing helps the energy body and is not directed at the material body. Is that right?"

~ ***"We can direct the healing at both bodies."***

Rod: "You say: some of your best doctors. Does that mean that they will have a stronger thought transmission?"

~ ***"There will always be those who are more powerful, yes."***

Back to energy again, which of course underpins everything. On the way to the meeting, some of us had talked about bio-fuels—alcohol and oils obtained from plants. This we mentioned to Bonniol who then added a little more on the plant energy: ~ ***"Yes, it is not quite the same. It (that used on Aerah) is an energy form which is NOT QUITE material. It is energy of the plants, but it is of an etheric nature. We are not able to do it ourselves. It is ONLY the nature spirits that are able to extract this kind of energy."***

I said regretfully: "Yes, we would have to, first of all have a population that *believes* in the elementals, and secondly be on good terms with them."

Sarah: "How do you get this elemental's-extraction-from-plant into your vehicles?"

~ ***"It is extracted by them and they change it a little. They are able to change it into something APPROACHING a material energy. But it is still not physical as such, but it is placed in containers for us to cut into."***

We are becoming aware of so much more than just material world and spirit world. There are 'in-between states'. We know of de-materialised matter and re-materialised matter. We know of ethers and ether beings, Astral Plane beings, and now 'not quite physical energy'! It seems that, as viewed by physical beings, there are degrees of insubstantiality. Some may prefer to think in terms of light or ghost forms, visible to some and not to others.

Sarah: "So how do you—with your thoughts, you ask the elementals to do this?"

~ ***"We have been communicating with them for many, many years. We have not always been on good terms but for a long time now we have been."***

Sarah: "That's interesting."

Rod: "Have we got the same kind of elementals here as far as you know?"

~ ***"We believe they are similar, yes."***

George: "And you would refer to them as 'ether beings', is that right? They live in the ether as opposed to the material world?"

~ ***"Yes, they are not of material bodies. They are lighter, yes."***

George: "Do you in your world have what we refer to as 'four elements': *earth, air, fire, water,* so that there are the four different types of elemental who inhabit each of those four elements (or ethers)? Would it be like that?"

~ ***"Yes, these are the four—the four—pause—representations of forces, yes."***

George: "Yes, 'states of matter' is another term you could use—"

~ ***"Yes, and these are common throughout known space, yes."***

Jim: "When you use energy, does this have any effect on climate? That's something we find on this planet."

~ ***"Yes, everything has an effect, but our fuel has probably the most minimal effect on our physical world. We have had other fuels***

in the past, and this one was given to us by those nature spirits so that we would have the fuel that would have least effect."

I wondered if the elementals might possibly have a vested interest but Bonniol assured that they would not see it in quite those terms, but he did agree the arrangement makes their work easier.

George: "And nature would be the better for the fact that a clean fuel is being used."

~ ***"Yes, this is true, yes."***

Rod: "This may happen on *this* planet in many, many years to come by the sound of it."

~ ***"It is not the only— there are many forms of energy and many of them will be clean, and available in large quantity. For us, this was a good solution with what was available to us. Your Earth may have better alternatives for YOU."***

Humanity will in time doubtless develop other less damaging energy. We referred to Bonniol's words on *needs* as opposed to *wants*, pointing out how the brainwashing of advertising and salesmanship steer many ever in the direction of *wants* instead of our much smaller and simpler *needs.* Our actual energy *needs* could be quite small if we would only adopt a rational approach to our future pathway, whilst having due regard for natural environs.

~ ***"Yes, when you reach out more spiritually, things that you would normally feel important often slip away so that you no longer NEED all your machines and buildings. So the amount of energy you use today could easily be reduced tomorrow, if you begin to reach out more spiritually as a people."***

There followed some lighter chat, then Rod was saying: "What I think is most incredible—I look up at the sky at night. I look at the constellations up there, and I think: Bonniol, you're up there somewhere, where *are* you? You find this tiny little house in Kingsclere—"

Jim: "Do you have any idea of our relative positions in the universe?"

~ ***"We have no way of reading where you are physically. None of our instruments would be capable of that."***

Turning to Rod and Jim, who had not been with us for earlier meetings, I explained: "Bonniol has spoken with us before, and we *can* say where in the universe Aerah is *not.* Bonniol is *not* in what we see as *the observable universe* (that is, he is beyond the heavens that we see with our most powerful devices)."

Rod: "Gosh!"

~ ***"And yet we are communicating instantly."***

Jim: "Spiritually, there is no time and there's no space—"

George: "That's right we're side-stepping space."

With that little reminder, Sarah returned us again to 'healing', wondering if Aerans would be able to give healing thoughts to those on this planet.

~ ***"It's more than possible. We've been doing it!"***

Sarah: "Oh right!"

~ ***"As have you!"***

Rod: "Yes, Salumet told us to do that!"

Our teacher has indeed encouraged, when giving healing thoughts, to include 'beyond Earth' and not restrict to just the one planet—we are all one. Sarah went on to explain she had been thinking of Aerah's healing doctors. Bonniol conceded that to be a little different:

~ ***"It is not always a simple sending light and healing. Sometimes there is dialogue between the doctor and the patient. There has to be the healing of the spirit, and this can involve the spirit having to face something or be more open in some way, before the healing can take place."***

George: "In your hospitals, do you also have a surgery facility to cope with accidents?"

~ ***"We have a surgery but we do not need to use tools. When you have the ability to use your mind, it can work in many ways, including on the physical body."***

George: "So if there is an accident and the physical body loses a limb and there is bleeding, the mind can cope with that?"

~ ***"If it is not too late we can often repair it, yes."***

Lilian, remembering an earlier session: "And did you say you *can grow* limbs?"

~ ***"Yes, this is something that not all of us would be capable of, but yes, in the hospitals."***

Bonniol then declared it time to depart. It had been another remarkable session and as ever, concluded by fond farewells.

Political symbol and energy resource are prime issues in shaping Earth's immediate future and they might well work together for us. Here, the current news is that accelerating thaw of polar ice brings with it dramatic change. Our forebears survived climate transition by yielding to nature's forces, by adapting, by retreating from rising sea levels, moving before advancing glaciers and donning the extra clothes to keep out cold. Those were the rational options then. In our present world little has changed. It is true there are alternative energies that can buy us a little time, but eventually we have to go with planetary exigencies. We must face starkly real and logical *needs*; not get ensnared in excessive *wants* beyond bounds of reck or reason. We have a crossroads situation. The old 20th-century unrestricted, broad highway ends here. Humanity must now throw past standards, chart course afresh and meet challenges set by nature's balancing wisdom.

CHAPTER: **40**

Crogarian Initiative and the Atlatl Rock … 25th Sep … 16th October 2006

SALUMET'S VISIT HAD been accompanied by exceptionally powerful energies, felt by everyone. When Bonniol arrived, Sarah enquired if he had been with us long.

~ ***"Yes, I was aware of the energies in the room."***

We expressed our surprise that the energy was so intense, to which our knowing friend pointedly replied: ~ ***"You will have much to ponder for this evening."***

True, but of course at this stage we had little idea of what was yet to come.

~ ***"I've been aware that we've not brought you the beings from one of the other planets as yet. We can do it this time if you wish."***

To the expressions of enthusiasm I added: "Certainly—we wish!"

~ ***"I will speak for them if that is okay."***

Lilian: "Yes, fine."

~ ***"They are wishing you to think of them as another one from far away."***

George: "Yes, and we would like to, on this occasion say, welcome to *both* of you—a very warm welcome!"

Lilian: "Do they mind travel as you do?"

~ ***"They are mind travellers, yes."***

Sarah: "So they mind travel to you, and then you're mind travelling to Paul?"

~ ***"We have a strong connection to them. They are as adept as us in this."***

Sarah: "And have they had contact with humans before?"

~ ***"Yes, they have visited this planet, but never in a group such as this."***

So they have visited before and now we have a *group* of them? Just as Bonniol's group of sixty or so are all here as a mind-travelling group, we now have with us on this wonderful evening, a further group of beings? Our friend went on to speak of past occasions: ~ ***"They have reached out to individuals. They have found those who are able to be aware of them."***

I still felt the need to clarify, and asked: "Is there one with you tonight, or more than one?"

~ ***"There are many. They are so pleased to be with you in this way."***

George: "Well we likewise are pleased. So they are able to travel as a group?"

Bonniol attempted to explain this just a little: ~ ***"They bring you something of a lighter—um—physical body than our own. They are less physical than either you or us, I believe."***

Again, we had to turn our thoughts to how beings might be much less physical than we ordinarily understand. But now we became aware of something that was again different. Jan began to get strong clairvoyance and spoke of it. This led to a three-way exchange between the visiting group, Bonniol and Jan, while the rest of us were able to continue to place questions. And Bonniol, of course, continued to speak through Paul as usual. An entirely new situation was unfolding!

Jan: "Can I talk to you please, because I have at least fifty transparent beings shown to me? They are completely transparent. They have dark eyes."

~ ***"You are able to see them, I believe—"***

Jan: "Yes I can. They have an outline."

George: "Well if they are less physical, then I guess it figures that they are seen as transparent."

Jan: "They are very, very light—extremely light."

~ ***"Yes."***

I asked if these might be from Suwax, a planet mentioned previously.

~ ***"They are not the Suwaxians, no. These are—more difficult to give the word, another race though, from another planet."***

Sarah: "Have you physically met these people, or do you just know them through mind travel?"

~ ***"No, we have not met physically. We have been connecting with them though for many years. They have not developed the physical machines for space travel. It is unimportant to them."***

Lilian: "Because of the body they have, would that make it easier for them to mind travel?"

~ ***"They are of a lighter vibration, which makes this easier, yes."***

Sarah: "Do they have speech, or do they communicate between themselves through mind?"

~ ***"External speech, yes."***

George: "So, I think I imagine them to be physical beings, but not *very* physical, with bodies, limbs, eyes, and mind of course. Is that fair description?"

~ ***"Yes, they are a similar shape, I would say, but they have not the need for the bone structures that you have."***

Sarah: "Similar shape to us or to you?"

~ ***"Your shape."***

Jan: "Similar to us, relatively large hands."

~ ***"Yes, they use their hands to direct their energy at times."***

Jan: "They have a sensory perception on the outside of the brain. They have a functioning brain within their skull / head, but they have an extra part of the brain outside."

~ ***"That is correct, they are not as enclosed as you are."***

Jan: "Their atmosphere is extremely—I want to say *dense,* through which they hurl themselves. I am being shown—I can *feel* it—"

~ ***"The atmosphere would be—"***

Jan: "Very difficult, Bonniol, to move around. It's like thick soup!"

~ ***"Yes, that is why—they are able to live in such conditions. They are unaffected by the—it is not exactly 'density' but—"***

Jan seemed to be within the atmosphere and *experiencing* it, and she was finding it hard going: "My goodness! It is *thick*!"

Graham: "Would it be like living under water on this planet?"

~ ***"There are so many alternative conditions. I would perhaps—um—say it is more like living in your earth—your—um—"***

Jan: "In soil."

~ ***"Yes, like moving through soil."***

Jan: "They could never feel free. I'm having a tough time!"

~ ***"There are so many planets with different environments."***

Jan: "Ah! I'm being shown a nursery. They *grow* their young in pods!"

~ ***"You are seeing their places where they—it is—um—something extraordinary, yes."***

Graham: "How big are these beings—our size or—"

Jan: "They're about four-foot-ten!"

Graham: "Mm! That's very precise!"

Fair comment—and I think we were all quite shaken by the quick answer given in feet and inches. It at first seemed ridiculous but Jan simply explained that that is what she had been given. It appears that she was receiving spoken information as well as the pictures.

Graham, to Bonniol: "Can they see through their atmosphere? Is it transparent like ours and yours?"

~ ***"You would find it difficult. They are able to see through it though."***

Sarah: "So what are these pods that Jan has seen? Can you explain a little more Bonniol?"

~ ***"You could compare these to—perhaps your tadpoles."***

Sarah: "Yes, oh right!"

Jan: "They've got an umbilical cord—I was going to say—like a potato—like a tadpole anyway, and they're all attached to an enormous nucleus. So they're not born—not of the body. I don't know how that works. They grow on a stem—"

~ ***"Yes, and they are able to survive in that condition until they are ready to—hatch, you could say."***

Jan: "To hatch."

~ ***"Yes."***

Jan: "Bonniol, they actually emerge, don't they? Emerge with a whole, not a 'brainy' (developed) brain as we know it, but with a juvenile brain?"

~ ***"They are quite—"***

Jan: "Developed?"

~ ***"Yes—when they emerge—"***

Sarah: "So does this mean that they don't live in family units as we do? How do they—?"

~ ***"They are already able to survive the—"***

Sarah: "Without a parent—"

~ ***"But they will be in groups, yes."***

Jan: "They are put into groups of juveniles that belong to a higher—part of the race. It's a bit like parenting but *en masse*."

~ ***"They are taken in and become part of the society, and the parentage is not important."***

Sarah was concerned about the lack of body detail and how they survive and grow. There was no obvious system of food intake and digestion as we might understand it: "So what is their nutrition?"

~ ***"They are able to get energy from their—"***

Jan: "Sun."

~ ***"Yes, there is sunlight. Their bodies absorb from the sun, and also from their planet. They do not EAT FOOD."***

Sarah then mused on how we spend much of our time buying food, cooking, eating and clearing up afterwards: "So what do they do with their time?"

Jan: "They sunbathe!"

~ ***"It is part of their nature to feast on the light. They have a well developed social system—they enjoy their lives."***

Sarah: "So are they a peaceful society or do they have troubles?"

~ ***"They are the most peaceful race we have encountered."***

George: "So the group who are with you, they have a kind of collective consciousness that is connecting with Jan. Is that the way it is working?"

~ ***"I believe Jan is able to see these—um—glimpses, or pictures which they are—well, she is tuning into their minds, yes."***

George: "I see."

Jan: "Bonniol—what is *The Crogarian*?"

~ ***"You have given their name! They are, or this is, their planet—'Crogaria'. I am having problems saying these planetary words."***

Graham: "Would you be able to draw them Jan?"

Jan: "Definitely—I won't forget this!"

Graham: "Do they have industry?"

Jan: "No."

~ ***"They have no need of machines or enclosures."***

I asked if there are any other life forms on the planet.

Jan: "They've not been visited because of their extremely difficult atmosphere."

~ ***"Yes, they are unable to receive visitors at this time. They of course have nature spirits."***

Jan: "Very much like our fairies—um—I don't think they are anything like people imagine fairies to be. But I am being shown in *their* time, going back in *our* time—if you understand what I mean—when *our* planet was *younger,* put it that way—they were able to come here, but conditions are not right for them now."

~ ***"They have an ability to appear in other places, yes."***

Jan: "They've actually visited the Nevada Desert!"

George: "Are you saying they are able to *apport* themselves?"

~ ***"They can appear to be in another place."***

[There are the accounts of Indian mystics and certain others appearing in other places and we have the term *apport* to denote this. It happens rarely on Earth and is dependent on a much more developed spirituality.]

Jan: "George, this makes so much sense. They can stay on their planet but can teleport themselves here without *physically* entering this atmosphere. Does that make sense?"

George: "Yes, I think it has to tie in with their being much less physical than ourselves."

Jan: "I'm not quite sure how that works."

George: "Having nature spirits means they also have nature."

~ ***"There is always nature but not as you would imagine it."***

The above dialogue happened exactly as stated, and Bonniol was then saying: ~ ***"I have been talking for enough perhaps, for this time. But they say they would like to try to visit you again. You were as much interest to them as they seem to you."***

We of course expressed our eagerness for a further meeting, with impassioned assurance that the interest was mutual, and Lilian thanked them for showing themselves to Jan. The session closed, Jan was able to draw her pictures in useful detail and I was able to take them home with me. It was as our friend had said, we had much to ponder!

Jan's contemporaneous sketch of a Crogarian being

Next day, the Nevada Desert was still on my mind, and a bell was ringing somewhere from distant memory—or was it a prompt from our friends in spirit? Anyway, whilst at the computer transcribing last evening's recording, I had the urge to look on the Internet and see if there was anything relating to 'Nevada Desert Rock Drawings'. Perhaps it was only an outside chance but there might just possibly be something to connect with Jan's drawings. It was just a vague notion that nevertheless felt right to pursue and I should perhaps not leave that stone unturned. A brief search produced the *Atlatl Rock Petro-glyphs*, part of a set of *Valley of Fire* photos. The petro-glyphs are described as *Anasazi Art* thought to date from around AD 500. The similarity to Jan's drawings was immediately striking; agreement wildly beyond any rational expectation! Two central figures had strong outline and were slim with large 3-fingered hands and wider-than-human heads. And below was the 'nursery picture' depicting pods growing on stems, and to the right, tadpole-like shapes and zigzag umbilical cords. When the downloaded picture of the Atlatl Rock was shown to Jan, she was in her own words 'blown away'. The correspondence was remarkable and with much amazing matching detail!

The Atlatl Rock Petro-glyphs, matching descriptions given during Jan's clairvoyance

The following week, all was recounted to Salumet and we asked for any comments he might have.

~ **"Indeed I do have a comment of course—it never ceases to amaze us that you as human beings feel that you are some kind of select race, when in fact I have told you many times, there is more to all of existence than this planet Earth. And you now have some further knowledge!"**

It was said rather tongue-in-cheek and we had to laugh as I replied: "I think we are becoming more and more aware of this all the time."

~ **"But I have told you my dear friends in past times, that all things that we would speak about would be given or shown in some other way. As you now realise, many of your ancient civilisations on this planet had much superior knowledge. And by their demonstrating what they know (in the form of the petroglyphs), today it has become a source of knowledge for those who are seeking. Therefore my dear friend I say only—why do you continue to be so surprised?"**

I explained that it was not only surprise but also our sheer delight that those who visited in past times had left their mark in this way. A further factor is of course that it is so nice to be able to place these facts in turn before others for *their* benefit.

~ **"—For you all now to discover in your own time and in your own way!"**

So perhaps at last, we begin to recognise that we are not a *select race* but share with others a place in the much wider picture of creation.

There had been others also on this occasion; the evening had been busy and it was already late as Salumet departed and Bonniol arrived. Lilian greeted: "Nice to have you back again after a very, very interesting evening last time."

~ ***"Yes, I am sorry I cannot stay this time for long."***

Lilian: "It's nice of you to call in."

~ ***"It was an excellent meeting, bringing you all together last time."***

I declared it to have been such a bonus that pictures were given as clairvoyance to Jan, so that it was very much a 3-way experience in which we were all able to participate.

~ ***"She will help us in our 'getting to know each other' with her pictures and her information."***

I referred very briefly to our new friends and the rock drawings.

~ ***"All I am able to say is, they have been your friends in the past and they have been less active of late. But they would like to come more often."***

We of course voiced our pleasure at the thought to which Bonniol replied: ~ ***"You will have another chance to meet them I am sure."***

We went on to speak of how humankind, over the years, appears to have taken steps forward and steps backward, and how we are only just beginning to move forward again following a lengthy period of lost direction, veering far off course into wars, slavery, exploitation and extremes of materialism.

~ ***"Just a blip in time—there is a period of growth, followed by some dying back."***

Sarah: "We haven't had such a gap for quite a long time!"

I think Sarah probably felt that, if the dating of the rock drawings is correct, then the Indians of that time had a certain spiritual strength, later lost, and now 1500-years later it is being regained in some small measure. And to us, one and a half millennia, seems a rather big *blip*. I enquired if Bonniol had any questions he would like to ask: ~ ***"I am aware that it is a little late, but I wanted to come and be with you again. I will save my questions for another time, and bid you all a beautiful evening."***

Our thanks and farewells concluded that evening, but our discussion of this same subject was to continue.

It was two weeks later when we were able to resume; explaining in better detail about the *Atlatl Rock* drawings and how there was this excellent record on the rock, of the earlier Crogarian visit.

~ ***"Yes it is one of those pieces of information that may surprise you."***

George: "Yes, and they gave the same information to Jan, as it would seem, they gave to the other people they met in that previous visit."

~ ***"Yes, and if they come again, they will probably give similar information, as it is one of the basic questions asked of other beings."***

Sarah: "Do you think it was actually them that drew the pictures on the rocks, or those they were communicating with?"

George: "I think it would have been the Indians that made the pictures. What do *you* think Bonniol?"

A pause then followed, after which Bonniol replied: ~ ***"I am being told it was your people that made the images, yes."***

I thanked our friend, but of course that thanks was also to the ever helpful guides.

Rod: "Are you in contact with them at all?"

~ ***"I am in contact with them only at certain times. When I brought them through last time it was arranged beforehand."***

George: "It was a very, very interesting visit, and the aftermath as well—finding out about their earlier visit seemed to make it doubly interesting."

Sarah: "How would they have communicated with the Indians? Would that have been thought, or do you know how they communicated with them?"

~ ***"Yes, your Indian peoples would have spoken in their own tongues, but these beings would still be able to understand because of the 'thought' behind the words."***

Sarah: "But then, how would the Indians have understood the—"

~ ***"The Indians were aware enough to understand a little of the mind projection that was given to them."***

Sarah: "Ah right."

George: "Would there have been a brain connection—a mind-to-mind connection in which the brain takes care of translation of the thought?"

~ ***"Yes. When you are able to receive and transmit thoughts, you do not need to speak the individual languages. Thought is universal."***

Lilian: "So they wouldn't have been able to come here in a craft of any sort?"

~ ***"They are able to—um—"***

George: "I think it would be rather like *apport*?"

~ ***"Yes, they do not need machines. They are able to appear in other places using the power of thought."***

George: "Yes—wonderful!"

Rod: "Could you do that Bonniol?"

~ ***"We are not able to do that."***

George: "So would the Indians have actually been able to see their image?"

~ ***"Yes, they would see the translucent beings."***

Rod: "That's wonderful!"

Sarah: "Well do tell them, we'll be very happy to have them here if they'd like to come, and we'll re-paint Lilian's wall—with the beings."

We of course laughed at the idea of emulating yesteryear's Indian art on Lilian's wall, and this prompted Bonniol to say: ~ ***"And how would you understand them?"***

Sarah: "We must practise our mind projection!"

~ ***"That is why it will be useful for you."***

As the laughter stopped we of course all had to agree.

Rod: "Until we improve our technique they won't be coming for a cup of tea!"

I attempted to sum up: "So I think we can say the Indians were sufficiently developed spiritually to be able to have awareness of them and to be able to see their image. But they haven't approached Earth in that way recently—because we do not at this time have that capability. Would that be a fair statement?"

~ ***"You are not ALL without the ability. There are still some who have these abilities."***

Sarah: "Are these groups or are they just individual people?"

~ ***"Yes, there are individuals, but they do come together in groups."***

Sarah: "Such as us, who meet together at certain times?"

~ ***"Yes."***

George: "And perhaps you were saying that there would be individuals rather like Jan, who would be able to receive the images."

~ ***"There are those able to receive, yes."***

Sarah: "When they visit, how long do they stay—moments, hours—days?"

~ ***"It would depend—I would think they would stay as long as they felt was beneficial."***

Bonniol then declared that some problems were arising and it was time to go. We thanked our friend and his team for making several points clearer, and that concluded the session."

The atlatl, pronounced at-lat-el, is a spear thrower used to project a lightweight spear. It was the forerunner of the bow and arrow. The Atlatl Rock is in the Valley of Fire State Park, Nevada, to the northeast of Las Vegas. And it is the 'west view' of the rock that displays the details described. None of us had visited the area. All information given has been researched since.

CHAPTER: 41

Cosmic Visits and Earthly Denial ... 13 November 2006

IT WAS A gap of four weeks before Bonniol again graced us with his presence; there being no fixed schedules in this work. We simply see ourselves as extremely fortunate, with every next visit a bonus. Not that we ever get lonely, and this evening had been busy. Firstly a guardian brought through two children. They had the problem of a 'fixed' memory of paralysis from the Earth life, and this required removal; a little healing job. Next there was a wonderful pre-Christmas message from a group who lived on the Earth in pre-Christian times, but who nevertheless were accustomed to year-end celebrations. Then Albert was with us for what amounted to a 'rescue re-run'; very unusual. The problem was that he had been left with no memory of his actual transition to spirit and it bothered him. With the re-run, he now had memory, and apparently there were many onlookers who also benefited; these having been in similar circumstance. We think they were fallen war comrades, and it is heart-warming that so many can be helped as a group, in the one session. So once again we had been busy and it was a late start for our old friend from across the universe.

Lilian: "Nice to have you back!"

~ ***"I have come a bit late but I am very happy to be here again."***

Lilian: "We have a saying: better late than never."

~ ***"Yes, we have had a little break, but we are hoping to continue in earnest from now on."***

There was mention again of the Crogarian visit, our brief debriefing that had followed, and what a visit that had been!

Lilian: "Wasn't it just!"

~ ***"We did have a little chat since that visit. Maybe you have a question about it?"***

Lilian looked in my direction: "George would have!"

Well I had and when the knowing laughter had abated, I referred back to that wonderful evening, then added: "I think we now realise that there are a number of ways of travelling great distances: there is mind projection and there is the *apport* method that the Crogarians seem to be capable of. There are the physical means of travelling, by rocketry, and by that accompanied by de-materialisation. Then there is also use of the *wormholes* in space that we have discussed. Is that a fair résumé?—those are the methods used?"

~ ***"Those are the methods you have knowledge of so far."***

George: "Yes, I was going to say—there may be other forms of which we have no knowledge."

~ ***"Yes, we are aware of many ways to connect with others—and to call it 'travelling' is a term for it. But of course, the connection to another may not involve physical travel, but it may SEEM like you are travelling when it is a small part of you that is travelling."***

George: "Yes and when you first came to us, you said: '*this is an incredible journey!*'—and I think the way the words were put, was for our understanding, which was more limited then than it is now."

~ ***"Yes, it is confusing to think of it as 'travel', when—ah—we are doing it instantly."***

Lilian: "Yes, it seems such an amazing thing to us."

~ ***"But we still use the words, because they are still valid I think."***

George: "Yes, and we must always bear in mind that others will read these transcripts of the meetings, and such words are well understood generally."

There was some further talk of Jan's clairvoyance and how useful it will be in future work, and Rod suggested she might do a sketch of Bonniol that we could frame and hang on the wall! We spoke of the scanty knowledge of visits to Earth from elsewhere and of the endeavours of Erich von Däniken [13, 14], an author who has seriously studied material evidence for extraterrestrial visits. We pointed out that his publications suggest there are many rock drawings, inscriptions and artefacts that relate quite clearly to visits from elsewhere in the universe.

~ ***"You have I'm sure had many visitors and you will have more. You are in a TIME OF DENIAL—I think is the word."***

George: "The population at large—yes—would be in denial."

~ ***"Yes, but you HAVE HAD visitors from other planets, yes. Perhaps the time will come when much more is available. Your world is still denying too much, but you've been told this will change."***

Lilian: "I think the younger people—they are not in such denial as the older ones."

~ ***"And you all here have open minds."***

I agreed, also pointing out that we here are nonetheless some of the older ones.

~ ***"And there are others. There have been many others IN THE PAST who have welcomed these visitors."***

George: "I imagine it has been similar on your own planet—you have had visits in past times and records of these have been made in various ways. Would that be correct?"

~ ***"Yes, we are all exploring and being explored!"***

Graham referred to our own moon exploration and how Salumet had indicated that some facts have been withheld, to which Bonniol suggested: ~ ***"Perhaps they saw other evidence of visits in space."***

Graham: "We have been told that some material has been kept quiet, but truth always eventually comes out, and we will find out more."

~ ***"It has been the case in your world that even when there were visitors from other planets, they did not visit everybody (only a few got to know). Now that your world is 'smaller' in some ways, it is more difficult to visit unnoticed. But there are still those who have a great interest in your world, and (they) continue to observe it."***

Graham: "I think if something happens, that this world cannot possibly deny it would have a very sobering effect. When people realise that there really is more than just this little planet, I am sure it would have a good effect in many ways."

~ ***"We will continue to try to bring you more—more of the wonderful people and possibilities that there are."***

We spoke further on 'denial', and how our thinking may become too fixed. I ventured that there are two major areas of denial widespread within population. There is denial of *visitors from space* and there is denial of *the spiritual existence*. There have of course been many over the years who have worked towards making the reality of spirit, undistorted knowledge of spirit, more generally known. To this end there has been a small minority who have been able to bring about 'materialisations' of those in spirit, and we asked if this phenomenon is known on Aerah.

~ ***"Yes, this is possible. We have achieved this in past times when we wished to 'physically' see our departed ones."***

George: "But you don't need to do that now. Would that be correct?"

~ ***"That is correct, yes."***

That substantially concluded our exchanges for the evening. But it is interesting to note that *spirit materialisations* like so many other things, are not confined to this one planet. It is well known that in past times there have been charlatans and exhibitionists who have sought self-aggrandisement by pretending to produce phenomena. Sadly, these have been responsible for much damage to true belief. They have given spirit world a bad press. Today, one has only to go to the Internet for clear updates[17] on materialisation evidence, but this type of evidence is of course a mere detail within the wider picture. Spiritual existence and space-travel are highly significant issues that warrant our careful attention. The phenomenon of materialisation from spirit versus its bogus misrepresentation should never have become a stumbling block to belief. Partly on account of such details and bad press, many at this time on Earth still remain in denial of both spirit world and other physical worlds that have long since developed the capability to explore this wonderful cosmos.

CHAPTER: 42

A Phenomenon Planned - Carbon is Universal ... 27th November 2006

AGAIN IT WAS late evening as Bonniol followed Salumet and others.

~ ***"Hello."***

Lilian: "Hello Bonniol."

~ ***"I have been told you have finished something, and you are now ready for a little talk before you close. I will not stay long."***

I replied: "Please stay as long as you wish. We have an expression: the night is young!"

Agreement and giggles followed.

~ ***"I will be happy to stay all night if I could."***

Lilian: "That's nice to hear."

~ ***"I am hoping to be allowed to help with your PHENOMENON work, which you have been hoping will come to you."***

George: "Yes, Salumet mentioned this last time and I did wonder if you would be involved. It's very good news to hear."

~ ***"We did try once before and we would like to try again, to bring an object from my world."***

Lilian: "Thank you."

Rod: "That would be wonderful."

~ ***"I hope this will—ah—not PROVE to you, because you do not need proof—but it may give you the absolute assurance that—ah—words are as we speak them."***

It was delicately put, and we explained there are many who read the transcripts of these meetings, and they in turn speak with others, so that many would benefit from knowing that the phenomenon of which we speak is possible.

~ ***"We will attempt to bring you at first something simple, made of a simple—metal—a metal coin."***

Jan: "So would we be able to actually keep this object?"

~ ***"You would be able to keep it if we manage to materialise it. It will be permanent."***

George: "And we could certainly photograph it for the record."

Sarah: "If it is a metal that we don't have on this planet, it would be convincing to non-believers!"

George: "It may well be a metal that we have, but its energy-density may be different. That would be interesting!"

We next asked if our friend would be happy to take questions.

~ ***"Yes, please ask a question if you have one."***

The first presented difficulties. I explained about 'carbon' and how it is a very special chemical element on Earth. All vegetable matter and life materials burn to yield carbon. Conversely, all life structures are *based* on carbon. It is the ELEMENT OF LIFE. I wanted to know if it is the same on Aerah. Bonniol hesitated. If he were of this Earth, I think he would have shuffled awkwardly whilst replying: ~ ***"We would have a different—um—I feel the answer is more complicated than I can deliver at this time. The whole system of chemistry is a little different—a different energy system, vibrating at a different rate. There are many factors involved in determining the nature of your elements."***

I suggested: "Perhaps things don't even burn in the way that they do on this planet—"

~ ***"They will not burn in the SAME way. There will be a different chemistry."***

Graham: "Is this because your planet vibrates at a higher frequency?"

~ ***"Yes, that is the main reason."***

Graham then enquired if vibrations had been slower in the earlier evolution of Aerah.

~ ***"The vibration—yes—was once slower than it is now."***

It was late evening, the going seemed tough and we felt it best to leave it there and skip to a lighter topic.

So I said: "Going onto something quite different, do you have fat people and thin people on your planet?" and midst a few titters,

"And do you get concerned about getting too heavy and eat to a regimented diet? Do you have fatness and thinness?"

~ ***"We have many different sizes. Some are perhaps what you would term 'fat', yes. There are always those who—"***

Lilian: "Eat too much?"

~ ***"Yes, this is something that we have not fully outgrown yet."***

Someone said 'good!' And perhaps it is nice to discover a shared distinctly human trait.

Sarah: "One problem at the moment is that there is an awful lot of what we call junk food and mass-produced food that isn't good. Do you have junk foods or do you eat all natural foods?"

~ ***"The food is natural, we do not have these highly manufactured foods."***

So the wise course to follow would appear to be to keep to natural diet, adhere more closely to gardening and agriculture, and to minimise food processing. But we explored further, wishing to know if Aerans worried about their weight, pointing out that we have weight-watchers clubs and slimming diets.

~ ***"I would say that we are not as concerned with how we look. If a person is overweight, they can easily change if they want to."***

George: "Yes, it sounds like you are more in control than some of us here."

~ ***"Yes, there is not really the addiction."***

Addiction! Yes, food can be addictive, and Bonniol has chosen a good word here. On Earth, the mechanism for over-eating is a current study area and addiction has been mentioned.

Lilian: "If you're mostly vegetarian, do families or groups grow their own food?"

~ ***"Yes, there is more locally produced food."***

Lilian: "And do you sometimes buy from each other?"

~ ***"We buy from the producers. We also share each others."***

Clearly then, this suggests much less transportation of food on our friend's planet. There is a local production emphasis, and perhaps this is another important issue that needs attention.

~ ***"I would like to tell you a story from a book I read recently, but I feel I must do it next time."***

Lilian: "Then we look forward to next time."

~ ***"Until then, our love goes with you."***

Rod: "Thank you Bonniol, it was wonderful."

Sarah: "Look forward to your story."

George: "It's been nice to talk again. Thank you, *all* of you."

That concluded Bonniol's visit, but then there was a surprise. The evening was not yet finished. There were indications of one with Eileen.

Lilian approached: "Hello."

~ *"I am here to say one thing. I'm sent to tell you: your discussion about CARBON—yes, I am instructed to tell you: IT IS A FUNDAMENTAL ELEMENT OF ALL THE UNIVERSE. And it will exist on the planet you have been speaking about, although as they have told you, at a different rate of vibration."*

I quickly acknowledged that we understood.

~ *"But in all the cosmos, this exists because it is a 'regenerative force' on all planets—all LIVING planets. The only time it (the situation) changes is in spirit. So that point has to be made, and that is why I am here."*

George: "Thank you! Are you also saying that this would be a basis for life structures throughout the (physical) universe?"

~ *"It is one of the elements, yes. It is a REGENERATIVE element, yes."*

I acknowledged, and the regenerative factor was being very much emphasised, the full import of which was still not yet with us.

~ *"But of course, you here call it carbon. But the actual vibration exists all over, because it is a 'regenerative force'."*

George: "Yes—mm."

~ *"And don't ask me questions! I am only the messenger!"*

Much laughter followed, as I declared: "A very nice messenger to have! And we do thank you for that information."

~ *"You are very welcome."*

George: "Thank you."

Our helpful communicator hesitated and added: ~ *"What a very pleasant people you are!"*

The compliment led us to declare our appreciation of those who watch over and bring additional data, pointing out that there are clearly many more pleasant ones than just those who sit in the chairs at these meetings. We were left with much to think on.

Our language is complex and sometimes a word has more than one application or meaning, take 'regenerate' for example. We are conditioned to think of the more general meaning, but the Concise Oxford Dictionary begins with: *Invest with new and higher spiritual nature* and then *breathe new and more vigorous and spiritually higher life into.* In relation to an element's regenerative value in the universe, that definition fits to perfection, and the meaning conveyed by our messenger from spirit becomes sharply clear. Having dealt with that aspect let me now as a chemist say just a little about the unique chemistry of carbon that facilitates this road to higher spiritual life. Carbon stands apart from all other elements. Unlike any other, carbon forms millions upon millions of different compounds because its atoms easily attach to each other and to hydrogen. And then all these resulting HYDROCARBONS (that may take the form of long chains, branched chains or rings of atoms) can also fix onto other elements. Confused already? There is no need because there is so much order in the way it happens. It will help if we take a look at *crude oil* which is a mess of broken down (and simplified) carbon compounds. So let us begin with crude oil. This includes many hydrocarbons known collectively to chemists as 'the paraffin series', and the entire series may be written as one general formula:

$$C_n H_{2n+2}$$

Where C = carbon, H = hydrogen and 'n' can be any number. So the *octane* of petrol, having n equal to 8, is a hydrocarbon chain having the formula:

$$C_8 H_{18}$$

This shorthand description means that a chain of 8 carbon atoms is combined with 18 hydrogen atoms to form one long molecule of octane. There are other well-known compounds and blends within this same series. They include: propane, butane, paraffin, diesel fuel, petrol, petroleum jelly, paraffin wax, and the simplest member with n = 1 being methane, alias 'marsh gas'. We have looked briefly at just one series. Crude oil also contains other series that can be represented by different general formulae. The point I would now make is that millions of years earlier, when the crude oil was living vegetable life, the compounds and the chemistry were very, very much more complex. The chemistry of carbon and its compounds is truly astonishing. In this regard it is an exceptional element, unlike any other. All vegetable, animal, human, insect and microbial life forms involve carbon-based structures. It underpins all physical life. That is the point to be made here. The further fact that, in conditions of high temperature and immense pressure, carbon atoms compact together to form *diamond*, seems to somehow endorse its special character. This is the underlying chemistry that supports carbon as a *regenerative force*, not only on Earth, but as we are now told, throughout all creation—a vital factor within the perfect plan.

CHAPTER: 43

Tales of Revelry – Clairvoyance – A Super-Computer ... 4th December 2006

THERE WAS A question to be put at the outset concerning clairvoyance.

Lilian: "Jan has been getting a picture of a green pyramid. Have you anything like that on your planet?"

George: "She was getting that image just before you came through and it happened last time as well—a sort of green, crystal pyramid image. Does that mean anything?"

~ ***"I've been sending her a picture of a pyramid, yes."***

George: "Oh good! Jan has picked that up!"

~ ***"We have been sending these things to you all, but we have waited for one to realise, yes."***

Jan: "To make the right connection—is it the right colour?"

~ ***"You have seen correctly. I have now some other pictures for you, and hopefully you will be able to receive them soon"***

Jan: "Right."

Lilian then reminded Bonniol of the story offered last time.

~ ***"I will tell you, yes."***

Lilian: "Thank you."

~ ***"It is a pity that we have to tell this story without our full powers of communication, but we will nevertheless try for you."***

Lilian: "Thank you."

~ ***"I will make the explanations brief, but leave the details to YOUR imaginations. There was a time on our planet when our people had unusual ways of celebrating their achievements. They would often adorn themselves in all kinds of colourful—"***

Jan: "Plumage?"

~ "Yes, with flowers, yes—and they would sing and dance, and perhaps become a little intoxicated. As these gatherings progressed, they sometimes fell to their knees and became a little sad. They would purposely hit their heads on the ground, because they forgot that they were celebrating and were not able to focus any more. They had literally exhausted themselves with their excess of euphoria. We have adapted our celebrations and no longer exhaust ourselves to this point."

Our attention faltered for the moment, returning to Jan's clairvoyant images. But we would return to the story in due course, and although short in words it reached deeply into the consciousness in a curious way.

Jan: "Tell me what I can see Bonniol, could you explain it?"

~ "Yes, you are—"

Jan: "Four—like paper—art paper—"

Outline shapes of Aeran palaces. Jan's contemporaneous sketch

~ "Yes—"

Jan: "Cream in colour, or off-white—pyramid shape, with a large hole in the top. Now, either this is an item of clothing, though I am not seeing the person in it, or—in fact—a building! Does that sound silly?"

~ ***"You are having a—you are seeing another building, yes. It is—"***

Jan: "It's very beautiful!" and, as more detail came into view, "You're showing me a city! You're showing me the equivalent to a city!"

~ ***"Yes."***

Jan indicated that it was as if her view was from about a mile above and looking down on the buildings, and how clean they looked!

~ ***"You are looking at our main housing areas. These are constructed for the people—"***

Jan: "Ten floors or more in one of *these* buildings!"

~ ***"You have seen the—palaces, yes?"***

Jan: "Yes, they are *very* palatial, in a pure sense."

~ ***"These palaces are found in the cities, yes, and are for—"***

Jan: "Your dignitaries—"

~ ***"Yes, are for special housing for guests when they visit our cities. They are not the permanent / usual homes of our people."***

Jan: "Right, there are not many of them."

George: "A little bit like our hotels perhaps—"

~ ***"They are used in that way at times."***

Jan: "Well thank you for that—and I've still got them."

As Jan declared that she would try to hold the images we suggested she may be able to draw them.

~ ***"I am happy that you are now sensing our world."***

Jan: "So am I!"

~ ***"You will soon be able to see US. I hope you found the story of some interest."***

George: "Yes—yes indeed. When you said: intoxicated—"

Jan: "They were drunk George."

George: "Yes, but was that a result of dancing around or was it a result of drinking alcohol?"

~ ***"It was mainly the intoxicating effect of their—"***

George: "Their euphoria?"

~ ***"Their celebrating, yes—but there were also those who will use drugs."***

George: "I see."

Jan: "Plant form—the drugs came from nature."

~ *"Yes".*

Rod: "Do you have that problem? Is it a problem on your planet?"

~ *"It has been a problem."*

Jan: "Obviously no violence, because what you've allowed me to see is just so peaceful. Unlike you, *our* substances are abused in many ways. I would imagine that use of it was purely for recreation or enhancement of their euphoria. Am I right?"

~ *"They only wanted to celebrate."*

George: "Some of our shamans of the past have used very vigorous dancing in order to put themselves into a trance state, and I just wondered if there might be a similarity or parallel, with your exuberance."

~ *"Yes, I feel there can often be parallels. This story has significance to many, and we use it to modify our behaviour."*

But now it was Eileen's turn to receive an impression from spirit, and it took us all by surprise because it related to something completely different. It concerned a development in computer science of which none of us had any knowledge whatsoever. It came as an obscurity from out of the blue, one might say.

Eileen: "Bonniol, I'm being very strongly impressed from spirit to say to you—can you explain to us what 'R21' is? I feel it is some kind of a robot. Can you explain please?"

~ *"Thank you. You are correct, yes. We (on Aerah) have another name for it of course. In your language you say it like this (R21). But it is a machine that we program for powering our homes and preparing our—propelling our—"*

Jan continued to be impressed: "It's a generator."

~ *"Yes, thank you. It generates power."*

Well, that was a start, but this Aeran version of R21 we were later to discover is something much more complex than just a generator, but that is the first part to be mentioned. Bonniol working together with Jan's further impressions would finally reach a fair and more complete description, albeit sketchy at first.

Jan: "It's solar powered—it doesn't have electricity in it like ours."

~ ***"It is powered by the—"***

Jan: "You've got to have a computer too."

~ ***"Yes, it has other uses. It is like a machine that is able to perform many tasks."***

Jan: "And a machine to take part in surgery."

~ ***"It can be made to follow certain procedures, so it can."***

Jan: "The intelligence is only—R21 is purely the intelligence. It's the artificial intelligence of the computer that they've produced. And they put it to use in different ways."

~ ***"Yes, this is—ah—a good summary."***

Jan: "It's extremely full of work. It has the ability and the knowledge of everything. It's extremely—an ENORMOUS COMPUTER. Our computers aren't anywhere near this yet. It's big—chips like ours—it's enormous!"

~ ***"It is linked to a large database."***

Jan: "It controls everything! It controls your temperature, your climate, your seasons—"

~ ***"It—um—is not CONTROLLING the climate. It—um—"***

Jan: "It works *with* it."

~ ***"It works with it, yes, and it's able to predict—"***

Jan: "Yes, it's like our weather forecasts."

~ ***"—And—um—make the right changes which may be needed. And it is a computer which has learned to—or is capable of adapting, predicting, and then—"***

Jan: "Calculates."

~ ***"Yes, it makes our lives far simpler."***

Graham: "The computers—where do you keep them? Are they in people's houses or around the neighbourhood?"

~ ***"We have the mother-computer in the main city and there are smaller units wherever needed."***

Lilian: "So do you have one in all your homes?"

~ ***"There will be some form of it in every home."***

Graham: "Do they check up on your lives and make sure you all behave?"

It was said tongue-in-cheek and we chuckled, knowing full well there would not be a 'big brother' situation on our friend's spiritually, and perhaps, technologically more advanced planet.

~ ***"We have talked I think about our computers a little. We have them for communicating."***

True, we had spoken a little, and now some more; and it becomes clear that Aerah is well advanced. Here on Earth we do not have a solar powered, linked system of computers connecting to every home. That we have to see as technologically advanced, but more than that, it demonstrates a neighbourly caring, sharing quality of life. But it might be said we have evolved to a parallel piecemeal situation in which Internet and email connect many of us. As the evening concluded, with as ever our parting warm wishes, I felt that what had just transpired was much to digest and difficult to grasp, but truly wonderful. On this evening, R21 was something new that none of us had encountered, but I have since found R21 intelligence applications recently listed on the Internet. We in the group were oblivious of that development until nudged from spirit! Amazing! I recall the early dialogue with Bonniol when he said Aerah has *something like our computers*, but we had not guessed a solar powered super-model spreading influence far and wide throughout their world to every household! I suspect there is also more to Bonniol's short story than face value. He says it has parallels and can be used as a behaviour modifier. Yes indeed, and it has since made me reflect on Earth's past great civilisations and how some were so much more advanced in matters issuing from spirit; Egypt for example. Past great civilisations had so much that was really well worth celebrating, and doubtless they celebrated. But eventually they forgot their motivation—the source of those spiritual gifts. They became attracted to different and more selfish ways; leading to the fighting of wars with the many trials, tribulations and heartache that followed. We all know about this only too well, perhaps reeled in disgust from the error of those ways; metaphorically banging heads on the ground. Through all of this, the teachings of love, laws given to Moses—*thou shalt not kill*—all forgotten. Yes, this evening left much, so much to think on, as Jan sketched in outline wondrous buildings, ten-floored palaces of truncated cone shape, rather like upturned flower pots;

the smaller green dwellings being quite different, reminiscent of 'Gaudi architecture' with decorative tops rising to a central point and having many windows. This had been our final intergalactic evening of 2006. If meetings continue like this, then prospects for the coming year might be seen as more than a little intriguing; so what next?

CHAPTER: 44

Suns and Moons – Seasons – Agriculture ... 29th January 2007

BONNIOL EXPLAINED THAT his team had been quite busy during our recess communicating with other friends about the universe. It seems that mind projection is the preferred and more standard procedure, but unlike this Earthly connection, mediums are not normally needed, it being a direct mind-to-mind link that is possible. When asked if the link could be done via a computer Bonniol replied: ~ ***"We are not THAT clever! It is something that might be possible but we are more used to mind contact."***

Lilian: "More spiritual—"

~ ***Yes. And it is a New Year for you."***

Lilian: "That's right. Do you have calendars as we do?"

~ ***"Yes, it is always important to count our days and mark them in some way. There is a need to make note of the changing seasons."***

When asked if everywhere followed this pattern, Bonniol indicated this not to be so, reminding that the *mushroom people* spend most of their time projecting, and they have no reason to count days.

Rod: "You mentioned that you have seasons. Does that mean that your planet is tilted in relation to the sun to give you the seasons?"

~ ***"Yes, we have seasons as you do."***

At this point Jan spoke of receiving more clairvoyance: "You have four suns don't you? We have one–"

~ ***"We have two suns, and several moons."***

Jan: "Why am I seeing four?"

~ ***"We are able to see some of our heavenly bodies brightly, but there are only—"***

Jan: "Two suns."

~ ***"Yes."***

George: "Perhaps what Jan was seeing includes two moons."

Graham: "Would they be very bright?"

Jan: "Two are brighter than the other two, so yes. One is very fat in relation to the others, so I presume that's different."

Rod: "You are obviously going around one sun. The other is too far away to affect you is it?"

~ ***"Yes, it has an effect in some way on the others. Each is giving something out, even if it is far away."***

Jan: "Bonniol, am I right in that one of your suns is actually dying?"

~ ***"Yes, one of the—"***

Jan: "One of the two is dying—is older than the other."

~ ***"It is in its stages of, where it is reducing, yes. But it is still many years from its final transformations. They will not happen for many years."***

George: "Bonniol, you are influenced by two suns. Could I ask—does your planet rotate around both of them or just one?"

~ ***"We are in a rotation which involves both."***

Graham: "The suns are relatively close together then?"

~ ***"Yes."***

Jan: "One underneath the other. One is high—the younger one."

Sarah: "So if that sun dies, will that have an enormous effect upon your planet?"

~ ***"When it finally transforms it will collapse and draw into it much of the material around it. I am hoping that this will be many, many years in the future."***

Sarah: "We are sorry that your planet—"

~ ***"Of course, everything is meant to last as long as it is needed, yes."***

We of course speak of inconceivably distant matters but 'final transformation' is a conversation stopper, even if remote. After a short pause, it therefore seemed a good moment to further express our pleasure at once again having Bonniol with us, and we asked if he had questions or would he prefer that we continue with some more.

~ "You will find I am not so in need of questions from now on."

George: "I see—you've been working on Paul's memories?"

~ "We have understood much in the time that we have been away, and there is less need of questions."

Sarah: "Were you listening in earlier on Salumet's words?"

~ "I was not around at first but I became aware towards the end."

Sarah: "We wondered if someone was with Paul earlier—"

~ "There are many who are drawn here."

Jan: "Bonniol, I believe I am beginning to have some flash-pictures of yourself."

~ "When you say 'flash-pictures'—"

Jan: "Nothing's clear or constant."

~ "You may be able to stabilise them."

Jan: "Of course, it may not be yourself I can see but I am seeing somebody. Are you pink?"

~ "We are pink, yes."

Rod: "Did he wave to you?"

~ "There are certain things which will distinguish us. We would prefer you to wait until you are able to notice them, and it will be better to build up naturally. There are many new doorways, you could say, to walk through, as we continue to learn more."

We seemed to need a fresh topic, so I asked if we might ask more questions concerning Aeran agriculture, explaining the current Earthly issue of farming with synthetic chemical fertilisers versus organic farming; the latter involving giving back to the soil compost and animal manure. The use of synthetic fertilisers seemed a strange idea to our friend: **~ "Your chemical fertilisers are nothing more than isolated chemicals from more whole (complete) organic material?"**

George: "Well, they are not necessarily *derived* from organic material. They can be derived, shall we say, from rock or minerals."

~ "Yes. We prefer to give our nutrients in a more 'whole' form."

George: "The natural way."

~ "Yes."

George: "Yes, and how would that be? Do you use animal manure?"

~ ***"It is one of the ways, yes, but I think you will find there are many ways to recycle. All matter—"***

George: "All vegetable matter?"

~ ***"Not just vegetable matter—all the materials that WE use can be recycled—much of it is useful as growing additives."***

George: "So you use *all* recycled material and you don't use straight chemicals. Is that correct?"

~ ***"Yes."***

George: "Would you have used straight chemicals in the past?"

~ ***"As far as I am aware we did not. It is for us a strange idea. Separating out what you need can create more work for yourselves."***

George: "Yes, it is a strange idea that has been with us for around 300-years, but I think now we are beginning to move away from it, and we are heading back towards what we call 'organic farming.'"

Lilian: "Well, I remember that you are mostly vegetarian. At any time did your people farm animals for eating?"

~ ***"We did go down that road, yes. And there are still some very close relationships with the animal kingdom, which could be seen as farming. But it is more like a symbiotic relationship."***

Lilian: "But not to kill them to eat."

~ ***"No."***

George: "Would it be possible to say what percentage of your population are vegetarian?"

~ ***"We are ALL vegetarian now."***

George: "All vegetarian now! Right, that's interesting!"

~ ***"It is very good to be with you again, and I look forward to more. It is time though, to leave you this time."***

Sarah, recalling the planned phenomenon said lightly: "Perhaps next time you can bring us a coin—"

I added: "This last month a year ago, you had a few problems coming to us—a bumpy ride—so *this* year you've missed out that New Year period, and very wisely perhaps."

~ ***"We have much to bring. It will be a most interesting year."***

George: "We certainly look forward to that, and are delighted that you have come back and resumed."

Sarah: "Yes, our good wishes to all your people."

George: "Thank you Bonniol and thank you team."

So the New Year visits were under way, and with much to look forward to.

It is known from earlier dialogue that Aerah has three moons and now we know of two suns. It is a fair assumption that Jan was seeing two suns and two bright moons. It is also clear that, as with Earth, the planetary axis of rotation is inclined to its plane of rotation to give seasonal variation. And having two suns would perhaps help to explain earlier information that days are longer than nights. As regards our farming, it was Johann Glauber in our 17th-century who first prepared potassium nitrate and recommended its use as a fertiliser. Much land has more recently been spoiled by over-use of manufactured fertilisers. But now, synthetic chemicals are being quite seriously questioned. It is therefore interesting to note that a more advanced culture chooses a natural organic system of food production heavily linked to a practice of recycling *all* waste back to the soil. They do not even consider synthetic chemicals as an option! That came as a surprise. Earth might do well to move further into organic farming and to recycle much higher proportions of waste to compost. And what may be said of vegetarian regime? There is good evidence that this equates to healthier and happier lifestyle. Surely we would do well to move towards some of the ways of newfound Aeran friends.

CHAPTER: **45**

Without a Doubt – A Date to Remember ... 12th February 2007

SO TWO WEEKS later Bonniol was saying: ~ ***"I am always happy to come here and the experience is becoming much easier. Finally, we have overcome many of the minor details of this type of connection. I think there is a little more fluidity about it now than in the earlier days. And now that it is easier we have a greater opportunity to bring our worlds closer together, in terms of the sharing of our ways, and the sharing of our views of life."***

We responded with enthusiasm as each point was made, and Sarah recalled that there had also been the process of building up the connection when Salumet's mission had first begun; this over some considerable period. Worthwhile ventures do not happen instantly.

~ ***"—and a growing friendship developing as we cut through the stillness of the universe."***

Bonniol now used phrases befitting a poet!

Sarah: "Well, we already treat you as a friend Bonniol—"

Lilian: "Once we got over the shock!"

Midst ensuing laughter, Sarah suggested Bonniol must have felt very uncertain at first.

~ ***"It is always an adventure."***

George: "Yes, and I have to say, we are much enjoying the adventure, and you are certainly *as an old friend,* and you have made quite a number of visits now—I think forty-eight."

~ ***"The ease with which it can be done now means the information can be a little clearer. We have struggled at times to answer questions, and understand the nature of your questions."***

This was logical pattern and Sarah referred to the helpful contribution of Jan's clairvoyance and enquired as to his awareness of her.

~ ***"I am aware of each of you in the room, yes."***

George: "Unfortunately, Jan is not with us this evening."

~ ***"I am not always able to tune in to you, but there is a little more tuning in, and we are very pleased to bring a little more visual side to our reality, through Jan. And we may be able to increase the—increase the—"***

Lilian: "Clairvoyance?"

~ ***"Yes—all of this linking our worlds."***

Sarah: "Very helpful, especially if she can draw some pictures."

~ ***"You are very keen to have visual understandings—"***

Sarah endeavoured to explain how pictorial representation reinforces understanding for us.

~ ***"You will all perhaps be able to glimpse us. It is about tuning in, in the right way."***

Sarah: "Yes, that would be wonderful."

~ ***"And for this meeting we are hoping to perhaps start the first steps of bringing to you something material. It will just be 'stage one', because we cannot achieve this in one session."***

Sarah: "That's fine by us."

George: "These things must be approached steadily sometimes—wonderful news—a wonderful prospect!"

We are hoping to pave the way and part of this is removing any doubts—any questions—so that we are all happy and vibrating on the same frequencies. Are we all able to believe that this is within our reach?"

Sarah: "I should think it is."

George: "Yes, it's something I've thought about and imagined—and yes, hopefully it is within our reach."

But this was clearly not enough—not good enough for Bonniol and neither was it good enough for those attending in spirit, as will become evident.

~ ***"HOPE is something where you are uncertain—"***

George: "Yes, I can speak for myself and say: I *know* it can be done, and in using the term 'hope', I was really thinking about everyone."

Lilian: "Yes, we know it can be done."

George: "Perhaps we all need to speak for ourselves, and believe wholeheartedly."

Rod: "Yes, I don't think there could be any problems with that."

Jim: "No."

Lilian: "Perfect—yes."

At this point, one in spirit who had been listening to our rather muddled affirmations, decided to join in via Sue. That one now spoke: ~ *"Have you not 'believed' in everything in the past years of your teaching?"*

George, midst knowing chuckles: "Yes—yes!"

~ *"Have you not accepted almost everything you have been taught?"*

George: "Oh yes."

~ *"—after a few questions?—well then, come along—"*

Lilian: "Well, we know materialisation can happen."

George: "We have trodden a wonderful pathway these last years, and yes I am sure we are all believing wholeheartedly."

~ *"Forgive the interruption."*

George: "Thank you for it."

Lilian reflected: "We just have a thought from another planet."

The extra input had come as a surprise, but I could not help thinking it is good to have the occasional reminder that we are not alone. And this was in no small way a reminder! Always others listen to what goes on in this room.

Rod: "You knew where that voice was coming from then Bonniol?"

~ ***"I am aware of everything in this room."***

Lilian: "Are you?"

Rod: "Wonderful!"

~ ***"So I will bring you a gift from our world."***

Lilian: "That's something to look forward to."

~ ***"But it will not be wrapped up!"***

The laughter subsided as Sarah promised there would be no squabbling over it. Following a short pause, we next attempted to compare calendars. It seemed an interesting idea to see how similar the passage of time might be.

Jim: "Can I ask you a question about your calendar? Can you tell us what the date is? We will tell *you* the date according to *our* calendar, and we can compare. Would that be possible?"

George: "And then, sometime in the future we can do the same again, and it will tell us how our planets rotate, relatively."

~ ***"You wish to do a time-check, yes?"***

We explained how our year is split into 365 days and the year also divided into twelve months. And today is 12th February in the year 2007 (counting from one of our incarnated masters). That equates to the 43rd day in our year 2007, and we asked if Bonniol was able to make a similar statement.

~ ***"We also have a calendar, yes, which I will give you in—yes—the year we are in is perhaps a little long, but for this purpose we can just say: 27—yes, 27th year, and we are at the 97th day—97th day of the 27th year."***

George: "Thank you—and I imagine the 2-7 to be the last two digits of a larger number—"

~ ***"Yes."***

Sarah: "And how many days are there in your year?"

~ ***"We have—ooh—3084."***

Sarah: "3084 days in a year."

~ ***"Yes."***

Sarah: "That's a big number."

Rod: "It takes a long time to get around the sun."

~ ***"Yes, it is a way of noting the rotation."***

Sarah: "So you are only just into the beginning of this year—your 97th day. Does that mean your seasons then are quite long?"

~ ***"It will be longer, yes."***

Sarah: "Do you just have four, or more seasons than us?"

~ ***"We have mainly three seasons, but you can always classify them differently."***

Sarah: "So each season lasts about a thousand days?"

~ ***"Not exactly, we mainly have the season which is dry and quite warm."***

Lilian: "Would it vary on different parts of the planet?"

~ ***"Yes it does, yes—I'm being told it's a little late now, but we will continue if you are willing, next time."***

We would of course be more than willing! But the evening was not yet quite closed. Our extra guest still sat with Sue and now gave us a few more words of spiritual wisdom: ~ *"Doubt—doubt is a negative vibration which could influence the communication from the other galaxy. It is a negative vibration which will be detrimental to the power required for what is to happen. It is human nature to doubt—you may THINK so—we KNOW, we KNOW! We can all have the same outlook—BELIEVE! Make the bond strong! Make the power glow—glow—a fiery ball of power, which will result in the phenomena which WILL happen. That is all I will say."*

We thanked our visitor for those further elegant words. To believe is paramount!

CHAPTER: **46**

An Intergalactic Gardeners Question Time ... 19th February 2007

SEVERAL WERE UNABLE to get to this meeting and those present ambled into a light chat, mostly about plants. Sarah was saying: "Have you done anything special this week?"

~ ***"I've been working outside a lot."***

Sarah: "May I ask what you've been working on?"

~ ***"—Working with plants, it is the busy time."***

It being our springtime in the UK with the daffodils blooming, I felt it right to say that we too like to get out in the garden, adding: it is our season for doing that.

~ ***"We have to prepare the plants for the changing temperatures and weather patterns."***

Sarah: "It's beginning to get warmer is it?"

~ ***"It's becoming a little heavier and colder, and they need some protection."***

We indicated our understanding of the need to protect, and Lilian enquired if it was mainly flowers or vegetables that Bonniol was growing.

~ ***"The plants that I have been working with are for eating, but we also plant others around them which are there purely for pleasure."***

Sarah wanted to know if there were separate areas for pleasure and for food production, or is everything mixed?

~ ***"We try to plant wherever we can. There is enough ground for growing our food and still plenty more for other plants."***

I asked if plants were grown for their fibre to make cloth and string, having in mind cotton, sisal, flax and such. The response was interesting: ~ ***"There was a time when we needed plants for ropes and string. We now have less need of that."***

George: "Do you use string for tying up some of your plants in the garden, to give them support?"

~ ***"You may find this unusual, but we have other plants for— other plants help to—um—"***

Lilian: "Support?"

~ ***"Support—yes. So it is using nature to support nature."***

Lilian then enquired about insects on Aerah, mentioning the valuable work of our bees and the beauty of butterflies.

~ ***"There are all kinds of creatures, yes. They all play their part."***

Returning to plant protection, we explained about greenhouses and how they let the sun in and keep the wind out, and wondered if they use anything like that to aid growth.

~ ***"We do not use greenhouses, though there could be some advantage. But we are able to work without them."***

It seems clear that the growing system on Aerah is kept 'as natural as possible', so greenhouses are simply not used if one can get by without. They might even be seen as an unnecessary complication.

Jim: "Are some plants grown for energy? Did you say once: the energy used in machines comes from plants?"

~ ***"That is correct, yes."***

George: "Is it a particular crop that you grow for that?"

~ ***"We have several crops which are used to harness this energy. The first crop is limited in terms of its availability all the year round, but other crops have a little longer period for harvesting this energy."***

George: "I see. So do you get some differences in the energy from different crops, or is it all much the same?"

~ ***"The energy is as far as WE are concerned—it is the same."***

Rod: "And do you use nuclear power as well?"

~ ***"No, we are able to cope energy-wise with our plant energy. It is not an energy that it is possible to harness without the nature spirits. They are the ones that draw it from the plants."***

Lilian: "That's marvellous. I believe you described it as 'milking'?"

~ ***"Yes."***

George: "Yes, I think Bonniol described it before as a non-physical energy, which is made a little more physical by the elementals."

Sarah: "Going back to your plants that you are tending as it gets cooler, what are you going to do if you are not going to cover them? How are you going to protect them?"

~ ***"We use other plants to shelter them and protect them a little."***

Lilian: "So it's nature taking care of itself—"

~ ***"Yes."***

George: "Yes, I suppose on Earth, a little bit of that happens in the rainforests, in that the canopy of the forest encapsulates other plants lower down, and it's an interesting ecosystem."

Rod: "And we do also have windbreaks in some areas.

Sarah: "And these plants that are protecting other plants—do you use those, or are they purely ornamental and practical for protecting?"

~ ***"Mostly they are there purely for support. The ones that produce our food are rather fragile, but they grow well when the climate is calmer and warmer."***

There was some talk of colours and it seems the fruits that are eaten are mostly purple and the leaves green or blue-green. There was some uncertainty regarding leaf colour, but finally this was referenced to the appearance of our oceans.

Rod: "When you've had a busy year do you go on a holiday—go to the seaside and swim in the sea?"

~ ***"We have different options of course. Our oceans are one of our places where we can have holidays, yes. We also journey 'inwards', of course."***

Rod: "Is it a danger for you to sit in the sun too much? Do you get burnt and get a reddish skin?"

~ ***"There is less danger I would say, for our people."***

Sarah: "Did you say your skin is pink? Is it a darker pink than ours?"

~ ***"Yes, it is a brighter pink, and darker, yes."***

Sarah: "So that probably protects you from the sun—"

Rod: "So if you go in the sun, do you get even darker? Do you change colour at all if you sit in the sun for a long period?"

~ ***"We actually become lighter."***

Sarah: "That's interesting."

Rod: "So when you see some of your people come back almost white, you know they've had a good holiday!"

~ ***"Yes!"***

George: "The reverse of us then!"

Sarah: "Why should that be? What happens to the skin if it goes paler?"

~ ***"Our skin is a different material to yours and its colour fades."***

Well, we have many dyestuffs here on Earth that are not colour-fast, many jeans, sunhats and so forth fade in the sun, so why not Aerans-on-holiday? Returning to the vegetable garden, we enquired about root crops.

~ ***"Actually, it is less common to eat the root systems. There are plants which make good roots. These have been eaten much in the past, but for today's people, we prefer to eat other parts of the plant."***

George: "So it's all fruit and leaves, and the harder fruits we call 'nuts'—and stalks? Is that what you eat?"

~ ***"Yes, we prefer to take from the plants that which they can give, without damaging them too much."***

Sarah: "Do all your plants actually grow in soil or can you grow some suspended in the air—taking moisture from the air?"

~ ***"There are plants that will grow suspended, but like yours, (they) mostly grow into the ground."***

Jim endeavoured to explain about the chlorophyll basis of photosynthesis powered by sun energy, enquiring if it is similar on Aerah, to which Bonniol replied: ~ ***"Yes, the sun is the main provider of energy, and yes, the leaves absorb this through the botanical processes."***

Some sketchy chat concerned colours, Paul's memory downloads and how the various planets are all so very different, then it was again time for our friend to depart. We were left much intrigued by the 'naturalness' of Aeran agriculture that shows unstinting respect for nature and her plants. Perhaps I shall be inspired to encourage the bean-rods to take root and leave them in for next year's crop. Already, some of us save seeds for next season rather than have them go through all that machinery to get double-packed!

CHAPTER: 47

Earth is Opening Up! – As the Days Slip By ... 12th March 2007

LILIAN WAS SAYING that if we were to speak with friends about these meetings they would mostly disbelieve and Bonniol had ventured that this was a shame. But then Rod had apparently briefed his twenty-five-year old grandson, who had happily accepted everything right away.

~ ***"I think the younger ones are more able to—"***

Rod: "Take it on board."

~ ***"Yes."***

Lilian: "Think for themselves."

~ ***"It is a problem for the ones who have their minds 'set' on this world."***

I explained that the recorded meetings are all being transcribed and will go into a book and hopefully enable many more to consider the true facts of existence.

~ ***"And I would think there will be a lot of people who will be curious."***

Lilian: "I hope so."

~ ***"It is within everyone."***

George: "The curiosity, yes."

~ ***"And also the knowledge of other worlds, though it is 'locked up', as you've been told."***

George: "Yes, people do get 'stuck' in their ways and ideas, and it's a hurdle to be jumped for some. Knowledge such as this they do not always accept readily."

~ ***"Well, there will be a time when it WILL BE accepted."***

George: "Mm—yes."

Rod: "Would I be right in thinking that *all* the people on *your* planet are aware of other beings on other planets such as us?"

~ ***"We are all—yes it is common knowledge for us."***

Rod: "Good gracious!"

~ ***"It is one of the differences. Our minds look more outwards."***

Lilian: "Yes, Salumet said that other groups such as ours would be having visitors. What I was going to ask—are you aware of any groups that your people visit?"

~ ***"YOUR WORLD IS OPENING UP, there will be more and more groups, and yes, hopefully we will be able to visit other groups as well."***

George: "Mm, that Earth is opening up at last is a very refreshing thought for us all here."

Rod: "Did you hear Salumet's words about, many of our children are going to be more spiritually aware?"

~ ***"Yes, I was aware of those words."***

Rod: "It might be slow at first but it's on the go."

There was a brief pause and Jim changed the topic to the passage of time: "Could I ask the question that I asked a month ago?"

~ ***"Yes."***

Jim: "I asked the date on Aerah—"

So Jim again asked the date. Bonniol with some hesitation indicated that they were now 3,056 days into their year, which sounds most unlikely. It would mean that Aerah spins roughly 100-times faster than Earth; but if by any chance our friend has clipped early digits from the number of days given a month ago (as with the year date), then it might be only twice as fast; or it may simply be that mind-linked Aerans get confused when it comes to arithmetic. And it may of course be that we are simply not allowed this information and that must be seen as one possibility. So relative planetary time remains uncertain, but it has been established that Aeran days are divided into 25 'hours' and each of these is subdivided into 100 smaller units, so that Aeran time is thought of as *something past the 'hour'*, as is the Earthly custom.

Sarah: "We have our meetings every Monday and we start at half-past seven. So for you, it's always at a different time, is that right?"

~ ***"Yes, we meet at different times."***

Sarah: "So that must be a bit awkward for you..."

~ ***"Why?"***

Sarah: "Well, for us it's easy, because we always know it's half-past seven, but for you, I suppose you always know what time it's going to be, do you?"

~ ***"We are all more connected and we SENSE when the meeting will occur."***

Sarah went on to point out that with our busy working schedules we operate on fixed times, while Aerans, would they not have other things to do?

~ ***"We are less fixed in our working schedules."***

Rod: "Called *flexitime* here."

Sarah: "So you can work around our meetings then—"

~ ***"It is often possible to—um—leave your work in order to join a meeting."***

Still concerning our meetings, Lilian wondered about the lightness of our summer evenings and the dark of winter, and would they be aware of the difference?

~ ***"It is our awareness of it. I am able to—um—interpret the memories."***

Lilian: "You are aware of the darkness or the light, yes?"

~ ***"It's for US, an understanding of how YOU perceive it. And we will have our own perception."***

It was elegantly put and I added: "But your personal awareness would relate just to the conditions in this room I imagine?"

~ ***"We are not confined to this room—only for purposes of communication."***

George: "Ah—yes, right."

Rod: "When Paul goes into a garden (to work), are you aware of all that beauty around?"

~ ***"Yes, we have looked at the memories and seen those. I am also able to project myself of course, into the—um—all over your planet, to become more aware of it in that way."***

Rod: "Gracious me! I'm intrigued. What kind of a job have you?—what is your work?"

~ ***"We are mainly involved in growing—um—working with nature."***

This led to more talk about colours, and it was confirmed that plants are in the blue-green range of colour similar to our oceans. Next Bonniol made an important announcement:

~ ***"We will be able to attempt the materialisation next time."***

This sparked general chat about positive attitude and choice of object, and it was decided to have a small white mat to hand, to be placed on the floor to receive the object. Rod asked if any further preparation might be required.

~ ***"Just simply to remember that for us it is an everyday occurrence, just like eating your food. So it should not be looked upon with (in) any special way. It is a simple act, which when you can do it, you will find it simple too."***

Jim: "Does the size of the object being materialised relate to the energy needed? Is it easier to materialise a small thing than a large thing?"

~ ***"Yes, the size—it is easier to visualise if it is reasonably small."***

It is understood that the item will be permanent, and Rod added: "But is distance any problem, because we are a couple of miles or so from you really, aren't we?"

When the laughter at such gross understatement subsided Bonniol aptly reminded: ~ ***"Once you have reached another mind, the miles are irrelevant."***

And that concluded the session.

It was two weeks later when one came through with a spiritual-energy-report, beginning: ~ *"No doubt you are aware of energy changes this time. We are trying to build it just a little more for you."*

We said that was interesting, and our visitor continued: ~ *"Yes, most interesting. We started by using your happiness and your laughter this evening, and of course you realise the one who comes to teach (Salumet) is not with you this time, because that takes its own special kind of energy, So I am here to tell you that we are working and utilising your energies in order to help those waiting to come."*

We chatted awhile about the energies but our visitor was unable to enlighten any further, finally departing with the words: ~ *"Anyway, my purpose with you is done. But I have to say: I have not felt a greater pleasure for a little while when joining with you Earth people; it is not always so comfortable."*

As she left, several became aware of energy change and spoke about a marked sensation of coolness in the lower part of the room; this despite the fact that it is the habit of several to use travel rugs during sessions. As Bonniol joined us he confirmed that the energy adjustment related to his proposed materialisation.

Lilian: "Do you wish us to sit quietly and not talk?"

~ ***"It is better to be quiet, yes, and I will see what we can achieve."***

Lilian: "Thank you."

There was silence for 11-minutes during which period some fancied there were swirling energies above the white mat but no material form.

~ ***"We are unable this time, because the—um—power is—is—"***

Lilian: "Not quite strong enough?"

~ ***"Yes, it is fading a little now."***

Lilian: "Yes, but thank you for trying."

Others: "Yes."

~ ***"And it is not a disaster. You WILL have your materialisation!"***

George: "Well, we are very grateful for your efforts in this."

In response to our further questions Bonniol added: ~ ***"It is simply a matter of making the conditions as right as possible."***

He went on to confirm that there are many in spirit helping with adjustments, and that this was the first time that he and his team had attempted an across-the-universe materialisation in this particular mode. There would of necessity have to be several attempts to hopefully each time bring the project closer to successful conclusion. We suspect that a tricky factor must be the matter density difference between our two planets. But then, this is what helps to make this particular aspect of the exchange so very interesting. It is a grand experiment. Watch this space!

CHAPTER: **48**

An Immensity of Existence – Glimpsing a Life Form ... 23rd April 2007

ON GREETING OUR wondrous friend, we wondered if he had been present the week before, since there had been an energy-adjustment made from spirit.

~ ***"Yes, I am never far from your meetings these days."***

There were exclamations of surprise all round at these words.

~ ***"We are very enthusiastic about these gatherings. It is one of our biggest hobbies, if you like, to learn of other peoples, yes."***

Lilian: "Is there another in your group that travels like you do?"

~ ***"Yes, there are several in our group who travel in this way, yes, to other worlds."***

Lilian: "Very interesting—a good thing to do."

~ ***"We hope that it is giving you some feeling of the immensity of existence."***

George: "Yes, it's a wonderful exercise for us. We have received Salumet's teachings and he has mentioned the more extensive universe far beyond Earth, and so it helps to explain and consolidate his teaching to hear your words. Yes, we appreciate that."

Sarah: "It makes the teaching clearer."

And I think we were all rather impressed with our friend's expression: 'immensity of existence'.

~ ***"Yes, I am happy that you are able to use this to expand your awareness."***

Lilian: "You can travel into the realms of spirit I believe—"

~ ***"Yes."***

Lilian: "Do you travel anywhere near the realms where our teacher comes from? Are you allowed in those realms?"

~ ***"Your teacher is in a place way beyond our experience at this time."***

George: "For want of a better expression, I think we can only think of that as 'deeper spirit.'"

Bonniol had given the expected answer. Such domain is really beyond our comprehension. There was further talk of materialisation prospects and Bonniol went on to say that all was going well from his end while something was not quite right here.

I referred to the week before: "I was impressed by the fact that some in spirit—three great Indians were mentioned—coming down to help with energy adjustment. So that tallies with the idea that the conditions were not quite right, and it may well be that those in spirit who, shall I say, are not too far away, will be able to help in this."

~ ***"Yes, I think there are so many people wanting this and wanting to help."***

Sarah: "That's good news."

Our friend added that another attempt would be made soon. Then, almost immediately, it became clear that Jan was receiving clairvoyance: "Is it you or is it one of your colleagues? Are you handing me an object?"

Bonniol hesitated in his reply: ~ ***"You are receiving an impression I think?"***

Jan: "Someone with *your* limbs—not human."

~ ***"That is probably us then, we are attempting to give you an impression of us."***

Jan: "So can it be a hand—no, two hands—very long—a long palm—very long fingers, and transparent? I can see all the veins, even the muscles."

~ ***"These are—it is one way of seeing us perhaps—"***

Jan: "But I do know that what I am seeing is from another world. I'm not to drop it. I'm being told I'm not to drop it."

Lilian sought clarification that it is indeed of Aerah, not from elsewhere.

~ ***"This IS from our planet."***

Jan: "Is this a picture of your hands?"

~ "They are perhaps more transparent than yours. WE would not call them transparent, because there are those who have much more transparent hands than these."

Transparency as perceived is of course relative, and when Lilian queried the extent, Jan described it as: translucent, like the scan of a foetus in the womb, and blood can be seen pumping in the veins.

Sarah: "How many fingers are there Jan?"

Jan: "It's very similar to us only much longer."

Sarah: "Four fingers and a thumb?"

Jan: "Mm—the thumb is longer."

~ "We have mentioned our thumb in the past I believe."

George: "Yes, more of a gripping device."

Lilian: "A gripping device Jan?"

Jan: "It's a bit like a pincer on a crab..."

~ "Yes! This is more apt description, yes!"

Bonniol was now certain that Jan was getting useful detail, and she began to receive more. The hands held an object.

~ "It is ah—"

Jan: "Shaped like a rugby ball—"

Sarah: "Is that something else Bonniol?"

Jan: "No, it's the object that the—"

~ "Yes, you are still seeing—"

Jan: "I'm very aware of this, and I don't want to move my feet 'cos it's there. Can I keep it?"

We laughed at first, but Jan clearly had serious feelings of a protective, even maternal nature, for this object—a bonding maybe.

~ "Yes, you are aware of its—"

Jan: "Form."

~ "Form, yes. And you know what is inside?"

Jan: "I am very aware that it is fragile. Although it's quite a hard substance it is fragile—the contents are fragile."

Eileen looked at the white mat that had been placed on the floor earlier just in case a materialisation was planned: "What if you placed it on the mat Jan?"

Jan: "I've got the impression that it's a life form—I don't know—that's just what I'm feeling. I'm very protective of this thing."

Sarah: "Did you hear what Eileen said—try putting it on the mat?"

Eileen: "Would it be possible Bonniol, to transmute that shape into something solid?"

~ ***"It would be easier now that it has been seen by one of you in the room—this would help."***

Eileen now sensed that we might be onto something intriguing and went on: "If it's not possible for it to become a solid object, could you perhaps show us the energy of the object? Is that possible?"

~ ***"I am willing to bring a little more detail and we will see what happens."***

A few minutes passed, during which time we watched and spoke quietly amongst ourselves.

Eileen: "If anyone sees anything please speak."

George: "I can see a pattern on the white mat."

Eileen: "Can you?"

George: "A sort of pattern, that criss-crosses and seems to be trying to come together."

Jan: "I can see that too."

Several more minutes elapsed and Rod spoke: "Interesting for you Jan!"

Jan: "Right—I know that it's not gone. It's strange, but I am drawn to it over there. I've kept my eyes firmly fixed to it."

George: "I've lost it now."

Bonniol broke the brief silence that followed: ~ ***"When the next time comes to attempt the materialisation we will bring something else, but we are pleased that this has been visualised—has been seen."***

George: "There was certainly something there. There seemed to be an elongated sense—I could see that quite distinctly."

Lilian: "It seemed to me like smoke coming up."

~ ***"There is the beginning perhaps but it is not finished. It is—um—what we come from, yes. It is our beginning in life."***

That was the signal for all to speak at once so that the recording at this point is jumbled, but phrases could be picked out.

Jan: "I knew it!"

Rod: "And you wanted to keep it!"

And midst the buzz of sound, Jan was thanking Bonniol for what had been revealed.

~ ***"We have something else for you for our materialisation. We wanted to bring you this as something of interest."***

Well, it was certainly of interest—held us spellbound. Jan could not quite work out how much of what she could see was actually known to Bonniol. He explained the team effort and how each of us *could* possibly be picking up on something: ~ ***"You are all open to our communications. We are trying to use this time to bring you more awareness of us."***

Jan: "And your colleagues are working away in the background—"

~ ***"Yes."***

George: "I think an uncertainty factor is *our* degree of awareness."

Sarah: "Actually, while I was looking at that white thing, it seemed that there was dark in the middle. Around the thing it was completely white but quite dark in the middle."

Jan: "May I just ask if your colleagues are patting me on the head?"

As we laughed at the thought, Bonniol replied: ~ ***"I am unaware of that one, so this must be from another."***

Lilian: "Yes, earlier Jan, someone was touching the back of *my* head very lightly."

~ ***"There are plenty of others helping at these meetings."***

Rod: "From your planet?"

~ ***"No they're from here. They are pleased."***

Well, Jan had certainly earned a pat on the head! Our friend then indicated it was time to leave, and we all expressed our thanks for a remarkable evening; to Bonniol, his team and to everyone involved. So many come together in some way or another in this venture, and this time we had come close to having an interplanetary film show!

CHAPTER: 49

Metric Numbers – More on Projection – Carrots & Parsnips ... 30th Apr 2007

HERE IN ENGLAND at this time, eye-catching tulips nodded with late flowering daffs and spring prettiness abounded. Several were away on holiday breaks and only five made the meeting. Sister Angelica, an old friend in spirit, had been describing in some detail the energies and auras as seen from her domain, and Bonniol followed on as that dear one departed: ~ ***"Hello, how are you?"***

Lilian: "Hello Bonniol. Have you been here for some time?"

~ ***"It is easy for us, but we don't always feel it is in our interest to speak because you have many interesting and wonderful speakers from spirit, like the one you've just had!"***

Lilian was saying that, had we realised our friend was around, he could have been invited to join in.

~ ***"I'm really touched, but we can also communicate from our side of course."***

Lilian: "Yes, more easily than we do, probably."

Sarah: "Do you have many visitors to you from spirit?"

~ ***"Of course, yes. We have regular contact with our guides."***

The exchange moved on to establish that Aerans experience regular contact with their guides, on an individual one-to-one basis, and they also receive teaching from advanced ones much as we do, with the difference that ours is more often the group situation.

Jim moved the conversation to mathematics; to numbers and the way we count: "We have a system called: the decimal system. We start at zero and count 1-2-3-4-5-6-7-8-9, then we use two digits."

~ ***"Yes, we also use a set of ten, so it is based on the same."***

Jim: "In our computers we use another system, where we've got zero and one, called a binary system."

~ ***"There is a different system for our computers. They have different processes to yours."***

Jim: "I see. After that it gets very complex for ordinary people like me to understand."

~ ***"We cannot find the words for these at this time."***

That may well be a recurring problem as regards more advanced scientific data. The words needed are too specialised and may well not be available in Paul's memory. Lilian observed that there must be so much that Aerans simply do not need to develop on their planet because of mind applications, and this prompted Bonniol to speak on bringing about planetary change: ~ ***"We have managed to change our planet to the way we felt it should be. You have not yet changed yours to how you feel it should be, but you have the right thoughts."***

Sarah: "In what way have you changed your planet?"

Lilian: "We think you live much more simply now, a much more care-of-the-planet life."

~ ***"Yes, we have learned to live with our natural world without destroying—but living together."***

Sarah: "Much more harmonious."

~ ***"There is more harmony now, yes."***

Lilian: "Hopefully we are improving."

~ ***"You are."***

Sarah ventured that the more ready contact with spirit probably leads to an easier life on Aerah, while it has been said how here on Earth we make difficulties for ourselves.

~ ***"When you ask for help, your decisions become clearer, and we ask for help. That is a simple but important thing. Your lives are more complicated—more busy. Asking for help would be even more important (for you)."***

That has to be seen as a mega-point to consider. That having been carefully noted, we moved on to the prospect of help in materialising an object and Bonniol was saying:

~ ***"And we are confident that this will work, though we were also confident before."***

Sarah: "Have you done this with any other planet?"

~ ***"Yes, we have materialised objects on other planets, but this is a different situation. But there is no reason why it will not happen."***

Sarah: "When you say it is a different situation, in what way is it different?"

~ ***"We are using the instrument (Paul) in a way that is not the same as we communicate with other planets. There are various ways to do mind projection."***

Lilian: "So there's more than one way. That's interesting."

~ ***"Linking with another mind, is usually a more two-way activity."***

Lilian: "Ah, I see."

~ ***"This is a more one-way projection."***

Sarah: "We are not so spiritually advanced as the other planets—is that a way to look at it?"

~ ***"In this respect, yes."***

Well perhaps this was a kindly way to put it. We moved on to clairvoyant images.

Sarah: "With Jan, when she sees these things, are *you* aware that she is seeing this clairvoyance?"

~ ***"We only know that we are sending these images. We do not know how they are received."***

Sarah: "Ah, so you send them on and hope that someone will pick them up—"

~ ***"Yes. When we are linking with another's mind, we have access to their memories, and we therefore share out OUR memories, and this is what Jan is picking up."***

On reflection then, this may in some measure reflect the two-way quality of which Bonniol speaks. Sarah went on to ask if Paul might become similarly perceptive and Bonniol affirmed that we could all have this capability with continued adherence. This then was an incentive to continue practising, and Bonniol pointed out:
~ ***"Because all our minds are linked you only need to have the intention to connect with another and your mind will begin to link. You can learn to communicate without words."***

It occurred to Lilian to explain the nature of twins to Bonniol and how they are often seen to share thoughts and emotions.

~ ***"They have already communicated with each other."***

Lilian: "Yes, before they were born!"

~ ***"Yes."***

Sarah: "So they've had lots of practice!"

~ ***"It is more natural than you realise."***

Lilian: "Yes, I'm sure. We've just lost it really."

Sarah: "We've lost a lot of things haven't we, over time?"

If twins can do it, then so can we all!

Jim considered for a moment; then, addressing Bonniol, boldly ventured: "I'm thinking of a vegetable—focussing my mind on that vegetable. So if you are able to see that thought, it would be very interesting."

Lilian: "Our vegetables are probably nothing like Bonniol's."

Jim: "The shape?"

A minute passed before our friend again spoke: ~ ***"Yes, there is an image in your mind. It is not the clearest but it is showing a form, which is a long form. It is a—parsnip—"***

Jim: "Did you say: parsnip?"

~ ***"Yes."***

Jim: "I was thinking of a carrot—very, very similar!"

Sarah: "I had carrot!"

Lilian: "I was thinking carrot too!"

Rod: "I'm sorry Bonniol but while that went on, I was thinking of a parsnip, so I probably fouled it!"

Some further discussion followed and we of course are never quite sure if we truly receive or imagine. But it appears that both Sarah and Lilian had got their result at the moment Jim began to send.

~ ***"Then I would assume it was the projection you were picking up."***

Sarah: "It's good that we all got carrot or parsnip. They are so alike aren't they apart from colour?"

Jim: "Yes, but the word would come from the memory bank in Paul's mind. Is that how it works?"

~ ***"Yes."***

Rod: "I know it doesn't sound crazy to *you*, but to sit here, just the five of us—chatting to you at a distance that we cannot imagine, as if we are in a pub having a drink!"

Midst howls of laughter, Rod continued: "You probably don't think it's wonderful because you are doing it all the time—for me, it's mind-blowing! Wonderful!"

Time for farewells again, but I think Rod's statement, clearly coming straight from the heart as it did nicely sums up the evening.

CHAPTER: 50

Halloween – Time to Put Aside the Pumpkins … 14th May 2007

WE SPOKE OF Aeran plants whereupon Bonniol replied: ~ ***"We are preparing a little something for you on our plants, but this evening we hoped to learn a little more from YOU. We have a question for you about your 'Halloween' tradition."***

The subject came as quite a surprise.

Lilian: "Halloween!"

~ ***"Yes."***

Sarah said gleefully: "With the pumpkins!"

But Bonniol was being on this occasion, deeply serious:

~ ***"Your religion has not been very clear on this festival."***

Jan: "Ah, that is because it is not a religious ceremony, it is a pagan festival."

In the terms of our sometimes wayward word definition, how very true! And it is a fact that our dictionaries still equate 'pagan' to 'heathen' and 'irreligious', so small wonder our religions are not clear on this festival! But the more logical mind of Bonniol had taken careful note and he continued: ~ ***"And have you been aware of its significance?"***

We stumbled on with uncertainty and I suggested: "Well, I guess one could see the pagan system as the younger religion, before the present formal world religions. Yes, it's an ancient tradition."

Jan: "A British tradition, carried over to the continent and Canada—"

Well, there was certainly that development in Druidic times that has been quite well documented, but the roots go back far; to the Great Mother, to the winged mother goddess Isis of Egypt and perhaps even earlier. We voiced an assortment of lesser notions:

Sarah: "They've enhanced it haven't they, with all the 'trick or treat' stuff?"

Jan: "It is a festival to ward off evil spirits."

George: "I think it was considered to be a time when the various spirits were loose and I think it went along with the idea of the 'hollow hills' opening their portals, so the spirits were running loose. I think that was the idea but I am uncertain in my own mind if it has any significance or not."

~ ***"It is apparent to us that this time IS SIGNIFICANT in your planet cycle, and it is a time when there is a powerful wave emitted from the energies of your Earth."***

We had rather ambled into this matter voicing bits and pieces picked up here and there, but now it became more serious.

Jan began: "Around *this* time period—and they celebrate—"

~ ***"Yes."***

Jan: "So it's something that our ancestors would have known, but we've only followed the tradition because it is fun to us but our ancient ancestors would have been aware, would they?"

George: "This energy release would have had the effect of making it easier for people to be sensitive to spirits. Would that be the connection?"

~ ***"I would not think that they would find it easier but they would perhaps feel the wave of energy flowing from their Earth, and be able perhaps to charge themselves a little from it. It is a powerful energy of your Earth, which you are all a part of."***

George: "Yes, this might have given rise to the idea of portals in the hills opening to release that energy—"

~ ***"I would not know about that."***

George: "I think people tend to stretch ideas a little."

~ ***"It is an energy release which can be felt, and which would have been felt more by your past peoples."***

Sarah: "Do you think it's still happening on our Halloween night now? Would you know that?"

~ ***"We understand that it happens at the time of your celebration. But it is a little confusing to us that this energy is not used in the way that WE would use this."***

Lilian: "We are not aware of it."

George: "How would you use that released energy?"

~ *"We would allow ourselves to open and bring it in to us and feel the power of your Earth planet. You would feel energised and connected to your Earth."*

George: "So this would be central to the ancient celebrations of that time of year?"

~ *"Yes."*

Jan: "What effect would it have on our offspring if born around this time, because I was born just after—are you a Scorpio George?"

George: "I'm on the cusp—last day of Scorpio."

~ *"You perhaps would be—um—if you were born whilst this energy was releasing, it might give you a special connection. It is an Earth-energy and very much a powerful energy for you."*

George: "Now that you have said that Bonniol, and consolidated some feelings that we've had, and things we've worked at—I realise now that the Avebury Temple, which is at the centre of a major energy ley line that runs across Britain—the temple, which consists of stone circles built into the countryside—this would have been a chosen place where the energy release would have been particularly marked. Does that make sense Bonniol?"

~ *"Yes, your ancient people would have brought this energy to the attention of as many as possible."*

George: "Yes, and that would account for the ancient tracks along the ridges leading to the Avebury Temple, and many people would have travelled along those tracks to meet, and I guess the energy released would have helped in their wellbeing."

~ *"Of course!"*

Lilian: "Do you have many of these energy happenings in *your* year?"

~ *"Yes, we also have times when our planet gives out its energy in a stronger than usual way."*

Sarah: "Why do you suppose this is? It doesn't just give out a smaller amount all the time—why does it give out at a particular time?"

~ *"These things are part of each planet's connection with the whole of creation. They are linked, they are pulsating, if you like. It is like your (tidal) oceans flowing."*

Jan went on to suggest the summer solstice as being included in this pattern.

~ ***"Of course, there are other times throughout the year."***

Jan: "And you're aware of that?"

~ ***"We have noticed another large one, but the one we mentioned was of the highest—"***

Jan: "Frequency?"

~ ***"Yes."***

Jan: "What I find surprising is that, of the two, an awful lot of people today celebrate the summer solstice, but Halloween is more of a fun thing for children and we are not really aware of that energy."

Sarah: "Let's not forget that in summer, people go out and celebrate, whereas October and November—"

Jan: "It's cold and miserable! I have never been aware of the energy around that time, so that's really interesting. This year, I think we'll be concentrating to see whether or not we can feel that energy ourselves."

~ ***"If you can make more connection with your Earth you will find there are so many lessons for you."***

George: "You have reawakened our interest in ley lines and the planetary energies. Do you on your planet, have beings who *watch over* the planetary energies with whom you are able to communicate?"

~ ***"We are aware of beings who work with our planetary energies. They are another—ah—"***

George: "Another type of non-material being?"

~ ***"They would perhaps be a little more similar to nature spirits, but they are not concerned with the animals or plants or the materialised forms."***

George: "Yes, I think the energy lines can change or be upgraded and they will look after that. That is one of their jobs. We have these beings."

~ ***"They are always present. They are beautiful and powerful beings."***

George: "Beautiful and powerful—yes, excellent description!"

Jan: "Of course, around that time, our plants and animals will be aware of that energy. It's quite a busy time isn't it—October? Our animals and plant life are probably more aware of that energy."

~ "You are correct I believe. Your animals are probably more aware than you, at this time."

Some discussion followed about how our sensitivity to Earth energy can be enhanced by divining rods, pendulum and the like, and how leys have been carefully mapped by some who have a sufficiently enhanced ability. And finally, Bonniol was saying: ~ ***"Perhaps I will come back to this subject. We feel we also need to explore it further. We looked into it and it was baffling us."***

It was explained to our friend that, although Earth's planetary energies are in the general sense known to us, we had been unaware of the extra pulses given out on calendar dates aligned to ancient festivals, or that these are orchestrated through a deeper cosmic rhythm. It had been a wonderfully informative evening again. On reflection, how amazing it is, that one or should I say a team, from across the universe was able to draw our attention to this Earthly matter! The powerful St Michael ley runs across Southern Britain from the southwest tip of Cornwall to the Norfolk coast, its detail has been meticulously dowsed, traced and recorded by Hamish Miller and Paul Broadhurst[15]. What remains of the Avebury Temple stands majestically at its midpoint. Today we are indebted to the work of John Aubrey and William Stukeley who drew attention to and recorded its more complete layout as it existed in the 17th-century. Running north-south is the nearby ancient Ridge Way and running east-west is the Wansdyke Path. The various leys clearly form part of Earth's energy system and the very existence of Avebury Temple bears testimony to the awareness of those in much earlier times who celebrated the energy-release festivals. Equally, early Christian churches built all along the St Michael line testify to the fact that their builders likewise had that knowledge. As to the beings who watch over our planet's energy lines, they are known as 'Ancient Site Guardians'; alternatively 'Earth Protectors'. Paul Bura[16] is one who has been able to communicate with these *beautiful and powerful beings*. Salumet confirms their existence and acknowledges the work of Paul Bura.

CHAPTER: 51

Volcanoes – Drifting Eggs and Sticky-trees ... 21st May 2007

EILEEN HAD RECEIVED several pieces of information from spirit guides to pass to others and she continued: "I think some of us should be receiving clairvoyance."

Jan: "Is Bonniol with us?"

Paul, replying in normal voice: "Not at the moment."

George: "He may take that as a cue."

Jan explained that she wondered because she was receiving a picture. It then became evident that both Jan and her son Richard were receiving clairvoyant scenes relating to Bonniol's planet. This being so, they began comparing notes; like two explorers in a 'lost world landscape'.

Jan: "If they're around, it's quite feasible that I'm going to pick up."

Richard: "What colour is Aerah predominantly in what *you* can see?"

Jan: "I think it's predominantly—"

Richard: "Purple."

Jan: "Yes—a purple tinge. Can you see any structures?"

Richard: "Yeah, but they are organic."

Jan: "Yes, well done! They are! When you say 'organic', are you seeing plant life, or are you seeing any buildings?"

Richard said 'no' to buildings and went on to describe a curious scene, with the ground appearing like 'gluey, swirled lava' and a tree 'shaped like a tepee with arms coming out of the top'. It was all very purple, and he conjectured this to be possibly on account of atmosphere.

Jan: "Yes, sometimes it can look purple or sometimes I've seen it with a greenish hue within."

Richard: "I haven't seen anybody yet, though."

Jan: "Just ask them to show themselves."

Richard: "It's really like jelly. The whole thing's like a big bowl of not-quite-set jelly!"

The short period of silence that followed was broken by a voice resonant with pleasure: ~ ***"It is good—you are seeing our planet."***

Jan, laughing: "Hello!"

~ ***"Hello!"***

Sarah: "Hello Bonniol!"

~ ***"You have a better way to describe it than I can at the moment."***

Jan: "Yes, because it's using our words."

Sarah: "—and our perception of it."

~ ***"You are able to see it from your point of view, relative to your own Earth. We often have problems describing, using your own symbols."***

Well, if you think about it, we are physical beings from two very different planets and of incomparable language. I have been astounded from the outset that there has been any cohesion of dialogue whatsoever. But despite these circumstances it has worked out surprisingly well, and once we learned how brain is able to convert thought to appropriate language, the logic of it became clearer.

~ ***"And it is becoming possible to give you more each time, especially when you are seeing the pictures. They speak a thousand words."***

Sarah: "It's a shame we can't all see."

Jan: "Perhaps in time we all will."

Sarah: "Richard was mentioning it was like unset jelly. That sounds quite plausible because you said about how you have to kick through the atmosphere."

~ ***"Yes, and it is a better term for you maybe. We have wanted this for a long time. It is like probably when you got your first television sets."***

Lilian reminded how fazed and uncertain we had been at Bonniol's first arrival, but now we take it all for granted. And we laughed as Sarah added warmly: "He's become an old friend."

~ ***"I wonder what will become normal in the future. You will be given much more as you continue to grow of course, and we wish you all to embrace it all—with excitement!"***

Sarah: "We've already got that!"

I affirmed: "We are excited!" adding: "In view of the pictures seen by Jan and Richard, would you wish to steer the conversation on that?"

~ ***"You have had a good description I think. It is important I think, for you all to open your minds to these pictures."***

Lilian: "Yes, that would be very handy."

Richard: "Bonniol, is your planet volcanic?"

~ ***"It—ah—yes—we have—"***

Richard: "Are they dormant or are they active?"

~ ***"At this time, they are mainly—alive, yes. They are acting."***

George: "Do your volcanoes produce lava?"

Richard: "I am assuming it is going to be the same process, erupting molten rock the same way that ours do. Does that shape your planet in the same way?"

~ ***"We have an understanding about these eruptions—so yes, it shapes the areas where they occur."***

George: "And, yes, you have earthquakes?"

~ ***"We have those also."***

Sarah: "I think the gravity is different on your planet. Does the lava fall in the same way as it does on this planet, or (does it) cover a much wider area?"

Richard: "I get the impression it falls very flat."

~ ***"Yes."***

Jan: "It disappears back into their earth..."

Richard: "It is like a layer—a crust."

~ ***"It is like this. The volcanic debris falls as I believe would be expected, but it is absorbed back—ah—"***

Jan: "I can help you with that Bonniol. What I'm actually seeing—it's like layers of cookies, and if you cut away the earth, it's like our sedimentary rock—layer upon layer of different colours. But it seems to absorb it into the earth. The top layer never seems to get too high, if you see what I mean—it sinks."

~ ***"Yes."***

Jan: "Lots of greens, lots of mauves."

~ ***"When it is in liquid form it will flow back into the ground."***

Richard: "Would I be right in saying there are plants that can grow in these areas?"

~ ***"Yes, there are—"***

Jan: "They've become like our deserts, that's what I think."

~ ***"They are—"***

Richard: "Yes, they're very like deserts."

~ ***"—adapted to this, yes."***

Richard: "Quite big."

~ ***"We have plants that will (grow in), and prefer these conditions, yes."***

Richard: "Is your ground very hot?"

~ ***"In these areas, yes."***

Richard: "Right, your ground in general or where it's volcanic?"

~ ***"Where we live, the ground has SOME warmth. It is perhaps like your beaches when the sun shines on the sand."***

Richard: "It can get *very* hot. I was given a very, very clear image, a bit more than a picture, and I was *there* placed on this ground, and it was quite warm by our standards. And despite the thick atmosphere, which to us would appear as water but it is not—and that is also—"

Jan: "Warm."

Richard: "Warm—but the ground is actually quite dusty. I wouldn't say it was sand, but it's dusty, and the rocks and dust move—move about, as when you have wind, but it's not—it looks like the atmosphere is moving it about. Am I right?"

~ ***"Yes, it is perhaps like your oceans moving."***

Richard: "It moves the pebbles—"

~ ***"Our atmosphere has more—it is thicker than yours, and when it moves, objects can move with it."***

Richard: "I see. It's very, very clear. It's a very weird sensation—strange to us anyway."

Jan: "You can feel—like treacle, can you? It's like wading through treacle."

Richard: "It is, but it's a bit strange because—I'm getting the feeling that we are able to breathe it. It's not so thick that it's obtrusive."

George: "In the early days, Bonniol explained how the atmosphere can be thinned by fanning it—by moving it. When it has been moved it seems to get thinner. Are you picking up any of that?"

Richard: "Yes, because the area in front of wherever you're moving then becomes thinner. It's perhaps not breathing. I'm not sure how their bodies work. I haven't been shown one."

~ ***"We will show you more when we come again."***

Richard: "Thank you."

~ "This has helped a lot, filling (in) the puzzles perhaps, but you may all begin to see these pictures now."

Lilian: "That would be very nice."

George: "Wonderful!"

~ "You can all begin to turn your minds in this direction and find this space which is no distance."

And now Richard placed a probing question: "Bonniol, do any on your planet grow from eggs?" He went on to describe the egg as seen, to be like an iridescent jellybean shape about a foot long. "You can almost see through it. But they float! They come off of something and float. Wherever they actually land they float! What is that?"

~ "Yes—"

Jan whispered: "I haven't told him any of this." She had glimpsed the egg shape four weeks earlier, but now we were getting more: ***~ "You have already begun to see our eggs then. This is how we begin."***

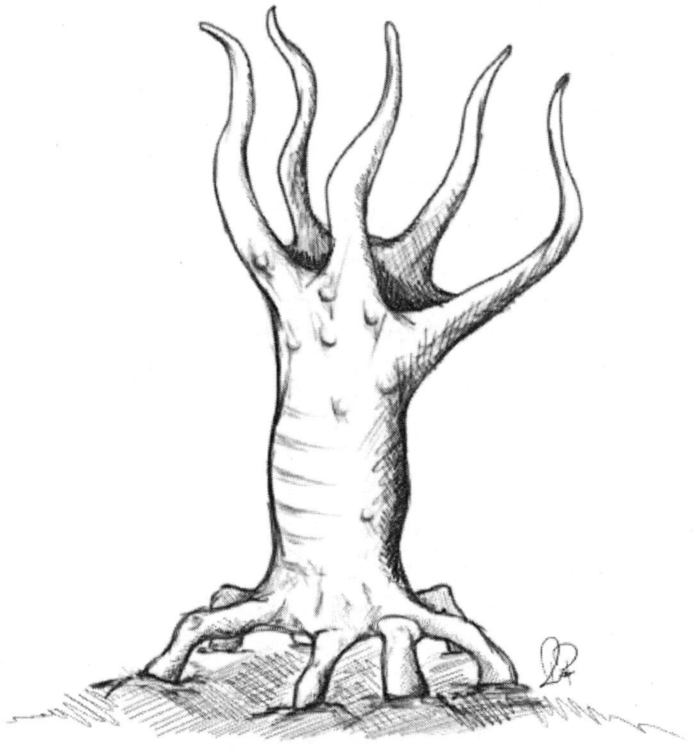

Aeran tree seen clairvoyantly and later drawn by Richard

Richard: "Do they come off of these large tree-like objects?"

~ ***"We lay our eggs on these plants."***

George: "Ah yes, and are a number of individual eggs laid at a time, one being coming from one egg?"

~ ***"We have to lay many eggs. We have mentioned this I believe."***

George: "Yes."

Lilian: "Because you have many children."

~ ***"We do have many children but not all of us have children."***

George: "Yes, I remember you explaining that."

Richard: "What happens to the eggs that float too far away? I'm getting this real feeling that these eggs aren't staying in one place."

~ ***"When you see this happening, it is like you're—you have—"***

Richard: "Transport?"

~ ***"Yes, they are moved by the currents."***

Richard: "Will they survive if they are separated from the larger group?"

~ ***"It is well known where they are going because we are in communication with them."***

Lilian: "Are they quite self-sufficient when they first hatch out?"

~ ***"No, they will need careful mothering, but they will not float too far away."***

Lilian: "Good."

Sarah: "So you go and get them back..."

~ ***"And we will know when they are ready."***

Bonniol reminded that only one gender-type actually produces but all may care for the juveniles, Jan adding: "That's the nursery that I saw before."

Richard: "I can see many of them around these areas now."

On departing, Bonniol exclaimed that they were very happy with what had transpired, and our discussion continued long after. The clairvoyance given was of a kind whereby the recipient was placed within the scene and was able to experience temperature as well as feel movement. A 'sticky-tree' is sought for egg laying. The eggs are mostly retained on the tree, but the few drifting away under influence of atmospheric eddies and currents are easily recovered; this due to the fact that communication with the unborn has already begun. The atmosphere might be described as thixotropic—it has a 'weak gel' character until worked upon (and our non-spill paints are deliberately formulated to have a more pronounced version of this very property). A scientific explanation would likely be: loose attraction between molecules that can only hold fast in still conditions. But there can be drifting movement of the gel capable of moving objects, just as our ocean currents move sand and pebbles. We can now better understand these Aeran atmospheric conditions that appear strange until one has some notion of the forces that underpin. And it is now known that there are profound differences of *gravity* and lower *matter density*, and we conjecture that such factors contribute to the observed conditions.

CHAPTER: 52
Transparency – Abductions – Materialisation Facts … 4th Jun – 30th Jul 2007

THERE WERE TWO short visits, before more lengthy dialogue again became possible. Bonniol declared how happy he and his team were with our working together and we replied that for us it was pure joy and how we look forward to these meetings! Then we had silence for eight minutes in a further materialisation attempt, but it was becoming clear that this was an ongoing experiment situation. It would not happen at the first or second or third attempt, but the project would steadily approach fruition with each try. It would take as long as it takes. Our friend was happy to stay just a little beyond the period of silence and we talked about the 'transparency' seen in clairvoyance.

~ ***"We are aware of it. It is something we take for granted I think, but there is something more etheric if you like, about it."***

It was explained that we are aware of our own transparency in strong light or with certain wavelengths, but have the impression that humans are generally rather more opaque.

~ ***"We are able to see you with some transparency, with our spiritual eyes."***

George: "Ah yes, the spiritual eyes would be more penetrating."

~ ***"When you are able to see the energy, the physical side begins to—um—reduce. The physical barriers are no longer as strong."***

Acknowledging that this could easily be accepted, we next briefly moved on to house-building. It came as a huge surprise that one complete house-materialisation is achieved from just a single session. No muddles or frustrations with building regulations, inspections, codes of practice, statutory requirements or red tape of any kind—one complete dwelling produced at a single sitting, just like that! Wonderful! Bonniol added: ~ ***"—though this would require perhaps many of us."***

Richard: "Do they come out very different?"

~ ***"They will come out differently, yes, because the minds are always different, but there is a preferred structure which we mainly aim for."***

Jan then made an interesting comparison: "May I just say please, that the structures that Bonniol's referring to are very similar in (principle of) construction to our spider's webs. Each web is of the same shape, but the make-up is different with each one. The Aerans are using their brain energy, the formations of which are vastly different. So each building will look characteristically different."

~ ***"Thank you. You have used a good analogy of the spider's web."***

Rod queried: "Do you have *them* as well?"

~ ***"We have something that you might think of as a spider, yes."***

That ended the first short session. It seems the energy available for an evening gets much depleted by attempting materialisation. Six weeks later, Bonniol again dropped by. It was late evening just before our closing, but he was warmly welcomed of course, as always.

~ ***"Hello, I'm here for just a little while. I will be coming for longer next time. We have much to build on and I am looking forward—"***

Lilian: "Yes, we are too."

~ ***"For now we will build our energies and be patient for what is to come. I believe you will be closing soon."***

And apart from farewells, that was it. I suspect Bonniol had been around earlier and possibly working with those energies, and he just wanted to say 'hello' before departing, that would likely be the way of it.

Two weeks later, Salumet had spoken at length on the reality of *UFO abductions* and how 'fear' can sometimes obstruct any help from spirit that would otherwise benefit the situation. He pointed out that 'curiosity' is the simple reason for conveying those few to and from visiting spaceships. Although the abductors will be in many ways more advanced than ourselves they remain imperfect physical beings like us. And Salumet had this to say about abductees: ~ **"Certain Earth beings are more prone to be taken, for many different reasons that perhaps at this moment in time you cannot understand. But they are 'chosen', if you like, to be abducted. And sometimes these other beings do not have the same emotional contact as you Earth beings, which therefore leaves many Earth beings traumatised by the experience. But open to all people is the love and protection of spirit, after all, I have told you, it is either 'love' or 'fear', which governs your lives and 'fear' is negative to the spirit, and it blocks out the help that is available. But we cannot place all responsibility onto those people who are taken; also, responsibility lies with those other beings who are intent on having their own way. In the same way that Earth beings, have to take responsibility for *their* actions, so too do *all* beings in the great scheme of life from all planets."**

Following this we had chatted amongst ourselves on the matter of curiosity, and how *we* in the past, might similarly have given insects and various Earth creatures a hard time. Curiosity can be a powerful driving force. Then we had spoken of general difficulties in the non-acceptance of spiritual knowledge and, arising from this, how sad it is to see so many people struggling and suffering in their ways forward. Then, just when it seemed to be verging towards one of those putting-the-world-to-rights sessions, the familiar voice broke in: ~ ***"Hello, how are you?"***

Lilian: "Hello Bonniol, nice to have you!"

~ ***"It's always wonderful to be with you."***

Lilian: "Have you been listening?"

~ ***"I have been around, yes."***

Sarah: "And you've picked up a few tips as well, have you?"

~ ***"We are often picking up tips, yes. But this evening, we would be interested in providing YOU with some tips, if we could put it like that."***

Sarah: "Yes please—lovely!"

~ ***"We have been particularly interested in your discussion about your fellow people, and how they are behaving, and how it is difficult to teach them your information. I am aware of your situation to some degree and how important it is to bring more awareness to everybody on this planet."***

Bonniol had spoken with some hesitation and one felt he was choosing words with extra care. I observed that the raising of awareness is a slow process.

~ ***"Yes, and I think that is the key word that we were looking for—SLOW."***

I responded: "And yes, so would I be correct in thinking we just have to give people enough time and not rush things?"

~ ***"Yes, there is, there is so much time—for everyone."***

Paul declared afterwards that he experienced such a feeling of endless space as the words *so much time* were uttered.

~ ***"There is no need to worry about teaching them at the same rate as you are learning here."***

Sarah: "The main thing that concerns us is the suffering that people have to go through whilst learning, but then I suppose that's all part of the evolution."

~ ***"Yes, if you think about all of the suffering it would be unbearable I think."***

Sarah: "So perhaps we should just give thoughts out to them that they can take heed of—"

~ ***"Yes, they have their awareness and you have yours, and maybe you are helping them just by maintaining YOUR awareness."***

George: "Yes, Salumet has spoken of setting example and sowing seeds."

~ ***"Yes, and there are so many wonderful seeds being sown on your planet at this time, it really is up to the individuals to—um—pick up on some of them."***

Rod: "Did you hear the question to Salumet about abductions by other planetary people? Is this something that your planet may have done—abductions?"

~ ***"This is something that we have encountered before but we have not practised it ourselves. Possibly, with our mind abilities, we are able to understand more quickly, other worlds."***

George: "Yes, and fortunately you are able to obtain your information through the mind process instead of going through a physical process."

~ *"But these beings who wish to study you physically, are being curious."*

George: "Yes, I was going to say, I can well understand their curiosity."

~ *"We would not judge them. We are assuming they are not harming you."*

Rod: "May I ask, if you wanted information not readily available to you, would you be able to steer Paul into a library or manoeuvre him in any sort of way?"

~ *"It is not in our nature to use individuals in this way. Our needs are not so extensive or that specific. We are curious and love to link and become friends with other beings."*

Rod: "Yes, understood."

~ *"However, we are not so curious about ALL their details."*

Sarah: "You say that you have never abducted. Has anybody ever abducted *your* people?"

~ *"I am not aware of anyone being abducted in our world."*

George: "I get the impression that the biggest problem is our own lack of understanding, and *fear*. If we were more advanced spiritually, I think we would have greater feelings of love and generate much less fear."

~ *"This I think is what your master was conveying. There is no need to fear them. They are seeking in their own way, as we are all seeking."*

We of course had to agree, providing they seek with sufficient respect. They would be technically more advanced and that being so, one would expect them to have developed a measure of respect for life.

Jim: "Can I ask about your recent attempted manifestation? I've a feeling Salumet said that creation and manifestation are similar or the same. Is this your understanding?"

~ *"I—um—yes, it is an aspect of creation to manifest something. It is not a trick or something that will not be there later. We are creating in that sense, yes."*

We suggested that to create an object from energy might be compared to the universe being created from energy, only the scale and complexity would be vastly different. Bonniol agreed this, and went on to explain that *his* proposed materialisation would relate to an *Aeran* object, using the energy available within *our* room; the energy being brought together by Bonniol's mind. If metal, then it would be a metal known on Aerah because that metal would be in Bonniol's mind.

~ ***"Yes, it does not have to be of your Earth. It is not restricted in that way."***

Jim: "Would the size be limited to a small or larger object?"

~ ***"The size does make a difference, yes."***

George: "I imagine it makes a difference in terms of energy requirement."

~ ***"Yes."***

Rod: "And having a large number of people in here helps—"

~ ***"It helps the conditions in the room and the communication."***

I added that if we sat in the middle of a football stadium with 20,000 people, the numbers might benefit but the conditions could be a problem. A few titters followed as our friend went on:

~ ***"There has to be that connection between you all. If people are of a similar energy, then there is more energy available. You are I believe well suited to each other, which helps your energies to blend."***

Lilian: "Without the blending we wouldn't have Salumet and we probably wouldn't have you."

~ ***"If there was disharmony, the vibrations would be difficult."***

The harmony, the blending, the unison are paramount. And that was a good note on which to end. As to that important matter of fear, it was made obvious during Salumet's visit and endorsed by Bonniol that fear-of-the-unknown is a problem that so many humans need to confront. We are aware of some who have bravely faced their fears or placed them to one side, with much benefit. It should, we feel help, if UFO data were brought out from the shadows, debated openly and accepted as the reality that it is. Clearly, serious media attention that squarely faces reality must eventually prevail. The unknown cannot and will not remain unknown and feared forever.

It will have become obvious to some that de-materialised physical space-travel, UFOs, abductions and crop circles are all connected. On 3rd September 2007, we were discussing amongst ourselves the wonderful crop pictogram that was made the previous week at West Kennet Long Barrow near Avebury. Others then came via Sarah and Eileen to add their comments. We had spoken of the designs as attempts to communicate and how this particular one had 3-dimensional character. Our visitors assured that this was indeed a 'genuine' UFO-made-design and not a foolish hoax; also that our thoughts were along the right lines. An intriguing statement was made: ~ "*I can tell you that this particular one is a significant contribution to the thoughts of this population. It has been given to you as an indication of the power that is about you, and it is not only a picture for you to decipher but it is also a message to you that there is much more to come.*"

As to power about us, we now have some awareness of the universal energy, and how the pyramid shape can enhance and reveal so well the effect of it, and in fact the pictogram can certainly be seen as a 3-dimensional pyramid. Then came one known to us as 'Nahashiwar', this her third visit. In Earth life she had been a 19th-century North American Indian lady and we adore her gentle etheric voice and gentleness. She spoke softly and teasingly: ~ "*In my time we looked upon these lights in the sky as messengers from the Great Spirit, and it was quite normal for us at that time to just look, to accept the brightness and the shapes and to KNOW—the connection between us was much greater at that time. But I now know from my time here in spirit that, throughout your planet Earth, all of these events have been happening from time as you have known it. So you see I had to just step forward to let you know.*"

So it has been from the very beginning of our time here; and when I ventured that present day Earth people have got rather stuck in their ways, she replied: ~ "*You are like children. You are in need of first education ... Ha! Ha! ... You do not recognise the signs in the sky! You do not recognise communication as we know it!*"

Clearly then, there is a need for us to open our minds to the sign language being presented.

CHAPTER: 53

Patience – Other Universes ... 6th August – 26th November 2007

As summer's warmth gave way to winter's chill, much changed; including the emphasis of our endeavours. Meetings were often silent or with limited speech, as we pursued a materialisation that stayed elusive. There were good signs; swirling energies seen by several during 'heady' sessions; sometimes gold with dark interlacing wisps; sometimes misty haze. It became increasingly clear that others in spirit showed keen interest, wishing to see this intergalactic event succeed. A clear and permanent result would be a firm incentive to 'believe' and some in spirit were lending a hand; even an arm! Contributions sometimes took on totally unexpected, even bizarre character. A team from ancient Egypt loaned each what was described as an 'extra arm', an 'energy arm' that should contribute to work in progress. This, we were told had helped *their* energies during pyramid work in earlier times, to get them through a problematical period. Others from spirit collected energies from us one week and stowed them in a glass of water, with instructions to hold over to the next meeting when those extra energies might be used. The eagerness to help was plain to see, and Bonniol acknowledged this to be so. We spoke briefly with our friend when opportunity arose—on the subject of 'other universes'. Graham had mentioned that our becoming aware of multiple universes was relatively recent, and asked if each goes on forever or is there an edge?

~ ***"We have never found any edges. Our understanding is that we continue into infinity, because there is no end to our universes."***

Graham: "I wonder if it is possible for our universe to truly go on forever, and yet there still exist other universes. I think that is something we have to learn in the future."

Sarah: "Perhaps like radio waves, they can all exist together—"

George: "That's an interesting thought."

~ *"It is not something to work out. It is something that you can only KNOW."*

George: "Exactly! One cannot work it out because one *thinks* in terms of mathematics, but mathematics does not handle *infinity* with any success."

~ *"This is because it is only a mechanical process and not a spiritual matter, where there are no limitations."*

George: "So one can deduce that *infinity* is a spiritual matter and not a mathematical matter."

~ *"Yes, I am not adequately knowledgeable to expand much on these thoughts."*

Rod suggested the form of a huge circle coming round on itself and Sarah pointed out that there would then be an edge.

~ *"This is a way your physical mind tries to explain it!"*

Bonniol's observation is correct of course, and while the physical mind and its mathematical constructs belong to the physical, *infinity* aligns to spirit. Clever thinkers have desperately sought to incorporate boundlessness into mathematics but only ever with partial success. That any number whatsoever divided by zero produces the same *infinity* result, offends the preciseness of logic. Perhaps it is more a situation than a number, and mathematics can only process *numbers* with success.

During this period of several further attempts to materialise, Salumet spoke on self-development, and he addressed Paul on the 'natural meditative state' that he continues to develop. Our teacher encouraged that he should stay on that course. I added that a factor in Paul's development has been the way Bonniol speaks through him, in such a way as to augment Salumet's own teaching to a very useful degree.

~ "Yes, I am pleased that you see that connection."

I went on to speak of the spiritual help received: "There have been many involved in this exercise, from spirit, but I think I would be right in saying that you were the guiding factor in making this arrangement."

~ **"Yes, because you needed to know (about) the connection of minds. It is something that can be developed by each individual."**

And continuing: "It has been so good for us to compare notes with Planet Aerah, a planet that has advanced more spiritually than the present Earth planet."

~ **"Yes, there are so many who are more advanced than you human beings. I have told you that Earth is a very young planet, so try not to be too amazed that there are others who have greater gifts, as you might say, than yourselves."**

It seemed opportune at this point to mention how the book of these exchanges now nears completion logging our interplanetary conversations, with Salumet's commentaries built into it, and I hoped that he would be happy with this arrangement. And so with fingers crossed I awaited his reply: ~ **"I would have said by now, my dear friend, if we had not been happy. But a word to you: it is not a topic which will be readily accepted by many, but what it will do, as I have often said, is to plant those seeds of knowledge, and as you know my dear friends, one little seed of knowledge grows and grows until you have a forest. Is that not true?"**

As our next meeting began, we received word that Salumet would work silently with Eileen, while others in spirit would go about their separate agenda. We were invited to 'think' unvoiced questions and those suitably versed in whatever topic would then come through our mediums to speak the answer. It worked well and was informative, but one of my own silent questions had queried the difference between 'Salumet' and 'angelic beings'. It was really one for our teacher, and this prompted Salumet to conclude a lovely evening by coming forward to say a little more about his own nature: ~ **"Good evening, I could not leave you this time without answering the question my dear friend has put, about the difference between myself and angelic beings. I do not wish him to struggle with this till next time! It is quite simple, this answer to your question. I, as you know, belong to a conglomerate of beings. I and others, come from that Divine Source of energy, as do those angelic beings. And to put it simply for you in your Earth language, let me say—it is only the difference in a 'job description'."**

So that energy that we know as Divine Source has 'job descriptions' within and these descriptions include 'masters' who teach, and 'angels' who watch over evolution and development. A little more information was sought: "Could I add one further thought?"

~ **"Yes—"**

"Your concern is with *all* universes*, not just this one?"

~ **"Yes."**

"And a word we have in our language is 'omnipotent'—"

~ **"Yes."**

"And perhaps this applies. The angelic beings—would they be less widespread in their influence?"

~ **"Not at all, but (they would be) in different guises for different planets. It is only in your association with them, and your recognition of them that is different."**

"So their tasks would extend to other universes as well?"

~ **"Yes, in the same way as, 'we' as divine energy, are more knowing of all things. You understand?"**

I think we understood so far as it is possible to grasp an understanding of 'Divine Source' and 'Omnipotence'; and it is at least clear that Earth, Aerah and all planetary living in all universes are included within the perfect plan of endless creation. Again, we come to a big statement.

It was Paul who placed the final question of the year to Salumet: "When we attempt the materialisation with Bonniol, is there anything else that we can do to help it along—any subtle changes that I could do to help?"

~ **"No—only to be positive—only to allow each one of you within the room to see it happening. Again, the power of the thought will create the energy that is needed for it to happen. Do not despair. All of these things take time, and however positive most people are, you will find within a room such as this, that there will be a few doubts or a little fear, perhaps not recognised but nevertheless still there. So I will say to all of you: be patient. It is something that humankind is not good with—PATIENCE."**

It was apt conclusion to the year's work with all that had transpired.

*Some may struggle with the notion of 'many universes'. Salumet has several times referred to *many universes.* As I write these words (2008), it can be said that astronomers have recently observed a huge cosmic hole—a void, nearly one billion light-years across, having very few visible stars and galaxies; in the constellation Eridanus. Standard cosmology cannot explain this, and cosmologists consider it to be the imprint of another universe beyond our own. It is cited to be the first experimental evidence for another universe; also vindicating 'string theory'. String theory sees the ultimate building blocks of matter (sub-atomic quarks and leptons), as strings of mass-energy vibrating in 10-dimensional space-time. The same void has also been revealed in maps of big bang afterglow and the string theory itself leads to there being *many universes.* It would appear that science and the words of Salumet converge towards agreement that there is indeed a multiplicity of universes.

PART THREE: *Oneness and Way Ahead, Energetic Void, Our Planetary Schoolhouse, Wonderful Help from Others and a Grand Cosmic Finale*

—No limit to that infinite domain.
And nature will not have it that the sum
Of things set any limits for themselves,
Forcing matter to be limited
By void, and void be limited by matter.
This alternation, this recurrence, makes
The total limitless— Lucretius, The Way Things Are, Book I [19]

The sum of space is infinite, reaching far
Beyond the ramparts of the world; the mind
Persists in questioning: what can be there?
What is there so far off, toward which the urge
Of the free spirit flies?
There is no end,
No limit to the cosmos, above, below,
Around, about, stretching on every side.
This I have proven, but the fact itself
Cries loud in proclamation, nature's deep
Is luminous with proof. The universe

Is infinitely wide—
There are, elsewhere, other assemblages
Of matter, making other worlds. Oh, ours
Is not the only one in air's embrace
—there are other worlds,
More than one race of men, and many kinds
Of animal generations— Lucretius, The Way Things Are, Book II [19]

The mind—the intellect, we sometimes call it—
The force that gives direction to a life
As well as understanding, is a part
Of a man's make-up, every bit as much
As are his hands and feet and seeing eyes.
Some say the sentient mind is not located
In any one fixed area— Lucretius, The Way Things Are, Book III[19]—circa 98 – 55 BC

CHAPTER: 54

Group Mind and Deep Philosophy ...
31st March 2008 – 11th August 2008

PATIENCE IS A virtue and quite obviously the timing of really major happenings involves many, many considerations; not least our group-condition or exactly how well we all knit together. And certainly there is the need to improve mind projection ability. So perhaps we should be more than just patient, and consciously be open to whatever helpful influences are on offer. And *timing* so far as the more general Earthly progress is concerned must always be observed and adhered to. These thoughts occurred as three months of the New Year slipped by with no cheery 'hello' from Bonniol. Uneasy uncertainties prevailed.

A team came through from spirit, making the salient points: ~ *"We are working together to bring you a gift of mind. This will enable you to better communicate with, not only each other, but with us in spirit. We, as you know, cannot interfere with you in any* ***physical*** *way. We are not doing this solely that each one of you can become more aware—the awareness is of the GROUP MIND. The main work that we will be doing with you is whilst you are together in the group."*

Lilian ventured: "So it is a blending together—"

~ *"It is indeed part of the blending. The blending you have already done and it can be improved, but what we are doing is working with the awareness, can I say, of this blending, so that each one of you, whilst you are in the group will attain the same amount of awareness."*

The following week, Salumet spoke on the difference between *belief* and *deep knowing*. He went on to ask that we voice our understanding of the phrase 'brotherhood of man'.

Jan: "I believe it is our *spiritual connection* to every spiritual being that walks the planet."

George: "I would say a oneness that has many details within."

Rod added: "Everyone being interlinked."

~ **"Yes. So you see, by your expression of those words, you show that your understanding of that phrase has meaning, whereas most people on your Earthly planet would say it was a connection to his fellow HUMAN being. But my dear friends, it shows to us that you have allowed the layers of materialism to drop from you."**

He compared this steady change to the emergence of a butterfly, declaring it to be a realisation of all that is already known within; then silence for 15-seconds.

~ **"Forgive my silence but to each one of you this time I extend that spiritual love that bonds between you all. I hope my dear friends that you feel it from us. There is a unity here this evening. Please accept the love that is being given to you this time—it comes not only from myself but from many, many others who have gathered here this time."**

The love-energy was felt; *thickly etheric* and maybe this added to that group-mind-unity.

One more month and we had flowers in abundance, Summer Solstice and Salumet but still no Bonniol. Our teacher commented that it is human nature to be not always full of sunshine. And it was an opportunity to reflect on wonderful Bonniol memories as 'sunshine in our lives' and I expressed my feelings that maybe we need to work on our mind projection, upgrade abilities and further improve group unity before we can expect more visits. In his reply, Salumet firstly reminded of the reasons at the outset for this development, and how the knowledge would benefit, not only our selves, but also so many others; then continuing: ~ **"And of course the purpose of that knowledge, is to grow and grow and grow. It would be an enhancement of communication with those from other worlds if you could try to perfect your spiritual gifts which you ALL possess. After all, you cannot allow spirit to be dormant."**

I referred to the loose end in the materialisation experiment, how there had been such positive indications but it had not quite happened.

~ **"Yes. There is more-than-one energy needed for what you term 'materialisation', and of course each person within the room**

is a conduit for that energy—therefore you have to be together first and foremost in your desire to use these energies properly. But firstly, as I have often said, you have to look inwards to yourself. You have the ability, all of you, for all of these happenings, but you must truly believe and want these things."

Yes indeed, the 'old' abilities lie within us all to be re-awakened. I explained that during the week I had projected a shape, a red triangle, to Paul and he had received a green one. That seemed to sum up our efforts; only partial success and sporadic.

~ **"But if you have part success, that is what should spur you on to continue, and I might suggest my dear friends that you keep it simple: instead of a red triangle, try either the colour or the triangle (shape) until you are more proficient."**

In fact, all of us, group members as well as readers, are encouraged in this development. Still the mind – exclude thoughts – picture a simple object – see if it is picked up by a friend. Play the game as mind exercise. We practise within the group, at home and at times with Bonniol. It works. It will come more naturally to some than others but all can steadily improve; it could in the fullness of time, replace the mobile phone!

Time rolled by; as August came, Salumet waxed philosophical: ~ **"In your world, since the beginning of human existence, we hear so often: 'Show us the way' or 'why are we here?—what is the purpose of life?' You my friends have travelled with me along a pathway of discovery, of knowledge, of truth—truth that has always been. You have made discoveries, not only about yourselves but about mankind—all those who exist within this planet. Not only that, you have been associated with mind connection, with planets further afield and this, my dear friends you have all accepted, you have all gained from this knowledge."**

I agreed that our teacher had *brought us gifts beyond measure* and it is our earnest wish and endeavour to place all communications before others. Salumet continued: ~ **"You know that when you discard these physical overcoats, you are once more reborn to spirit—you have accepted that mind belongs to spirit and there is much that is open and waiting to be experienced. So we come to the first question:**

Show us the way. This, my dear friends is what I have tried to achieve with you over the many years that we have come together. You have moved forward in your thinking, in your experience of spirit, in your understanding of all things greater than your selves, because you have accepted that you are more than your selves. You are all as one—you belong to the wider picture. You are finding your way in beginning to know what the plan of life is.

Why is there existence? Why does mankind strive for this knowledge? Because my dear friends, it is a natural inquisitiveness within you to find the reason why. That is why mankind has in time past become more interested in that—outside of this planet—of this universe. I wish to tell you that, as you leave these many universes behind, you realise that still you remain within a VOID. Your scientists and those who are interested in other life forms are beginning to understand how little they know—each star, each planet, has a form of communication. If you accept that all life, all consciousness is expansion and knowledge, then of course there has to be a form of communication, not in the sense that you would understand, by words, but by energy."

I said: "Yes—and Bonniol spoke of a pulsing light, seen from out in space on approaching planets and suns."

~ "Yes. This is an experience open to all within the many universes but I am trying to take you just a little further."

Salumet went on to develop the point that beyond all lights, planets, suns and universes there is still the void, and within that void there is all-knowledge; of planets, universes and all that is—all the knowledge that is the 'why' of existence. We asked if 'void' is synonymous with 'Great Creative Force / Creative Principle'.

~ "The 'void' is the *result of* the 'Creative Force', it is this seeking, the returning of the energy of the 'Creative Force'. We are speaking of deep matters here."

As Salumet continued in response to questions it became clear that the void encapsulates all creation, is intelligent to the extent of energy exchanges within, that we should see as communication and holding all-knowledge. So the void is as a first breath of the creation; deep matters indeed.

~ **"Do you therefore see the expansion, the continuity of life, the knowledge, the growth—all part of the Creative Force—yet here you are, one little being and how really insignificant you are within the whole."**

Even so, Salumet agreed, we beings connect throughout, going on to describe how the Creative Force is looking for expression in all forms of existence; most humbling. Rod asked about control and our teacher indicated there are 'laws', a word he preferred to use reservedly, since these details are really beyond Earthly vocabulary and comprehension. This was very deeply philosophical and we sought further answers as best we could: ~ **"There has to be expansion—the Creative Force needs to have some form of expression. But that basically answers the question 'why?', a question which has puzzled mankind and those on other planets for so long. Nothing has changed, it has always been, but consciousness has grown, evolution has changed planets."**

I mentioned the attempt to answer the question: 'why', currently in progress in Switzerland; the huge CERN hadron collider experiment, that has taken many years of dedicated work to approach fruition.

~ **"Yes, I am aware of what you speak, and of course, any attempt to try to understand can only be for the good because it shows that mankind is opening up in his own consciousness."**

It was I thought refreshing that the project is at huge cost shared between twenty nations but for no actual monetary gain. Salumet responded: ~ **"That is why I say it can only be good, because it is affecting the *consciousness* of man, not the *emotional* being, not the 'monetary-gain-being'—but because they are seeking. And remember, if you seek, you will be given answers."**

It had been a brainstorming session, and that 'heady' quality has to continue a short while so that we may realise the full import. The significance of all this that comes via Salumet from that deeper spirit becomes apparent when considered against a general backcloth of scientific developments. We have come a long way since that darker mid-20th century period when the majority who taught physics asserted astronomical space to be empty—simply 'nothing', and I recall as a young student being 'put down' for daring to think otherwise. There were just a few of us who thought that if we are obliged to assign properties to space then it cannot be written off as vacuous 'nothing'. And the notion of 'all-knowing intelligent communicating void' was out of sight and out of mind in those days. Now, with refreshed awareness we should look again at the new terminologies of science:

VOID—IN ASTRONOMY: A term used to denote areas in the sky of 'cosmic nothingness' loosely called 'empty space', containing no normal and no dark matter. 'Normal matter' is planets, stars and galaxies. 'Dark matter' does not respond to sunlight but its presence is inferred from gravitational data. The largest void, discovered recently in the constellation Eridanus, is almost one billion light-years across and in astronomy remains a hot topic.

QUANTUM PHYSICS: A tremendously significant and successful branch of theoretical physics based on the assumption that energy is comprised of 'quanta' or minutely small units.

VOID—OF QUANTUM PHYSICS: This is the exciting concept that connects strongly with the Salumet teaching. The void is seen as an 'energetic' mass of virtual particles that forever appear and disappear—a phenomenon termed 'quantum fluctuations'. The void has huge or infinite intrinsic energy known as 'zero-point energy'. And theoretical calculations equate to the creation from this, of whole new universes! A general statement of the quantum theory is that every particle of our universe is a waved excitation of an underlying field—all solid matter of our familiar knowing derives from the underlying field energy.

HENRIK CASIMIR: As early as 1948 Casimir predicted entirely from theory that two facing mirrors in 'empty space' one micrometre (1/1,000 millimetre) apart will produce a disturbance in the 'quantum fluctuations' that will pull the mirrors together. In this last decade nanotechnology has advanced sufficiently for his theory to be tested using the 'atomic force microscope'. He is perfectly correct! 'Zero-point energy' is now a scientifically proven property of the void! Therefore, the enormous energy of the void that may give birth to universes and to which Salumet refers, is embraced by contemporary physics.

SALUMET: It was 27th May 2002 when we first got to hear the term 'zero-point energy' or 'zero-point field' and we checked with

Salumet if this might be one of the newly discovered energies that he had previously mentioned as being a significant advance. He replied: ~ **"I have held back my words to you, because, did I not tell you that there would be many discoveries on your planet that were unknown to you at the time?"**

And so now, 6-years on, he has considered it the time to take this matter a step further.

CHAPTER: 55

Void Analogies – A Time of Challenge and Greatness Within ... 25th August 2007

AT THE START, Salumet was saying: ~ **"As I came close this time, I listened to you speak about the good feeling around your Earth, because of the joining together of many nations. It gladdens the heart to know that peoples can live in harmony, be happy for another human being's success—it is a very good example of unity."**

The Beijing Olympic Games had contributed to the mood on this occasion. It was a grand opening, and soon Salumet was making the gross understatement: ~ **"I know that my words last time gave you much to think about,"** adding **"my purpose was not to confuse but rather to stretch your thinking."**

Well, it certainly did that! And hoping for a little extra clarity I suggested that 'zero-point field', 'Akashic Field' and 'Source' would be much the same thing, each being beyond space-time and involving communication.

~ **"Of course as always, words are limited for descriptions such as these. But because of the expansion of knowledge within many scientific communities** (with Akasha coming from Indo-European Sanskrit) **these things are given human terms. I would say to you: they are related, but 'The Source' will never fully be defined, because consciousness is still expanding to that point—is always seeking, always growing. But yes, I would go along with the names that you have used for the understanding of something that is not yet quite understandable to the human brain."**

The additional factor in respect of 'Source' was acknowledged. And Salumet now continued in response to several questions from us all, giving some idea of how the system builds: ~ **"The void I speak of is of course ever-growing, ever-expanding knowledge, because it contains all-knowledge and is partly a mirror-image of 'Source'. Your own consciousness will become part of a wider consciousness, which then belongs to a wider consciousness, and so it continues. You cannot use the mind, which after all is spirit, without some effect."**

Paul suggested 'void' as a 'manifestation' of 'Source'.

~ **"It is an expression of 'The Source', yes."**

On suggesting that a mathematician might have a view of the Creator as a summation of all expressions from zero to infinity, Salumet quickly responded: ~ **"Yes, that is 'creation'."**

A movie analogy may help. The cinema consists essentially of: the silver screen, the projection room and the zone between which carries the process of projection. What we call 'the real world including ourselves' is the screen image. The ever-changing projection zone that somehow throws images onto screen is the void. It yields all the information needed, gathered from the film's spinning spool. The projection room is 'Source', and contains more than that which is projected. But all analogies are not modern. Ancient Greece had the Legend of the Cornucopia: the father god Zeus, raised by a goat, accidentally broke a horn from the animal and returned it. The horn, normally depicted laden with fruit and flowers, and in the hands of the goddess 'Fortuna' would produce any wish. The Cornucopia, Horn-of-Plenty, yields worldly fortunes, Zeus identifies with Source, and the horn itself is the void that produces worldly things. Salumet responded to this concept: ~ **"I accept your analogy. Within Greek mythology there are many elements of truth, as in many of your ancient civilisations, because in those times many people were closer to what today you call 'The Creator'. Therefore, to make these truths palatable to others, they were given in the form of stories of gods and—dare I say—magic. But yes, I understand how you see the relation between what you have spoken of and the void."**

Salumet then gave us one more analogy: ~ **"You as human beings are houses of the mind. Within the human form the mind is restricted, but in actual fact the mind contains all-knowledge. So you could say that the mind was the analogy of the void. The mind knows all things but is only a shadow of what it truly knows."**

I suggested: "So the human mind would connect with the universal mind and—"

~ **"Yes and therefore expand in that way. The mind holds the knowledge of all things and it is only in the process of expansion that that knowledge is made available, whether it be housed within the body, whether it be taken home to our world—then the mind is freed to continue with that expansion of consciousness."**

Finally we moved onto other matters and there was brief comment on portentous claims for the year 2012, closing with my comment: "That is the next—", but there was no chance to finish.

~ **"—Olympics, that you speak of,"** illustrating just how slick with dialogue our teacher can be; then: ~ **"Now my dear friends, I will take my leave of you and allow the rest of your evening to continue."**

The evening continued with Lilian noticing that Paul was 'away', and she enquired: "Are you okay Paul?"

~ ***"I am—ah—waiting to speak."***

Several surprised voices superimposed.

George: "Is this Bonniol?"

Again the several voices: "Yes / Yes / Yes!"

~ ***"I was—um—"***

George: "Wonderful!"

~ ***"—unsure whether to begin."***

Lilian: "Well, please do!"

George: "Well, you are an old dear, dear friend and we are delighted that you are with us again."

~ ***"I have been waiting for reasons that may not be—ah—known to you, but we have our reasons for our interval."***

Lilian: "I'm sure you do."

~ ***"There has been much happening in our different worlds, I am sure. But there is the same feeling as when we were here before."***

Sarah: "I had been wondering if you had been working on bringing us an object, but there have obviously been other things as well."

~ ***"We have waited for what we think would be the best time, and we will wait a little longer for that time."***

George: "Will it help in the meantime if we just have nice conversation again as we did before?"

~ ***"I was hoping for another chance to speak with you. There are points of interest for us, and perhaps now there will be a better understanding on both sides in that we have had some digestion time."***

George: "Yes, it's certainly been a valuable period of going through what has transpired, and as you say: digesting. And I hope all has been well with you and your group since we last spoke."

~ ***"There have been a few changes and that is as it should be. There are always some changes in our world, so we are happy that these are intended."***

Sarah: "Salumet has said that in our group we will have people coming and going. Maybe it's the same with your group?"

~ ***"That is what we were thinking of, yes."***

Sarah: "Right."

George: "And is there a question you would wish to put to us this time?"

~ ***"Perhaps we have been assessing this one's memories enough now. We have worked through so much of your different experiences."***

George: "And that's all through the downloaded memories that you have—"

~ ***"And it has been of great value to us, and we have reached a point where we can accept that you have—a very challenging place to live. Your world is—it is in many ways far more full of unrest—"***

George: "Yes, sadly."

~ ***"—than ours."***

Lilian: "When you first came and we talked about our different worlds, I said to my daughter at home, explaining yours. And she said: well, when can we go?"

~ *"You would be very welcome. And when you no longer require your physical body, we can then give you safe passage over."*

George: "That's a very nice thought, thank you for that."

Sarah with enthusiasm: "Or we could just come over to your place when the meeting's over; that would be nice!" And laughter followed that!

~ *"I will bring to you others, when I come again."*

George: "Oh that would be wonderful!"

~ *"There is one race of beings who we believe are a little nearer to your location. They have agreed to allow us to bring them to you."*

Sarah followed our positive responses with: "Are they similar to us?"

~ *"They are—ah—similar in their size and their shape is—humanoid—in their general shape. They have of course their—they are unique—there is no one the same of course."*

Sarah: "Yes, this we understand. I wondered, if they are a bit nearer to us, maybe they have visited us in a physical way?"

~ *"They have craft but they are not yet able to traverse that distance. They are not particularly advanced technologically. But they are ahead of you in things. They have developed their minds, and used their mental work abilities in a way that—is more in line with the large—the universal love consciousness."*

Sarah: "We can well believe that they are more advanced. We've been told we are the least intelligent of the lot!"

~ *"I am nevertheless in luck, now that I am more aware of the challenges that you face. I can only say that there must be greatness within for these challenges to be placed before you."*

Sarah: "It seems to be what we need to grow; I think it is part of our learning. How *you are* helps with *your learning*, and how *we are* is obviously what we need to grow spiritually."

Lilian: "The next time you come you will be relaying messages for that person, will you?"

~ *"I will, yes, that will be the way I believe."*

Lilian: "Yes, I see. They'll be very welcome."

~ *"Though we may have a blending of Paul's thoughts, but I will prepare you in advance."*

Lilian: "Thank you. We'll look forward to that."

I asked if this would be one of the eight that we know of or another contact since developed.

~ ***"There are 'nine' now."***

George: "So you have developed the ninth! Well done!"

~ ***"This is not the latest, these people have been known to us for a long time. I think they will be of interest to you."***

We responded that this meeting would be welcomed wholeheartedly.

~ ***"I will not keep you further this evening."***

George: "Can I just ask you one silly question that I have wanted to ask since we last spoke? If we jump from a great height, say from the top of a building, our gravity pulls us to the ground and we hit it very hard and we die. Is it the same with you, or do you survive jumping from a great height?"

~ ***"Yes, we would—ah—have to prepare ourselves, and fall—um—"***

I suggested: "In the right way."

~ ***"Yes. There would not be the same damage because we would not fall heavily like you—we are much lighter."***

Sarah: "That's interesting."

George: "And your atmosphere is thicker, perhaps that makes a difference too—"

~ ***"There are places where this changes on our planet."***

George: "Yes, well thank you for that. It is a question I have wanted to ask for a long time."

Sarah spoke of those who commit suicide from tall buildings, suggesting that might not be a possibility on Aerah.

~ ***"Not from our buildings—there are locations where falling into certain canyons would be very dangerous. But there are always ways to kill one's self if that is one's purpose—one's intent."***

Sarah: "Yes, not the best thing to do. Could I just ask before you go: did you hear me saying earlier 'we'd like to have you', before our meeting started, or were you coming anyway?"

~ ***"We did not hear that but we are sometimes listening in."***

George: "Yes, I mentally wondered if you might be about this evening, and indicated that you would be very welcome."

~ ***"Thank you. I will say our best goodbyes."***

General heartfelt farewells followed and expressions of delight at Bonniol's return.

~ ***"I leave you with our love."***

Lilian: "And our love goes with you and to all your family and friends."

It must be said that we were over the moon to be speaking with Bonniol again after an absence of nine calendar months. It just goes to show how unpredictable these evenings are, yet we remain so lucky. Bonniol's *'full of unrest'* and *'challenging place to live'*, apply so well to Earth, and as later intimated, we are clearly *'less in line with the universal love consciousness'*; hence our wars, wayward politics, aspects of greed and self-indulgence, disrespect for nature and our urban violence, all aligning to that portrayal. That our severe challenges must relate to *greatness within* is profound commentary. Salumet has referred to the greatness of earlier civilisations and how their superior ways continue in consciousness. It all rests there within, to one day re-awaken. We have discussed earlier the low matter density of Aerah. This is now clearly illustrated by the fact that Aerans survive falls from great heights in the grip of their planet's less pronounced gravity. And as to communicating planets, now we are ten. This has to be seen as the hot news item.

CHAPTER: 56

Timing is Everything – The Earth as a Schoolhouse ... 15th September 2008

LILIAN, SENSING SOMETHING was happening looked to Sarah, who gestured to Paul saying: "I think it's Bonniol."

~ ***"Hello!"***

He quickly explained that they had not brought the others this time and still worked on modus operandi for that. We said not to worry and warmly welcomed our dear friend.

~ ***"There is a chance that it will not be possible at the moment because they have not yet become as able to project their minds as our people, but we hope it may be possible."***

Lilian: "Well it would be nice but we do understand if it's rather difficult for them."

And needless to say we can well identify with those having inabilities in this area!

~ ***"You are so like them in some ways, but of course, there are many differences too. We are waiting for the right time to do the things we mentioned before, so from our side there is nothing needed to say. This is because we have gained so much information already."***

Sarah: "Are you waiting for the energy levels to be right?"

~ ***"It is to do with that yes, and to do with the right time, for these things, TIMING IS EVERYTHING."***

George: "Yes indeed, we do appreciate that. On the matter of time, we have had this, what you would probably call: a slight break, in our exchanges, which in our timing amounts to ¾ of a year. Is it possible to say how long that period is in the way you count time on your planet?"

~ ***"We have had—um—1½ years, yes."***

Lilian observed the Aeran year to be shorter.

~ ***"We have of course different timescales."***

George: "Your yearly planetary season change seems to be just twice as fast as ours. Yes, it is interesting to have that comparison."

~ ***"Thank you."***

Lilian: "Can you, with your mind, travel to *any* planet that you would like to visit?"

~ ***"Yes, of course our minds can go anywhere that we have the knowledge—where to go. We have to know where we are going, but—um—"***

Lilian: "It has to be arranged before—"

~ ***"It has to be within our minds."***

Lilian: "With spiritual help—"

~ ***"Yes, there has to be an awareness of where we wish to go."***

Sarah: "So how do you find out the places that you want to go to?"

~ ***"We have our libraries which contain more than just books, but we are also able to, of course, gain much knowledge from experiences such as this. We, as I have said before—um—use the memories in the one I am using to gain much knowledge of YOUR planet."***

Sarah: "Tell me again how you found Paul's mind."

~ ***"We became aware of this planet through—um—ah—"***

George: "I think your guides would have been involved. Is that—"

~ ***"Yes. Close guides brought us here—in a sense."***

George: "When you say 'close guides', would they be close to your planet or close to our planet?"

~ ***"My own personal guide—"***

Lilian: "Yes."

George: "Ah!"

~ ***"—brought me here as a learning experience."***

Lilian: "We all have our helpers from spirit."

~ ***"You are also guided in your lives."***

Lilian: "It's absolutely wonderful!

George: "You have been able to study the downloaded memories. Has that raised any puzzles or problems? Are there questions that arise from that, that you would like to place to us?"

~ ***"We—um—now feel we understand the stage of your planet, and we understand the particular learning available here—the teachings. And we understand the place Earth has as a learning planet."***

George: "Ah—and the learning to be had would be a little bit different from the learning ventures of *your* planet. Would that be correct?"

~ ***"Each learning planet is different—yours caters particularly well—um—(when it) comes to learning about very physical matters—the material world, so there is a very concrete—um—very physical side of life, which is in a sense, the—um—the furthest away from the spiritual side. But it is also a very, very—the word escapes me—"***

George: "A necessary journey?"

~ ***"Its spiritual teachings become very clear once they are learned here, almost as clear as the structures you build here. They become deeply embedded."***

Sarah voiced that we have been told, if there were a league table, then we are a lowly planet, so maybe we need a firm base to build from.

~ ***"It is—um—a very useful experience for us to see this part of creation. I cannot express it (quite) the way we feel at this time, but it has given us much clarity ourselves, much 'definition'—perhaps that comes closer. Your emphasis on the physical interpretations of life, provide a very strong framework. But perhaps this is more the way WE see it."***

Sarah: "Your view of course—you are able to communicate everything by mind, so everything is freer. But we have lost that ability and are searching for it. So we don't work in the same way. So I suppose that's another reason for structures."

George: "I think the stronger framework is providing a base from which we can move with some clarity in a spiritual direction. Does that make sense?"

~ "Yes, I think once you establish your firm physical base in the universe, you will be able to move forward with great power—with great direction."

Sarah: "That's good. We've got a long way to go yet though."

Lilian: "I think we are improving slowly."

George: "Could I just ask a silly little question stemming from last time? We talked about jumping from great heights. To help us in this, we invented the parachute—a cloth and cord device, enabling us to go down to the ground more slowly. I imagine that, on your planet, this is something that has not been invented because there is no need?"

~ "Yes, we understand, the contraption is well-designed for your conditions. Yes, we do not need it, but we can have fun with similar equipment."

George: "Ah, so you have similar inventions that enable you to glide and float and have fun—"

~ "Yes, they can help us learn about the wind and have fun with the elements. But they are not used in the same way as your parachutes."

George: "Well, that helps us to understand the conditions on your planet. Thank you."

~ "I have something a little like your kites, which can allow me to—um—fly a little, but it is not for travelling with. There is no guarantee which direction you will go in."

Sarah: "If you are able to float in your atmosphere—things that you want to keep on the ground—how do you, if they are lighter than you are?"

~ "We have gravity, there is some pull. So unless there are winds to move objects, they will stay put. But they may need anchoring, as objects on your planet."

Sarah reflected: "You would not be able to play football as we do. The ball would just float about."

~ "We would need—"

Sarah: "A different ball."

~ "Yes."

Rod: "I guess you can run a lot quicker than we can."

~ "I would imagine, yes. It would make this a lot easier."

Sarah: "You skip more, don't you, on the ground?"

~ ***"Yes, it (the atmosphere) is also in some ways 'thicker' for us to move through. So we are able to float or glide a little, but perhaps moving through (and disturbing?) the atmosphere slows us down."***

I mentioned how every four years we have the Olympic Games and how athletes cannot jump much more than their own height; and suggested that Aerans might be able to jump much higher.

~ ***"Yes, there are of course 'games' like that, and there are people able to jump well above their height."***

Lilian: "Some are better than others—"

~ ***"Yes, not everyone likes to develop their physical attributes much. You I believe develop these, for it is more important. We only ENJOY IT, yes—not a competition."***

Rod enquired if Bonniol had picked up on our world's economic downslide.

~ ***"It has been looked at, yes. But we only look at it for a short time, because you will no doubt also know that they are natural ups and downs."***

George: "Yes, we realise that our planet is in the process of change—faster change than usual. And people have to get used to changes in climate, in monetary system and use of resources. And it is easier for some to accommodate the stringent changes than others. But certainly our conditions are changing in a number of ways at the present time."

~ ***"Yes, these are natural cycles to keep the balance right. It is always balancing out and it, I am sure you realise—your whole world has many cycles to work through before you achieve your goals."***

George: "Yes, again, some of us realise that more so than others."

~ ***"There may be a time when everything is much more predictable and your structures are more peaceful."***

Lilian: "Yes, we hope so."

~ ***"But this is the point where we are now, and it provides the best possible teaching for the people at the moment, and that is what is being provided by your teacher."***

George: "He is taking us on a very nice journey."

~ "You have many teachers on the Earth all around you."

Rod: "Are you aware of them when you say that?"

~ "It is not so much 'an awareness' when I say it. I am speaking from my knowledge of the way life works. THE EARTH IS A SCHOOLHOUSE. We're here in it, and I'd better finish I think now."

George: "Well, that's a very good note on which to finish, Bonniol—'The Earth is a schoolhouse.'"

Our fond farewells followed.

Rod: "Love to you all."

~ "Our love to you too."

As ever, we had much to think on. The few words on parachutes brought memories of my own youth and conscripted military service. Para training had been intensely physical but jumping from aircraft, I would say is something more. Putting down the underlying fear of leaping into space seemed in some strange way to awaken an inner knowing of life, love and spirit; so much more than mere emotion. And perhaps a basic rather physical structure was felt, to be later built upon. Bonniol refers to our underlying structures and cycles and balancing. There are many, with the media focus on health and medication in recent months; some advanced treatments being unaffordable, yet taxation funds are huge. Two large tax expenditures are 'hospitals / health' and 'weapons of mass destruction'. These two outgoings are opposites, and surely we need to simply choose between 'respect for life' and 'death threat'. It is a powerful physical structure to confront, and choosing 'respect for life' embodies with that choice, love and compassion, and this must clearly be our ultimate spiritual pathway. And we should not forget the date May 2000 when five leading nuclear nations signed a document agreeing to rid the world of nuclear arms; so that pathway has entered consciousness at least. Bonniol dismisses our economic downturn as part of a *natural cycle to keep the balance right*. Some may prefer the expression 'pendulum of change', that has swung too much into materialism, so that we naturally now swing back to less material inclination. It is in any event an important part of learning curve that lengthens by the minute as we progress through grades in this *planetary schoolhouse*, where yesterday's encounters yield tomorrow's dream-child.

Salumet subsequently also spoke on the economic 'crunch': ~ **"No matter what time in your Earthly history, there has always been highs and lows of Earthly living, whether it entails the many wars, the ravaging of land, or as you speak now, the deep depression of trade and moneys. All of these things are part of the evolution of your world. This crisis that you are all feeling at this time, of course will pass, but it will leave behind the recognition for change and that is the true purpose of these things—the realisation and change that must take place. It is to help mankind recognise what is important—that importance is not gain-through-wealth-and-materialistic-things, but by going inwards and recognising the brotherhood-of-all-mankind, and the goodness and the love that should be extended to all peoples in your world. That is what mankind must strive for."**

CHAPTER: 57

Cosmic Party and Concluding Notes ... 10th November 2008

OUR JOURNEY FORWARD continues, so that firm conclusion to these chronicles becomes inappropriate, and certain doorways must of necessity stay open. That this might be a problem seems to have been realised by our friends in spirit. Anyway, a grand party was arranged for this particular evening, in the nature you might say, of a finale. Wonderful! Firstly, one spoke via Sarah explaining that many were gathered, our cooperation would be required, and one or more would be assigned to each of us. That control withdrew, and several minutes elapsed, while Sue struggled with a tickly throat, then another, with powerful steady voice, addressed us, again via Sarah: ~ *"Good evening ... I was not expecting to come through this instrument but I feel the other lady is not quite ready for my presence."*

Lilian explained about the tickly throat.

~ *"This could be the reason why I am being sent to this lady; so, first of all, I am happy to be with you and am very pleased that so many from our world are joining with you this evening. We have noted that many of you have been lacking in your thoughts for 'THE UNIVERSES' and they have been wishing to make some cosmic contact. We have brought to you many who have been (lived lives) on other planets on other universes."*

Staggered by such announcement, all I could manage was: "That is most interesting!"

~ *"And these are those that are standing close by you this evening. You will I hope be aware that you will feel changes to your body—to give you a little insight into the structure of other beings. Once you feel some slight changes, we will be able to help with your mind, and hopefully you will be able to get a feeling of the spirit with you. We would ask that each one of you asks (mentally) that one with you a simple question and we will try to give you the answer. So I will draw back, and each one of you can we hope sense that one, or maybe there will be two or three, all from the same planet (to boost energy).*"

After four minutes of silence: ~ "*I am here if you need to ask for help.*"

Another two minutes and Lilian enquired if any had feelings.

George: "I asked if they have limbs similar to ours, and following that I have a 'solid' feeling in the fingers, and the feeling is getting more so."

Lilian: "I feel as if my mouth is very small."

Rod: "I feel a movement around my cheek and mouth."

Paul: "My nostrils are hairy, I think."

In response to several questions from us the clarifying statement was made: ~ "*The ones with you are from spirit, but they have been (lived) on these other planets and are able to impress upon you how they were. The exercise is for you so that you can use your mind, and this is part of your development, where we hope that you will be able to achieve much with your minds. So I hope that each one of you has asked a question, so that you may receive mind-to-mind, the answer.*"

Sue: "I have asked about stature and I have a feeling I'm being pushed down, and I think that's my answer."

Lilian: "Anyone else?"

Ann: "I asked about sound and my mouth opened."

Paul: "I asked what they look like—very prickly face, very rough skin—greenish 'cactus' colour."

Well that was a start, and a few more minutes passed in silence.

George: "I asked if they have limbs similar to our selves, and I got this solid feeling in the fingers—not the little finger, just the others. I extended the question: do they have arms and legs? And I now have that same feeling in the lower legs."

~ "*The two gentlemen are quite correct in their thoughts.*"

Lilian: That's nice to know."

~ "*The last gentleman to speak—you have indeed one digit free and the others are welded together.*"

George: "Thank you, that's nice to know, and certainly there is that feeling."

~ *"And yes, this other gentleman—do you have any other feelings, any shape you can feel?"*

Paul: "I have quite small red eyes. I wasn't sure about the shape of the head—fairly round—"

~ *"Would you like me to tell you?"*

Paul: "Yes please."

~ *"You are more like the lizard."*

Paul: "Ah yes—that had crossed my mind."

~ *"That did?"*

Paul: "Yes."

~ *"That is good, it is not quite like you would get here but that is the nearest description I can give you. But you are both quite correct!"*

Rod: "Is my face rounder and am I not quite so tall? Am I more elliptical?—I feel cramped here (pointing down)."

~ *"You have a much thicker body and you are not quite as tall, but you are not short. I think this feeling comes from the fact that you are much thicker. You are much more solid, and on the planet that your spirit came from, you did not have the need to move. So you are much more rigid in your shape. That is not to say that you did not move—you had no reason to move. Your people were most advanced in mind projection, and this is the reason why."*

Daphne: "I feel as if I've got cobwebs on my face and on my head."

~ *"You are beginning to get the sensations dear lady. You need to just sit a little longer, and you should get a reply to your question. And the lady, who is next to this one, who spoke of the smaller mouth (Lilian)—do you have other feelings or answers?"*

Lilian: "I'm thinner, much thinner—small mouth, yes. That's all I feel at the moment. The question—because we have colds and coughs at the moment, where we live—I did ask if on their planet, they have similar colds and coughs. I thought there was a chuckle."

~ *"I will tell you—you are like a fish."*

Lilian: "A fish—with a small mouth!"

~ *"And you are indeed more elongated, and I can tell you that although you do not live entirely in liquid, you do spend quite a considerable amount of time in—I say 'liquid' because it is not like your water—and the answer is that disease is not known."*

Emily: "I feel like I am—I don't know if it's a tree or a mermaid or something. My legs feel like they are just one."

~ *"Dear one, I believe you were not at this group when we had a visitation from one who came from a planet where the bodies were (shaped as) 'mushrooms'. You have indeed a 'mushroom', of that planet."*

There were delighted cries at this as we recalled meeting with those we know as 'the mushroom people'.

~ *"You, like the gentleman, did not move. You also had very good mind projection. And the one who is close by you (Paul) I can tell you, had influence with the bringing together of that planet at this meeting. That one has quite a 'soft spot' for this group, and I think you will find in the future, you will have more contact with that one."*

George: "We shall certainly look forward to that!"

Paul: "I think they like the elephants of this planet—"

Lilian: "Talking to the elephants, yes."

~ *"I think you have, like the elephant, a very good memory!"*

George: "The one who is with me, I feel is a very 'solid' form, perhaps almost 'leathery' exterior."

~ *"The one who is impressing you was indeed a solid type, but was able to move at great speed—but the reason for the toughness of this one was, the hostile conditions that it had to live in."*

George: "And there would be arms *and* legs I think."

~ *"There were indeed arms and legs, and I can also tell you that the nose was not quite like 'a trunk', but it was certainly much—"*

George: "Projected forward?"

~ *"Longer than the ones you have here."*

George: "Yes, I have a feeling—almost ape-like, and I think two eyes."

~ *"There were two eyes, and have you an impression of ears?"*

George: "I felt hair about the head but I have no impression of ears."

~ *"They, I can tell you, are somewhat like gills of a fish but longer, so you have many small openings."*

George: "Ah yes, thank you—most interesting."

Paul: "Yes, an interesting bunch of people!"

Lilian: "I don't know if it is anything to do with it but I feel I want to chuckle again—and realising how different we all are!"

~ *"Yes, I think some of the amusement started with the disease, because they are aware how fragile you are and, I could say, how lucky they were that they did not suffer from diseases."*

We can understand that!

Sue: "I feel like a sphere—possibly liquid-filled, like a bubble, no arms, no legs, translucent—like we would see bubbles when we blow them—a pulsating movement to get around—"

Sue's overshadow must have felt really strange.

~ *"You have some of the feelings. I can tell you that the lower part of your body is not unlike an octopus, but the top half is quite different. You also were in a liquid, but not as thick as water."*

Sue: "That makes sense—a liquid."

~ *"And you were able to float on the top, but the top part of your body is subjected to heat, and you have a skirt that flows over the top of the 'octopus', if I can put it that way, which protects it from the heat. This top part also has a shell-like formation which protects the body. So you were part correct."*

Sue: "Thank you."

~ *"And now we have one more lady—"*

Ann: "I don't know that I have got on very well—the middle part was quite bulging, perhaps a small head, and there was quite a sense of heat, and a reddish colour—I'm a bit uncertain really."

~ *"You must not doubt what you are given. You are quite correct! The red that you speak of is not actually the colour of you, but it is a reflection from the red sand. Your body is like a type of glass and it absorbs the colours around it. You are describing one aspect of your life. This is the aspect on the red sand and you talk of the round part in the middle. This is indeed because you roll—you roll over the sand and your glass-like structure reflects this. But at other times you are another colour. Do you have any feeling of what this colour might be?"*

Ann: "Greenie-blue?"

~ *"The blue is near, it is violet—a deeper violet, and what happens to you is that in one part of your life you are rolling about on the sand, but like the butterfly, you then develop into a much lighter being and you rise off the sand into the atmosphere, and you absorb the colour of the skies, a deep purple. So this is a two-part being."*

Ann: "Thank you."

Daphne: "I might come back to my cobwebs—I feel rather tight around the middle and around my shoulders."

~ *"This is good—you are a form of—not human and not tree but something in between. Do you feel quite stiff?"*

Daphne: "I do, yes."

~ *"That is the tree aspect, but if you were to move your head, would it move quite freely?"*

Daphne: "Yes, it does."

~ *"So that is the human side. I use the words you understand, just for your understanding."*

Daphne: "Yes, thank you."

Our visiting friend then addressed our gathering: ~ *"I am pleased you have been able to get the information. You all have been much impressed by many and have had help from many—not just those with you, but many who have come to help. And we would say to you: do try to use your mind projection as much as you can, because exercises like this will become much easier in the future and much more will be able to be brought to you, with your minds more trained."*

Lilian: "It just shows how important the mind is."

~ *"So I will now leave, and thank you for your time, patience—"*

George: "Well, *we* must thank *you* before you depart. And this has given us a valuable insight into the great variety of form that is possible, and I'm sure we all feel very much indebted to you for that, and yes, for the exercise. Thank you very much!"

Paul: "Yes, a very enriching evening!"

~ *"We are pleased to have been able to help you, and may I just say that the variety of shapes and forms that you have been made aware of ARE SO FEW IN RELATION TO THOSE THAT ARE AVAILABLE."*

Following 'gulps' and 'mms', Lilian added: "We are just grateful to everyone."

Paul: "If we practise our mind projection, maybe one day we can have another go."

~ *"I am sure there will be many opportunities for you. And I can tell you, there are many who wish to make contact when the opportunity is right."*

We were again reminded of that phrase: timing is everything, and Lilian added that we would be more relaxed and less surprised next time.

~ *"So again I thank you, and I will return back to my place in spirit."*

Warm farewells followed as over-shadows withdrew, leaving us with never to be forgotten memories of an incredible party. In physical domains there are separations; of countries, continents, planets, galaxies, entire universes; that we can well understand. But not so in spirit, where in circumstances of evolved mind, all may come together.

It is difficult for human intellect to grapple with exactly how physical and spiritual worlds entwine; how in spirit, individual form and character prevail and can come together as an organised event. As physical beings, our desire to understand this universe and our environs is a natural endeavour. Two entirely different methods of enquiry are open to us: 'physical exploration' and 'mind work'. As part of the physical approach, a telescope directed across the heavens, sees how it once was, because it takes many, many years for starlight to reach Earth. So we see a remote past. Due to the accelerating expansion of the universe we cannot possibly see further back than 15-billion years, because at that furthest point galaxies recede at light-speed. So, all that can be seen is but a part, a fraction of unknown size, of this universe as it once was. A universe created in space-time is controlled by laws appropriate to that physical system. But since mind is exterior to space-time, the same laws do not apply. All mind-encounters are strictly in our present and such encounters may be anywhere within this universe, and sometimes 'beyond the observable universe', and may even involve 'other universes'. And this has just been demonstrated! It may help to clearly state the comparisons between physical exploration and mind exploration.

PHYSICAL EXPLORATION: The various forms of telescope are of course restricted to the 'observable universe', likewise photography. Dialogue between beings is possible by means of crop circles or similar sign language. Any more detailed communication would have insurmountable difficulties and cultural data would simply not be forthcoming. Rock sample collection would be restricted to our own solar system and any collection of artefacts most unlikely. The cost of physical exploration in terms of both time and money is huge, while media attitude is one of enthusiastic acclaim.

MIND PROJECTION EXPLORATION: The criteria are completely different with no range limitation. Pictures may be given by clairvoyance. Dialogue is by use of words without language difficulty. Much information exchange regarding cultures is therefore possible. Artefacts may be obtained through materialisation, once procedure for this is perfected. Costs are minimal and media interest is thus far likewise minimal.

The above chapters give a clear indication of what is possible, and one must remember of course that all communications with others will be 'overseen' and subject to spiritual protocol. Some restrictions will always be required to suit our progress status. Intergalactic materialisation remains at this moment undemonstrated; we are assured that it will indeed happen but only when the time is exactly right. That could be in the not too distant future, and possibly when we have developed our own skills a little further. Any news of this event will be immediately posted on the Salumet Websites: www.salumet.com and www.salumetandfriends.org. You are invited to watch for this and for the many other posted news items and updates.

One further statement should be made. If you recall, we began sitting on the topmost step of the Mayan sun temple at Palenque. There were thoughts about the workings of the universe and a message was received concerning this: LOVE IS THE MOST IMPORTANT THING. Yes, love is so enmeshed in all the wonderful workings. Love is intrinsic and reigns supreme throughout. The sun temple experience was twenty years earlier; much has happened since. Now, thanks to Salumet, Bonniol and the many others who have contributed to the Kingsclere evenings, I and my friends understand so much more clearly the meaning of that message.

"For so long, individuals could see nothing other than what stood before them, but all that is changing. You know that 'universes' exist—your astronomers would confirm that there is one so far that they can see, but they *believe* that there are other universes."

Salumet – 25th April 2005.

There has also been wise statement made by some who have walked the physical Earth in times past:

"And therefore as a stranger give it welcome. There are more things in heaven and Earth, Horatio, than are dreamt of in your philosophy".

William Shakespeare, Hamlet 1, V, 165-167.

APPENDICES

APPENDIX 1
THE KINGSCLERE GROUP

USUALLY 8-10 OF us sometimes more, meet on Monday evenings, at Lilian's house in residential Kingsclere. But the group is larger than those numbers suggest, since there are also many in spirit. These include spirit guides, controls, healing groups, teachers, some who like to 'sit in' on the informative teaching, past life connections, some who bring messages for humanity and some who bring good cheer to uplift. We owe much to Leslie Bone, who originally established the group and presided in earlier years. Under Leslie's guidance much good work was done, including many 'rescues', aiding those who experience difficulties of transition from this world to the next, where lives continue. Many valuable contacts were made. Then a message was received that there would be a major event. This happened in June 1994 when the Ascended Master we know as 'Salumet' first came to us through Eileen, who then quite rapidly assumed full-trance status. Much has followed since, with Salumet's visits ongoing most Monday evenings, plus visits from wonderfully interesting individuals arranged by Salumet.

Leslie, our dear founder, president and good friend, passed to spirit in the autumn of 1999, but he remains very much with us and on several occasions has dropped by for chats. Lilian now hosts the meetings. When a project continues to go forward for a decade or two, there are bound to be changes along the way, with some moving abroad, new ones joining the fold, family exigencies and so on. The present team meets as ever on Monday evenings, travelling from homes scattered across four counties. A few notes on each might be appropriate. We are:

Lilian Pearce: Our warmly welcoming host, whose counselling of 'spirit rescues' is well known, and who provides a much appreciated cup of tea at the close of proceedings. This is a chat-over-a-cuppa time when the events of the evening are reviewed and Eileen, who will have been 'away' in full trance, is brought up to date with how it all went.

Eileen Roper: Full trance medium through whom 'Salumet', speaks with so much love, wisdom and spiritual knowledge for all humanity. Many others also have ventured forth, some being historic figures, each having individual voice character. Eileen is also a healer and member of the National Federation of Spiritual Healers.

Sarah Duncalf: Trance medium through whom several speak with individual voices of character that we have got to know. These include South American tribal connections from the time of the Inca Empire and a head farmer from Egypt in the days of the Pharaohs. We are grateful to Sarah for regularly typing the Salumet transcripts from digital recordings.

Sue Grandjean: Trance medium through whom several speak, including eminent North American Indians and Sisters of Holy Orders who have visited intermittently for more than a decade.

Jan Pearce: Trance medium who on occasions has remarkable clairaudience and clairvoyance, and these gifts have contributed wonderfully during some of the Bonniol visits. Jan has been able to sketch objects of clairvoyant vision that have been confirmed by Bonniol.

Richard Pearce: One of our younger team members and another who experiences detailed clairvoyant images and can subsequently sketch their form. Richard and Jan, his mum, are able to compare visions during a session and discuss their implication with Bonniol. And Richard has recently built a Salumet website: www.salumet.com .

Sara Martin: 'Receives' inspiration to lead the group in meditation journeys at Salumet's request. It is clear that Sara also receives inspiration during sessions as a musician and hotel pianist.

Graham Martin: Special needs teacher and accomplished artist. Graham has been able to place some of our more searching questions to Salumet and Bonniol.

Paul Moss: Mind-link medium through whom the Aeran being, our very dear friend Bonniol, speaks. We are also grateful to Paul for transcribing a backlog of pre-2000 meetings held as tape recordings, and for producing CDs and a CD-ROM of all meetings from June

1994 to the present. This latter was a marathon task that has made our records more accessible and leads to wider and more efficient distribution.

Jim Howship: Retired chemist from a well-known international organisation has joined us during the Bonniol era having read much of our literature. Jim's clear thinking and scientific reasoning has been a much appreciated input.

Rod Taylor: With a passing resemblance to his silver screen namesake, Rod, a retired Horse Guards sergeant brings warmth and laughter to our meetings; a more recent team member who has joined during the Bonniol era.

Daphne Taylor: Rod's dear wife often accompanies him; bringing good cheer, and as a senior girl, helped to keep me in order when we were at primary school together!

George Moss: As a retired scientist I am well familiar with writing reports. In the group, it is my job to see that everything gets recorded and I transcribe the Bonniol proceedings; endeavouring later to put some of the Salumet and Bonniol material into article and book form.

Ann Moss: My dear wife who is a pillar of strength and who has been able to come along to the more recent meetings. Ann is a great help with transcribing the recordings.

Emily Duncalf and **Natalie Moss:** It is so nice to have 'youth' represented, and these two join with us when their busy schedules permit.

The Team, L > R from top: Lilian, Eileen (Salumet speech), Sarah, Sue, Jan, Richard, Sara, Graham, Paul (Bonniol speech), Jim, Rod, Daph, George, Ann, Emily, Natalie

All members: In addition to what is listed above, all contribute their energy, healing prayers and of course enquiring questions. These things are important and we frequently hear back from those in spirit regarding the living *group energy* and our *healing prayers.* These are answered in various ways, and sometimes produce results that have been described as miraculous. We should of course not overlook the fact that some of us have more free time than others. We are all at different stages in our living; some are retired, some in full-time demanding jobs and some are busy mums and dads, and such commitments can make a difference! That accounts the Earthly team.

Those in spirit: Many in spirit are involved in the present project and this fact should of course not be overlooked. If names were named it would make a formidable list and not all names are known to us. Salumet, is so frequently with us that I am tempted to think of him as one of our number but he is of course formless divine energy and not of this Earth. But let me just reiterate that this dear friend of so many evenings is a being of light and an ascended master; he is of all-knowledge and has chosen to enter dense Earthly matter in the way that he does to teach the truth of existence. He brings with him so much love, knowledge and upliftment. The voice that issues from Eileen is vibrant with love and compassion. Those of pure energy, who come to teach, usually choose an apt name that we may know them by, and 'Salumet' is a name of salutation. (Names are irrelevant in the deeper spirit where communication is by direct thought process, not cumbersome spoken language.)

There are two books. The first, *A Smudge in Time* [3], published 2000; is a millennium book tracing the development of human consciousness and knowledge of spirit from our early days as Homo erectus in the African Rift Valley. Several chapters of Part 4 are devoted to modern spirit communication and this latter part of the book includes a first published introduction to Salumet. The second work, *Salumet* [1], followed in 2005 and is a presentation of the first ten years. Much is accounted concerning topics that might be anticipated of a spiritual teacher, such as meditation, prayer, love, angels, the creation, and power of thought. But because this is a 21st-century mission, our exchanges have also included topics within present day consciousness that were simply absent in earlier times. And collectively, our small team has knowledge and experience of several disciplines, including healing, psychology, geology, chemistry, forensic investigation and education. Hence, question-and-answer dialogues have on occasions been quite searching; equally, contemporary topics such as space-travel, terrorism and 9/11, the Bible Code, healing of modern diseases, vegetarian diet and cutting-edge research topics are included. The teachings sometimes make authentic connection to Earthly literature and 37 references are listed to illustrate this. And then amazingly, the final chapter of this second book was actually delivered by our founder-president Leslie himself during his visit from spirit of 25th August 2003.

APPENDIX 2

A CASE FOR TWO UNIVERSES / Scientific paper / 2005

A DISCUSSION OF how the *physical universe* appears to connect with the *spiritual universe.* The former, with some reservation, is quite well defined. The latter is much less so and may even be dismissed by many as 'mystical nonsense'. It is of course incumbent upon those attempting to describe the nature of spirit, to use physical language, and this has to be seen as a stumbling block. But acceptance of a spiritual-universe-basic-format could not only lead to an improved understanding of the *physical* universe, but also its origin. Our current thinking is dogged by some difficulty in getting our heads around expressions such as 'singularity', 'infinity' and 'imaginary number'. These terms are the 'outlaws' of conventional mathematics, so that even our accepted science has within itself a measure of the mystical. Furthermore, it has become clear in recent years, that 'nothing' is an abstract notion having no place in the real world. Even the deep space between stars can no longer be viewed as nothing. Our science has definitions, and well-constructed theorems, but there is always the feeling that there is a not quite perfect connection to reality. This leads to the idea that there surely has to be a missing factor that will eventually clarify. I believe that factor to be the recognition of two coincident universes with some subtlety of connection between them.

1. **The Physical Universe:** Firstly let us briefly recap on developments in astronomy during the past century.

The huge advances that have been made were in fact triggered earlier, with the discovery (1784) by John Goodricke, of the pulsating nature of the star Delta Cephei in our galaxy. There are now many known pulsating Cepheids throughout the universe, for which luminosity values have been measured. These values provide a basis for estimating distance from Earth. Luminosity has, in this way, become a celestial yardstick. The other significant measurement to have been catalogued is the recession velocity of stars and galaxies. This step came with the understanding of the Doppler or Red Shift phenomenon. In this, the bars of absorption spectra are seen to shift towards the red end of the starlight spectrum due to apparent increased wavelength (as seen from Earth). This led to the universe being mapped, to show the distances as well as recession speeds, of the galaxies.

Edwin Hubble made the observation (1929), that in whatever direction you look, the distant galaxies are moving rapidly away. He went on to establish that there is an empirical relationship between distance and recession speed (that Alexander Friedmann had in fact already predicted); speed of recession being proportional to distance, and the factor of proportionality became known as Hubble's constant. Therefore, the universe in which we live is expanding. It follows that at an earlier time, its galaxies must have been closer together, and if we could travel far back, we might find a beginning; a creation point. George Gamow developed the idea of an extremely high temperature initial explosion and this led to what has popularly become known as the 'big bang' theory.

In recent decades much has been said on the subject of *expanding universe* and valuable theorems have been deduced concerning a *big bang singularity*. Stephen Hawking points to three possible solutions that emerge from the original Friedmann universe expansion model, all three emerging from the postulated initial singularity of physical existence. Measurement of the cosmic background radiation left over from the big bang and the discovery of dark matter have further supported the concept. Several statements have been made concerning the moment of creation:

1. It would have happened between ten and twenty billion years ago
2. There would have been zero distance between galaxies (distance would simply not exist)
3. The curvature of space-time would be infinite

4. At this point, time as we know and experience it, first came to be.

We can say then, that in the first moments of the big bang, time, space, space-time, physical matter and all laws that govern it, first came into existence.

The Friedmann model of the physical universe is based upon Einstein's general theory of relativity that predicts: at the singularity point, the theory breaks down. It is also a fact that scientific theory presupposes space-time to be smooth and approximately flat, so that under infinite curvature condition, scientific theory must more generally break down. And neither can mathematics handle with confidence, infinity. We have therefore arrived, through scientific process, at a very interesting destination: the very edge or limit of intellectual reason. Now this has to be seen as an intriguing place, and it is to the great credit of speculation by the *physical mind* that it has led us to this furthest outpost of human perception.

It has therefore become clear, from purely scientific observation and reason that, the physical universe was suddenly created or came into being, in its initial form as a singularity. We cannot say 'at some point in time' because that moment of creation is seen also as the birth of time itself, and neither did physical space exist before this sudden event. There are several questions that arise. They are:

1. Why? The intellectual process itself springs from reason, and there must be a reason for such a significant event, deduced from our reasoning process. The idea of 'a spontaneous free lunch' that has been suggested in the literature, is hardly an acceptable raison d'être.

2. What was there before the creation of a physical universe? And we cannot easily say 'nothing' because our physical reasoning has indicated that 'nothing' has no place in reality. Some form of reality is required in order to give birth to a universe, no matter how invisible that reality may be. (Equally, some form of reality is required to produce through quantum mechanical argument, a particle from nowhere tangible, and this is considered acceptable.)

3. What would be the nature of a reality that has no time or space? Can we imagine its format without these parameters? Perhaps

the physical mind is capable of perceiving only in terms of the physical laws.

4. Three further factors should be mentioned before we leave this part of the discussion. One is the long-revered axiom that energy can neither be created nor destroyed (but it may be transmuted). The second is Einstein's mass-energy equivalence $E = mc^2$, and of course reading the equation left to right, it strongly represents much of the ongoing creation process. Thirdly, the physical universe has a speed-restriction. 'C' is the maximum velocity permitted within it, and this imposes a spherical limit to the 'observable universe', where c is the speed of its recession. Beyond this limit, light from the galaxies never reaches Earth (and similarly for any other observation point within the universe.)

2. <u>Mind:</u> Before proceeding further, I think a few words on mind would be appropriate. As has already been intimated, reason and perception link to mind, and as with many things not clearly understood, several alternative words appear in language. Psyche, spirit, nous, soul and mind have all become fairly interchangeable terms, although we could further break down each into stricter definition. It was Plato in the 4th-century BC who described mind as the ultimate nature of reality. Two thousand years on, René Descartes deduced the ultimate first perception: *I think, therefore I am.* Mind and perception are clearly fundamental to our being and indeed fundamental to this issue. It is no surprise that philosophers across the centuries have addressed the subject of mind and how it relates to brain, knowledge, reason, inspiration, conscience and soul.

Some have developed the idea that there are two distinct kinds of knowledge: *empirical,* that springs from experience and reason, and *a priori,* that comes to us from elsewhere. A notable exponent of this view was Immanuel Kant, who maintained the latter to be independent of experience, and coming to us directly from heaven. Not only did he recognise this as the essential nature of the best form of knowledge, but he also saw it as relating to every possible universe and not just the physical universe of our immediate familiarity. The notion that brain is capable of accessing knowledge from elsewhere, (whether it be heaven, soul, spirit, a remote physical being or another universe), leads to the proposition that the physical brain is capable of functioning in several completely different ways. It may function as:

1. A generator that produces scientific/intellectual thought and reason
2. A transmitter of information located elsewhere
3. A 'personally guided' form of transmission from elsewhere. The several aspects of this may all be placed under one broad heading, that of *mediumship*.

There is today much evidence for the brain functioning in the three ways listed.

The generator mode is well understood and accepted, since it involves the *physical mind* and physical thinking, with which we all feel entirely comfortable. The brain's transmitter mode requires a more careful consideration because it presupposes information held elsewhere that has the potential to be an influence. Such influence has various guises and has been referred to as *conscience, inspiration, guidance* etc. Gifted artists and composers will have been open to inspiration from beyond themselves, and young children are sometimes found to have abilities far beyond their years that cannot be the result of their own experience.

Personally guided transmissions are collectively known as 'mediumship'. I have familiarity with four quite different aspects of this kind of transmission. They may be listed as:

1. The psychic / clairvoyant who receives information from elsewhere and passes it to another, whilst all the time remaining fully conscious.
2. The partial-trance medium through whom another speaks, either in the recognisable voice of the medium or in another voice. The medium will be aware of what is being said at the time of delivery.
3. The *full*-trance medium whose own awareness becomes *completely* switched off. Afterwards, the medium will have no awareness or memory of what has transpired during séance.

Such mediumship is both rare and impressive to behold, and the voice that speaks will carry its own character, knowledge, humour, and qualities of love, compassion and the ability to teach. These may well bear no resemblance to the persona of the one entranced.

4. 'Mind projection' is another most remarkable category. In receiving a communication by mind projection, the medium's own voice as well as own vocabulary and phrasing are used for speech. The medium is aware of what is being said, but the knowledge presented is likely to bear no resemblance whatsoever to that of the medium! The knowledge given in this kind of communication may well be from unimaginably far; for example, from physical beings beyond this galaxy. There is quite simply no limit where distance is concerned, for reasons that will become clear later. However, such a phenomenon does not arise from chance; much preparation and protocol being required. A necessary prerequisite for all categories of guided transmission is that physical / intellectual and everyday thinking is switched off. The shutting out of worldly thoughts requires quiet and practice, and may be achieved through daily meditation. This has to be seen as a very important first step, and it is clear that by shutting down the physical thinking, a different mind happening / connection is allowed.

A careful consideration of the above data leads us to the notion of: duality of mind.

1. Physical Mind: The basis of scientific method and intellectual reason.
2. Spiritual Mind: Providing the modus operandi for receiving inspiration, for conducting all forms of mediumship and for spectacular transactions within the spiritual universe.
3. It is possible, during a lifetime, to dwell so much within physical thinking that the spiritual mind goes almost unnoticed. The reverse situation is scarcely possible because of the all-embracing nature of spirit.

3. **The Spiritual Universe:** It has been possible to firmly map out a picture of the *physical* universe with historic sequence of discovery, measurements and remarkable photography, leading to ingenious theories and scientific testing. The perception of and evidence for a *spiritual* universe are rather different, being more *experiential* than a process of objective reason. There are historical milestones, and it was Aristotle who said of the mysteries: *"Those who are being initiated are not to learn anything but to experience."* He clearly sensed the experiential need in comprehending spirit. In addition to understanding coming from experience, there have been the teachings about spirit received from Masters. Within such teachings, an often-repeated phrase has been: *spirit has always been.* Repeated phrases are usually important and this one would certainly appear to be so. It answers the question: what was before the big bang? And the notion of the physical universe being created from a spiritual origin is somehow much more plausible than a creation from 'nothing'. As has been said, 'nothing' has no place in our reality, but the alternative source, *a spiritual universe,* or *spirit* will become self-evident, as we continue.

Our conception of a spiritual universe is a system that has predated the big bang and therefore is without time, space or space-time and has within itself, no physical laws. It follows also, that there will be no light-velocity speed limit. The ongoing absence of linear time and space dimensions in spirit is also consistent with the data received through types-3 and -4 medium communication listed above. We can therefore tentatively say of the spiritual universe at this stage that:

1. It has always been
2. Linear time does not exist
3. Dimensions of space do not exist
4. Space-time does not exist
5. Physical matter does not exist
6. There is no speed limit, so that whatever dialogue ensues has no time-delays

Then what *does* exist within the spiritual universe? Keeping as far as possible to a scientific format of presentation, the answer to this question has to be: INFINITE, PRIMORDIAL, INTELLIGENT ENERGY, which many would see as THE CREATIVE PRINCIPLE and which many would prefer to call GOD or simply THE INFINITE. Some would also lay claim to sub-categories of energy called: love, soul, thought etc.

That the spiritual universe is comprised of limitless energy is of course, a fundamental requirement of our scientific reason, in order to satisfy $E = mc^2$.

There can be no physical universe having particulate matter and light-velocity speed limit, without huge energy input. As has been stated, Einstein's much revered equation is an equation of creation, and it is fundamental to the creation of all that we know. Perhaps it is even more fundamental than its author realised at the time of its most brilliant conception. It surely must enfold the very first moment of creation, with 'E' representing primordial energy and 'mc^2' representing the physical universe. If no energy preceded the big bang, then Einstein's equation, that veritable bastion of scientific reason, becomes violated, and this would be plainly unacceptable. Therefore a spiritual universe of spiritual energies exists and has always existed, even before the big bang.

Some may feel that there is something odd about this conclusion. Have we been here before? The fact is, the criteria listed for the spiritual universe are very similar indeed to those describing the perceived initial singularity: zero time, zero space, zero space-time (or infinitely curved space-time which amounts to the same) and no physical laws. Furthermore, both (the singularity and spirit) are cited as the origin of the physical creation. I suggest that they are, to all intent and purpose, the same; the only real difference being that the deduced singularity is at *time zero* whilst the spiritual universe per se, is permanently timeless. The singularity is as seen and deduced by the physical brain/mind. The spiritual universe is as experienced / felt by the spiritual mind with brain-in-transmitter-mode. The two approaches lead to different perceptions of the same origin.

4. Testing Elements of the Theory: It is customary to test a theory by finding out if it can explain known facts or shed light upon observed phenomena. It is appropriate therefore that we explore a number of observed phenomena to see if they fit the proposition that a spiritual universe as described exists; also, that we can look to it as the true progenitor of physical creation.

Non-linear time: In the material world, 'time' is in general regarded as absolute and travelling in one direction from past to future. This suits us for our everyday needs. But following the development of relativity theory and quantum mechanics, it has become clear that time has an elusive, more fluid quality not evident in the macro-physical world of our daily living.

Recent Random Number Generator (RNG) experiments reinforce this view. (Thought energy directed at an RNG can bias its results. Not *all* thought applied has influence. It is likely the deep thought energy from the spiritual mind that influences the machine's output, while physical thought is ineffective. This would explain why some are successful in inducing a bias and others not.) During this work, deep thought energy may be applied, then results examined, or the results may be first recorded and the deep thought energy applied later. Either way, the results are found to be the same! It matters not when the thought is applied, it could be yesterday, today or tomorrow. The rational explanation of this is that the RNG machine is 'Earthbound' and fixed in linear time, whilst the deep thought comes from the spiritual mind and so is 'of spirit' where time is non-linear.

I would also refer to the large peak of *collective consciousness* energy recorded by 40 linked RNGs at the time of the terrorist atrocity of 9/11/2001. On the chart, the peak-rise began three hours before the first plane's impact. It is clear and readily accepted that the main peak represents the energy of the collective consciousness of those of us who live in the physical world. Those who have moved on and now continue in spirit, also have consciousness energy. Their knowledge of the happening and thoughts would not be fixed in linear time, and so their consciousness energy began to show up three hours earlier. This explanation is consistent with time being non-linear in spirit. The British Premonitions Bureau has catalogued premonition and strange feelings that occur just prior to major disasters. It is my view that these recorded feelings would also relate to the thought energies of those in spirit, and this observation further supports the premise.

Prophecy: The matter of prophecy connects in no uncertain way with time's absolute nature in the physical universe and its fluidity within the spiritual universe. Due to a lack of understanding, acceptance of the principle of prophecy has been much maligned, despite analysis. But analysis has often overlooked vital factors and not all claimants to the gift have been genuine. Two genuine examples that come to mind are Saint John (Book of Revelation, AD 96-97) and Nostradamus (The Centuries, 1555). The latter is closer to our time and perhaps easier to interpret. It is often overlooked that Nostradamus makes it clear that his quatrains continue to the year 3797 and it of course follows that many of his prophecies will not yet have come to fruition. Some that *have* are very precise and have been wonderfully accurate. I therefore present as proof of the gift, some of his precise dating:

'666...................Great Fire of London
1792..................New calendar of the French Revolution
June 1991.........Break-up of the Soviet Union (given as *'73 years and 7 months'* from the October Revolution)
July 1999..........Refers to a key move by the terrorist leader *'King of Terror'* whose war *'reigns happily'* both before and after this date

In addition he names a number of notaries from our history (and his future), including the French chemist Louis Pasteur. The ability to prophesy with such precision, involving both dates and names, therefore requires explanation.

Within the concept of the proposed two universes, an explanation is simple. Those having the true gift are able to go into trance state and be guided in spirit (as Nostradamus himself in fact describes), where time is not linear, and where events happening in the (our) future can be observed. On returning to Earthly linear time, those events can then be divulged to others. This is the way of all true seers.

Synchronicity: A satisfactory explanation for synchronicity has long been a thorn in the flesh of rationality. Carl Jung has said much and has given wonderful observed examples, not least the account of Monsieur Fortgibu and the plum pudding [5]. I think my own most remarkable one was meeting our youngest son in Palenque whilst in Mexico. We had lost touch for several months and he had been travelling in four Central American countries. Then my wife and I met him in the street! It is a common factor in such experiences that to attempt to calculate the mathematical chance is mind-blowing. And Jung has stated himself that: *the connection of events may in certain circumstances be other than causal, and requires another principle of explanation.* How very true!

The physical universe, as has been said, is subject to physical laws and embraced within these are mathematics and probability, and we are familiar with the causal factors that naturally follow from this arrangement. It may well be however, that in certain circumstances the spiritual universe acts directly upon elements of the physical. In this situation, the normal physical laws would be circumvented. In this eventuality, what we term synchronicity would be seen as an unusual but nevertheless entirely rational occurrence, befitting of *another principle of explanation* to which Jung alludes. Therefore, acceptance of the reality of a spiritual universe could offer the basis for an explanation of synchronistic events.

A similar explanation might also apply to the controversial *Bible Code.* Data within the original Hebrew Torah appear to be accurate but not fixed to any one point in time. There is much Earth-history accounted, spanning across the centuries from the 13th century BC (when it was written down), to the present time and beyond. This data is encoded and has become accessible by computer program, and it appears by design, that it should come to light now. One reference to that timing is: *'and seal the record, until the fixed period, when many will travel and knowledge will be increased', Daniel 12, 4.* References also occur in the Books of Daniel, Exodus and Revelation and in communications received from spirit. The presence of the code is indeed well attested. It presents a form of retrospective prophecy, which could arise as an induction from spirit into the physical universe, and its purpose might even be to demonstrate that the two exist and work together.

Spirit Communication Work and the Kingsclere Group: It is appropriate that brief mention is made of some of the work of this particular group, for two reasons. Firstly, although only a small group of dedicated members in Earthly terms, (but there are more in spirit), it is so active and has particular spiritual connections. Secondly, I have been privileged to sit in séance with this group for more than a decade and am therefore well familiar with and share in its activities. I shall make reference to the two categories of mediumship, listed as type-3 and -4 above.

Full-trance work: In the manner that has been described above, Eileen Roper has, from June 1994, regularly received 'Salumet', a Master who teaches and with whom we are able to have dialogue. The visits are most enlightening and continue still. All sessions are recorded and transcribed. Full records are kept. During the sessions, much valuable data and insights are received in regard to the ways of spirit, and facts about our planet and universe. Two books have so far been published [1, 3] and scientific papers. The present paper is very much in line with the experiences of the Kingsclere Group and information received. And indeed, we have been fortunate enough to have question-and-answer dialogue with Salumet on such topics as RNGs, the big bang, 9/11 and the universal Creative Principle / God.

Mind projection work: As yet (2006), the Kingsclere Group has not aspired to mind project to others, but for the past two years, one of our number has 'received' on a quite regular basis, from a group within a civilisation living on the planet Aerah. He has been 'chosen' for this work. Aerah is unimaginably far from Earth and beyond our own and other nearby galaxies. It will not surprise me if this information, is considered by many as dubious. But I can say that its authenticity is confirmed by Salumet and by spirit guides, and data received is of an intelligent, well-structured, consistent standard and we gladly accept it as entirely plausible. I shall make only a very brief statement on actual data received at this point in time:

We are the eighth planetary culture to have been contacted by this, in many ways more advanced, civilisation. Aerah is spiritually much more progressed than Earth (revering the Creative Principle, marvelling at all creation, respecting nature and living 'love thy neighbour' to the extent that war exists only as a remote memory). We are told that the Creative Principle / God is recognised by cultures throughout the universe. The majority of dominant physical species on planets are animal-evolved, having body, limbs, mouth, 1+ eyes, 1+ ears and mind. Those on Aerah recognise as we do, that the universe is expanding and that light velocity imposes its limit on the 'observable universe'. They affirm that mind projection operates within the spiritual universe, which is void of time and space, so that dialogue is instantaneous. A large and increasing amount of information has been compiled from this valuable source. It is both our experience and instruction, that there are no time delays in dialogue encompassed by mind projection.

United States Military Surveillance Work: I refer to data published [2] under this heading, as further confirmation of the reality of mind projection communication, as described above. It is clear that the principle has been successfully developed and used by the US military for espionage purposes. Since this is an example of mind projection having been developed in a totally different field and for different purpose, it is no surprise that own terminology is used to denote and describe. But it is obvious from description that the factors encountered are the same as those found in spiritual work in general. Examples of corresponding terminology are:

1. Scientific remote viewing (SRV)	=	mind projection
2. Subspace	=	spirit realm / spiritual universe
3. Midwayers	=	spirit guides

In this work, the projected mind of one who is entranced is controlled by the conscious mind of a partner, and a time-fluidity is encountered in what is called 'subspace'. The point being made is that mind projection work is clearly not just the preserve of spirit communicators. The principle and details are recognised by others working independently in a completely different field. This endorses the reality of mind projection. It is a phenomenon that must be taken seriously.

Quantitative Kinesiology: I refer to the published work of David R Hawkins [6]. Part of this work indicates that the original teachings delivered by spiritual Masters such as Jesus, calibrate much higher than subsequent Earthly religions that have evolved from those teachings. It is worthy of note, that this scientific finding upholds the principle that what comes to us from Masters in spirit, is indeed *superior* knowledge.

5. <u>The Two Universes:</u> Having reasoned the existence of two universes, a number of points emerge about their general form. The physical universe is based on space-time, expands outwards and has its time arrow. The spiritual universe is without these factors but is in some way omnipresent to all existence. All elements of the physical universe are connected to spirit. Using physical means, only the 'observable universe' may be reached and with the disadvantage of light-years of delays. Communication by physical means within the physical universe has its restrictions, whilst if we work within the spiritual universe, all physical targets may be reached instantaneously. Some brief mention of modes of connection between universes is relevant. Several interactions have already been mentioned: the non-linear time observed in experiments, accurate prophecy, observed synchronicities, spirit communication, inspiration etc. Our connection to cultures on physical planets seems to take a particular form. The realms known as 'Astral Planes' (where life continues following physical death) might be seen as 'intermediate spirit', between a planet and what one might call 'spirit proper'. I think I would be correct in suggesting that life is more similar to Earth-life in this zone, compared to deeper spirit. Some feeling for the passage of time would persist, as would continuation of Earthly thinking. Spirit guides would work here, seeing to between-worlds communications and mind projection protocol. Messages from those who have passed on would, through the good offices of 'controls' and 'psychics', originate here. Masters such as Salumet and angels who watch over planetary evolution and other light-beings are from that deeper spirit beyond. The Astral Planes are then as intermediate zones between the deeper spirit and all planetary cultures that exist throughout the universe. Each planet has its own intermediate zone.

This is the picture that emerges from spirit communication, and from the teaching of Masters who venture from that deeper spirit.

6. Discussion: Early religious record refers to a time of creation of the physical, for example: *In the beginning was the Word, and the Word was with God, and the Word was God. The same was in the beginning with God. All things were made by him; and without him not any thing was made that was made.* – The Gospel According to St John, Ch 1, 1-3. It is a curious but perhaps significant fact that our more recent scientific work has led us to this very same conclusion, albeit phrased differently. The term 'big bang' describes an event from time-zero and not earlier. Our science does not encroach beyond the physical; and yet it does. Einstein surely takes us beyond the singularity to a condition of pure energy? If $E = mc^2$, is not to be violated, then the physical universe must have been derived from energy; infinite energy. Add to this the axiom 'energy can neither be created nor destroyed', and we have a 'belt-and-braces' claim to energy as progenitor. It follows that, if we can equate Infinite Energy to Creative Principle to God, then ancient religion and modern science are in excellent accord.

The question: 'what preceded the big bang' is clearly important. The simple answer is: energy, but energy is in no way simple. Our knowledge grows rapidly and much progress has been made in recent decades. It is our current knowledge that thought, individual consciousness, world collective consciousness, group meditation / prayer and personal aura, are all energies that can be detected by scientific instruments and in some measure quantified. Therefore we are now in a position to firmly state that 'consciousness' and 'thought' are indeed energies.

In the world, *thought* is truly powerful; preceding all new things that we are able to devise or become conscious of and consciousness evolves. It can be said that thought and consciousness lie at the cutting edge of evolution. A case has been made for some such energies coming to us from beyond the brain, from timeless spirit. And just as those energies of timeless spirit play their part in evolution today, they might well have initiated at the very start … the big bang. In the absence of scientific ethos, such names as Creative Principle, Infinite or God would seem apt.

The teaching that comes to us from Masters in spirit is that *spirit has always been,* both before during and following the physical creation. We can of course experience only the present spiritual status quo. Those Masters who come to us speak of *oneness with God* and are blessed with all-knowledge. This is clearly consistent with that supreme consciousness of the spiritual existence equating to God / Creative Principle. The evidence is that all elements within the physical creation are touched by the spiritual consciousness. Hence, we have a case for two universes; the one compounded of time, space and a limiting light velocity, and the other of more subtle energies. These more subtle energies are non-physical, yet are detectable by modern scientific means. But the spiritual universe, being free from physical constraints, has very different possibilities within itself, not least instantaneous communication by (spiritual) mind projection.

Conclusion: A case has been presented for two coincident universes; the one comprised of *physical* energies, and the other of non-physical *spiritual* energies. They each within themselves clearly have very different properties, but they interact in a variety of ways. The interactions have in the past been cloaked in mystery and sometimes ridicule. But acceptance that both universes exist could lead to our much better understanding of those factors that continue to be viewed by many as unbelievable or mysterious.

[Scientific Remote Viewing: It has since become clear that SRV work is not the sole preserve of the United States. RAW, for example, India's equivalent of America's CIA, utilises SRV as a means to help counter terrorism.]

APPENDIX 3

NOTES ON MODERN PYRAMID WORK BY RUSSIAN SCIENTISTS:

PYRAMID ENERGY EFFECTS that have been observed:

1. Water does not freeze (even as cold as – 40° C).
2. Razor blades are sharpened, (comparable with ultrasound polishing).
3. A vertical energy column extending 2 Km above a 44 M pyramid was detected by a radar station.
4. Salinity of water decreased.
5. Altered resistance of carbon materials.
6. Effects on animals and disease incidence.
7. Human aura is brightened
8. Foods stay fresh longer.
9. Domestic pets thrive well in situ.
10. Patient's burns heal faster.
11. Meditation enhanced.
12. Plant growth found to be faster in early phase.
13. Structural changes in various materials.
14. Can cause nausea in too much pyramid environment (Compares observations for some crop circles!)
15. Seeds: crop yields increased by 20-100%. (Compares with wheat seed from some crop circles!)
16. Immune systems are enhanced.
17. Pathogenic strengths of viruses and bacteria reduced.
18. Radioactivity decreased.
19. Crystalline materials kept within a pyramid, then transferred to surround jails, reduce crime.

Ancient pyramids have been described as being aligned to the pole star. This would mean that the other pair of sides is aligned east-west to planetary rotation, which would be the real intention of their builders.

The Russian pyramids are built to phi ratio and are described as having 70-degree slope. The Egyptian pyramids are less steep and to pi ratio.

Further information in English on Russian pyramid work is currently available on the Internet.

REFERENCES

1. Salumet / George E Moss, *SALUMET – His Mission to Planet Earth,* Trafford Publishing, Victoria BC, Canada, 2005.
2. Courtney Brown, *Cosmic Voyage, A Scientific Discovery of Extraterrestrials Visiting Earth,* Hodder & Stoughton, London, 1997.
3. George E Moss, *A Smudge in Time,* Gemma Books, Wittering, 2000.
4. Helen Greaves, *Testimony of Light,* Neville Spearman Publishers, Saffron Walden, 1969.
5. C G Jung, *Synchronicity, An Acausal Connecting Principle,* Ark Paperbacks, London, 1955.
6. David R Hawkins, *Power vs. Force, The Hidden Determinants of Human Behaviour,* Hay House Inc, Carlsbad, California, 2004.
7. Oliver Lodge, *The Survival of Man, A Study in Unrecognised Human Faculty,* George H Doran Co, New York, 1909.
8. Upton Sinclair, *Mental Radio,* Hampton Roads Publishing Co, 1929.
9. Russian Pyramid Information from Internet: A tremendous amount of information on this subject is available in English. Google search 'Prof I Krasnoholovets' and 'Prof A Golod, pyramids'. *On the Way to Disclosing of Mysterious Power of the Great Pyramid* and *The Divine Cosmos / Chapter 9 – Pyramid Power.*
10. The History of Herodotus, Book II – Euterpé 142-144; also included in: Great Books of the Western World Vol. 5, Ed. Mortimer J Adler, Encyclopaedia Britannica Inc., 1990, p. 79-80.
11. Peter Lemesurier, *The Great Pyramid, Your Personal Guide,* Element Books, Shaftsbury, 1987.

12. Akbar-Ezzeman MS, *Abu'l Hassan Ma'sudi,* Bodleiean Library, Oxford
13. Erich von Däniken, *Chariots of the Gods?,* Souvenir Press, London, 1969.
14. Erich von Däniken, *In Search of Ancient Gods ... My Pictorial Evidence for the Impossible,* Souvenir Press, London, 1973.
15. Hamish Miller & Paul Broadhurst, *The Sun and the Serpent,* Pendragon Press, Launceston, 1989.
16. Paul Bura, *Stepping to the Drummer, The Extraordinary Tales of a Psychic Man,* Honeystone Promotions, Newstead, 2000.
17. Sheila Ostrander & Lynn Schroeder, *Handbook of PSI Discoveries,* Sphere Books, London, 1977.
18. 'Earthly' materialisation Information from Internet: www.victorzammit.com
19. Included in: Great Books of the Western World Vol. 11, Ed. Mortimer J Adler, Encyclopaedia Britannica Inc., 1990, pages 14, 28, 31.
20. Peter Tompkins & Christopher Bird, *The Secret Life of Plants,* Harper & Row, New York, 1973.

ABOUT THE AUTHORS

BONNIOL: AS PROJECT leader in more ways than one and as the main spokesperson, Bonniol is cited as principle author of this book. Domiciled on Planet Aerah, he is one who has a very large family and he leads a team of sixty colleagues in this work. Whilst our Earthly group always meet at 7.30 pm on Monday evenings, Bonniol and his team manage to match our routine by sitting in session at all hours, for which we are extremely grateful. Their knowledge, dedication and abilities are truly amazing.

Salumet: This dear one, Light-being and Master of all-knowledge from the far soul integrations has regularly visited our lower Earthly vibrations to teach the truth of existence. He began his mission in June 1994 and has described Earth as a *learning planet*. In addition, Salumet has arranged for many notaries and interesting ones from spirit to visit and speak their truths. And he has organised the mind-link dialogues with Bonniol that began in October 2004. His valuable commentaries that have accompanied the Bonniol dialogues are included as an essential part of this work. Since the value of pyramid form and our first Egyptian pyramids are one fascinating subject of the exchanges, Salumet's discourse on the origin of the earliest structures on the Giza Plateau is included.

George E Moss: As co-author/editor and as a human, I take Earthly responsibility for presenting the material in book form. I do not work alone of course, but feel guidance from many in spirit and there are my much valued companions: the Kingsclere Group. We have all worked together in bringing this project to fruition.

www.salumet.com and **www.salumetandfriends.org** : Please do visit these websites for news items, latest Salumet transcripts, topic compilations, dialogues with some from our history and journal postings.